Animal Revolution

Changing Attitudes towards Speciesism

RICHARD D. RYDER

Basil Blackwell

British Library Cataloguing in Publication Data

A CIP catalogue record for this book is available from the British Library.

Library of Congress Cataloging in Publication Data

Ryder, Richard D. (Richard Dudley)
    Animal revolution: changing attitudes towards speciesism /
Richard D. Ryder.
        p.   cm.
    Bibliography: p.
    Includes index.
    ISBN 0-631-15239-3
    1. Animals, Treatment of — History.   2. Animals — Public opinion —
History.   I. Title.
HV4705.R93   1989
179'.3—dc20   89—32199
                                                                CIP

Typeset in 10 on 11.25 pt Garamond
by Setrite Typesetters Limited, Hong Kong
Printed in Great Britain
at the University Press, Cambridge

Contents

Acknowledgements

I have received assistance and advice from so many, among them Harriet Barry, Anne Campbell-Dixon, Birgitta Carlsson, Meg Clark, Brian Davies, John Douglass, Ian Fergusson, Mark Glover, Mark Gold, Hugh Hudson, Gill Langley, Andrew Linzey, Olive Martyn, Frank Milner, Julia Mosse, Julia Neuberger, René Olivieri, Helen Pilgrim, Peter Roberts, Derek Sayce, Michael Shaw, Angela Smith, Ann Heather Smith, Ginny Stroud-Lewis and Caroline Vodden.

My thanks go to them all and to Penny Merrett who typed (and retyped) the manuscript.

Richard D. Ryder

Abbreviations

AHA	American Humane Association
ALDF	Animal Legal Defense Fund
ALF	Animal Liberation Front
ASPCA	American Society for the Prevention of Cruelty to Animals
AWI	Animal Welfare Institute
BFSS	British Field Sports Society
BUAV	British Union for the Abolition of Vivisection
CALL	Central Animal Liberation League
CITES	Convention on International Trade in Endangered Species of Wild Fauna and Flora
CIWF	Compassion in World Farming
CRAE	Committee for the Reform of Animal Experimentation
FAWC	Farm Animal Welfare Council
FAWCE	Farm Animal Welfare Co-ordinating Executive
FOE	Friends of the Earth
FRAME	Fund for the Replacement of Animals in Medical Research
GECCAP	General Election Co-ordinating Committee for Animal Protection
HSA	Hunt Saboteurs Association
HUSA	Humane Society of the United States
IFAW	International Fund for Animal Welfare
IPPL	International Primate Protection League
ISPA	International Society for the Protection of Animals
IUCN	International Union for the Conservation of Nature
IWC	International Whaling Commission
MFH	Master of Foxhounds
NAVS	National Anti-Vivisection Society
PETA	People for the Ethical Treatment of Animals
PsyETA	Psychologists for the Ethical Treatment of Animals
RSPCA	Royal Society for the Prevention of Cruelty to Animals
SELFA	Stop the Export of Live Food Animals
SPCA	Society for the Prevention of Cruelty to Animals
UFAW	Universities Federation for Animal Welfare
WFPA	World Federation for the Protection of Animals

TO BRIAN, GLORIA AND HAPPY

1 Introduction

This book is not another catalogue of cruelties. Lists of atrocities perpetrated by humans against other sentients have been widely and effectively published in recent years.[1] Rather, this is an attempt to look behind such phenomena to establish explanatory links, and to examine the changing relationships between human and nonhuman over the centuries, using history — chiefly British history — as a framework for new ideas.

The positive side of this human-to-nonhuman relationship — that is to say its manifestation in the writings and campaigns of those concerned to improve the protection of nonhuman animals — is given priority. Sometimes I have only scratched the surface of a large but relatively unexplored field — as when I cover the active period of the nineteenth century — and I hope such inadequacies will stimulate further research. I do not claim to be writing a comprehensive or definitive history, but to be providing a few findings and observations.

We are, I believe, discussing a matter of fundamental importance for the future of our planet. The struggle against speciesism is not a sideshow; it is one of the main arenas of moral and psychological change in the world today. It is part of a new and enlarged vision of peace and happiness.

The time has come for a revolution in our attitudes — attitudes which can and must change because there has been a huge and rapid shift in power. For hundreds of millennia our ancestors were one weak species in the struggle for survival, but now we rule the world. For almost our whole existence as a species we have been shaped by our environment, but now we are shaping it. We can destroy rain forests, alter the weather, cultivate deserts or make them. We can even change the other animals to suit our whims for meat, fur, laboratory utensils or playthings. We have wiped scores of species off the face of Earth and are now beginning to create new ones. Our power is already immense and, in the future, it will be greater still. Such power demands, at least, a reappraisal.

A NEW LANGUAGE

Some aspects of the language I use may surprise the reader. This is because I have tried, when appropriate in the context, to dismantle the speciesism inherent in the words we use. Phrases like 'men and animals', for example, insult not only women but nonhumans also, for humans are animals too.

Using the word 'animal' in opposition to the word 'human' is clearly an expression of prejudice. So how can this be avoided when describing those sentient creatures who are not of the human species? Does a phrase such as 'animals and human animals' help? It might, but it is rather clumsy. Slightly less cumbersome is the phrase 'nonhuman animal' and its inevitable abbreviation 'nonhuman'. To some this may itself sound speciesist, in that it could be asserting that human is the norm and that nonhuman is inferior. All I can say is that no such inferiority is intended or understood. In the absence of other appropriate words I use 'nonhuman' or 'nonhuman animal' in the hope that their use reminds the reader, as it does me, of the kinship between those of my own species and others.

Admittedly, in dealing with the past, it is difficult to use new terms and concepts consistently, so the early chapters do contain some speciesist phrasing. I defend the use of the word 'animal' in the title on the grounds that the revolution to which I refer applies to the human animal as well as to others; and because the revolution, to a large extent, is about the concept of 'animal' itself.

The hostility towards so-called antropomorphism during this century has been so extreme that the use of certain adjectives, pronouns such as 'he' or 'she' and verbs in a nonhuman context has been abhorred, particularly by those intellectuals who should have known better. Nevertheless, if I believe it appropriate I have, and without shame, deliberately attributed behavioural and emotional qualities to nonhumans which some may regard as far-fetched. So, if I believe a dog is angry then I say so, and if she is a dog who feels angry with speciesists, then I sympathize!

THE MODERN REVOLUTION

This book considers the history of humankind's changing attitudes towards the other animals; the story, by and large, of the gradual triumph of reason and compassion over habit, vested interest and convenience. I have tried to analyse causes and to provide arguments for further progress at a period when our relationships with other sentients and the environment generally are under scrutiny. Progress may not be a fashionable concept, yet I consider that some progress *has* been made towards a greater respect for nonhumans on our shared planet, and that the 1970s and 1980s have seen a quickening of this progress. The historian W. E. H. Lecky asserted over a century ago that 'the general tendency of nations is undoubtedly to become more gentle and humane in their actions; but this, like many other general tendencies in history, may be counteracted or modified by many special circumstances'.[2] There is much evidence to support this hypothesis.

The connections between animal liberation and the modern environmental movement are complex, yet the differing rationales of the two movements often lead to similar actions. When environmentalism arises from a generalized 'respect for nature' the step to animal liberation is a short one; but where the environmentalist's motive is an anthropocentric desire to preserve for the benefit of the human species, then therein lie seeds of conflict. Both movements have, in recent years, become more ideological and more effective. Environmentalists have illegally sailed ships into nuclear test zones and animal rightists have broken into factory-farms and animal research laboratories. They have lobbied with spectacular results.

The change in phraseology from a concern for 'animal welfare' to a concern for 'animal rights' indicates the movement's increasingly ideological complexion, its emphasis on the right to *life* as well as the avoidance of *suffering* and, perhaps, the youthfulness of many of its adherents. Whereas some of the great religions of the East have emphasized the desirability of protecting nonhuman *life* while tending to ignore nonhuman *suffering*, the animal welfare movement of the West has emphasized the reduction of suffering while condoning killing for food and other purposes. Now the modern animal rights ideology brings both threads together in its quest to conquer suffering and to protect nonhuman life universally.

Since the 1960s the pace of the change in outlook towards other species has accelerated and a powerful moral concern has emerged for the well-being of the other individual sentients of our planet. To an extent, this arose in the context of the still maligned 'hippy' culture of that decade which placed a new value on compassion and allowing others to 'do their own thing'. The return-to-nature element of this 'Flower Power' philosophy helped to blur the dividing line between human and nonhuman, implying that *all* sentients should be respected. Hippydom (a view of life rarely claimed to be, yet in some ways not far removed from, the teachings of Jesus) also questioned the priority of the commercial motive and consciously tried to demote the power of the 'macho' ideal after the disillusionment of the Vietnam war.

As Harlan Miller has suggested, there are also other reasons for the new interest in the relationship between nonhumans and humans.[3] First, anti-speciesism is a logical extension of the liberation movements against racism and sexism which flourished in the 1960s and 1970s. Secondly, we live in a scientific and science-fiction age which has given us a completely new perspective of the human animal as being possibly only one sentient species among many in the universe, some of whom may be far more intelligent than ourselves. Thirdly, various scientific disciplines – psychology, anthropology, zoology, ethology, neurophysiology and other biological sciences – have permeated popular thinking to an unprecedented degree and have helped to 'demystify' the human being, putting us on a level with the other animals. Finally, our greater scientific knowledge of nonhumans and of their capacity for intelligence, for rudimentary language and for suffering pain, has helped narrow the conceptual gap between us.

The dissemination of such information through higher education and television is now practically universal in the West and challenges the blind acceptance of the old speciesist status quo. The reawakening of interest in the 'rights of animals' in the 1960s and 1970s was not due, initially, to proselytizing, but to the spontaneous conclusion arrived at by many people that it was plainly *illogical* as well as unjust to discriminate so grossly on the basis of species. We recognized the huge extent of suffering in this Fourth World – the world of the nonhuman sentients.

Just as animal liberation of the 1970s had its roots in the swinging sixties, so the 1960s were, in part, born out of the concerns of the 1950s. The reaction against the semi-militaristic culture of the Cold War period eventually encouraged the liberation movements in America. Individualism was trying to assert itself against authority – an authority which appeared to deny pleasure, justice and freedom. It was not a class war but the mainly middle-class product of prosperity and education. Furthermore it was augmented by the attentions of an increasingly internationalized media, television particularly. The hedonistic hippy subculture survived well into the 1970s, with a strong emphasis upon sexual freedom and an insistence that each individual had a right to find his or her own pleasures. In America, genuine progess was made against racism and sexism and the liberation of thought of this period naturally and logically was extended to cover the oppression of nonhuman sentients. This development became clear from 1969.

Unlike the two previous periods in Britain of rapid progress in the movement against speciesism, which occurred around the end of the eighteenth century and the end of the nineteenth, on this occasion the revolution attracted support from men and women of *all* classes and now permeates the whole of the developed world. Initial developments in Britain have been followed in Australia and then in the USA and other Western nations. Whereas Europe followed the USA in its Women's Liberation and Civil Rights movements, it is America which followed Britain in the animal revolution.

A revolution, to be a revolution, does not merely entail a total change of attitude; it must affect aspects of the human condition which are fundamental. Too often a concern for nonhumans has been dismissed by politicians and intellectuals as being of only peripheral importance. Yet a moment's reflection will show that the whole development of human civilization has depended on the relationship between the human and nonhuman animals, and how that relationship was perceived and justified in the moral, cultural and religious contexts of the time. Humans have conquered the planet, taking control over the other species, some of whom have been both rivals for food and territory and often downright foes; we had to pit our brains against their brawn. Now that that war has been all but won, and the human ape has emerged triumphant over the other vertebrates, surely it behoves us to be magnanimous in victory? Only the battle against the microbe remains important.

Our cave-dwelling ancestors depended upon other sentients for food, and needed their skins for clothing and their bones for tools. But human exploitation and domination of nonhumans is no longer the urgent necessity that once it was; we now have alternative foods, clothing materials, methods of transport and sources of power. Yet we continue to trap, poison and shoot our evolutionary cousins, inflict agonies upon them in the name of science, imprison them in factory-farms and devour them, quite unnecessarily, by the million. Changing all this will have revolutionary consequences, affecting what we wear, what we eat, the price of food, the development of science, the appearance of our environment, the character of industries and the way we spend our leisure.

The twentieth century has been a remarkable period of anti-speciesist enlightenment, but, paradoxically, it also has been an era of worsening exploitation and encroachment. While the human population explosion has made ever-greater demands upon habitat, and expanding worldwide industry has destroyed wildlife with pollution, science and agricultural technology have devised new means of oppression and justified all by results.

SPECIESISM

The Battle of Ideas

The moral basis for animal liberation has been given much attention by modern philosophers since the publication of the well-known novelist Brigid Brophy's major article entitled 'The Rights of Animals' in the *Sunday Times* in 1965. Brophy wrote:

The relationship of homo sapiens to the other animals is one of unremitting exploitation. We employ their work; we eat and wear them. We exploit them to serve our superstitions: whereas we used to sacrifice them to our gods and tear out their entrails in order to foresee the future, we now sacrifice them to science, and experiment on their entrails in the hope — or on the mere offchance — that we might thereby see a little more clearly into the present.[4]

Six years later *Animals, Men and Morals* was published, a book edited
by three young Oxford philosophers, Stanley and Roslind Godlovitch
and John Harris; Roslind Godlovitch's essay 'Animals and Morals' came
out in the same year.[5] Anti-vivisection letters in the *Daily Telegraph*,
the first entitled 'Rights of Non Human Animals', were my own opening
shots.[6] At that time I had no contacts with the then rather stagnant
animal welfare movement, nor with the other people in Oxford who
were beginning to think along similar lines; for me, it was spontaneous
eruption of thought and indignation arising out of the conflict between
my natural sympathy for nonhuman animals and what I had witnessed
in university laboratories in Cambridge, Edinburgh, New York and
California in the 1960s. Brophy, reading my letters in the *Daily Telegraph*, put me in touch with the Godlovitches and John Harris in 1969,
and I was able to contribute to *Animals, Men and Morals*. This was
reviewed in the *New York Review of Books* in 1973 by Peter Singer,
who had known us in Oxford two years earlier.[7] Andrew Linzey then
became part of our circle and so did Stephen Clark; we formed what,
retrospectively, can be called an informal Oxford Group. With the
support of John Harris, the Godlovitches and others, I organized campaigns against otter-hunting and animal experiments. Years later the
Group was superseded by Oxford Animal Rights – a body run by
Macdonald Daly of Balliol.
   A spate of serious books on the subject followed, many or most
written by members of this group, including my *Victims of Science* in
1975 and Peter Singer's *Animal Liberation* published in America in the
same year and in Britain in 1976.[8] The Oxford Group's powerful contingent of academic philosophers started a discussion which has continued ever since among their colleagues around the English-speaking
world and in Europe. Academic journals such as *Ethics* (January 1978),
Philosophy (October 1978), *Inquiry* (Summer 1979) and *Etyka* (1980)
have published special editions on the moral status of animals. Indeed,
animal liberation is possibly unique among liberation movements in the
extent to which it has been led and inspired by professional philosophers; rarely has a cause been so rationally argued and so intellectually
well armed. Albert Schweitzer had once complained that philosophy
had ignored the question, playing 'a piano of which a whole series of
keys were considered untouchable'. Yet this modern revolution in
thought, which experienced a remarkable surge after the *annus mirabilis*
of 1969 (see chapter 11), was heralded by the philosophers themselves.
   Our moral argument is that species alone is not a valid criterion for
cruel discrimination. Like race or sex, species denotes some physical and
other differences but in no way does it nullify the great similarity among
all sentients – our capacity for suffering. Where it is wrong to inflict
pain upon a human animal it is probably wrong to do so to a nonhuman
sentient. The actual killing of a nonhuman animal may also be wrong if

it causes suffering or, more contentiously, if it deprives the nonhuman of future pleasures. The logic is very simple.

Geneticists tell us that humankind is physically closer to a chimpanzee than a horse is to a donkey. Surely if animals are related through evolution, then we should all be related morally? The species gap is not an unbridgeable gulf, even physically; some species, such as lions and tigers, can interbreed naturally and produce fertile offspring. Even primate species can do so and, in the laboratory, species can now be mixed like cocktails. One day, if human apes are interbred with other apes, will it be justifiable to hunt or eat or experiment upon the hybrid child, or should he or she be sent to school?

In order to produce cheaper meat, pigs have already been born who contain human genes. Yet surely this makes a nonsense of our speciesist morality? Is it not partial cannibalism to eat such a humanopig? How many human genes are required to make a creature human in the eyes of the law? The Oxford Group has been warning of such genetic developments since the early 1970s.[9] In the 1980s transpecies fertilization became a reality and in April 1988 the US Administration awarded to Harvard University the first patent for a new animal species – a cancer-prone mouse containing a human gene.[10]

The findings of a scientific RSPCA committee under Lord Medway[11] in 1979 to the effect that there now is strong scientific evidence that all vertebrate classes can suffer because all have been found to possess in their bodies those biochemical substances known to mediate pain, supplemented the older biological, neurological and behavioural evidence which pointed in the same direction. Furthermore, we have seen the scientific definition of nonhuman suffering widen to include disease, starvation and mental states such as fear, despair, and those arising from the deprivation of exercise, companionship or stimulation, or from the frustration of other psychological needs.[12]

As if to assert our superior moral status it is sometimes claimed that Homo Sapiens is the only altruistic species. But this may not be accurate, for there are authenticated cases of elephants and cetacea trying to assist ailing individuals of their own species, and reports exist of dolphins allegedly trying to help humans. There are also many instances of symbiosis in nature, where one species depends upon another; a predatory fish, for example, allowing cleaner-fish of a different species to cleanse his or her scales in safety. Perhaps our greater toleration of nonhumans may have similar survival value for ourselves, in terms of physical, ecological or even moral benefits. But even if it were true that humans are the only unselfish species, how could this justify our exploitation of other sentients? Should it not reinforce our sense of duty towards them?

The answer to the question 'But isn't it *natural* to be speciesist?' is that it may *not* be, and that even if it is, speciesism and selfishness are still wrong; rape and murder, after all, can spring from 'natural' impulses, but this consideration does not transform rape or murder into virtuous behaviour. We are not slaves to our genes; genetic tendencies can, to a large extent, be overcome through education and by the restraints of civilization.

Other excuses have been used by humans to justify our speciesism, for example, that we are the only tool-using or tool-making species, or that we are the only animal capable of language. In recent decades, all such distinctions have been eroded by science. Other apes, in particular, have been found to be tool-makers capable of learning human sign-language.

One is left in the startlingly simple position, already stated, that whatever is morally wrong in the human case is probably wrong in the nonhuman case as well. When faced with a particular type of exploitation one can apply some such 'human test'. *Veal calves:* would it be right to separate babies from their mothers while still suckling? *Laboratory rats:* would it be right to inflict severe electric shocks upon unwilling men and women? *Bullocks:* would it be right to castrate boys and fatten them to be eaten? *Foxes:* would it be right to chase vagrants across the countryside and to encourage hounds to tear them apart?

The implications of such a revolutionary conclusion are inconvenient, yet they remain entirely rational. What holds for humans, especially for such categories as the mentally handicapped and infants, should also apply in the case of nonhumans.

Self-deceptions

Powerful classes have often rationalized their exploitation of weaker beings by minimizing the latter's capacities for suffering or denying them entirely. African slaves, being of a different race, were barely sensible of their harsh conditions, or so it was sometimes argued by their exploiters; indeed, in 1799, the Duke of Clarence claimed that the slave trade had the virtue of rescuing negroes from savagery.[13] Similarly, a whole host of self-deceiving tactics have been used to defend speciesism, ranging from pragmatic arguments through to more subtle psychological deceptions.

If, as I consider to be the case, all human beings experience some sympathy with other animals, then do we all feel some guilt when we exploit them? Guilt can be suppressed, denied or reduced by various means: we can blame others for what is done; we can distance ourselves from the bloody act; we can attempt to shut it out of our mind or we can try to convince ourselves that the victim of our exploitation deserves to die or feels no pain. When these defences are stripped away, tell-tale anger can erupt, or 'necessity' − 'the argument of tyrants' as Pope reminds us − is defiantly proclaimed and exaggerated.

The exaggeration of the need for meat, for example, has been a feature of Western cultures for several centuries, and over the last hundred years scientists have exaggerated the importance of their scientific research on animals, just as Alderman Newman exaggerated the value of the slave trade two hundred years ago: 'If it were abolished altogether, he was persuaded it would render the City of London one scene of bankruptcy and ruin.'[14] Of the revolutionary proposal to prevent orphan boys being made to climb chimneys, Sir John Yorke warned that the only alternative was the use of brushes which would destroy the mortar in the chimneys and thus cause devastating and uncontrollable fires.[15]

The fierceness of wolves was once exaggerated just as the 'verminous' natures of dingoes, coyotes and foxes are today. Emotive words worthy of the best propagandist are deployed against nonhuman sentients in order to stifle compassion – 'pest', 'vermin' and 'trash'.

Just as men in battle find it easier to kill at a distance without seeing the suffering of the enemy or getting to know him intimately, so people distance themselves from the nonhumans they exploit. They arrange for those who have not known the cows or pigs or sheep to do the slaughtering, or they give numbers or contemptuous names to their laboratory animals.

In general, with the exception of individually motivated cruelty, the greater the intimacy with an animal the harder it is, psychologically, to abuse or exploit it. Even aboriginal hunter-gatherers, who may show no compunction about cooking wild animals alive, would not dream of eating their pets – they are treated as members of the family. In some Amerindian cases such peoples will not even eat the eggs laid by the domesticated fowl they keep.[16]

Exploiters use many stock excuses to reduce their sense of guilt. Serpell has found that, in Britain, hunters claim to be conservationists and may take pride in following certain rules of 'fair play', pest-controllers blame their employers for their work or attribute deliberate wickedness to the pests they kill, farmers blame consumers for the demand for cheap meat and scientists claim that their experiments on nonhumans are done highmindedly for human benefit.[17] Similarly, veterinarians blame the need to keep good relations with their clients and the latter's legal rights of ownership for their reluctance to take firm action to protect animals under their care.[18]

Those who exploit directly are sometimes shunned as being inferior, as slaughtermen are in some societies; in Japan, for example, meat and leather goods traditionally have been processed only by the Untouchable caste. Alternatively, animal exploiters can be ritualistically elevated so as to counteract the underlying guilt and to put them 'above' blame: scientists and 'sportsmen' are thus glorified.

Language has been pressed into the service of exploitation. Bland euphemisms or even self-aggrandizing quasi-religious terms have evolved:

scientists 'sacrifice' their animals, the hunter 'accounts for' a fox, the slaughter-house becomes a 'packing factory'. Special words are used to conceal the true animal origins of products: skin becomes 'leather', cow becomes 'beef', pheasant becomes 'game', deer becomes 'quarry', tail becomes 'brush', dogs become 'experimental subjects', screams become 'vocalizations'.

All these defences are used in our institutionalized system of speciesism; abattoirs are hidden away, meat is elaborately packaged, laboratories are locked, foxes are characterized as too evil to be pitied, and language is changed to disguise reality. In the ensuing chapters we shall encounter many more excuses, ranging from the religious idea of 'man's dominion' to Descartes's claim that nonhuman animals feel no pain; from the assertion that speciesism is justified because animals lack immortal souls to more modern economic claims. As each generation has exploded the speciesist myths of previous periods it has tended to look for new arguments to support humankind's exploitation of the other animals.

Power

Humans now have almost total power over other animals, yet sometimes we like to pretend that it is an equal fight. Does power alone justify exploitation? Did it justify the persecution of Jews or would it justify the exploitation of humans by a super-intelligent species of aliens from outer space? Does morality stand only upon a fear that the oppressed may one day retaliate? If so, then why not exploit and experiment upon unwanted babies or the mentally handicapped? They cannot effectively strike back, nor do they exercise duties towards the rest of us; they would certainly produce far more reliable results scientifically. Such a proposition rightly appals.

As C. S. Lewis once put it in an attack upon vivisection:

If loyalty to our own species, preference for man simply because we are men, is not sentiment, then what is? It may be a good sentiment or a bad one, but a sentiment it certainly is. Try to base it on logic and see what happens!

But the most sinister thing about modern vivisection is this. If a mere sentiment justified cruelty, why stop at a sentiment for the whole human race? There is also a sentiment for the white man against the black, for a *Herrenvolk* against the Non-Aryans, for 'civilised' or 'progressive' peoples against 'savage' or 'backward' peoples. Finally, for our own country, party, or class against others. Once the old Christian idea of a total difference in kind between man and beast has been abandoned, then no argument for experiments on animals can be found which is not also an argument for experiments on inferior men. If we cut up beasts simply because they cannot prevent us and and because we are backing our own side in the struggle for existence, it is only logical to cut up imbeciles, criminals, enemies, or capitalists for the same reason. Indeed experiments on men have already begun. We all hear that Nazi scientists have done them.[19]

This is surely true, although far from being the only reason for attacking speciesism. If knowing, as we now do, of the community of pain among animals and of our evolutionary kinship, we still persist in the total subordination of nonhumans, then are we not paving the way for a more callous attitude towards the weak generally, whether nonhuman or the children, the elderly or the handicapped of our own species?

Speciesism is indeed sheer sentiment, and its irrationality is easily exposed, yet despite its profound moral blindness it continues without any real excuse and for a number of reasons: first, there is profit in it; secondly, it is enjoyable; thirdly, it is habit.

Does the habit element derive largely from our own distant past when the struggle with nature was a real one and the threat posed by our vertebrate kindred was like the threat still posed by earthquake, fire and flood? A combative approach towards rival species and dangerous predators was then highly necessary, as it is towards terrorists today, and if there were conditions in which other food was scarce, then there was a need to kill to eat. In much of the modern world humans are no longer in such a condition, yet almost everywhere they continue to treat other animals as rivals, enemies or prey.

A distinction has to be made between the cases of cruelty committed by individuals in their private lives and the large-scale institutionalized cruelties. The former are usually instigated either by human anger or neglect (which is often associated with equal anger or neglect to children and to other human beings). The institutionalized cruelties, on the other hand, ranging from the overworking of horses and dogs in Victorian times to the plight of nonhumans in factory-farms and laboratories today, are motivated usually by greed, ambition and an unthinking adherence to convention.

The experiments begun by Stanley Milgram in the early 1960s demonstrated how strong is the normal human drive to conform, even if conformity is believed to involve the infliction of severe suffering upon other people. Milgram's experiments showed that most people will give apparently agonizing electric shocks to others if they are led to believe that this is part of a scientific experiment. Like Eichmann, and hundreds of soldiers, torturers and executioners throughout the ages, they did what they were told to do. Normal people who are part of an evil system do evil deeds. Is not speciesism such a system?

Although it is true that most people will do terrible things motivated merely by the desire to conform, thus overcoming the natural restraints of compassion and squeamishness, is it wrong to assume that sadism is often an additional motive? It may be that pleasure in dominating another and in inflicting pain is a basic human tendency, albeit much denied and rarely discussed. In the average human it is probably no stronger than many other impulses, but it may be there, nevertheless, perhaps associated with sexual excitement or accentuated by frustration and the spirit of revenge. Its antithesis to civilization makes it a taboo subject and, although disguised in human-to-human relationships, it is sometimes blatant in human-to-nonhuman interactions. The child who cuddles the puppy at one moment can all too suddenly switch to sadistic teasing in the next.

SOME QUESTIONS RAISED

Do any of our speciesist excuses hold water? If not, what drives us to continue our tyranny? Is it just material gain, convenience and habit, or is there also a deep-seated drive to dominate, and if so, is this drive innate or acquired?

On the other hand, why is there a countervailing *concern* for non-humans? Is this streak of compassion learned or spontaneous? Is it linked with that powerful yet ignored feeling of squeamishness at the sight of blood? If we try to deny squeamishness because we think it is a sign of weakness, how far do such 'macho' motives explain our cruelty to nonhuman animals? Does the conflict between compassion and cruelty, often within the same person, explain the remarkable inconsistency shown in the human attitude towards nonhumans?

These are just some of the questions to be addressed as we consider the history of the subject. Other questions concern the rate at which more humane attitudes have developed. Has it been a smooth continuous progress, or were the middle ages less anthropocentric and therefore slightly kinder towards nonhumans than the later Renaissance period? Were our hunter-gatherer ancestors more respectful towards other animals than later agricultural ages? What has affected the development of the animal welfare and animal rights movements? Has it been urbanization or affluence, the effects of religious or secular teaching, or the implications of science and, particularly, of Darwinism? Why, when so many outstanding men and women have sided with the animals, has so little changed? If Christianity has been the most speciesist of all the major religions, why have supposedly Christian countries led the modern animal welfare movement? And why have Protestant countries done better than Catholic ones?

To explore and answer such questions I have reviewed the history of the relationship between humankind and the other animals. In Part I, which deals with events from antiquity up to about 1960, I have arranged the chapters approximately in chronological order. Part II deals with a more personal view of the modern movement. As this covers the period in which I have been closely involved as a campaigner, out of necessity my own role has had to be included, although I hope not egocentrically. In Part III, the philosophical and psychological issues are discussed and summarized.

I have been at least four people while writing this book – campaigner, psychologist and 'ideas man' as well as historian. I have wanted to include my knowledge of the national and international aspects of the movement which come from first-hand experience, while at the same time recording the results of some original library research. Where the research has turned up little-known information I have sometimes given this in the notes. I hope this has worked to produce a readable text for the general reader while offering further information for the academic.

Part I
THE PAST

Introduction

It is all too tempting to assume that the intellectuals and writers of any period represent the common opinions of their times. Similarly it is easily insinuated that these same writers are the leaders of society and that their doctrines substantially influenced the conduct of their less articulate contemporaries. How far are these two assertions true? Is it not possible that, in some instances at least, the writer who is remembered was not typical of his age and that the masses scarcely noticed or were affected by what he or she had to say?

Unfortunately for the historian, the records of the lives of the inarticulate are less well preserved, and so it is simpler to rely upon the written record. Besides, the historian, being a scholar and a writer, may naturally prefer to believe that it is the written word which fashions the deed and that the pen is always mightier that the sword! Yet there is a tide in the development of cultures which ebbs and flows as much through the tendency of human thinking to swing spontaneously between extremes, and by the natural response to events, as under any influence from intellectuals and theorizers. Sometimes, perhaps, the shift in doctrine *follows* rather than precedes the change in practice. Nevertheless, a survey of the written word on the subject of cruelty is a necessary element in any attempt to grasp the development of the past. There are many disturbing questions to be answered.

2 The Ancient World

Stone-age cave paintings of animals reveal that the human preoccupation with our fellow creatures is an ancient one, whether or not such paintings were to worship beasts, propitiate them, assist in their capture by means of magic, or to express Homo Sapiens's admiration for their strength, speed and beauty – the Palaeolithic equivalent of a twentieth-century child's doodlings of tanks, aeroplanes and racing cars. One thing is certain: nonhuman animals were among the most important elements in the lives of the people of those times, more than ten thousand years ago.

Two themes stand out in the extraordinary history of Homo Sapiens's relationship to the other animals: first, its perennial *importance* in the human psyche and, secondly, the *ambivalence and inconsistency* of that relationship.

It is in sculpture and pictorial art that we find the earliest records in this story. The cave paintings of Lascaux and Altamira are succeeded by later prehistoric effigies of animals suggesting a religious use. Some portrayals indicate that the gods take on animal forms, other imply that the animal itself is to be worshipped.

The prominent place occupied by bulls in the Palaeolithic cave paintings of Spain, as well as in those of the Neolithic Near East several thousand years later, have suggested the worship of a long-lived bull deity which continued in Crete and as the sacred bulls of Egypt. After the later development of Mithraism in the West, its crowning myth became the killing of the bull by the divine Mithra, portrayed as an idealized human figure. This cult, a rival to Christianity, excluded female participation and appealed to the militaristic mind. Its bull-killing myth – possibly one origin of modern bullfighting – was perhaps an early example of the association of speciesism with manliness; the male human figure being extolled in an act of domination over the bull who, in previous centuries, himself may have been worshipped as the epitome of dominance and strength. Man had conquered Beast.

EGYPT

In ancient Egypt the preoccupation with sacred animal forms reached a high level: the goddess Hathor is often represented as a cow, the moon god Thoth as a baboon or ibis, Bastet as a cat, Anubis as a jackal, Horus as a falcon and the midwife goddess Taurt as a hippopotamus. Mixed human and nonhuman forms are also characteristic and appear in later (Dynastic) periods. In Egypt, these hybrid forms of the deities usually had humanoid bodies with nonhuman heads. Later, it was the other way around when the Greeks gave human heads and torsos to their animal-bodied centaurs, mermaids and harpies, and the Mesopotamian civilizations did likewise. Such hybrids seem to imply a basic assumption of the physical inter-relatedness of humans and nonhumans, as Hindu religious sculpture does to this day. Not that the part-animal nature of the gods would necessarily imply respect for their earthly counterparts.

At some periods in Egyptian history, the hunting of lions, hippos, birds, wild oxen and even elephants were regarded as kingly sports. In the Late Period, 664 to 332 BC, however, the manifestation of gods in individual animals (such as the three sacred bulls, Apis, Minevis and Buchis) was extended so that *every* animal of a species in which the power of a god was revealed was regarded as sacred and therefore protected and accorded ritual burial; extensive ibis, crocodile and cat cemeteries have been recorded.[1] Furthermore, Herodotus, perhaps unreliably, states that in later years *all* wild animals in Egypt were held to be sacred and that their murder incurred the ultimate penalty:

Anyone who deliberately kills one of these animals is punished with death. Should one be killed accidentally, the penalty is whatever the priests choose to impose. But for killing an ibis or a falcon, deliberately or not, the penalty is inevitably death.[2]

Such a draconian and comprehensive wildlife conservation policy has not been seen since. Nevertheless, prohibitions upon the killing of members of totem species have been widespread and continue in some parts of the world to this day.

The cat enjoyed a special status in Egyptian society after its domestication in about 1500 BC. Earlier (about 2500 BC), while still wild, the cat had been proclaimed a sacred animal. The portrayals of cats in Egyptian art are often of great beauty and sensitivity, apparently motivated as much by affection as veneration. Herodotus reports that killing a cat also became a capital offence, and there are stories of a Roman soldier and Greek tourists getting into trouble on this account. Thousands of cat and other animal mummies have been found in Egypt and are signs that an after-life was believed to await them. Other pets included dogs, gazelles, ornamental fish, monkeys and even palace-trained lions, although none of these ever gained the popularity of the cat. The Egyptians gave names to their dogs such as 'Ebony', 'Grabber', and even 'Cooking Pot', and a distinguished government official, Sen-Mut, had his pets ceremonially buried, placing a bowl of raisins in his monkey's coffin as food for the afterworld.

There is no indication, however, that food animals in general were treated with any greater respect than those of today. Meat was an important, if rare, item in the Egyptian diet, and Old Kingdom tombs depict the forced-feeding of oxen, calves, antelope, cranes, ducks and geese, presumably not for their benefit but for that of people who were to eat them. Some creatures, such as flies, rats and scorpions were regarded as pests, but other dangerous species such as crocodiles, lions and snakes were incorporated into religion and worshipped in the belief that the gods had chosen to inhabit the bodies of these animals or, at least, to manifest their power in them.

It is tempting to speculate that, if more written works had survived from Egypt, in the later periods we would find references to the sufferings of animals and exhortations, even laws perhaps, against cruelty towards them. One conclusion we can draw tentatively from Egyptology is that out of a worship of nonhuman forms emerged the first recorded signs of affection for nonhumans. Literature which has survived includes moral tales in which animals play the central roles, as well as poetry rich in animal imagery. But at the same time some animals were being hunted and sacrificed barbarously. The perennial ambivalence of people's feelings for nonhumans is certainly detectable in the Egypt of three thousand years ago, yet the balance favoured the animals more than it did in the Greek and Roman civilizations that followed.

MESOPOTAMIA AND GREECE

In Mesopotamia, laws survive from the beginning of the second millennium BC which list penalties for the theft of animals, and stipulate that anyone killing a hired ox through negligence or blows must replace it. A veterinary surgeon received payment only if he cured an animal; if it died after treatment then he was required to recompense the owner. The Mesopotamians, as much obsessed in their art with dogs as the Egyptians were with cats, also gave them names like 'Spot' and 'Red', but no indication of any real respect for them has been found.

The Greeks, although they thought little of cats, obviously highly regarded dogs, and it is in Greek literature that we find the first written concern for the treatment of animals in the West. Indeed the status of nonhumans and their relation to humans were important concerns of Greek philosophy, as they are in ours today. Four differing schools of thought emerged. We can call these animism, vitalism, mechanism and anthropocentrism. Animism's central figure was the great mathematician

Pythagoras (active around 530 BC) who contended that animals and people have souls that are the same in kind. These souls are indestructible, he said, composed of fire or air, and move from human to animal or human in succeeding incarnations. Pythagoras himself was a vegetarian and advocated strict moral self-examination each evening with three questions: In what have I failed? What good have I done? and What good have I not done? Pythagoras certainly regarded kindness to animals as a fundamental good, and is reported to have bought live creatures from fishmongers and fowlers in order to set them free.

Vitalism similarly recognized a difference between organic and inorganic entities. But unlike the animists, vitalists such as Aristotle (384–322 BC) stressed the interdependence of soul and body. Aristotle did not deny that men and women are animals, but placed them (as the most rational of animals) at the head of a natural hierarchy, and proposed that the less rational exist to serve the purposes of the more rational. Even slaves, although human and capable of feeling pleasure and pain, were considered to be less rational and, therefore, open to justifiable exploitation by the more rational: 'Since nature makes nothing purposeless or in vain, it is undeniably true that she made all animals for the sake of man.'[3] Unfortunately for the animal kingdom, Aristotle's philosophy eclipsed the influence of Pythagoras over succeeding centuries and was influentially revived by Aquinas and the Dominicans in the thirteenth century.

A third view, mechanism, was that people and animals are mere machines. They were thus seen as beings essentially the same but without any 'soul' differentiating them from inanimate matter.

Finally, elements of the Aristotelian view were simplified and popularized by Xenophon and others. Their simple creed was that everything in the world has been made for the benefit of mankind. If Aristotle's more sophisticated arguments subsequently helped to build the pinnacles of Western thought, then Xenophon's crude anthropocentrism was one of its foundation stones. The animists (such as Pythagoras), the mechanists and the vitalists (such as Aristotle) all accepted the similarity in kind between people and animals. Only the anthropocentrists proclaimed the gulf between us which became such an anxious preoccupation in Europe over the succeeding ages.

ROME

The Romans' cruelty to animals in the arena is notorious. Countless thousands of animals, maddened with red-hot irons and by darts tipped with burning pitch, were baited to death in Roman arenas. At the dedication of the Colosseum by Titus, five thousand died in a day; lions, tigers, elephants and even giraffes and hippos perished miserably. Nevertheless there were several remarkable humanitarian writers in later

Roman times who showed compassion for animals. Pliny recounted anecdotes about the alleged intelligence and religiousness of elephants, the medical skill of the hippopotamus and the love that dolphins showed for music and young children.[4] A tender feeling for animals is a distinctive feature of the poetry of Virgil, and Lucretius and Ovid also touch upon it.[5]

As a militaristic society the Romans consciously suppressed. their tender feelings, but they could not cut off entirely their natural springs of pity. In 55 BC, Cicero wrote to a friend that the agonized trumpetings of some elephants, being slowly butchered in the amphitheatre, had excited the compassion of the spectators, who had cursed Pompey for his cruelty. Interestingly, Cicero adds that the spectacle in the Circus had aroused not only pity but a feeling that the elephant was allied with man.[6] There was also the favourite story of the slave Androcles who was recognized by a lion from whose foot he had removed a thorn. The lion greeted Androcles affectionately and declined to eat him. [7] Sometimes even an emperor could show flickerings of mercy. Marcus Aurelius (AD 161−80) did not like the public entertainments; their cruelty repelled him.

The philosophers Porphyry and Plotinus, and the statesman Seneca, all followed a vegetarian diet, but the most outstanding exponent of this habit was Plutarch, the Greek-born philosopher, who lived in Rome around AD 46−120. He wrote that he would never sell an ox who had served him well, and he defended animals in his two tracts on eating flesh and in his *'Life of Marcus Cato'*. Unlike Pythagoras, Plutarch did not base his vegetarianism upon the idea of reincarnation, but upon a general duty of kindness to human and nonhuman alike. He argued that much of the world's cruelty arose from humankind's uncontrolled passion for meat:

For the sake of some little mouthful of flesh, we deprive a soul of the sun and light and of that proportion of life and time it had been born into the world to enjoy...let us kill an animal; but let us do it with sorrow and pity and not abusing or tormenting it as many nowadays are wont to do.

In Plutarch's day these gastronomic torments included trampling and inflaming the udders of sows about to give birth, sewing up the eyes of swans and cranes, and skewering live pigs on red-hot spits, allegedly to improve the taste of the meat.

The range of meats eaten by the nobility at banquets in both Antiquity and in the middle ages was probably dictated by more than mere gluttony. It seems to have symbolized humankind's conquest of the 'animal kingdom', as well as the superiority and opulence of the host. Thus, meat-eating became a symbol of social status. Later, and possibly in consequence, arose the erroneous belief that meat was an essential

PLUTARQUE.

1   Plutarch (AD *c.* 46–120) was a Greek-born philosopher who
lived in Rome. Like Pythagoras before him, and Porphyry and
Plotinus, he was an ardent vegetarian. Furthermore, he based his
vegetarianism upon a general duty of kindness.
(The Mansell Collection)

part of the human diet. Today both these connotations are in decline, and there is a corresponding decline in meat-eating in some advanced countries.

THE GREAT RELIGIONS

It is tempting to try to trace the origins of Pythagorean morality back to Hinduism or to the other faiths which were quite newly founded in Pythagoras's day. Pythagoras, as a traveller, may have encountered people with knowledge of Zoroastrianism (which advocated the protection of useful animals), Jainism or Buddhism, which probably all began between 500 and 650 BC. As many major religions were founded in this era it seems best to discuss them in this chapter; but this is not to deny their continuing importance.

Based upon the idea of the transmigration of souls and the belief that all living creatures are the same in essence, Hinduism provided an entirely different basis from Christianity on which to build society. Animals, like humans, were arranged in a complex social hierarchy. According to this tradition, to kill a cow was as serious as to murder a high-caste man. Elephants and horses also held elevated status, but the penalty for killing even the despised dog was no less than that for the murder of an 'untouchable' human being.

Buddhism springs historically from Hinduism and shares the belief in the rebirth of the soul in human or animal form. Buddha 'trained himself to be kind to all animate life', taught that it was a sin to kill any living creature[8] and observed that 'the key to a new civilization is the spirit of Maitri, friendliness towards all living things.'

Hinduism and Buddhism quite early in their development abandoned animal sacrifice, and the feeling against unnecessary destruction of life led to widespread vegetarianism in both Hindu and Buddhist societies from the third century BC onwards. Animals were held to possess the same feelings as people, and several kings of ancient India are known to have founded hospitals for old and sick animals. Indeed, Asoka, emperor of India from about 274 to 232 BC, became a Buddhist and a vegetarian and, in accordance with the doctrine of 'ahisma' (nonviolence), suppressed the royal hunts and ordered the curtailment of the slaughter of animals throughout his empire. Among some Buddhists respect for all life is still the central ethic. Modern Hindus are still taught that the human soul can be reborn into other forms such as animals and insects – they are all considered part of the Supreme Being. Those who have lived wicked and selfish lives are more likely to be reborn in nonhuman form, whereas good living can mean eventual escape from the world. Hindus feel a duty to care, therefore, for all living things. Failure to observe this duty is believed to create bad 'karma' which increases the likelihood of rebirth as a nonhuman.

Of all the Eastern religions, Jainism in India carried the respect for life (rather than the avoidance of suffering) to its most radical position. The first vow of the Jain is not to kill. This leads to fastidious care for all living beings; 'vermin' may be removed, but never killed, and the mouth is covered and the path swept before it is walked upon, in deference to insect life.

The strict followers of Mani, the third-century Persian, were also forbidden to kill any living creature. The ordinary secular Manichaeans, however, observed a more relaxed code, and it is doubtful whether a respect for nonhuman life survived this religion's contact with Christianity over the subsequent centuries.

The Shinto religion of Japan, too, displayed a reverence for nature, emphasizing gratitude towards its benevolent forces and appeasing the malevolent; monkeys in particular were revered and depicted in the famous sculptured triplet 'see no evil, speak no evil, hear no evil.'

To this day, humankind's relationship with the other animals is an important part of the world's religions and many still believe in an active and magical kinship between human and nonhuman. Some South American Indians, for example, believe that all living things, including themselves, were created by animal spirits. Some animals, like the Harpy Eagle, are partners of members of the tribe and to kill one of them will mean the instant death of the human partner. For this reason some species of animal are carefully preserved. When an animal is killed for meat, it is feared that its angry spirit may seek revenge upon those who killed or ate it, making them ill. Killing for food thus becomes an action which requires special care. Similarly, in Babylon, priests would whisper in the ears of their sacrificial victims that it was the gods who killed them;[9] such is the guilt people feel about their speciesism.

The Australian aborigines for centuries have seen themselves as brothers and sisters of certain totem species. They believe that they and the totem animals share the same ancestors, who are still magically alive. Although they hunt animals for food, the totem species are never harmed and in some sacred places other animals are also protected. Aborigines feel a duty to care for the land and to preserve water-holes not just for themselves but for the nonhumans also.

Muslims believe that God created both human and nonhuman, although people were created in a special way when God breathed his spirit into Adam. Rather like Jews and Christians, Muslims are taught that God has given people power over the animals, yet to treat animals badly is to disobey God's will. They believe that the world belongs to God and that people are answerable to Him for their treatment of it; it is wrong, therefore, to hunt merely for pleasure, to use an animal as a target, to use its skin, to cause animals to fight each other, to incite them to act unnaturally in entertainments, or to molest them unnecessarily. Muhammad, so it is said, left his coat upon the ground rather than disturb his cat Muezza, who was sleeping on it, and was angry with his followers for capturing young birds, not least because this upset the mother bird. In practice this aspect of the Muslim religion has declined in its observance over the years, probably under Western influence, though several modern Muslim writers, such as Sayyid Abu A'la Maududi and Al-Hafiz Basheer Ahmad Masri have sought to re-emphasize Muhammad's concern for nonhumans.[10]

The Prophet taught that an animal should only be killed out of necessity. To do so unnecessarily was a deadly sin: 'He who takes pity (even) on a sparrow and spares its life, Allah will be merciful on him on the Day of Judgement;'[11] and 'if you must kill, kill without torture'.[12] He urged humane methods of slaughter: animals should be killed by the best means possible, should not be bound at slaughter, and should not be made to wait. When he saw a man sharpening his knife in the presence of the animal he was about to kill, he asked: 'Do you intend inflicting death on the animal twice?' Muhammad is also recorded as telling his followers to ride their camels 'only when they are fit to be ridden and let them go free when it is meet that they should rest'. He was opposed to the mutilation or disfigurement of animals caused, for instance, by cutting of forelocks, manes or tails.[13] He said that a woman would be sent to Hell for having locked up and starved a cat and, conversely, that Allah had blessed a serf who had saved a dog's life – 'there is a reward for acts of charity to every beast alive.'[14]

What is remarkable about Muhammad is his equal concern for saving life and avoiding suffering. Furthermore, as indicated by the stories of the animal seeing the knife being sharpened and at the feelings of the mother bird, the Prophet clearly included mental suffering in his considerations.

In most cases where religions lay down rules affecting human exploitation of nonhumans, however, the emphasis tends to be on restrictions on the *taking of life* rather than the *infliction of suffering*.

The religion which could have changed this emphasis through its principle of Love, Christianity, did not do so, as we shall see, because it magnified the gulf between human and nonhuman, eventually espousing the anthropocentrism of St Thomas Aquinas. Christians certainly believe that God is the creator of all things and that he (or she) cares for what he has made. Most also accept that people are responsible to God for the way in which they treat creation, and some feel a unity between all living things and are aware that they should be loving and caring at all times. Yet, strangely, animals were, and still are, usually omitted as appropriate objects of this Christian charity.

In the first book of the Bible, Genesis, it is stated:

And God said, Let us make man in our image, after our likeness: and let them have dominion over the fish of the sea, and over the fowl of the air,

and over the cattle, and over all the earth, and over every creeping thing that
creepeth upon the earth.

So God created man in his own image, in the image of God created he
him; male and female created he them.

And God blessed them, and God said unto them, Be fruitful, and multi-
ply, and replenish the earth, and subdue it: and have dominion over the fish
of the sea, and over the fowl of the air, and over every living thing that
moveth upon the earth.[15]

This gift of dominion is the key to the Christian understanding of
humankind's relation to the other animals. The humanitarianism of the
law of Moses, based as it may have been upon the kindly elements in
ancient Egyptian and Babylonian cultures, is quite evident for all who
wish to find it. On the other hand, a warped interpretation of the
concept of 'dominion' in Genesis has often overridden this in practice.[16]
The exact meaning of 'dominion', translated as 'rule' in the *New English
Bible*, must of course depend partly upon how a ruler of that day and
culture was supposed to behave. What connotations were customarily
attached to the idea of dominion? Was tyranny the norm or was there
an ideal of stewardship in which the lord and master should care for his
subjects as a parent does a child? It is worth noting that the same word
for dominion was used to describe God's relationship to humankind.
But whatever was originally intended by the word, surely it should not
be made to cover the full range of exploitation which it has been used to
justify in the case of human dominion over the other animals? What
Jewish ruler, for example, merely because he had dominion, would have
been regarded as justified in hunting his human subjects, or killing and
eating them? Even at the height of Roman cruelty such a state of affairs
would hardly have passed without comment!

The Jewish attitude towards nonhumans, as displayed elsewhere in
the Old Testament, was quite humane. In the book of Isaiah, for
example, who was preaching around 730 BC, we find opposition to
animal sacrifice when God says: 'I delight not in the blood of bullocks,
or of lambs, or of he goats'.[17] And in the book of Hosea, who was also
prophesying at this period, a similar sentiment is found:

And in that day I make a covenant for them with the beasts of the field, and
with the fowls of heaven, and with the creeping things of the ground: and I
will break the bow and the sword and the battle out of the earth, and will
make them to lie down safely.[18]

One of the strongest statements comes from Isaiah: 'He that killeth an
ox is as if he slew a man',[19] and in the first chapter of Genesis God
instructs man to be vegetarian.[20] It is only after the Flood that God
gives Noah permission to eat meat.[21]

These are not the only merciful passages to be found in the Old Testament. Cattle are to be allowed to rest on the Sabbath;[22] oxen treading the corn should not be muzzled; kids should not be cooked in their mother's milk; [23] parent birds should not be taken if sitting on eggs or with their young;[24] and men are enjoined not to yoke together the ox and the ass.[25] Proverbs recognizes that 'a righteous man regardeth the life of his beast'[26] and in Ecclesiastes it is stated that 'a man hath no preeminence above a beast: for all is vanity'.[27]

Even the strict injunctions of the Old Testament against sexual union between human and nonhuman were similar to those against incest; nonhuman animals were in this respect to be regarded rather as relatives.[28]

The decline in nonhuman sacrifice in Europe and Asia over the last two thousand years should not be taken to be a sign of growing respect for nonhumans, but of a belief that the gods were not to be placated in this way. Paradoxically, animal sacrifice works best, surely, when nonhumans are perceived as being kin, and thus qualifying as human sacrificial surrogates.

A LOST EDEN

What *was* the origin of meat-eating? Why are so many people repelled by the sight of blood, and why can so few easily kill and gut an animal until they get used to doing so? This reaction must tell us something about the basic programming of the human psyche. We do not seem to be designed as thorough-going carnivores. Nor do our teeth appear strong enough to tear and chew uncooked flesh. So, if it was not always present, when did our humanoid ancestors start this strange habit? Was it when the Ice Ages encroached slowly upon their fertile habitats, blighting the fruits and nuts upon which they had flourished and leaving vegetation suitable only for true herbivores? Perhaps there was indeed once an Eden in which men and women were all vegetarians because there was no shortage of fruit and vegetables; perhaps this economic, healthy and humane paradise will return.

Animals have been domesticated for thousands of years, kept as sources of food, clothing and services. New archaeological discoveries have pushed back the earliest dates of domestication far further into the past than had previously been recognized. Pigs, cattle and goats were kept as long ago as 6000 BC, dogs and sheep by 8000 BC. Did domestication improve the relationship between human and nonhuman? Some anthropological evidence suggests that modern hunter-gatherers show more respect for wildlife than agriculturalists do for their stock. But opposite cases can be found: the pastoralist Nuer, for instance, show considerable respect for their cattle, whereas some primitive hunters treat their quarry with appalling callousness, as in the case of the Baka pygmies of the Cameroon who use the same word for 'meat' as for 'animal' and see nothing wrong in cooking their prey alive.[29]

Serpell has eloquently asserted that typical hunter-gatherers see wild animals as their 'mental and spiritual equals or even superiors, capable of conscious thoughts and feelings analogous, in every respect, to those of humans'.[30] This is a pleasing idea. It may be true of some hunter-gatherer cultures, but it is doubtful if it is typical, except in the important case of totem species. On the contrary, it is reasonable to suggest that it was only after the domestication of agricultural and pet species that relationships between human and nonhuman could develop. In the absence of fear on either side, the solitary shepherd, for example, might begin to develop the feelings of companionship and protectiveness which this book is all about.

Maureen Duffy takes rather the same line as Serpell in arguing that 'it must have been the introduction of farming which led to the abandonment of respect for other animals and of a perception of humans as one species among many'.[31] The greater control exercised over nonhumans by the farmer indeed may have reduced his or her fear, and hence 'respect' for them. But this does not necessarily imply that it reduced his or her sympathy for nonhumans or increased his or her cruelty towards them. Surely the general rule is that familiarity breeds sympathy. It is easier to identify with a creature one knows, and although on occasions this will also lead to irritation at the other's failings, it at least allows him or her to be included in the moral circle.

Among primitives the moral circle is a small one, including only the tribe or group. Within this group nonhumans *can* be included provided that, as individuals, they are well known. Pet-keeping and even pet-suckling are common practices in hunter-gatherer societies, as Serpell notes,[32] and it is in relationships of this sort (rather than in the hunter–prey relationship) that kindness develops.

Farming comes somewhere between pet-keeping and hunting in the degree of intimacy which usually prevails between human and non-human, and typically creates a position for the animal which is on the periphery of the moral circle, closer to the centre of compassion than wild animals but further out than pets. It was probably because peasant Europeans in Antiquity still felt a closeness to other animals that the theologians of later times were so often prompted, as we shall see, to stress the desirability of maintaining a distance between human and nonhuman.

3 The Christian Legacy: Medieval Attitudes

Christianity can be seen as, in part, a reaction against the Roman cult of violence, but its concern was limited to human victims. Perhaps it was as politically unrealistic to try to save the thousands of creatures slaughtered in the Roman games as it would be today for a religious or political group to seek the abolition of football; the games were so central to the Roman way of life that not even emperors dared to interrupt them.

EARLY CHRISTIANITY

Except for his remark about the value of sparrows in the eyes of God, Jesus' own attitude towards animals is simply not known, perhaps because it was considered too unimportant to record, and St Paul – by far the most influential figure in early Christianity after Jesus – failed to include animals in the moral in-group. This is perhaps surprising in view of the revolutionary character of St Paul's teachings and his explicit opposition to prejudice based on class, sex and race.

The New Testament hardly mentions the human–nonhuman relationship. But this silence may have been only because it was conceived largely as a 'crisis document', written hurriedly to prepare people for Christ's return, which was believed to be imminent. The more comprehensive moral teachings of the Old Testament still stood.[2] One possible reason for the early Christian failure to include nonhumans more emphatically within the circle of Christian love, its central principle, is that early Christianity had to overcome pagan religions which included the worship of animals. To make matters worse, some early opponents had actually accused Christianity of donkey-worship, thus, possibly, putting its leaders on the defensive on this subject. Furthermore, the Christian and Jewish god, unlike many others, was explicitly manlike in form, rather than animal-like in any way. According to Lecky, no Christian writings equalled Plutarch's emphasis upon kindness to animals for another seventeen hundred years after his death.[3]

It was, however, Christianity which established the prevailing opinion on animals in the West, based to some extent upon one short remark made by St Paul. When commenting upon the law of Moses which states (Deuteronomy 25:4): 'Thou shalt not muzzle the ox when he treadeth out the corn', St Paul writes (I Corinthians 9:9–10): 'Doth God take care for oxen? Or saith he it altogether for our sakes? For our sakes, no doubt this is written: that he that ploweth should plow in hope.' Although the modern historian, Keith Thomas, has questioned St Paul's meaning, theologians usually did not.[4] They interpreted Paul as indicating quite definitely that God does *not* care for oxen.

Early Christianity continued to flourish in a world of declining civilization. Barbarian invasions from the North and East and the collapse of the Roman empire led to the erosion of law and order and the lowering of educational and administrative standards. Men and women of learning may have felt that human society was slipping back into a state of nature, and, in order to arrest this process it may be that they were further inclined to assert humankind's separateness from the beasts. Men and women definitely were *not* animals, they claimed; they alone were made in the image of God and alone possessed immortal souls.

The differences between human and nonhuman were thus exaggerated. Indeed, humankind's superiority over the other animal creation came to be regarded as almost synonymous with civilization itself, and those who behaved in an uncivilized way were dismissed as beast-like. This attitude continued through to the medieval and Renaissance periods, and, latterly at least, the characteristic view was one of exultation in the 'Empire of Man' and the hard-won conquest of nature.

ST THOMAS AQUINAS AND ST FRANCIS

The ambivalence of Christians in their attitude towards nonhumans is typified by the contrasting attitudes of St Thomas Aquinas and St Francis of Assisi.

Aquinas was born in Sicily in 1225, only a few months before St Francis died, into a world riven by religious dispute. Throughout the south of France and northern Italy at that time the Cathars had replaced Catholicism as the dominant religious influence, teaching that nonhuman animals as well as humans had immortal souls and forbidding the consumption of meat. At the age of nineteen Aquinas joined the austere Order of St Dominic, recently founded to suppress such heresy by the instigator of the Spanish Inquisition. Aquinas was very much influenced by Aristotle,[5] many of whose works had only recently become available to European scholars, and it seems he absorbed from Aristotle the idea that less rational beings, such as slaves and animals, exist to serve the interests of the more rational.

In his *Summa Contra Gentiles* Aquinas wrote:

If in Holy Scripture there are found some injunctions forbidding the infliction of some cruelty towards brute animals...this is either for removing a
man's mind from exercising cruelty towards other men, lest anyone, from
exercising cruelty upon brutes, should go on hence to human beings; or
because the injury inflicted on animals turns to a temporal loss for some
man, either the person who inflicts the injury or some other; or for some
other meaning, as the Apostle expounds Deuteronomy 25:4.[6]

Here he is referring to St Paul's remark about the oxen mentioned above
– 'Doth God take care for oxen?' And in his *Summa Theologica*,
Aquinas states: 'God's purpose in recommending kind treatment of the
brute creation is to dispose men to pity and tenderness towards one
another.'[7]

St Francis had been born forty years before Aquinas in Assisi and,
after a turbulent youth, had experienced visions and voices which led to
his conversion; he renounced material goods and began to preach the
imitation of Christ. Francis saw all nature as a mirror of the creator and
called not only living creatures but also the sun, moon, wind and water
his 'brothers' and 'sisters'; even illness and death were similarly greeted.
Francis was a visionary and a poet more than an intellectual. His
mystical sense of oneness with creation, his all-embracing love and his
frenzied life-style are in total contrast with the reserved, courteous and
scholarly character of Thomas Aquinas. The one was warm and intuitive
almost to the point of mania, the other cool and academic.

A medieval collection of anecdotes tells how St Francis preached to
his 'little sisters', the birds, and how he rescued some wild doves being
taken to the market and made nests for them. On another occasion he
tamed the fierce wolf of Agobio who had been eating people from the
town. St Francis spoke firmly to 'brother Wolf' and made him an offer:
if he would stop eating people then the townspeople would give him
food for the rest of his life. The wolf solemnly shook St Francis by the
hand and agreed. Such charming stories underline St Francis's love of
creation. Yet, as Peter Singer points out, he still accepted the orthodox
anthropocentric view that all creation exists for humankind's benefit.[8]
Indeed, he hardly distinguished between animate and inanimate; nor
is there any record of vegetarianism in the rules of the Franciscan
Order.

The Order did somewhat develop its ideas two centuries later in
the treatise *Dives and Pauper*,[9] written about 1410 and probably of
Franciscan origin, which implies that the commandment 'Thou shalt not
kill' (Exodus 20:13) applies in principle to nonhuman as well as to
human, although *not* applying in certain major cases such as the killing
of noxious animals or for meat and clothing. *Dives and Pauper* goes on
to state that men should not harm animals without cause and that it is a
grievous sin to torment beasts or birds for cruelty or vanity.

EARLIER SAINTS

Although Aquinas's doctrine towards the treatment of nonhumans eventually triumphed in Christian theology, it is important to emphasize that
kindness to animals was a hallmark of saintliness long before St Francis.
Far from being an isolated example, as is sometimes suggested,[10] St
Francis was really the culmination of a long saintly tradition. St John of
Chrysostom and St Basil of Caesaria, for example, both in the fourth
century, had preached kindness to animals. St John of Chrysostom, who
was a powerful influence in the Byzantine Church, is even quoted as
saying 'The Saints are exceedingly loving and gentle to mankind and
even to brute beasts...Surely we ought to show them great kindness
and gentleness for many reasons, but above all, because they are the
same origin as ourselves.'[11]
   In the Liturgy of St Basil can be found this prayer:

The Earth is the Lord's and the fulness thereof. O God, enlarge within us
the sense of fellowship with all living things, our brothers the animals to
whom thou has given the earth as their home in common with us. We
remember with shame that in the past we have exercised the high dominion
of man with ruthless cruelty, so that the voice of the earth, which should
have gone up to Thee in song, has been a groan of travail. May we realise
that they live, not for us alone, but for themselves and for Thee, and that
they love the sweetness of life.[12]

Both these texts are remarkable and explicit in their compassion.
   Many other saints are portrayed performing individual deeds of mercy
to animals: St Jerome (373–420), like the Roman slave Androcles, is
credited with taking a thorn from the paw of a lion who repaid him by
becoming a vegetarian and serving the monastery until he joined St
Jerome in death. St Columba, so it is told, ordered his monks to care for
an exhausted crane, and his follower, St Walaric, was wont to caress the
woodland birds. Some saints even anticipated the tactics of the modern
Animal Liberation Front: St Neot saving hares and stags from huntsmen,
and the twelfth-century Northumbrian, St Godric of Finchdale, rescuing
birds from snares.[13] St Aventine, who lived around 438 in Gascony,
rescued a stag from the hunters. St Carileff (c.540) protected a bull that
was being hunted by King Childebert, and both St Hubert (646–727?)
and the Roman general St Eustace (died 118), saw visions of the cruci-
fixion between the antlers of stags they were hunting; in the case of
St Hubert this led to his renunciation of the pleasures of the chase.
St Monacella (c.604) in Wales is said to have protected a hare from the
hounds, as did St Anselm (1033–1109) and St Isidore in Spain about a
century later.
   In 1159, a monk of Whitby, who was living in Eskdale, rescued a wild

2 St Anselm (1033–1109), Italian-born Archbishop of Canterbury, condemned cruelty to animals and once rescued a hare from huntsmen. A number of saints are reputed to have 'sabotaged' hunts in this way. The closeness of the relationship between St Francis (1181–1226) and nonhumans, far from being unusual, marked the end of a long saintly tradition, not yet revived in the attitudes of the modern Church.

(The Mansell Collection)

boar from the hunt. So outraged were the huntsmen at the disruption of their sport by this early hunt saboteur that they attacked and mortally wounded him. The abbot rallied to the support of the hermit who, before he died, forgave his murderers but ordered them, as a penance, to build a breakwater on the beach to prevent erosion of the land. Until the twentieth century this penance was remembered by the driving in of stakes into the sand on each Ascension Day.[14] The hermit of Eskdale surely must rank as one of the first great environmentalists, showing concern for wildlife and for habitat alike.

The remarkable St Cuthbert, too, was fond of wild animals and seems to have felt a sense of unity with them. A seventh-century Scottish shepherd-boy, he was fifteen when he became a monk in Melrose Abbey. Later, he became a hermit, living on Farne Island in a small cell. There he made friends with the birds, giving them his protection from the depradations of men, and, so the story goes, receiving food from them in return, as they shared their meals together.

Whether or not these stories are historical fact, it is true that they were part of Church lore for many centuries. If such compassion for beasts was attributed to the saints, it is clear that many ordinary men and women would have striven to follow their example. Regardless as to what the theologians were saying at the time, kindness to nonhumans must have been widely regarded as a saintly virtue.

In general, perhaps, later Christian theologians have not really faced up to the issue; rather than being actively speciesist they have ignored the problems intrinsic in the human—nonhuman relationship. Yet many in the Catholic Church continued to follow Aquinas's line and, as late as the nineteenth century, Pope Pius IX refused to allow the foundation of a society to protect animals in Rome on the grounds that human beings had no duties towards lower creation.[15]

THE MEDIEVAL RELATIONSHIP

Yet what did ordinary people think and do about the other animals in medieval times? It seems that Aquinas's anthropocentrism did not really percolate down to the masses for several centuries. Although it is evident that the middle ages were no exception to the age-old rule of ambivalence in the human—nonhuman relationship it seems that at least the non-humans were given a place in the community. Keith Thomas, in *Man and the Natural World,* mentions instances of everyday compassion contrasting with the better-known cruelties of the period,[16] and one can dimly discern that many in the medieval era perceived a kindred feeling with the beasts and that the natural impulse of compassion was often felt and acted upon. Nevertheless, the equally elemental sadistic desire to dominate was also present, as displayed in baiting, and the habitual contemporary exploitation of human and nonhuman alike bred an

3 This Victorian stained glass window in Whitby Museum commemorates the Hermit of Eskdale, who was mortally wounded by huntsmen while protecting a wild boar from them in the year 1159. Before he died the monk forgave his murderers on condition that they annually drove stakes into the water's edge at Whitby, reputedly to protect the land. This custom is still remembered on each Ascension Day. (Reproduced by kind permission of Whitby Museum; photograph John Tindale)

insensitivity to suffering and a thoughtlessness that we have with us to this day.

The record of the medieval relationship between human and nonhuman is, of course, rather sparse. Yet a feeling of kinship seems to have been taken for granted, with both kind and unkind consequences.

Country folk in Britain, after all, frequently slept under the same roof as their livestock until the sixteenth century. Even in towns it was not unusual to find horses, pigs and chickens sharing houses with men and women, rather as today our houses are inhabited by pet dogs, cats and budgerigars. It was not unknown to bedeck animals with bells or ribbons, to speak to them and to call them by name. Their alleged moral or immoral behaviour, or their social standing, could save or condemn them and, to a degree, the human class system was extended to the nonhuman community; falcons, greyhounds, spaniels and thoroughbred horses being regarded as 'noble', ferrets and cats as 'base'; and eagles, whales and lions as 'kings' of their respective orders.

Sometimes the 'social class' of an animal was simply a reflection of the class of human being who exploited it or the use to which it was put. This is clearly exemplified in the case of dogs, divided by Dr John Caius in 1576 *(Of English Dogges)* into three sorts − a 'generous' kind used for hunting or as pets, a 'rustic' sort used for necessary work, and a 'degenerate' type which included turnspits and stray curs.[17] As with human society, class was determined largely by breeding and partly by occupation.

Even more revealing is the old practice of holding animals responsible for crime, based perhaps upon Exodus 21:28: 'If an ox gore a man or a woman that they die; then the ox shall be surely stoned, and his flesh shall not be eaten: but the owner of the ox shall be quit.' Trials in England seem not to have occurred, although on the continent of Europe and particularly in France they were commonplace. A sow who killed a child in Falaise in 1386, for example, was sentenced to death by strangulation after being mutilated by the executioner, and during the following century sows were executed, usually by hanging, in Meulan, Lavegny and Laon for similar offences; in 1497, in Chavonne, a sow was condemned to be beaten to death for wounding a child, and another was executed in Nancy in 1572. Bulls were usually strangled, as at Moisy in 1314. A dog was hanged in the Netherlands in 1595, the carcass being duly suspended from the gallows to deter other dogs from biting babies, much as some modern gamekeepers will still display the corpses of 'vermin' they have shot.

Affronts to the dignity of the medieval church rarely went unpunished, as some sparrows had discovered in 1499 when they were excommunicated for leaving their droppings on the seats of the pews in St Vincent.[18] The famous Jackdaw of Rheims, who was cursed by bell, book and candle, was clearly not alone.

At least, one might say, nonhuman delinquents in the middle ages had the benefit of due process of law; they were not summarily executed as they are today. They were at least accorded the dignity of being treated, to some degree, as 'people' and not as things. Such trials may have satisfied the human need to 'make sense' of terrible events such as the killing of a child,[19] but it was surely because the medieval mind saw nonhumans as being very much like humans that it could not accept the modern explanation – that the child's death had been an accident caused by a less rational and unculpable being.

Insects often escaped with lighter sentences, most commonly being ordered to move to alternative accommodation. Beetles in St Julien, for instance, were ordered to move away from the vines they had damaged, and some leeches, convicted of killing fish in Lake Geneva in 1431, were excommunicated and banished to another home by the Bishop of Lausanne. Caterpillars in Valence and mosquitoes in Mayence suffered similar fates.

It can be seen that many regarded nonhumans as part of a wider class system, and the relationship between a peasant and his lord was considered similar in kind to that between an animal and his master. In short, the animals were often treated rather like poor relations – with a mixture of contempt and pity. Indeed this feeling of hierarchy was formalized in the popular philosophy of the Great Chain of Being which, as it derived from Aristotle, depicted nature as a huge feudal structure; at the top was God and beneath came archangels, seraphs, angels, man, animals, plants and minerals – in that order. However, the old pagan idea of transmigration persisted too; in medieval England the souls of the unshriven were commonly believed to roam, sometimes taking the form of seagulls or geese, or spectral dogs, and indeed some fishermen until quite recently believed that seals were the reincarnation of their comrades drowned at sea.

Perhaps as a reaction to such folklore, the denial that animals possessed a soul which would survive the death of the body became an important assertion among churchmen and one on which, rather inexplicably, many based their justification for the exploitation of nonhumans. Only a few splendid exceptions, like Cardinal Bellarmine, maintained the more logical opinion that because they lacked an afterlife nonhuman animals therefore deserved special consideration in this one: 'we shall have Heaven to reward us for our suffering, but these poor creatures have nothing but the enjoyment of their present life.'[20]

The large place filled by animals in the psychology of the middle ages can be seen in their heraldry, bestiaries, inn-signs and folk tales. Even their riddles and jokes reveal an often affectionate (and even anthropomorphic) interest in nonhumans:

Question: What day in the year be the flies most a-feared?

See here how Natures Book vnclasped lies, | Who y^th wise Apologues from Beasts, deriu'd,
Whose Pages Æsop reads with pearcing eyes. | Tells man they for his conduct were contriv'd.

4 Aesop's Fables are typical of literature popular in the late medieval and Renaissance periods, which condoned human 'dominion' and portrayed nonhumans as symbols for human exploitation.
(Barlow's Aesops Fables, Bodleian Library, Oxford, Douce A Subt. 48. Sig.a.2.verso F)

Answer: That is on Palm Sunday, when they see everybody have a handful of palm in their hand; they ween [think] it is to kill them with.

Question: Why come dogs so often to the church?

Answer: Because when they see the altars covered, they ween [think] their masters go thither to dinner.

Question: Why doth a dog turn him thrice about ere he lieth him down?

Answer: Because he knoweth not his bed's head from the feet.

Question: Wherefore is it that an ass hath so great ears?

Answer: Because her mother put no biggin [bonnet] on her head in her youth.[21]

Rude Sports

One of the main indications of how humans treated nonhumans in the medieval period is in the sporting record, for throughout the middle ages in Europe, as in classical times, the hunting and fighting of wild beasts were extolled as sports and entertainments. Although in later times Tudor ladies participated, and indeed sometimes delighted, in shooting and cutting the throats of captured animals, these activities were principally pursued in earlier days by men.

Such country sports can be divided into two major types. In the first a wild quarry is sought and killed, while in the second a captive animal is tormented. Both sports probably tap basic instincts — those of searching and bullying. The secondary reasons for these activities are fairly obvious. There were the usual social rewards associated with any sport: the displays of fashion, the conviviality and companionship. Furthermore, the fact that hunting (rather more than baiting) was for centuries the pastime of kings and nobles gave it an aristocratic appeal, and countless thousands of creatures have in consequence died on this altar of snobbery — and, indeed, still do so.

Throughout the middle ages, Europeans indulged in sports of both principal types; connected with both was the widespread idea that they were manly. Both had been founded upon the once essential tasks of the physically strongest and bravest of the tribe or family: the acquisition of food and the defence against predators. In prehistoric Europe, as in some parts of the globe to this day, these tasks had been necessary and dangerous. It did indeed take courage for Stone Age men to attack the mammoth with their primitive spears and to defend their families against the sabre-tooth tiger, but, gradually, as nature was conquered and food became cultivated, the necessity for hunting and conquering dwindled. Yet men did not wish to relinquish the pleasures they had derived from proving their manhood in these ways.

In the twelfth century, John of Salisbury criticized hunters thus: 'By constantly following this way of life they lose much of their humanity and become as savage, nearly, as the very brutes they hunt.'[22] Such early criticisms, however, were rarely recorded, unlike the better-known contemporary resentment towards the draconian laws against poaching which prevented the common man from killing for food.

The Norman kings had claimed a monopoly of hunting over large parts of the country and enforced this through a highly unpopular policy of 'afforesting' other people's land, penalties being imposed upon those who killed game species without authority. Indeed poaching was suppressed with brutality all over Europe for many centuries and, as late as 1537, the Bishop of Salsburg tied a poacher in the skin of a deer and threw him to the hounds to be torn to pieces in the market place.

It appears that hunting, although recognized as primarily a sport, had long been justified on the grounds that it produced food. Indeed, at least from Chaucer's day, the edible hare and deer were acceptable quarries while the fox, like the badger, was not. It was only in the early sixteenth century that fox-hunting became established,[23] and was then justified on the grounds that the fox was the utmost villain.

Cockfighting, according to Lecky, was a favourite sport for children in England as early as the twelfth century,[24] although it was, like football, suppressed for a time by Edward III because it was considered to be diverting men from learning the valued skills of archery. Bull-baiting goes back at least to the reign of King John in the thirteenth century, but in this case again the justification given was a culinary one. Baiting, so it was claimed, was necessary to make the bull's flesh wholesome, and for many years butchers in England were prohibited by law from killing a bull until it had been baited.

4 The Renaissance and its Aftermath

It seems that as the medieval period drew to a close, the human treatment of nonhumans in Europe actually worsened. The influence of the saints faded and the growing anthropocentrism of the Renaissance heralded several centuries of outstanding cruelty. It was at this time that the speciesism of Thomas Aquinas became a useful doctrine in helping to allay any qualms of conscience.[1]

TUDOR AND STUART BRITAIN

Whereas in earlier times hunting in Britain had been associated mainly with the killing of edible species, such as deer and hares, around the end of the fifteenth century this began to change. In 1539 Robert Pye informed Thomas Cromwell that foxes could be got rid of entirely, but the gentry would not allow it because they enjoyed hunting them. Foxhounds, he added, did more damage to farmers' chicken and sheep than did foxes.[2] Nevertheless, fox-hunting gained steadily in popularity throughout the sixteenth and seventeenth centuries. From the fifteenth century onwards hunting practices seem to have become increasingly bloody, the quarry (usually deer) being dismembered and disembowelled on the spot, its less noble portions being thrown to the hounds and blood being ritualistically splashed upon the onlookers. The hapless Henry VI (1421–71), although he hunted, could not bear to see the animals killed.[3]

In England, the scarcity of game after the fifteenth century encouraged the development of parks from which the deer could not easily escape and in which poachers found it more difficult to follow their craft. Seated in a bower surrounded by servants, Queen Elizabeth I, in later years, would shoot deer at close range, rounded up especially for the purpose. On one occasion, in 1591, she shot and killed four out of thirty deer brought to her and, while music played, one of the ladies shot another. On other occasions she hunted in the conventional manner, dismounting to cut the animals' throats. Once she contented herself by cutting off the ears of a terrified hart as 'a ransom' before allowing it to return to the herd. James I, too, would personally dispatch his cornered quarry, and he maintained contact with the latest hunting techniques from France, employing French riding and hunting masters to teach his children.

In many European countries, hunting became a spectator sport involving carefully staged mass executions of confined animals. In Germany, for example, deer were driven through triumphal arches or into lakes to be hacked to pieces with swords by men in fancy dress. Indeed it was towards the end of the sixteenth century that hunting and baiting became barely distinguishable. When Queen Elizabeth visited Kenilworth in 1575 she first watched a hart being killed in the water by hounds, then saw a pack of mastiffs let loose on thirteen bears – 'a sport very pleasant', said Robert Laneham, 'to see the bear...shake his ears twice or thrice with the blood'.[4] In Scotland the animals were driven into especially prepared dykes to be slaughtered, or rounded up in huge herds and then attacked with any sort of weapon that was to hand. James I used to paddle in the resulting gore, convinced that it strengthened the sinews of his somewhat spindly legs.

Baiting became increasingly barbaric and almost any creature unfortunate enough to be taken alive in the fifteenth and sixteenth centuries might be used for this purpose; bears, bulls, monkeys, cats, even horses, were chained to a post and then attacked. Dogs were the usual assailants, but men would also bait tethered bears, provided they had first been blinded. Paul Hentzner, a German tourist in England, reported in 1598 that he saw such a blinded bear scourged:

by five or six men standing circularly with whips, which they exercise upon him without any mercy as he cannot escape because of his chain; he defends himself with all his force and skill, throwing down all that come within his reach and are not active enough to get out of it, and tearing the whips out of their hands and breaking them.[5]

In Tudor times bear-baiting reached its zenith of popularity and herds of bears were maintained throughout England. The most famous bear-garden was on Bankside in Southwark, which admitted a thousand spectators at a penny a head to view bears set upon by mastiffs, who would often be so mutilated that they would also die cruel deaths.

In some parts of the country cock-fights were staged in churchyards, and many new cockpits were built in the reigns of Henry VIII and Elizabeth I. The other great bloodsport was cock-throwing. This involved tying a cock or hen to a stake and then hurling sticks at it until it was dead. Turner notes that 'if its leg was broken, rough splints were applied so that it could still stand to receive punishment. Sometimes it was buried in earth with only its head visible; or it might be thrust in an earthen vessel, with head and tail protruding, and become the prize of the first person to break the vessel.'[6] Throwing at cocks was a sport especially indulged in on Shrove Tuesday, although the reason for this is unclear. (A similar sport, involving throwing stones at live rabbits hung on stakes, persists in parts of Spain to this day.)

Despite royal patronage, towards the end of Elizabeth's reign there were signs that baiting was losing some of its popularity and that Londoners, at least, were beginning to prefer the more intellectual pleasures of the theatre. Elizabeth herself deplored this trend and, with the support of the Lord Mayor, she prohibited the performance of plays on Thursdays, which were reserved for baiting.

There seems to be no evidence that this gradual disenchantment with baiting was due to any organized opposition, and especially not on humanitarian grounds; such overt campaigns were only to begin in the following century. So we see the dwindling of a cruel custom without any accompanying reform movement to account for it. Was it just that William Shakespeare was writing such excellent plays? Was it the growing fastidiousness of the new middle classes, or was it the stirrings of conscience?

It is likely that in Britain in the sixteenth century there had been more tormenting of nonhumans just for sport than at any time before or since. But matters did not much improve in the following century. The cruelty of children, in particular, was marked. They would indulge themselves by throwing at cocks, tying pans to the tails of dogs, skinning live frogs, dropping cats from heights, inflating toads by blowing into them through a straw and pushing needles through the heads of chickens.[7] Throughout the Tudor and Stuart periods the long-established view had persisted that animals were given life in order to be of service to humankind, and this opinion was the usual justification given for barbaric sports. Keith Thomas aptly describes the attitude of the preachers of this period as 'breathtakingly anthropocentric'. Every beast was believed either to have a practical function or a moral meaning for human benefit.[8]

The medieval bestiaries, the best known of which was that of the perennial Physiologus, probably the most popular tome after the Bible itself, had been a wonderful mixture of inaccurate observations of animals laced with fantastic and religious overtones. The main intention of the bestiaries was to display virtues and vices in animal behaviour and to exhort the reader to imitate the former and abjure the latter. In some quarters these arguments were carried to extremes and even the most unlikely instances of creation continued to be explained in this way, even into the eighteenth century. Horseflies, according to William Byrd as late as 1728, had been created so 'that men should exercise their wits and industry to guard themselves against them'. The louse was indispensable, the Reverend William Kirby explained, as an incentive to cleanliness. Even horse manure had been given a sweet aroma, George

Cheyne explained in 1705, because God knew that man would often be close to it.[9]

The earlier emphasis upon the Fall and the consequent imperfection of nature was replaced in the late seventeenth century by arguments of this sort, intricately demonstrating the benevolence of the creator. Not only medics, but scientists in general, consciously espoused this position, arguing that the object of their studies was to discover God's benevolence to man through nature.

Post-Renaissance Europe had become exceptionally dependent upon animals as sources of food, motive-power and clothing, and from the seventeenth to the nineteenth centuries England was probably one of the most carnivorous societies of any age, reinforced by the theories of contemporary medicine (in the late twentieth century to be entirely revised) which held that meat was an essential part of the human diet and was of particular value to health.

The Renaissance had ushered in a process of refinement in manners, dress and attitudes, upon which men and women prided themselves. The rough simplicity of the early middle ages was looked down upon, and humankind's 'animal' functions such as excretion, copulation and suckling became increasingly matters for embarrassment – a long-lasting trend which only began to be reversed during the early twentieth century under the influence of Freud. The word 'beast', in common use during earlier centuries, began to be replaced by the more contemptuous 'brute' (literally 'stupid' or 'irrational') from the late sixteenth century onwards.

Middle-class Englishmen of the period were anxious to assert the difference between themselves and the brutes, partly to reassure themselves of their intellectual and social status and partly out of a genuine belief in the process of civilization. The Renaissance was, moreover, about humanism; the claim that man was of prime importance, dignity and potential. This opinion left the 'lower animals' out of the picture and compounded the anthropocentrism already being expounded by contemporary Christian theologians.

From about 1450 till 1700 the situation in Britain was at its blackest for nonhuman creatures. Nevertheless, although as we shall see it was only in the eighteenth century that the humane reaction really took off, the spark of compassion was far from being entirely extinguished by the rampant speciesism of the preceding two centuries.

SIGNS OF COMPASSION

Little is known of Leonardo da Vinci's concern for animals save that it is reputed that he became a vegetarian, that he used to buy caged birds in order to release them, and that he saw humankind as tyrannous.[10]

He is quoted by John Vyvyan as expostulating 'Oh, Justice of god! Why dost thou not wake and behold thy creatures thus ill used?'[11] When he died in 1519, there could have been few other contemporaries who had publicly committed themselves to such a view. But then Leonardo in so many ways anticipated the thinking of later centuries.

It is perhaps a feature of genius to feel sympathy with nonhuman animals. Isaac Newton, for instance, more than a century later, would become noted as a cat-lover, and is reputed to have invented the 'catflap' for his pets; that other great cosmologist, Albert Einstein, would urge 'widening our circle of compassion to embrace all living creatures', and Albert Schweitzer, in almost identical words, would warn 'until he extends the circle of his compassion to all living things, man will not himself find peace'.

In 1516 Sir Thomas More (1478−1535) published his *Utopia*, and thus qualifies as one of the first writers since classical times, albeit implicitly, to advocate mercy towards nonhumans. He wrote of his Utopians: 'They kill no living beast in sacrifice, nor they thinke not that the merciful clemencye of God had delite in bloude and slaughter, which hath geven liffe to beastes to the intent they should live.' They also despised the 'foolyshe pleasures' of hunting and hawking: 'Thou shouldest rather be moved with pitie to see a selye innocent hare murdered of a dogge: the weake of the stronger, the fearefull of the fearce, the innocent of the cruell and unmercyfull.'[12]

William Shakespeare's writing reflects the perennial ambivalence of human towards nonhuman. Throughout his plays animals are referred to in allegory and metaphor and dogs, for example, are depicted as figures of contempt. Yet the author reveals a humanitarian attitude in several instances. Isabella, for example, in *Measure for Measure*, claims that

> the poor beetle, that we tread upon,
> In corporal sufferance finds a pang as great
> As when a giant dies.

In *As You Like It* the First Lord describes Jacques in the Forest of Arden watching:

> A Poor sequester'd stag,
> That from the hunters' aim had ta'en a hurt,
> Did come to languish; and, indeed, my Lord,
> The wretched animal heav'd forth such groans
> That their discharge did stretch his leathern coat
> Almost to bursting, and the big round tears
> Cours'd one another down his innocent nose
> In piteous chase.

Tho: Moor L.ª Chancelour.

5 Sir Thomas More (1478–1535) was one of the few Renaissance figures whose writings indicate a concern for nonhuman animals. Living at a time when cruelty and callousness in the human– nonhuman relationship reached a peak in Europe, he wrote that his Utopians despised hunting as 'a foolyshe pleasure'. Leonardo da Vinci and Michel de Montaigne were contemporaries who held similar views.

(The Mansell Collection)

King Henry VI, in the play of the same name, is made to say:

> As the butcher takes away the calf,
> And binds the wretch, and beats it when it strays,
> Bearing it to the bloody slaughter house;
> Even so, remorseless, have they borne him hence:
> And, as the Dam runs lowing up and down,
> Looking the way her harmless young one went,
> And can do naught but wail her darling's loss,
> Even so myself bewail good Gloster's case...

In *Cymbeline*, the Queen proposes to experiment upon animals in order to test poison:

> I will try the forces
> Of these thy compounds on such creatures as
> We count not worth the hanging but none human,
> To try the vigour of them, and apply
> Allayments to their act, and by them gather
> Their several virtues and effects.

But she is warned off by Cornelius:

> Your Highness shall from this practice but make
>   hard your heart;
> Besides the seeing these effects will be
> Both noisome and infectious.[13]

One or two other thinkers of the sixteenth century are believed to have shown some compassion for animals. Tycho Brahe (1546−1601), the great Danish astronomer, is reputed to have been an animal-lover, as is Pierre Charron (1541−1603), the French theologian whose friend, Michel de Montaigne (1533−92), published his essay *Of Cruelties* in 1588. Montaigne has been hailed by Singer as the first since Roman times to condemn cruelty to animals as wrong in itself. Montaigne certainly does this, although his grounds appear emotional rather than reasoned:

Amongst all other vices, there is none I hate more, than crueltie, both by nature and judgement, as the extremest of all vices. But it is with such an yearning and faint-hartednesse, that if I see but a chickins necke puld off, or a pigge stickt, I cannot chuce but grieve, and I cannot well endure a seelie dew-bedabled hare to groane, when he is seized upon by the houndes...As for me, I could never so much as endure, without remorse and griefe, to see a poore, sillie and innocent beast pursued and killed, which is harmelesse and void of defence, and of whom we receive no offence at all. And as it commonly hapneth, that when the Stag begins to be embost, and finds his strength to faile-him, having no other remedie left him, doth yeeld and bequeath himselfe unto us that pursue him, with teares suing to us for mercie, was ever a grievous spectacle unto me. I seldom take any beast alive, but I give him his libertie.[14]

Montaigne repeatedly quotes Plutarch and Pythagoras rather than holy scripture. His sympathy for animals is clearly a 'gut' reaction and the texts he uses for support are pagan rather than Christian. Although himself a sceptic, he does produce one religious argument in support of his compassion:

Divinitie it selfe willeth us to shew them some favour: And considering, that one selfe-same master (I meane that incomprehensible worldframer) hath placed all creatures in this his wondrous palace for his service, and that they, as well as we, are of his household: I say, it hath some reason to injoyne us, to shew some respect and affection towards them.

Montaigne, like St Francis, goes on to express a feeling of:

respect, and a generall duty of humanity, which tieth us not only unto brute beasts that have life and sense, but even unto trees and plants. Unto men we owe Justice, and to all other creatures that are capable of it, grace and benignity. There is a kinde of enter-changeable commerce and mutuall bond betweene them and us. I am not ashamed nor afraid to declare the tendernesse of my childish Nature, which is such, that I cannot well reject my Dog, if he chance (although out of season) to fawne upon me, or beg of me to play with him.

He roundly rejects the anthropocentric view. He sees human and non-human animals as being qualitatively the same and therefore on the same level morally:

We are neither above nor under the rest: what ever is under the coape of heaven (saith the wise man) runneth one law, and followeth one fortune... Some difference there is, there are orders and degrees: but all is under the visage of one-same nature.[15]

Although Montaigne's works were promptly translated into English and were read by many, probably including Shakespeare, their message had already been somewhat anticipated in England by Philip Stubbes in 1583. Stubbes (1555–1610) was of a very different mould from the gentle but worldly Montaigne. A Puritan theologian, he attacked cock-fighting and hunting partly on the grounds that these sports tended to be accompanied by swearing, brawling, drinking and whoring: 'I never read of any in the volume of the Sacred Scriptures that was a good man and a hunter.' Stubbes's principal argument was that it is an insult to God to abuse his creatures. Yet one can also detect some genuine sympathy for the animals themselves:

What Christian heart can take pleasure to see one poor beast to rent, tear and kill another, and all for his foolish pleasure? And though they be bloody beasts to mankind and seek his destruction, yet we are not to abuse them for his sake who made them and whose creatures they are...[16]

Even the great Protestant reformers, Martin Luther (1483–1546) and John Calvin (1509–64) showed feelings of compassion for the beasts, although both reinforced the anthropocentric view of creation. Calvin wrote that God 'will not have us abuse the beasts beyond measure, but to nourish them and to have care of them'. Man still comes first, but a beast is 'a creature of God' who gave man dominion 'with the condition that we should handle them gently'.[17]

At the end of the sixteenth century, at the height of British speciesism, the humanitarian spark still glows dimly, fanned partly by secular compassion and partly by religious feeling, epitomized by Philip Sidney's (1554–86) gentle injunction: 'Thou art of blood, joy not to make things bleed. Thou fearest death; thinke they are loath to die'.[18]

In Catholic states, too, there were signs of compassion: in 1588 an anonymous Spanish officer on board one of the ships of the Armada noted the pitiable plight of horses thrown overboard into the sea, and in 1567 Pope Pius V prohibited bull-fighting and the baiting of wild beasts, and denied Christian burial to bullfighters killed in the ring. The motives are unclear, but his Bull states that such exhibitions are 'contrary to Christian duty and charity'.[19]

A trickle of arguments in favour of the nonhumans slowly appeared during the seventeenth century. The fashionable writer Francis Quarles, for example, expostulated in 1641:

> The birds of the aire die to sustain thee;
> The beasts of the field die to nourish thee;
> The fishes of the sea die to feed thee.
> Our stomacks are their common sepulcher.
> Good God! With how many deaths are our poor lives patcht up!
> How full of death is the life of momentary man![20]

Quarles demonstrated a practical and down-to-earth sort of decency towards animals which remains part of British culture to this day: 'Take no pleasure in the death of a creature; if it be harmless or uselesse, destroy it not: if usefull, or harmefull destroy it mercifully.'[21]

A significant figure of this period was the Chief Justice, Sir Matthew Hale (1609–76), who worried about eating flesh, yet assumed that it was necessary. He wrote, in about 1662: 'I have ever thought that there was a certain degree of justice due from man to the creatures, as from man to man.'[22] Sir Matthew abhorred cruel sports and saw all cruelty as 'tyranny' and 'a breach of that trust under which the dominion of the creatures was committed to us'. It was said of Sir Matthew that the only occasion on which he was known to be thoroughly angry was when a servant allowed a pet bird to starve.

The distinction falls to the remarkable Gloucestershire shepherd, Thomas Tryon (1634–1703), to be the first to introduce the word 'rights' in the nonhuman context, when he made the 'fowls of heaven' complain, in about 1683:

But tell us, O Man! we pray you tell us what injuries have we committed to forfeit? What law have we broken, or what Cause given you, whereby you can pretend a Right to invade and violate our part, and natural Rights, and to assault and destroy us, as if we were the Agressors and no better than Thieves, Robbers and Murtherers, fit to be extirpated out of the Creation?[23]

Tryon, who was a vegetarian, wrote extensively about diet and was an active opponent of slavery. Later, he wrote in his *Wisdom's Dictates* in 1691: 'violence and killing either Man or Beasts is as contrary to the Divine Principle as light is to darkness…Man's Soul nor Body can never be at rest or peace, until he do suffer the inferior creatures to have and enjoy that Liberty and quiet they groan to be delivered into.'[24]

During the early seventeenth century Puritan opinion began to come round to the view that animals did indeed have souls. John Milton, Robert Fludd and the Leveller Richard Overton were of this opinion. In the following century, Joseph Butler, John Hildrop and Richard Dean concurred. Nevertheless, Puritans during the Civil War decided that the best way to stop bear-baiting, souls or no, was to kill the bears. Cromwell himself ordered this to be done when, upon entering Uppingham, he found a bear-bait in progress on the sabbath: the bears were tied to a tree and shot. General Ireton acted similarly, and in 1635 Colonel Pride shot the bears at Southwark – an action which plagued his conscience on his death-bed. How far the Puritans were acting out of compassion is debatable. Later historians such as Hume and Macaulay were certain that it was the spectators' pleasure and not the bears' pain to which they objected.[25]

Baiting, like other blood sports, had become associated with the Royalist cause and with the rough hedonistic side of Old England. The Puritans were thus acting politically in their suppression of these kingly pleasures. They disliked the accompanying crudeness and immorality which attended them, and in addition may have had grounds for fearing that these sports were a breeding ground for Royalist sympathy or a pretext for Royalist gatherings.

At the Restoration, however, baiting did not experience the revival that some may have anticipated for it. The theatre, which had threatened to usurp the affection felt for baiting in the previous century, had also been suppressed by the Puritans, and after 1660 its popularity soared, along with that of horse-racing, while baiting continued to languish.

Two other figures of the seventeenth century must be mentioned: Henry More and John Locke. More (1614−87) had studied philosophy at Cambridge; although he put humans far above the other animals, he told Descartes that his doctrine that nonhumans were unconscious was 'murderous'. More tended to the view that animals, like men, had immortal souls, and in 1655 he wrote that animals had been created to enjoy themselves as well as to be of service to man, and that to assert otherwise was sheer pride, ignorance and 'haughty presumption'.[26]

John Locke (1632−1704), the great English philosopher, was another who could see through Descartes's contention. The idea that animals had immortal souls had caused some people considerable anxiety, Locke suggested, and this was the real reason why they argued that animals were unfeeling machines. He considered it wrong to waste any food that might sustain wild animals or birds. Locke argued that compassion was natural and cruelty unnatural, and in his *Thoughts on Education* he wrote: 'Children should from the beginning be bred up in an abhorrence of killing and tormenting any living creature...and indeed, I think people from their cradle should be tender to all sensible creatures.'[27]

EARLY LEGISLATION

The first modern laws to protect animals appear to date from the seventeenth century, one in a Puritan setting, the other originating from a more Royalist source. Thomas Wentworth, Earl of Strafford (1593−1641), a powerful and ambitious English statesman, was made Lord Deputy of Ireland in 1631, and as part of his 'civilizing' and 'anglicizing' reforms in that country, passed a law in 1635 prohibiting the pulling of wool off sheep and the attaching of ploughs to horses' tails; one of the two reasons for this law being given as 'the cruelty used to the beasts'. This is probably the earliest legal reference to this concept in the English language.[28] Strafford's motives are unknown. He seems an unlikely candidate to be a pioneering humanitarian, being better known for his arrogant pursuit of power, which eventually led him to the scaffold in 1641. If such a measure meant no more to him than being part of an accepted 'anglicization', it may reveal that by the early seventeenth century, condemnation of cruelty to animals was becoming part of English culture.

The other example of seventeeth-century legislation comes from the other side of the Atlantic where, in 1641, the Puritans of the Massachusetts Bay Colony printed in their first legal code 'The Body of Liberties':

OFF THE BRUITE CREATURE. LIBERTY 92.
No man shall exercise any Tirranny or Crueltie towards any bruite Creature which are usuallie kept for man's use.

LIBERTY 93.
If any man shall have occasion to leade or drive Cattel from place to place that is far of, so that they be weary, or hungry, or fall sick, or lambe, It shall be lawful to rest or refresh them, for a competent time, in any open place that is not Corne, meadow, or inclosed for some peculiar use.

These liberties were framed by Nathaniel Ward (c.1578–1652), who had been born in Haverhill in England and had graduated in law from Emmanuel College, Cambridge. Ironically, it was Strafford's friend Bishop Laud who had driven him from England in 1634 for heresy.

Of course, there had been some far earlier precedents. Besides the commands to be found in the Old Testament, Lecky records that for a time among the Greeks and early Romans it had been a capital offence to kill an ox. This is typical, suggests Lecky, of societies in which legislators are trying to establish agricultural habits among a warlike and nomadic people. He also cites Quintillian's first-century account of a child being put to death for cruelty to birds.[29] Among the Egyptians it had been a capital offence to kill almost any wild animal, and Asoka in India had similarly decreed (see chapter 2).

In other words, legislation in this field was not new. However, in the English-speaking world, the statutes of Thomas Wentworth and the Reverend Nathaniel Ward are the earliest records so far discovered. Yet for a hundred years after the passing of Martin's Act in 1822 (see chapter 6) this was believed to be an unprecedented step. Only in the last few years have the statutes of the seventeenth century been rediscovered, and so it may well be that others of even earlier date are yet to be found.[30]

THE VIRTUES OF BEASTS

The seventeenth century also saw a revival of interest in stories about the alleged virtues and abilities of beasts. These had been common themes in later Roman literature, as we have seen (chapter 2), and in stories of the saints in early medieval times (see chapter 3).

By the early seventeenth century animals were being promoted on several counts: first, it was claimed that they were almost as clever as men and perhaps wiser; secondly that they were morally superior. It was pointed out that animals did not tell lies, get drunk or wage war,[31] and Montaigne himself used such arguments to bolster his claims for their fairer treatment. Indeed these themes prepare the ground before almost all the major advances in humanitarian legislation. We find them in the late sixteenth and early seventeenth centuries in the fifty years prior to the first legislative protection of Strafford and the Puritans. They also are a feature of the movement at the end of the eighteenth century before Martin's legislation of 1822, and again in the middle of the nineteenth century prior to the Cruelty to Animals Act of 1876 (see chapters 5 and 7). In a more sophisticated form in such works as Desmond Morris's *The Naked Ape* (1967) and in the celebration of the intelligence of whales, dolphins and apes, these themes reappeared in the 1960s and 1970s. In each century, it seems, humans go through a period of reminding each other that the chasm between themselves and non-humans is not so wide. This process often anticipates political campaigns and legislative reforms, although all too often these have been postponed during periods of war, as for example, in the cases of the Napoleonic wars and the two World Wars in the present century.

John Locke himself postulated that animals share some mental processes with human beings. Sir Matthew Hale thought that many displayed sagacity. The Dean of Winchester in 1683 agreed that animals showed the capacity for reason. Indeed by this date this was orthodoxy in some circles, as is noted in the very revealing comment made by W. Howell in 1679: 'That there are some footsteps of reason, some strictures and emissions of ratiocination in the actions of some brutes, is too vulgarly known and too commonly granted to be doubted'.[32] It has been suggested that the scientists, whose experiments began to reveal the general similarity between the physiology of animals and themselves, were responsible for narrowing the gap. Up to a point they were, for the more they searched for the seat of the soul in the hearts or pineal glands of men and animals, the more it became clear that the physical differences between the species were more of degree than kind. It was not, however, the scientists themselves who drew the obvious moral conclusions from this. Sheltering absurdly and selfishly behind Descartes, they left it to the men of letters to call for justice for the animals.

DESCARTES AND VIVISECTION

Towards the end of the seventeenth century there seems to have been a rapid increase of interest in the practice of vivisection. Anyone could do it and almost everyone with intellectual pretensions did: princes and charlatans, serious scientists and quacks, all jumped on the bandwagon. No sooner did the rude sport of baiting begin to lose support than this new and even more frightful form of torture swept into vogue.

As E. S. Turner puts it:

In France fashionable ladies who used to attend the disembowellings of dead criminals for the frisson now watched living dogs turned inside out. There was no attempt to coordinate research, if research it could be called; anyone who could think of an audacious or amusing experiment proceeded to carry it out. Nor was it always pretended that the overriding object was to save human suffering, or to improve the human lot. For every experiment conducted to elicit new information, a score were performed to demonstrate what was already well known, or to show off the manipulator's skill...the new intellectual pursuits were dismembering, poisoning, drowning, suffocating, gutting, burning, impaling, draining, starving and injecting.[33]

Whereas the two great diarists of the seventeeth century, Samuel Pepys and John Evelyn, condemned baiting as 'rude' and 'butcherly', they both enthusiastically attended vivisections, Evelyn showing only minor twinges of concern.

During the middle ages vivisection was almost unknown. It was Renaissance Italy which had revived the practice established in classical times by Galen (AD c.130−201). In the sixteenth century, the anatomist Realdus Columbus of Cremona (1516−59) had dissected living animals; so also had Paracelsus (1490−1541) and Andreas Vesalius (1514−64). Later, William Harvey (1578−1657) had conducted research on deer in the parks at Hampton Court and Windsor, put at his disposal by Charles I, although it has been alleged that Harvey's initial postulation of the circulation of the blood arose not from such experiments but from his observation of valves in the blood vessels of dissected human cadavers,[34] and Robert Boyle himself related that Harvey had told him this.

Whether the influential contribution of René Descartes (1596-1650) helped to expand the practice of vivisection, as some such as John Vyvyan, suggest,[35] or whether his argument that animals do not feel pain was an attempt to justify an expansion which had already occurred and in which he participated, is not easy to ascertain. Certainly Descartes's fatuous assertion that animals do not feel pain helped to ease the consciences of many experimenters in the years to come.

Descartes, a neurotic young man, had peeled away the concretions of superstition and the other unprovable cultural beliefs that he had accumulated and found inside only one statement of which he could be sure: *Cogito ergo sum* ('I think, therefore I am' or, to parapharase Spinoza's rendering, 'I am conscious, therefore I exist'). Descartes's very fundamental sense of personal uncertainty led him to put great store upon the one thing of which he *was* certain − his consciousness. For the same reason he espoused a faith in mathematics 'because of the *certainty* of its proofs', and the definiteness of the new science of mechanics similarly attracted him. But Descartes also clung to his Christianity, although his faith seemed to be in conflict with his belief that the bodies of men and women are machines. He solved this problem by emphasizing the importance of the human soul (which, he said, does not have its origin in matter) and by equating this immortal soul with consciousness. As only men and women have immortal souls, he argued, then it follows that animals cannot have consciousness; they are machines only and experience neither pain nor pleasure. When burnt with a hot iron or cut with a knife their writhing and screaming are like the creaking of a hinge, no more. He proceeded to alienate his wife by experimenting upon their dog.

As Singer points out, Descartes was aware that such an argument had several other advantages, moral and practical. In the first place it helped avoid the assumption that people are like animals in that they can expect no after-life — an error that could lead to immoral conduct.[36] Secondly, Descartes's line of argument solved the theological problem of why a good God should allow animals to suffer, since they were not responsible for Adam's original sin. Finally, as Descartes put it in a letter to Henry More dated 5 February 1649: 'My opinion is not so much cruel to animals as indulgent to men...Since it absolves them from the suspicion of crime when they eat or kill animals.'[37]

Two outstanding British scientists of the period seem not to have taken Descartes too seriously. Both Robert Boyle (1627–91) and Robert Hooke (1635–1703) experimented on animals, but did so knowing the suffering they caused. Indeed both declined to repeat cruel experiments on the same animal and, in their correspondence, discussed the use of opiates to reduce their subjects' pain.[38] Most thoughtful people, then as now, probably remained convinced that nonhumans *do* feel pain, but the fact that the so-called 'father of modern philosophy' should make such an extraordinary claim remained a refuge for many subsequent vivisectors who were haunted by guilt or attacked by humanitarians.

An eye-witness account by Nicholas Fontaine (1625–1709) survives, which illustrates the attitude of contemporary Cartesians:

They administered beatings to dogs with perfect indifference, and made fun of those who pitied the creatures as if they felt pain. They said the animals were clocks; that the cries they emitted when struck were only the noise of a little spring that had been touched, but that the whole body was without feeling. They nailed poor animals up on boards by their four paws to vivisect them and see the circulation of the blood which was a great conversation.[39]

Fontaine was clearly critical, and so was the Parisian Jesuit, Gabriel Daniel (1649–1728), who mocked Cartesianism in his *Voiage du Monde de Descartes* in 1690. In England Descartes's view that animals feel no pain continued to be received with scepticism over the ensuing years and, writing in 1742, the Reverend John Hildrop remarked chauvinistically: 'Surely nothing but the Vanity of a Frenchman could ever expect that so absurd a scheme could pass upon a learned world for sound Reason and true Philosophy. For my own part, I could as soon expect to see Gallantries between a couple of amorous Clocks or Watches, or a Battle betwixt two quarrelsome Windmills.'[40]

As early as 1665 vivisection had been opposed on grounds of cruelty by the Irish physician Edmund O'Meara (c.1614–81), who had also pointed out that the subject's agony might well distort the results of the experiment.[41] Nevertheless, the practice continued to have a relatively free run until the turn of the century, before intellectuals in any number began to voice their criticisms. The darkest age of speciesism was then passing.

5 The Age of Enlightenment: The Eighteenth Century

By the eighteenth century there was no monopoly on compassion. The Quakers, and especially George Fox (1624–91), were noted for their concern for animal life. So were the Methodists, whose founder John Wesley (1703–91) opposed cruel sports, and thought it probable that animals had souls and that children should not be allowed to cause them needless harm. Anglicans and sceptics were equally committed to the cause.

MEN OF LETTERS

In the early years of the century, however, it was the secular writers who began to outnumber the theologians in their support for 'brute' nature. Some witty magazine articles are worth noting, written by Richard Steele in the *Tatler* of 1709, Joseph Addison in the *Spectator* in 1711 and Alexander Pope in the *Guardian* in 1713.

Richard Steele attacked the continuing practice of cock-throwing on Shrove Tuesdays and also the violence portrayed in the contemporary theatre, describing the unnecessary killing of animals as 'a kind of Murder'.[1] Joseph Addison (1672–1719) referred to 'a very barbarous experiment' on a dog and attacked it as 'an instance of cruelty'.[2] He believed that 'True benevolence, or compassion, extends itself through the whole of existence and sympathises with the distress of every creature capable of sensation.'[3] Alexander Pope (1688–1744) referred to the writings of Plutarch, Ovid, Montaigne and Locke, and concluded that 'there is certainly a Degree of Gratitude owing to those Animals that serve us.'[4] Like Addison, he narrowed the gap between men and beasts, seeing all creatures as 'but parts of one stupendous whole'; and in attacking vivisection he asked: 'how do we know that we have a right to kill creatures that we are so little above, as dogs, for our curiosity or even for some use to us?'[5]

Pope went out of his way to criticize the doctrine that animals are created for the benefit of humankind — 'is it for thee the lark ascends and sings?' He disliked the shooting of animals for sport[6] and, echoing Locke, urged that children should be taught kindness: 'I cannot but believe a very good use might be made of the fancy which children have for birds and insects.' The whole tenor of these early eighteenth-century writings is the awareness that humans themselves are animals. This is also made clear by Bernard de Mandeville in his *The Fable of the Bees,* published in 1714. For these sophisticated members of the intelligentsia there seemed no need to assert otherwise; their sense of their own civilized status was sufficiently secure.

French and German Writers

It should not be assumed, as it too often is, that England was the only country whose literate classes began to attack cruelty. Nearly all European countries had their humanitarians. Philipp Camerarius of Nuremburg advocated 'gentleness towards brute beasts' as early as 1621, and in France there was the priest, Jean Meslier (1664–1729), whose horror at human cruelty to nonhumans was so intense that he lost his faith; he deplored even the killing of insects.[7]

Voltaire (1694–1778), a Frenchman who lived in England between 1726 and 1729 and was a member of the same literary circle as Pope, subsequently attacked vivisection, pouring scorn upon Descartes:

How pitiful, and what poverty of mind, to have said that the animals are machines deprived of understanding and feeling. . .

Judge (in the same way as you would judge your own) the behaviour of a dog who has lost his master, who has searched for him in the road barking miserably, who has come back to the house restless and anxious, who has run upstairs and down, from room to room, and who has found the beloved master at last in his study, and then shown his joy by barks, bounds and caresses. There are some barbarians who will take this dog, that so greatly excels man in capacity for friendship, who will nail him to a table, dissect him alive, in order to show you his veins and nerves. And what you then discover in him are *all the same organs of sensation that you have in yourself.* Answer me, mechanist, has Nature arranged all the springs of feeling in this animal *to the end that he might not feel?* Has he nerves that he may be incapable of suffering?[8]

Voltaire, citing the compassion of Isaac Newton for the 'lower animals', went on to claim that compassion is not merely an acquired trait, but an instinct.[9]

Another great Frenchman, Jean-Jacques Rousseau (1712–78), also spoke out. In 1755 he wrote: 'It appears, in fact, that if I am bound to do no injury to my fellow creatures, this is less because they are rational than because they are sentient beings.'[10] In *Emile* in 1762 he claimed that animals could form ideas rather as men do, and went on to attack meat-eating on the grounds that it is bad for the character, as well as unnatural:

One of the proofs that the taste of flesh is not natural to man is the indifference which children exhibit for that sort of meat, and the preference they all give to vegetable foods, such as milk-porridge, pastry, fruits etc. It is of the last importance not to de-naturalise them of this primitive taste and not to render them carnivorous, if not for health reasons, at least for the sake of their character. For, however the experience may be explained, it is certain that great eaters of flesh are, in general, more cruel and ferocious than other men.[11]

In Germany, too, humanitarians were active. As early as 1684 a man had been pilloried in Sagan for cruelty to his horse, and in Leipzig, in 1765 and 1766, there had been imprisonments for inhumane behaviour.[12] Although Immanuel Kant (1724–1804) argued that we have no direct duties toward animals and that they exist to serve humankind, he recounts how the philosopher Gottfried von Leibnitz (1646–1716) had stressed the continuity between human and nonhuman, and would carefully replace a worm upon its leaf after observing it 'so that it should not come to harm through any act of his'.[13]

But the mid-eighteenth-century German scientists such as Christlob Mylius and Albrecht von Haller, rather like Hooke and Boyle in England before them, at least saw that vivisection posed a moral dilemma and admitted that they were causing pain. In general they justified their researches on the grounds of possible medical progress and by pointing to the routine killing of animals for meat. In the following century their fellow-countryman, Arthur Schopenhauer (1788–1860), in 1841 would fulminate against cruelty to animals: 'The assumption that animals are without rights, and the illusion that our treatment of them has no moral significance, is a positively outrageous example of Western crudity and barbarity. Universal compassion is the only guarantee of morality.'[14]

FLESH-EATING

The late seventeenth century provides the first modern evidence of revulsion at the slaughter and eating of animal flesh, and many distinguished men such as Milton, Pope and Isaac Newton began to commend a vegetable diet. Voltaire in 1736 attacked 'the barbarous custom of supporting ourselves upon the flesh and blood of beings like ourselves', although he remained a carnivore. Similarly, Jean-Jacques Rousseau in 1762 attacked meat-eating. In England, Thomas Tryon was a vegetarian

on moral grounds, and wrote at length about diet.[15] In 1741 David
Hartley argued that flesh-eating was unnecessary, and that 'taking away
the lives of animals, in order to convert them into food, does great
violence to the principles of benevolence and compassion.'[16]

William Paley, although justifying meat on religious grounds, emphasized in 1785 that it was not necessary and was poor economy: 'A piece
of ground capable of supplying animal food sufficient for the subsistence
of ten persons, would sustain, at least, the double of that number with
grain, roots and milk.'[17]

John Oswald, the Scottish atheist and soldier-poet who died for the
French Revolution in 1793, commented that:

The tender-hearted Hindoo would turn from our tables with abhorrence.
To him our feasts are the nefarious repasts of Polyphemus; while we
contemplate with surprise his absurd clemency, and regard his superstitious
mercy as an object of merriment and contempt.[18]

Indeed, by the end of the eighteenth century the inconsistency in eating
animals while advocating their rights began to worry some humanitarians.
As Oliver Goldsmith remarked drily, 'they pity and they eat the objects
of their compassion.'[19]

Vegetarianism was the main object of George Nicholson's 1797
anthology of writings against cruelty.[20] He argued that humankind had
been vegetarian for 1,600 years before the deluge and is not by natural
inclination carnivorous. Nicholson cited medical sources such as Dr
Cheyne's *Essay on Health* of 1725 to the effect that a vegetable diet
renders 'the circulation more free and the spirits the more lightsome,
that is, the better the health be'. He quoted a Dr Buchan's opinion that
meat 'induces a ferocity of temper' and a Dr Graham's even more dire
warning:

Do not degrade and beastatize your body by making it a burial place for the
carcases of innocent brute animals, some healthy, some diseased, and all
violently murdered. It is impossible for us to take into our stomachs putre-
fying, currupting, and diseased animal substances, without becoming ob-
noxious to horrors, dejections, remorse, and inquietudes of mind, and to
foul bodily diseases, swellings, pains, weaknesses, sores, curruptions, and
premature death.[21]

Finally, Nicholson argued on grounds of justice and compassion, and
asserted that 'there exists within us a rooted repugnance to the spilling
of blood; a repugnance which yields only to custom...'[22] Surely,
Nicholson had a point. This question of natural repugnance or squeamishness is a fascinating one, which will be explored in later chapters.

A CRUEL NATION

Often the impression is gained that England was regarded by others as the cruellest country in Europe. In the *Tatler* of 1709, Richard Steele had remarked that foreigners were shocked by the pastime of cock-throwing: 'Some French writers have represented this Diversion of the Common People much to our Disadvantage...as they do some other Entertainments *peculiar to our Nation*, I mean those elegant Diversions of Bull-baiting, and Prize fighting, with the like ingenious Recreations of the Bear Garden.'[23] Pope reiterated this view in the *Guardian* in 1713.[24] In 1751 Lord Kames remarked that 'the bear garden, which is one of the chief entertainments of the English, is held in abhorrence by the French and other polite nations,[25] and Rousseau condemned the English as 'coarse'.[26] In 1756 Adam Fitz Adam, writing in the *World*, was sorry to have to record that in the streets of London there are to be seen 'more scenes of barbarity than perhaps are to be met with in all Europe besides'. Arthur Broome noted that in 1768 the King of Denmark, on a visit to England, was shown a bull-baiting, but 'retired with expressions of abhorrence'. James Granger in 1772 saw England as 'the Hell of Horses'. In 1798 Thomas Young thought 'that the English have more of cruelty to animals in their sports in general, than any of their neighbours'.[27] Susanna Watts in the early nineteenth century could still argue in her *Animals' Friend*:

It is a very striking fact, that though the present age is boasted as highly enlightened, refined, and as far removed from barbarism as science, art, and literature can make it, no nation which we call savage, practices more degrading cruelty towards animals than the people of Great Briatin. The inhuman amusements of bull-baiting, cock-fighting, pigeon-shooting, etc. followed with such indefatigable ardor by the great and little vulgar, certainly contradict the vaunt of polish and refinement.[28]

An occasional sport at country fairs was the eating of live cats. The *Sporting Magazine* records several instances, one at Beverley in 1777 and another at St Albans in 1788. Earlier in the century it had been claimed that a man had eaten five live fox-cubs for a wager. Biting the heads off sparrows, beating rams to death and tying cats together by the tail were contemporary schoolboy games.

E. S. Turner describes how aristocrats in England, often following the example of the uncouth 'Butcher' Duke of Cumberland, would seek to stage various bloody encounters between animals. Yet towards the end of the century this crudeness was in retreat. In 1772 Dr Charles Burney was disgusted to see an advertisement in Vienna for the baiting of bears, boars and bulls which he felt was 'hardly fit for a civilised and polished nation to allow'. (It was stopped in 1791.) When Nelson was taken to a bull-fight in Cadiz in 1793 he felt sick and wondered if he could sit it out.[29]

Thus we see the beginnings of English criticisms of foreign behaviour on the very same grounds on which they themselves had been criticized – an attitude which persists to the present day. Goose-pulling, that is to say horsemen attempting to pull off the heads of live greased geese suspended upside down, currently continues in Spain and is roundly attacked by British and American organizations. Yet it was a favourite sport in Britain, and especially in Scotland, until the eighteenth century.

THE HUMANE REACTION

Perhaps it was partly because Britain had been the cruellest nation in Europe that it led the humane reaction over the next two centuries.

In 1742 John Hildrop published what appears to be the earliest example in Britain of a book devoted almost entirely to the subject of humankind's relationship with animals. Besides ridiculing the ideas of Descartes, he stressed the closeness of animals with uneducated humans. Animals, wrote Hildrop, were made to be happy, and it is an injustice to deprive them of this except for our own happiness.

Anonymous contributors to staid organs such as the *Gentleman's Magazine* were quite frequently attacking cruelty by mid-century. In April 1749 one such writer composed the dying speech of a hen martyred at the stake on Shrove Tuesday:

Perhaps the legislature may not think it beneath them to take our sad case into consideration or if the Government (taken up with great affairs of the nation) should think poultry below their regard; who can tell but some faint remains of common sense among the vulgar themselves, may be excited by a suffering dying fellow creature's last words, to find out a more good natured exercise for their youth, and idle fellows, at this holy season, which tends not to harden their hearts, and taint their morals?[30]

The same magazine recorded in May 1754 that a butcher had cut out the eyes of an unruly sheep. This had caused indignation in all who saw it, 'except the executioner'.[31]

In eighteenth-century England the unorthodox compassion of previous centuries rapidly became the established view among artists, poets, theologians and other leading intellectual figures. Even the popular scientist, James Ferguson (1710–76), criticized the 'agonies' of animals used in air-pump experiments, and in his public demonstrations he employed instead a model utilizing a bladder to simulate lungs. Ferguson must go down in history as the pioneer of humane alternatives to the use of animals in research.[32]

6 *Experiment on a Bird in the Air-pump* (1768) by Joseph Wright of Derby shows a cockatoo being suffocated in a vacuum chamber. Such experiments were popular in the eighteenth century. The expressions of the onlookers indicate some common reactions to cruelty, among them the spontaneous horror felt by children. The scientist (centre), inured to his work, appears desensitized. (Reproduced by courtesy of the Trustees, The National Gallery, London)

By mid-century the relatively mild exhortations of Rousseau's friend, the philosopher David Hume, to the effect that people should show 'gentle usage' to the animals, began to sound out of date.[33] The more robust views of Dr Samuel Johnson (1709–84) were more typical of the age; he chastised the 'race of wretches' who perform experiments on animals:

It is time that a universal resentment should arise against those horrid operations, which tend to harden the heart and make the physicians more dreadful than the gout or the stone. Men who have practised tortures on animals without pity, relating them without shame, how can they still hold their heads among human beings?[34]

Boswell recorded Johnson's fondness for animals, and in particular for his cat Hodge, for whom Johnson was in the habit of buying oysters. In

1776 Johnson remarked that there was 'much talk of the misery which we cause the brute creation' and indeed the references to animals and the injunctions against cruelty became numerous in the final third of the century.

Richard Dean, writing in 1767, referred approvingly to the earlier work of Hildrop. But for Dean the animals' sentiency is the main reason for treating them kindly: 'As Brutes have sensibility, they are capable of pain, feel every bang and cut and stab, as much as he himself [the reader] does, some of them perhaps more, and therefore he must not treat them as stocks or stones or things that cannot feel.' That this new, almost revolutionary, fashion in thought was limited chiefly to urban intellectuals is suggested by the reaction received by the Reverend James Granger from his rural Oxfordshire congregation when he preached a sermon at Shiplake on 18 October 1772 entitled 'An Apology for the Brute Creation or Abuse of Animals Censured'. He notes in a postscript: 'the foregoing discourse gave almost univeral disgust to two considerable congregations. The mention of dogs and horses, was censured as a prostitution of the dignity of the pulpit, and considered proof of the Author's growing insanity.'[36] His sermon was, however, more kindly reviewed by the literary press.

Religious thinkers of all denominations matched secular writers in their new concern for nonhumans. The Quaker John Woolman (1720–72), for example, in his journal in 1740, argued against 'cruelty towards the least creature' as a contradiction of the love due to God, and in 1772 he opposed any lessening of the 'sweetness of life in the animal creation which the Great Creator intends for them under our government'.[37]

Perhaps the most outstanding of all theological contributions of this period was that published by Dr Humphry Primatt in the year 1776. God would require a strict account from man for the creatures entrusted to his care, Primatt warned. Yet, despite this somewhat archaic imprecation, Primatt's book is otherwise remarkably modern in tone and entirely comprehensible to the animal liberationist of the twentieth century: 'Pain is Pain, whether it be inflicted on man or on beast; and the creature that suffers it, whether man or beast, being sensible of the misery of it whilst it lasts, suffers Evil.'[38] Primatt, like Tryon before him and Wilberforce afterwards, was also active in attacking the slave trade and frequently drew the analogy between racism and the exploitation of nonhumans: 'The white man...can have no right, by virtue of his colour, to enslave and tyrannise over a black man...for the same reason, a man can have no natural right to abuse and torment a beast.'[39]

Primatt's was an important work for the additional reason that it was read (and republished) by the Reverend Arthur Broome who, nearly half a century later, in 1824, was to help found the society which became the RSPCA. Interestingly, Primatt's Old Testament references, cited to support his thesis, outnumbered those of the New Testament by about five to one, and the RSPCA's educational tracts of the 1860s show a similar ratio. Primatt anticipated Jeremy Bentham's opinion in many ways:

Now if amongst men, the differences of their powers of the mind, and of their complexion, stature and accidents of fortune, do not give to any one man a right to abuse or insult any other man on account of these differences; for the same reason, a man can have no natural right to abuse and torment a beast, merely because a beast has not the mental powers of a man. A brute is an animal no less sensible of pain than a man. He has similar nerves and organs of sensation.[40]

Primatt went on to regret that cruelty to animals was inadequately controlled by law in the England of his day and unreproved from the pulpit. As G. H. Toulmin noted in 1780, the common view was still that 'everything is created for our practical use',[41] and although the sophisticated opinion of the London coffee-houses was now overwhelmingly on the side of the animals it is clear from Primatt's sarcasm that general public opinion was still far from sympathetic:

I am well aware of the obloquy to which every man must expose himself, who presumes to encounter prejudices and long received customs. To make a comparison between a man and a brute, is abominable; to talk of a man's duty to his horse or his ox, is absurd; to suppose it cruel to chase a stag, or course a hare, is unpolite; to esteem it barbarous to throw at a cock, to bait a bull, to roast a lobster, or to crimp a fish, is ridiculous.[42]

The gluttons of the eighteenth century indeed had much to answer for. Pope described 'kitchens covered with blood and filled with the cries of creatures expiring in tortures'. The whipping to death of pigs, in the mistaken belief that this improved the meat, was to continue in England until the following century. Turkeys were very slowly bled to death suspended upside down from the kitchen ceiling. Salmon were crimped (cut into collops while still alive), living eels skinned, and the orifices of chickens were sewn up, supposedly to fatten them. Geese repeatedly were plucked of their feathers while alive in order to provide writing quills, and many were nailed to boards for their entire lives, some with their eyes put out, while they were subjected to forced-feeding.

Meat was cheap in England at this time and its consumption continued to be gargantuan. Receipts for large houses indicate that it was ordered by the stone rather than the pound, and include details of the typical contemporary menu – lambs' tails for the first course for example, tongues and udders for the second, followed by ox palates with cheese-cake for the third.[43]

William Hogarth depicted some of the common cruelties of his day.

Although his strongly expressed objection to such activities was partly on the grounds that cruelty to beasts could lead to cruelty to people, it is clearly the case that he was also concerned for the well-being of the animals themselves. Animals were important to Hogarth, and in many of his pictures dogs appear as symbols of sincerity, contrasted with human affectation and hypocrisy. In 1750 he published 'The Four Stages of Cruelty', a series of prints depicting not only cruelty to animals but murder, in part the outcome of the former. Hogarth wrote of these prints: 'The four stages of cruelty were done in the hopes of preventing in some degree that cruel treatment of poor Animals which makes the streets of London more disagreeable to the human mind than anything whatever, the very describing of which gives pain.'[44] When told that his prints were much admired, he replied:

It gratifies me highly, and there is no part of my works of which I am so proud, and in which I feel so happy because I believe the publication of them has checked the diabolical spirit of barbarity, which, I am sorry to say was once so prevalent in this country...I had rather, if cruelty has been prevented by the four prints, be maker of them than of the [Raphael] cartoons.[45]

Trinity College, Cambridge, produced two Fellows of this period who applied their pens to the animals' cause: Thomas Young, who wrote *An Essay on Humanity to Animals* in 1789, and the Reverend C. Hoyle, whose 'Ode to Humanity' was published as its preface. Young marshalled all the usual arguments against cruelty to animals — that it renders people cruel to others of their own species, that it is opposed to the will of the creator who wishes to see the happiness of his creatures, that it is sometimes inconsistent with mankind's pecuniary interest, that it creates a bad impression socially and that it is contrary to scripture. He went on to describe the robbing of birds' nests as the commonest cruelty committed by contemporary schoolboys: 'we shall be sensible of this if we only reflect how many thousand boys make this their principal diversion during the greater part of spring.'

Indeed, the unbridled cruelty of young males is frequently remarked on. At Eton the annual clubbing to death of a hamstrung ram provided by the local butcher had been notorious from about 1687 until it was stopped in 1747. The tying of a duck to an owl and the hunting of the struggling pair over water, as well as the baiting of bulls, badgers and cats, and the fighting of dogs, continued to be regular public-school pastimes, approved by the educational authorities in the eighteenth century. Young cited bull-baiting, cockfighting and throwing at cocks as the principal sports common to men and boys, of which the most prevalent was still cockfighting, despite attempts from some magistrates to suppress it by refusing licences to publicans who allowed it on their premises. He also noted that in 'many large and respectable towns' cock-throwing had been banned by proclamation.

Forms of cockfighting included the 'battle royal', in which an unlimited number of birds were pitted, the last survivor being proclaimed the victor. In the Welsh Main form of the sport sixteen pairs of cocks were fought; the sixteen victors then were pitted a second time; the eight victors a third time; the four victors a fourth time; and then the two victors were pitted in the final. In such an event thirty-one cocks, said Young, 'are sure to be most inhumanely murdered for sport and pleasure'. Young referred to 'the Rights of Animals', and his philosophy was that of the applied Utilitarian:

A man who has made a tolerable progress in humanity, will adopt, and ever bear in mind, the principle of increasing, as far as lies within his power, the quantity of pleasure in the world, and diminishing that of pain: he will establish this to himself as a constant and inviolable rule of action, and in carrying it into practice he will not overlook one created thing that is endowed with faculties capable of perceiving pleasure and pain.[46]

Naturally enough, Young was also strongly opposed to the chase.

THE POETS ARISE

Among poets, cruelty was ardently decried in the eighteenth century. For his contemporaries it was the Scotsman James Thomson (1700–48) who was seen as the outstanding poetic inspiration of the humanitarian movement, as he attacked 'the steady tyrant man' who 'for sport alone pursues the cruel chase…to joy at anguish and delight in blood'. Thomson was especially critical of hunting by the female sex, fearing that it would 'stain the bosom of the british fair'.[47]

In his *Canterbury Tales* Chaucer had written that his prioress 'wolde weepe if that she saw a mous caught in a trappe', yet subsequent medieval verse and the great body of Elizabeth and Jacobean poetry is almost silent on such matters. Only when we get to Andrew Marvell (1621–78) do the poets begin to catch up the theologians. Marvell's 'Nymph complaining For the Death of her Faun' bemoaned:

> The wanton troopers riding by
> Have shot my fawn, and it will die.
> Ungentle men! They cannot thrive
> Who killed thee.

'Nothing', wrote Marvell, 'may we use in vain; ev'n beasts must be with justice slain…'

After Pope and Thomson came Oliver Goldsmith (1728–74) and William Cowper (1731–1800), closely followed by William Blake (1757–1827) and Robert Burns (1759–96), all showing a tenderness for nonhuman life. They were part of a society in which the cultivated mind had adopted a far more romantic view of all nature; no longer was it something simply to be subdued. Gardens which had previously been regimented and in which flowers and shrubs had been tamed with an almost military discipline were now allowed to unfold naturally. Animals, too, began to be regarded as lovely in themselves.

Cowper, who kept a pet hare, attacked hunting as a 'detested sport, that owes its pleasures to another's pain' and added: 'I would not enter on my list of friends (though graced with polish'd manners and fine sense, yet wanting sensibility), the man who needlessly sets foot upon a worm.'[48] Burns roundly condemned the hunter who wounds the hare:

> Inhuman man! Curse on thy barbarous act,
> And blasted be thy murder-aiming eye.[49]

He was another who saw man as tyrannizing the animals:

> Man; your proud usurping foe,
> Would be lord of all below:
> Plumes himself in Freedom's pride,
> Tyrant stern to all beside.[50]

Burns claimed kinship with a mouse[51] and Blake with a fly: 'Am not I a fly like thee?'

Towards the end of the eighteenth century, into a society in which cruelty was being routinely condemned in educated circles were born the poets William Wordsworth (1770–1850), Samuel Coleridge (1772–1834) and Robert Southey (1774–1843); all three defended nonhuman animals. Wordsworth, in his elegy on the legend of the hunted deer which leapt to its death near Richmond in Yorkshire, warned 'never to blend our pleasure or our pride with sorrow of the meanest thing that feels'.[52] Southey, in his poem 'The Dancing Bear', revealed the state of average opinion in 1799:

> We are told all things were made for Man:
> And I'll be sworn there's not a fellow here
> Who would not swear 'twere hanging blasphemy to
>   doubt that truth...
> And politicans say...that thou art here
> Far happier than thy brother bears who roam
> O'er trackless snow for food.
> Talk of thy baiting, it will be replied
> Thy welfare is thy owner's interest...[53]

Much of the poetic concern with cruelty at this period was not centred upon baiting, nor on culinary tortures, nor on vivisection, but continued the attack on hunting with hound or gun. Besides Burns and Cowper, other poets also reviled themselves for having indulged in such sports.[54]

Byron (1788–1824) wrote a moving epitaph to his dog Boatswain in 1808:

> to mark a friend's remains these stones arise;
> I never knew but one – and here he lies.[55]

Percy Bysshe Shelley (1792–1822), besides criticizing the chase, was one of the first to record being moved by the plight of ordinary farm animals:

How unwarrantable is the injustice and barbarity which is exercised towards these miserable victims. They are called into existence by human artifice that they may drag out a short and miserable existence of slavery and disease, that their bodies may be mutilated, their social feelings outraged. It were much better that a sentient being should never have existed, than that it should have existed only to endure unmitigated misery.[56]

It is believed that in 1816, while living in Wales, Shelley put out of their miseries several diseased or dying sheep belonging to neighbouring farmers. This so incensed local opinion that three shepherds attacked Shelley one night, firing three pistol shots at him. Shortly afterwards, the Shelleys fled to England. Shelley advocated vegetarianism out of respect for our 'kindred' the animals, who 'think, feel and live like man',[57] and in 1819 in *Prometheus Unbound*, he wrote: 'I wish no living thing to suffer pain.'

In America the poets were awakened in the early nineteenth century. Henry Wadsworth Longfellow (1807–82) wrote:

> Among the noblest of the land,
>   Though he may count himself the least,
> That man I honor and revere,
>   Who, without favor, without fear,
> In the great city dares to stand
>   The Friend of every friendless Beast.[58]

Oliver Wendell Holmes (1809–94) pitied the caged lion – 'poor conquered monarch'[59] ('To A Caged Lion') – and Ralph Waldo Emerson (1803–82) extolled the titmouse and the bumble-bee.

THE PARAGON OF ANIMALS

Long before Darwin's day, man had been regarded as an animal. In classical literature, Epicureans and writers such as Lucretius, Cicero, Diodorus Siculus and Horace had suggested that humankind had only slowly developed from the animal condition, gradually forming language and civilization. Aristotle viewed man as being at the top of the natural hierarchy, superior in reasoning to any other animal, but not different in kind. Shakespeare, through Hamlet, had seen man as 'the paragon of animals'. Yet, as we have seen, the full awareness of humankind's animality by many people was intermittent and discouraged by the Church; most behaved as if Homo Sapiens was a creature of an altogether different order, 'made in the image of God'.

Perhaps it was at opposite ends of human society that the consciousness of animality was least clouded. The medieval peasant, and later the poor townsman, living with beasts under the same roof, could not escape noticing the similarity in bodily functions and behaviour between themselves and their animals. Indeed the common assumption that sexual intercourse with animals was the cause of human deformity and handicap indicates some sense of underlying awareness that human and nonhuman were of a kind, despite the Inquisition's fierce opposition to such views.

At the other end of the scale, scholars and thinkers often had the time to reflect and the intelligence to realize the zoological facts of life. Whereas the common man might sometimes feel his social status threatened by his closeness to the brutes, and would react by emphasizing his dominion over them, the more elevated members of human society, sure of their social standing, could sometimes risk a more liberal view. The theologians disliked such liberalism, but could not entirely prevent it.

The discovery of the great apes made it more difficult than ever to deny the similarity between men and beasts. In 1613 the first reliable descriptions of the great apes were published by Andrew Battell – 'hairie all over, otherwise altogether like men and women'. In 1661 Samuel Pepys saw an ape exhibited, 'so much like a man in most things'. In 1653 John Bulwer reported the contemporary opinion that man 'was at first but a kind of ape or baboon'. Scientists like Edward Tyson in 1699 noted the resemblance of ape and human anatomy. Sir Thomas Browne remarked in 1643 that in the brains of people he could find no organs not also discoverable 'in the crany of a beast'. By 1700 it was acknowledged that the nervous system mediated feeling and it was accepted that animals had nerves similar to those of humans.[60]

In 1735 the *Systema Naturae* of Carolus Linnaeus (1707–78), the great Swedish naturalist, was published. In it, Linnaeus classified man as part of the Primate order which also included, he said, apes and bats. Indeed, Linnaeus even put man into the same genus as the orang-utang.

This view was opposed by other zoologists, most notably by Georges Leclerc, Comte de Buffon (1707–88), although his translator, William Smellie, placed man in the class of mammalia: 'Man is arranged with them, because he nearly resembles them in structure and organs, though', Smellie adds cautiously, 'raised in reality far above them by the possession of superior intellectual and moral powers.' Smellie thus enforced the view that man is an animal and, specifically, a mammal.[61]

Of all eighteenth-century pronouncements on this subject, those of the eccentric Scotsman James Burnet, Lord Monboddo, caused the greatest sensation. In 1774 he asserted that Jean-Jacques Rousseau was correct in identifying orang-utangs as a race of men who had not yet acquired the art of speech. With training, Monboddo claimed, animals could be educated. He could produce evidence, he said, to prove that a school-teacher in Inverness had a tail six inches in length which was only discovered after his death. The gulf between men and beasts disappeared under Monboddo's sturdy rhetoric.[62]

At the time that Monboddo was using such arguments to elevate animals, others were using them to lower the status of men – or at least certain races of men. Edward Long in 1774, for example, argued that the orang-utang was closer to the negro than the negro was to the white man.[63] Joseph Ritson, writing in 1802, could assert that man could properly be 'arranged under the monkey kind; there being the same degree of analogy between the man and the monkey, as between the lion and the cat'. The apes, said Ritson, were intermediate between man and monkey. 'Man, therefor, in a state of nature, was, if not the real ourang-outang of the forests...at least an animal of the same family.'[64] Ritson goes on to relate many amusing travellers' tales about the intelligence, language and sensitivity of apes.

Eighteenth-century writers from Rousseau onwards also recounted stories of wild children and adults found living in the woods with wolves, bears or other animal companions. These reports were often used to illustrate the closeness of mankind to nature, and to show that civilized behaviour was not spontaneous but learned.

By the eighteenth century, horses, cattle, sheep and dogs were all being bred with scrupulous care, so the fact that their physical and behavioural characteristics could change radically over the generations had become a self-evident truth; this was helping to prepare the ground for the acceptance of Darwin's ideas on Evolution.

In northern Europe it had become fashionable for country curates, gentlemen and ladies to be keen naturalists, although such a pastime did not develop so much in southern European countries. In England the libraries of country houses were filled with contemporary zoological best-sellers from authors such as Oliver Goldsmith, William Mavor, John Hill, William Smellie, Thomas Pennant and William Bingley. Although earlier writers had categorized animals according to their

7 Sir Joshua Reynolds's picture of Miss Jane Bowles was painted in 1775 during the great upsurge of interest in the rights of animals associated with the relative peace and affluence of the late eighteenth century. The picture portrays the natural bond of affection between child and pet which forms one of the foundation stones of the animal welfare movement.
(The Wallace Collection, London)

usefulness for man or their edibility, gradually such criteria shrank in importance as interest grew in the nonhuman animals themselves.

By the end of the century, therefore, not only the poets but the scientists, too, albeit more or less unwittingly, had done much to remove the human species (although not themselves) from a self-established pedestal.

PREPARATIONS FOR LEGISLATION

We have seen that by the 1780s pain had clearly emerged as the main matter for concern in humankind's treatment of the other animals. Earlier worries about the welfare of the oppressor's character and pre-occupations about the intelligence of animals, their capacity for language or the quality of their souls, if any, were finally swept away by the philosopher Jeremy Bentham (1748–1832), who wrote in 1780:

The day may come when the rest of the animal creation may acquire those rights which never could have been withheld from them but by the hand of tyranny...a full-grown horse or dog is beyond comparison a more rational, as well as a more conversable animal, than an infant of a day, or a week or even a month old. But supposed the case were otherwise, what would it avail? The question is not, can they reason? Nor, can they talk? But *can they suffer?* Why should the law refuse its protection to any sensitive being? The time will come when humanity will extend its mantle over everything which breathes...[65]

Bentham, like Montaigne and Johnson, is another example of a cat-lover who has contributed significantly to the history of the animal protection movement. His favourite was a cat called Mr Blackman who, because of his solemn demeanour, was progressively promoted to being addressed as Dr Blackman and, finally, the Reverend Dr Blackman.[66] Bentham's biographer, John Bowring, himself an advocate of humanity to animals, records that Bentham, as a boy, had burnt some earwigs in a candle flame and had been reprimanded for this cruelty by a servant called Martha.[67] His uncle also had occasion to rebuke him for teasing his dog Busy. Bentham never forgot these two experiences. Bowring also recalls Bentham's claim that he had been impressed by the fondness for animals shown by Cowper, George Wilson and Romilly. The philosopher had shown affection for 'a beautiful pig at Hendon' and 'a young ass of great symetry and beauty' at Ford Abbey, and his genuine feeling for animals is most convincingly displayed in his relationship with mice:

I became once very intimate with a colony of mice. They used to run up my legs and eat crumbs from my lap. I love everything that has four legs: so did

George Wilson. We were fond of mice, and fond of cats; but it was difficult
to reconcile the two affections.[68]

Bentham opposed hunting, fishing and baiting, but for him it was the
infliction of pain, and not death, that was the main evil. In line with this
principle, he saw no objection to dispatching a cat who had become
'despotic' and 'clamorous', sending him 'to another world':

It ought to be lawful to kill animals, but not to torment them. Death, by
artificial means, may be made less painful than natural death: the methods of
accomplishing this deserve to be studied and made an object of policy. Why
should the law refuse its protection to any sensitive being? The time will
come, when humanity will extend its mantle over everything which breathes.
We have begun by attending to the condition of slaves; we shall finish by
softening that of all the animals which assist our labours or supply our
wants.[69]

Thus, by the end of the eighteenth century in England the basic principles of the modern animal welfare position were established. These are
that nonhumans, like humans, can suffer pain, and that pain entitles
them to legal as well as moral rights. Pain had emerged as the central evil
and, as Walter Savage Landor later put it − 'cruelty is the chief, if not
the only sin.' The old preoccupations with the immortality and intelligence of nonhumans were dismissed as quibbles. Indeed, if animals,
unlike men, had 'no mind to bear them up against their sufferings', as
Thomas Chalmers (1780−1847) had it, and no hope of everlasting peace,
then their torment surely would be the greater.

Cruelty to animals remained quite a major subject of interest in
certain circles right through to the end of the century and beyond. And
those circles were widening. For example, John Oswald, the soldier
mentioned above who was carried off by a cannon-ball in 1791, wrote
on the topic, and recommended vegetarianism.[70] Soame Jenyns (1704−
87), an influential and popular Member of Parliament, could see that
much customary cruelty was the result of force of habit and of the loss
of sensitivity caused by habituation to the normally repugnant sight of
blood; he described this with memorable metaphor: 'The butcher knocks
down the stately ox with no more compassion than the blacksmith
hammers a horse-shoe; and plunges his knife into the throat of the
innocent lamb with as little reluctance as the taylor sticks his needle into
the collar of a coat.' In 1794 Thomas Paine briefly urged kindness to
animals in his radical classic *The Age of Reason*. In 1797, George
Nicholson, a printer living in Manchester, published what is probably
the first anthology of writings on the subject (also mentioned above).
He strongly advocated vegetarianism and attacked some appalling cruelties in his home town, recording the state of the law at the time, which

8 Jeremy Bentham (1748–1832), one of the most influential philosophers of his day, argued that all creatures who are capable of suffering should be included in moral and legislative calculations. Modern academic philosophers have led the recent revival of opposition to speciesism.
(The Mansell Collection)

permitted cruelty on the grounds that animals were mere property:

In November, 1793, two butchers of Manchester were convicted in the penalty of twenty shillings each, for cutting off the feet of living sheep, and driving them through the streets. The sheep were not their own property or, we suppose, they might with impunity have been allowed to dissect them alive.

A butcher in the same town has been frequently seen to hang poor calves up alive, with the gambril put through their sinews, and hooks stuck through their nostrils, the dismal bleating of the miserable animals continuing till they had slowly bled to death. Such proceedings frequently struck the neighbourhood with horror. Attempts were made to prevent the hellish nuisances caused by this man, but in vain, for he did but torture his own property! Such are the glaring imperfections of the laws of a civilised, a humane, a Christian country![72]

He concluded:

We have said that animals should be protected by the legislature, but there exists no statute which punishes cruelty to animals, simply as such, and without taking in the consideration of it as an injury to property.

Nicholson's anthology in its first edition in 1797 was dedicated to the 'generous, enlightened and sympathising few'. However, such was the demand for his book that he published the fourth edition in 1819, noting that 'the few have increased to a numerous and decided body.'
A writer in the *Gentleman's Magazine* of January 1789 provided a revealing description of contemporary cruelty:

The infant is no sooner able to use its little limbs, than they are exercised in procuring diversion by torturing every animal that comes within its reach, and which it is able to master: and the pleasure it manifests in these malevolent employments is such that the tender parents generally provide the pretty innocent with a constant supply of insects, birds, kittens, and puppies, to keep it in good humour. As years and strength increase, tearing flies piecemeal, sticking crooked pins through the tails of cockchafers to make them spin to death; misusing, laming, and killing, all the animals they are supplied with...they then prowl about to rob innocent birds of their nests, for the pleasure of destroying their eggs, and killing the unfledged brood. They catch dogs, tie old lanterns or faggot-sticks to their tails, and then drive them away with shouts, to be hunted to madness and death by all who meet them. They set dogs upon stray cats with the utmost glee, and enjoy their struggles while they are worried to death; and the hanging of a dog or a cat collects all the children in the neighbourhood as eagerly as the execution of a criminal, or a fire, draws together their fathers and mothers. They will tie two cats together by the tails and then throw them over a line, for the luxury of seeing them tear each other's eyes out. They will tie a string to a rat's tail, pour spirit of wine over it, set fire to it, and betray the most rapturous joy at seeing the unhappy animal run about covered with flame till it expires under this refinement in barbarity. The most agreeable sports of youth have for their common object a delight felt at the sufferings of animals appropriated to our diversion: thus harmless fowls and pigeons are set up to be knocked down with sticks: ducks are hunted in ponds by dogs; an owl is tied on the back of a duck, and both thrown into the water; while this glory of the creation, with the stamp of divinity on his mind, is worked up to extasy in contemplating their mutual distresses.

The writer, who signed himself only as 'Mr Humanus', concluded:

It is hard that there should be no law for brute animals, when they carry so large a proportion of representatives to every legislative assembly.[73]

To a certain extent cruelty to animals had become, by the end of the eighteenth century, a mark of distinction between the refined and the vulgar, between the uneducated and the cultivated. Many of the latter felt it was time to curb cruelty with legislation, and it seems to have been the public spectacle of cruelty to horses and farm animals in the street, and their witnessing of bloodsports which prompted this move.

Most humane eighteenth-century writers, including Pope, Jenyns, Nicholson, and Bentham, were explicitly critical of hunting, shooting and angling, and although his ambivalence on fox-hunting, is not typical, perhaps the most influential (besides Bentham) in this secular group of writers was gentleman-farmer John Lawrence, who proposed 'The jus animalium, or the rights of beasts to the protection of the law, on the ground of natural justice in the first intance, and in sequel, on that of expedience, regarding both humanity and profit.'[74] He published prolifically on sporting and agricultural topics, invariably advocating the duty of humanity. Like Young, he gave currency to the idea that animals have rights. 'Life, intelligence, and feeling, necessarily imply rights', Lawrence claimed, and he applied this principle in defence of human and animal rights alike. After his death in 1839 in his eighty-sixth year, he was almost entirely forgotten until forty years later, his writings were rediscovered by E. W. B. Nicholson. There is a copy of his *Philosophical Treatise* in the Bodleian Library, Oxford, into which Nicholson said he transcribed annotations made by Lawrence during the years 1835 to 1837; among these is the note: 'Mr. Martin M.P. for Galway, subsequently took up this cause on my recommendation, and got the animal protection bill with much difficulty thro' Parliament. Mr. M. and myself had many conferences on this subject.' Lawrence's political importance stands largely on this claim.

Apparently ashamed of his addiction to hunting, Lawrence published his book *British Field Sports* in 1818 under the pseudonym of William Henry Scott. His favourable view of certain forms of hunting and cockfighting − he condoned animals fighting if they did so voluntarily, and the hunting of ferocious (rather than timid) animals who, he believed, feel no fear — lays him open to the familiar charge of inconsistency. Nevertheless, Lawrence admitted that the cruelties perpetrated by drovers and other members of the lower orders were in no small part due to their emulation of the habits of the gentry: 'Since the most exquisite pleasure is supposed by their betters to be derived from hunting, worrying, and tearing the living members of the most harmless and timid animals, why not hunt bullocks as well as hares and deer?'[75] Lawrence was particularly concerned about the welfare of horses, who, he claims, were being 'literally whipped and goaded to death'. In a later edition of his book, Lawrence noted in 1812 that in the hot July of 1808 many stage-horses had died upon the roads and 'on the great road to Edinburgh fourteen or fifteen were killed in one day.' He drew an analogy between defending the cruelties committed by carmen and postilions and defending the African slave trade, and repeatedly called for comprehensive legislation to protect animals.

Lawrence paid tribute to a number of politicians for their humane interest in animals, among them Lord Erskine, Sir Charles Bunbury, Sir Samuel Romilly, Sir Richard Hill and the black Haitian leader, Toussaint L'Ouverture.

Although literate opinion was by now on the side of the animals, this had little effect upon the postilions and cowherds — 'The misfortune is the writings of an Addison are seldom read by cooks and butchers', regretted Adam Fitz Adam.[76] It was clearly time that the law should play its part in persuading the illiterate.

6 Time for Action

Gradually, naturalists, educators, politicians and campaigners had rejected the old view that nonhumans had been created to serve humankind. The time had come to take action. As soon as the Napoleonic wars were over, great advances were made towards putting into effect the ideas of the humanitarian writers of the eighteenth century.

The cultivated section of society felt it their duty to civilize the less educated. Three hundred years earlier the elite had been anxious to enlarge the conceptual gap between human and nonhuman; now the process was in reverse. The early nineteenth century saw a surge of activity which included the publication of numerous humane educational works for children, the foundation of the RSPCA in Britain, the first signs of organized vegetarianism, and a successful campaign to introduce effective legislation.

Under the so-called 'Black Act' of 1723 it was a capital offence, under some circumstances, to destroy the property of others – and this included their animals. In 1749, for example, two men at Gloucester had been convicted of killing a mare to spite its owner, and one had received sentence of death. On the other hand, a Quaker was convicted at Sussex Assizes in 1806 of pouring sulphuric acid on a dog, causing its intestines to fall out through the wound in its belly, and the court was able only to award compensation of £5 to be paid to the dog's owner for damage to property.

THE FIRST ATTEMPT: BULL-BAITING

John Lawrence noted that some magistrates, especially in London, had been trying to take a firmer line on cruelty during the last few years of the eighteenth century. They were, however, handicapped by the lack of appropriate legislation. Cruelties to dogs, horses and meat animals, notably those being driven to the Smithfield Market in London, were all contemporary causes of concern, but it appeared that among the 'softest' targets for legislation was bull-baiting. Few members of the upper classes still subscribed to the sport and it was widely regarded as vulgar and disreputable. In addition, it could become a public nuisance. In 1756 Adam Fitz Adam, for example, had complained that such cruelties 'frequently run me into great inconveniences', and it was certainly true that bull-baitings could severely disrupt the ordinary business of a town, especially when ancient custom or covenant decreed that bulls should be run through the streets before baiting. Usually the bulls were disinclined to fight and had first to be maddened. Various methods were used, ranging from pepper or gunpowder in the nostrils, fireworks under the tail, soap in the eyes, or tail-breaking. 'We have heard of a hot iron being thrust up the animals' fundament', Henry Alken recorded in 1821.[1]

Most infamous of all were the bull-runnings and baitings at Stamford in Lincolnshire. Bulls were let loose in the blocked-off streets, chased by men and dogs, beaten with cudgels and thrown off the bridge into the river before being baited. Despite attempts by the Earl of Exeter and the mayor to stop these customs, they continued. On one occasion the mayor called in dragoons, but they refused to intervene and joined in the sport.

The first Bill designed to put down bull-baiting was introduced into Parliament on 18 April 1800 by Sir William Pulteney, an independent-minded Scottish MP and an old friend of David Hume. He was tortuously opposed by William Windham on several grounds, not least that the Bill was an attempt by the rich to interfere with the sports of the poor. 'Why should the butcher be deprived of his amusements anymore than the gentleman?', Windham demanded. Besides, bull-baiting helped to cultivate the sterling qualities of both dogs and men.

John Lawrence, angered by Windham's sophistry, subsequently wrote in *The Sportsman's Repository*:

That man had in an eminent degree the gift of the gab; and at the same time, the pre-eminent art of confounding every subject beyond all possibility of its being developed and comprehended either by himself or others. He was the very Hierophant of confusion and his mind the chosen Tabernacle of that goddess. He had in truth been so much in the habit of shaking up right and wrong in the bag together that he had long lost the faculty of distinguishing one from the other.

Windham, however, was aided by George Canning, who thought the Bill absurd, and despite support from Rowland Hill, Richard Martin and Richard Sheridan, the Bill was narrowly lost by forty-three votes to forty-one. Windham was toasted in ale-houses all over the country and bulls, bears and badgers were subjected to celebratory baitings. *The Times* of 25 April 1800 supported Windham; its editorial fulminated against 'undue interference with private life', proclaiming that 'whatever meddles with the private personal disposition of a man's time or property is tyranny direct.'

In 1801, at Bury St Edmunds, a baited bull broke loose. As punishment, its hoofs were hacked off and it was again baited. An editorial in the *Sporting Magazine* expostulated: 'God of Nature, in what country am I? The bull of St Edmund's Bury is tormented for the amusement of Christian savages who take delight in inflicting torture. Can the philosophic Windham, the champion of Christianity and Social Order, stand up in Parliament and vindicate such amusements?'[3] He did, and repeatedly.

The Bill against bull-baiting was eventually reintroduced by a Mr Dent, and although he was supported by William Wilberforce − 'wretched indeed must be the condition of the people of England if their whole happiness consisted in the practice of such barbarity' − the Bill was again defeated.

THE EFFORTS OF THOMAS ERSKINE AND RICHARD MARTIN

In 1809, a new champion of the animals, Lord Erskine of Restormel, entered the arena by introducing into the House of Lords his Bill designed to prevent any 'wanton cruelty' to animals. This stipulated that any person maliciously wounding or cruelly beating any horse, mare, ass, ox, sheep or pig should be found guilty of a misdemeanour and sentenced, on first offence, to not less than one week and not more than one month in prison. Once again it was the drovers and others of the lower classes who were seen to be threatened by such legislation.

Thomas Erskine (1750−1823), had been born in Edinburgh and had risen to become Lord Chancellor in the years 1806 and 1807. Before he took up law, he had served as a young officer, first in the Navy and then in the Army. His success at the bar was rapid and spectacular, and by the 1780s he had become rich from his practice.

In Parliament he generally followed Fox and supported Whig policy, advocating the emancipation of slaves with a conviction that grew over the course of the years. He was well known as an admirer of animals, and his pets included a dog, a goose and even two leeches. He is reputed to have been an amiable and witty man and a great lover of puns. When he met Dr Johnson in 1772, he impressed Boswell with his 'vivacity, fluency and precision'. A little later he had become a friend of Jeremy Bentham, and it is possible that Johnson's and Bentham's views on animals were impressed upon him at this early stage in his career. Once aroused, his enthusiasm for a cause could lead him to forget the conventional dignity of his position. It is said, for example, that one day on Hampstead Heath Erskine saw a carter beating a horse. On remonstrating with the man he received the familiar reply: 'Can't I do what I like with my own?' 'Yes', replied Erskine, striking the carter, 'and so can I – this stick is my own.'

In his speech on the Second Reading of his Bill on 15 May 1809, Erskine complained:

Nothing is more notorious than that it is not only useless, but dangerous, to poor suffering animals, to reprove their oppressors, or to threaten them with punishment. The general answer with the addition of bitter oaths and increased cruelty, is 'What is that to you?' If the offender be a servant, he curses you, and asks 'Are you my master?' and if he be the master himself, he tells you that the animal is his own. The validity of this most infamous and stupid defence, arises from that defect in the law which I seek to remedy. Animals are considered as property only. To destroy or abuse them, from malice to the proprietor, or with an intention injurious to his interest in them, is criminal, but the animals themselves are without protection; the law regards them not substantively; they have no rights.

On 9 June the Bill was passed by the Lords. Sir Charles Bunbury, with William Wilberforce once more in support, then tried to pass it through the Commons, but it was defeated by thirty-seven votes to twenty-seven, much to the disgust of the *Gentlemen's Magazine,* whose editorial stated: 'Surely few subjects in the whole compass of moral discussion can be greater than the unnecessary cruelty of man to animals which administer to his pleasure, his consolation and to the very support of his life!'

It was another thirteen years before any reforms on behalf of animals finally became law. In 1821 Erskine joined forces with Richard Martin MP, and these two men qualify as the first people, anywhere in the world, to succeed in legislating against cruelty to animals by means of parliamentary procedure.

Richard Martin (1754–1834) was a similarly robust character and in his early years he had gained a reputation as a duellist. In 1781 George 'Fighting' Fitzgerald, a provocative eccentric, had deliberately and cold-bloodedly shot dead an Irish wolfhound belonging to Lord Altamont. Martin, friend of both dog and owner, was so angered at its death that two years later he fought a duel with Fitzgerald in which both men were injured. Educated at Harrow and Cambridge, Martin was the owner of vast estates in Galway. He sat in the House of Commons from 1801 till 1826, where he actively supported Catholic emancipation and championed such humane causes as the abolition of the death penalty for forgery, and the establishment of legal aid at the state's expense for those charged with criminal offences who could not themselves afford to employ counsel. Such attitudes show that Richard Martin cared as much for human as for nonhuman beings. Indeed he provided shelter for the

9 Richard Martin MP (1754–1834). The flamboyance and virility
of Martin and his collaborator Lord Erskine (1750–1823) undermined the criticism that a concern for nonhumans was 'unmanly'
and helped them to introduce their anti-cruelty legislation in 1822.
With William Wilberforce and others, Martin went on to establish
the SPCA two years later.
(BBC Hulton Picture Library)

homeless at his own castle, and his life-story is sprinkled with anecdotes that illustrate his kindness towards his own species, which earned him the nickname 'Humanity Dick' from his friend, King George IV.

From about the beginning of 1821 Martin was in touch with John Lawrence. Both men of the land, they had much in common. Together with Erskine, they planned the new legislation. On 18 May Martin printed his Bill, proposing:

that if any person or persons having the charge, care or custody of any horse, cow, ox, heifer, steer, sheep or other cattle, the property of any other person or persons, shall wantonly beat, abuse or ill-treat any such animal, such individuals shall be brought before a Justice of the Peace or other magistrate.

By preserving the rights of owners of animals to 'do as they liked with their own' Martin no doubt reduced the opposition to his Bill. Its targets, too, could be seen to be the drovers and carters of the London working classes rather than anyone with political connections. The Bill was amended in committee to include mares, geldings, mules and asses, and then triumphantly passed through the Commons on 1 June 1821, by forty-eight votes to sixteen. In the Lords, however, Lord Erskine's influence was not enough and the Bill was defeated.

Undismayed, Martin and Erskine reintroduced their Bill the following year, and it was passed in both houses. On 22 July 1822, it finally received the royal assent and became the first national law anywhere in the world, passed by a democratically elected legislature which dealt specifically and entirely with cruelty to animals.

Entitled 'An Act to Prevent the Cruel and Improper Treatment of Cattle', it quickly became known as Martin's Act. Over the next four years, until he was unseated in 1826, Richard Martin continued to present Bills to protect animals. His main targets were bull-baiting, slaughter-house conditions, dog-fighting and the general protection of cats and dogs (who were not included in the species protected under his Act of 1822). Martin was a determined parliamentary tactician. On several occasions he succeeded in bringing up his Bills late at night before a thinly attended chamber well stocked with his friends. However, all these efforts at further reform were narrowly defeated, either in the Lords where he lacked the skilled support of his old friend Erskine, who had died in 1823, or in the Commons, where Martin encountered persistent opposition from Sir Robert Peel.

Some time shortly after the passing of his Act, Martin himself brought the first prosecution. A costermonger, Bill Burns, was charged with cruelty to his donkey. It is alleged that Martin, as usual never afraid to flout convention, insisted that the donkey be brought into court so that his wounds could be seen. This episode created quite a lot of publicity,

which was probably Martin's intention. The occasion was celebrated by
a popular song entitled 'If I had a donkey that wouldn't go', and
commemorated by a print bearing the legend:

> Bill Donkey then was brought into Court
> Who caused of course a deal of Sport.
> He cock'd his ears and op'd his jaws,
> As tho' he meant to plead his own cause.[4]

On 11 August 1822, Martin brought a case against Samuel Clarke and
David Hyde for savagely beating tethered horses at Smithfield. Both
men were fined twenty shillings. Martin was determined that his legislation should be enforced and he methodically brought a number of such
prosecutions; anxious to educate rather than punish the poor too harshly,
he frequently paid the fines himself.

There is little doubt that Martin and Erskine succeeded where men of
milder temper would have failed. In an age when sexual stereotypes
were even more pronounced than they are today, a concern for animals'
welfare might well have been discounted as effeminate. The subject was
still regarded by many as essentially ludicrous, yet few could argue,
when faced with these two virile firebrands, that it was womanish. The
Celtic vigour of the Irish Martin and the Scottish Erskine spiked the
guns of those, like Windham, who tried to argue that opposition to
cruel sports was unmanly. It was said of Martin that 'he lets drive at the
House like a bullet and the flag of truce is instantly hung out upon
both sides.' The same source added: 'he holds the House by the very
test of the human race, laughter, and while their sides shake, their
opposition is shaken and falls down at the same instant'.[5]

Martin was a flamboyant witty figure; eccentric, quick-tempered, yet
kind. With his extensive holdings in Ireland he had also been bequeathed
debts of an equal magnitude and, hounded by creditors, he was to end
his days as a refugee in Boulogne in 1834, mourned by the poet Thomas
Hood as:

> Thou Wilberforce of hacks!
> Of whites as well as blacks,
> Piebald and dapple grey,
> Chestnut and bay —
> No poet's eulogy thy name adorns!
> But oxen, from the fens,
> Sheep in their pens,
> Praise thee, and red cows with their winding horns![6]

His Act of 1822 did not specifically mention bulls; the bull-baiters
therefore continued their sport. Martin's Act sought to prevent the cruel

and improper treatment of horses, mares, geldings, mules, asses, cows, heifers, steers, oxen, sheep and other cattle. Martin failed in 1823 and 1826 to outlaw bull-baiting specifically, but nevertheless tried to apply his Act to this sport, arguing that the phrase 'other cattle' clearly covered bulls, and in 1825 he vainly attempted to have convicted two baiters from Hounslow Heath.

CALL IN THE CAVALRY

Much agitation was caused by a lion-bait at Warwick in the summer of 1825, the first for some two hundred years. The lion, Nero, had been bred in captivity. Like some lions of the Roman theatre, Nero was disinclined to fight. Instead of biting the dogs who were set upon him, he politely pushed them away with his paw; when that failed, he rolled upon them. Eventually, after Nero had been severely bitten, the bait was stopped. Later in the show another lion, named Wallace, was baited with similar disappointment for the spectators.

The Times, now on the side of reform, attacked the events as 'a disgusting exhibition of brutality'. Baiting continued to wane in popularity, under growing middle-class disapprobation. Not until 1835, however, was it finally outlawed under an Act introduced by Joseph Pease MP. This legislation prohibited 'wantonly and cruelly ill-treating or torturing any horse, mare, gelding, bull, ox, cow, heifer, steer, calf, mule, ass, sheep, lamb, dog or any other cattle or domestic animal.' It also banned the keeping or using of 'any house, room, pit, ground or other place for running, baiting or fighting any bull, bear, badger, dog or other animal (whether domestic or wild) or for cock-fighting.'

But the battle was not quite over. At Stamford the traditional bull-baiting assumed almost revolutionary significance, as some of the 'lower orders' continued to defy not only the law, the mayor, the magistracy, and the local aristocracy, but subsequently the London police, the Home Secretary and the Dragoon Guards as well. At times the bull-baiting mob, swollen by outsiders, was estimated to be four thousand strong. In November 1836, the annual Stamford bull-running and baiting took place as usual and a subsequent prosecution was brought by the newly established Society for the Prevention of Cruelty to Animals (SPCA), resulting in two defendants being bound over under Pease's Act. (For an account of the founding of the SPCA see below.) The following year two hundred special constables, abetted by local magistrates, declined to enforce the new law.

In 1838 Lord John Russell, then Home Secretary, at the request of the SPCA, drafted in a force of Dragoons and police who guarded the only two available bulls. But in the afternoon a bull calf, recently sold by Lord Spencer and *en route* to its new owner, was seized by the crowd and briefly run before it was recaptured by the Dragoons. In 1839 it was a similar story, the bull again being saved by the cavalry. Finally, the cost of the forces of law and order became too much for the citizens of Stamford and they themselves ensured the end of the sport.

Attitudes certainly had changed, and one can discern a pattern of development. The prevailing anthropocentric view of the intelligentsia during the Renaissance, which had emphasized the chasm between human and nonhuman, had been challenged during the sixteenth and seventeenth centuries. Dissent then became the established view of the literati in the eighteenth century. The masses at first resisted this change, but gradually, the growing middle classes, motivated by a desire to seem civilized and respectable as well as by genuine humane feeling, came to accept the new opinions. At this time politicians began attempts at legislative reform, motivated not by a desire for popularity, but by the same sincere sympathetic feelings that had driven several of them to become opponents of the slave trade. Although the Evangelical element was pronounced, it is striking that animal welfare reformers came from all sects and from none: Catholics, Puritans, Quakers, Methodists, Anglicans, Tories, Whigs, Utilitarians, atheists and cynics all contributed to the movement, their common motivation, it seems, being a sense of compassion.

THE FOUNDING OF THE SPCA

The British instinct for forming committees and societies had led to the formation of the Society for the Suppression of Vice in 1802, one of this Evangelical committee's aims being the abolition of animal-baiting. In Liverpool in 1809 the short-lived Society for Preventing Wanton Cruelty to Brute Animals was established; its two main concerns appear to have been the treatment of hamstrung sheep being driven through the streets of Liverpool, and cruelty to horses. It was not until 1824, however, that a society was formed which survived its first few gatherings. On 16 June 1824, a meeting was called in Old Slaughter's Coffee House, St Martin's Lane, London, at which Fowell Buxton MP, the active anti-slavery campaigner, took the chair. The Society for the Prevention of Cruelty to Animals was launched at this meeting, and the Reverend Arthur Broome, subsequently to be described as the society's founder, was appointed its first secretary. Two committees were set up. One was to 'superintend the Publication of Tracts, Sermons, and similar modes of influencing public opinion' and consisted of the Utilitarian Sir James Mackintosh MP, A. Warre, William Wilberforce MP, Basil Montagu, the Reverend Arthur Broome, the Reverend G. Bonner, the Reverend G. A. Hatch, A. E. Kendal, Lewis Gompertz, William Mudford and Dr Henderson. The other committee was 'to adopt measures for Inspecting the Markets and Streets of the Metropolis, the Slaughter Houses, the conduct of coachmen etc.', and consisted of Fowell Buxton MP, Richard Martin

MP, Sir James Graham, L. B. Allen, C. C. Wilson, John Brogden, Alderman Brydges, E. A. Kendal, E. Lodge, J. Martin and T. G. Meymott.

Of the twenty-one people mentioned in the first minutes, three were clergymen and five were Members of Parliament. Three were already well-known humanitarians – Wilberforce, Buxton and Mackintosh. All were established figures but none, at this stage, were titled aristocrats. There were no women members, although the publications committee, which got off to a cracking start, decided at its third meeting on 25 June to publish 'a tract on cruelty to brutes by Mrs. Hall'. It also decided, at the same meeting, to publish a sermon on compassion as well as the late Lord Erskine's speech on the introduction of his Bill of 1809.

It was not until 1829 that women were again mentioned in the society's minutes. It was then decided to establish a ladies committee, initially to consist of Mrs Thompson, Mrs Fenner, Mrs Tattersall, Miss Milne and Mrs L. Gompertz. The heyday of the ladies committee came under the presidency of Baroness Burdett-Coutts (1814–1906), the outstanding humanitarian, although until 1886 ladies were not considered sufficiently business-like to be allowed to join the general committee governing the society's affairs.[7]

The Reverend Arthur Broome (1780–1837), who became so important in the SPCA's history, had gone up to Balliol College, Oxford, in 1798. In 1803 he was ordained in the Church of England and became curate at Brook and Hinxhill in Kent. From 1820 he was vicar at St Mary's, Bromley (now Bromley-by-Bow), in London, until he resigned his living in 1824 to devote himself entirely to the society's affairs as its secretary. In 1822 and 1831 he published abridged editions of Humphry Primatt's work *A Dissertation on the Duty of Mercy and Sin of Cruelty to Brute Animals,* with extensive footnotes.

Initially, the society was funded by donations, not least from Broome himself (although he was not a wealthy man). By January 1826, however, the society was in debt to the tune of nearly £300, and the committee sadly contemplated its closure. At that juncture, however, a legacy of £100 was received from the estate of the novelist Mrs Ann Radcliffe. This saved the society, but did not prevent Arthur Broome from being thrown into prison for the society's remaining debts, from which he was quite quickly rescued by the redoubtable Richard Martin (himself heavily in debt) and the ingenious Lewis Gompertz.

Early in 1828 Gompertz was appointed to succeed Broome as secretary, though the reasons for the change are not clear. A minute indicates that Broome had 'not been attending to the duties of his office', nor been present at meetings. Nevertheless, the committee's attitude remained one of respect rather than censure. Perhaps Broome had been made despondent by the society's financial problems and his own imprisonment.

In its first few years the society had, nevertheless, been a success. In

1824 alone it had brought nearly 150 prosecutions, mainly of drovers and others involved in the Smithfield Market. At Broome's expense the society had employed its first inspector, a Mr Wheeler, to gather evidence of cruelties, and the publication of tracts had begun in earnest. By the end of 1828 Gompertz had succeeded in putting the society on a sound financial footing, for which he was awarded the society's Silver Medal four years later, along with Inspector Wheeler. Gompertz, who was a practising Jew, had the reputation of being an eccentric, albeit an effective one. He was also a writer and an inventor, and among some thirty-eight inventions one, the expanding chuck, has proved to be of lasting value. It is clear that he was a man of 'advanced principles', for he not only was a vegetarian, but he also refused to ride in horse-drawn carriages because of his opposition to animal exploitation of any sort. In 1824 he wrote *Moral Inquiries on the Situation of Man and Brutes,* in which his argument for animal protection was based on 'the similitude between man and other animals'. In 1852 he published *Fragments in Defence of Animals* in which he attacked cruelties to horses and cattle, hunting, vivisection and the 'barbarity of whale fishing'.

How this radical man related to the hunting Martin and the shooting Buxton is not recorded, but, for whatever reason, he fell out with two other members of the committee, Dr John Fenner and the Reverend Thomas Greenwood. Fenner and Greenwood attacked Gompertz on three grounds: first, because he used 'informers' (i.e. the society's inspectors) to prosecute offenders; secondly, for his professed 'Pythagoranism', by which was meant his advocacy of a vegetarian diet; and thirdly, because he was not a Christian. In the summer of 1832 the SPCA committee resolved to suspend the inspectorate and insisted that 'the proceedings of this Society are entirely based on the Christian Faith and on Christian Principles.' Gompertz resigned, giving as his reason his opposition to behaviour 'inimical to the institution' on the part of one of the society's leading members.

So, within eight years of its foundation, the society had lost both its founder and its first saviour. Even before Princess Victoria's association with the society, therefore, which began in 1835, it seems that its conservative character had become established. We cannot attribute this with certainty to Martin, Wilberforce or Buxton, since these three men, all establishment figures in their fashion, had by this time ceased to be actively involved with the society. In the years 1833 and 1834 the character of the society became increasingly aristocratic, although quite how this came about is unclear, and it seems that those responsible for alienating its outstanding first two secretaries were otherwise men of little significance in the history of the movement. Although Broome and Gompertz are today honoured by the RSPCA, it appears that they were the first victims of the society's tendency to reject its more controversial and effective figures.

After his departure, Gompertz founded the Animals' Friend Society, with the aim of continuing 'those operations which the Society for the Prevention of Cruelty to Animals, when United, so successfully performed'. He ran this society with considerable success, and apparently with the approval of Richard Martin, until 1848, when he gave up because of ill health.

In 1840 Queen Victoria granted the prefix 'Royal' to the SPCA, thereby marking the final arrival of animal welfare as an entirely respectable concern. The first great golden age of reform in this field was over, but the royal patronage and prefix assured its continued advance during the remainder of the century.

EDUCATION

Shortly before the politicians started their attempts at reform, and at the height of the serious eighteenth-century outpourings on the subject of animal protection, there had been an increase in the number of educational books for children which, following the advice of Locke and Pope many years earlier, began to refashion nursery attitudes on the topic. Nearly all, until the end of the nineteenth century, were by women – such as Dorothy Kilner, Sarah Trimmer, Mrs Charles Bray, Edith Carrington, Charlotte Elizabeth, Emily Cox, Arabella Argus, Mary Turner Andrewes and Susanna Watts. Writers were not only continuing to use animals as mouth-pieces and exemplars of virtue, as 'disguised humans'; they were also beginning to teach children kindness to the nonhumans themselves.

In one of the first books of children's fiction in English, *Goody Two-Shoes,* published in 1765, the heroine was depicted as taking great pains to care for mistreated animals, and in 1783 Dorothy Kilner's *The Life and Perambulations of a Mouse* was the first children's book to stress kindness to nonhumans as a moral duty;[8] the author pretends to have been asked by a moralizing mouse to take her under her protection and to write her history of callous treatment at the hands of humans. But it was Sarah Trimmer's story, three years later, which was destined to become the classic in this field. Sarah Trimmer (1741–1810) was a noted educationalist who, as a young woman, had met and become a friend of Dr Johnson. Her first work was her *Easy Introduction to the Knowledge of Nature*, published in 1780, which was shortly followed by the remarkably enduring and most popular of her books – *The History of the Robins* in 1786.[9] This famous work continued in print until about 1911. It concludes with the words:

Happy would it be for the animal creation if every human being consulted the welfare of inferior creatures, and neither spoiled them by indulgence nor injured them by tyranny! Happy would mankind be, if every one acted in conformity to the will of their Maker, by cultivating in their own minds, and those of their children, the Divine principles of general benevolence.

Mrs Trimmer established a trend which continued for several generations after her death, and, for a century after the *History of the Robins,* publishers like Griffith and Farran, the Religious Tract Society, and S. W. Partridge produced numerous publications of this sort, explicitly aimed at inculcating kindness to animals.

Among the first to follow Mrs Trimmer was the pioneer feminist Mary Wollstonecraft (1759−97), whose *Original Stories from Real Life,* published in 1788, told of a kindly Mrs Mason who commented to some children upon her reluctance to kill insects: 'You are often troublesome − I am stronger than you − yet I do not kill you.'

Later, she advised them to 'Be tender-hearted. . .it is only to animals that children *can* do good. Men are their superiors.' Obviously Wollstonecraft's concern for women's rights cannot be separated entirely from her concern for nonhuman animals. Her famous feminist work *Vindication of the Rights of Woman* was published in 1792, shortly before her death after giving birth to Mary, who was to become the creator of Dr Frankenstein and second wife of the anti-speciesist Percy Bysshe Shelley. Ironically, her feminist views were subsequently ridiculed by Thomas Taylor, the contemporary philosopher, in an anonymous satirical work entitled *A Vindication of the Rights of Brutes.*

Early educational publications argued strongly against bloodsports and angling, as in the anthropomorphic *The Hare, or Hunting Incompatible with Humanity: Written as a Stimulus to Youth Towards a Proper Treatment of Animals,* which was published by John Gough in 1799 and was followed by similar injunctions in the *Youth's Magazine* of 1813, *The Picturesque Primer* published by W. Fletcher in 1837, and *Holiday Amusements* by William Belch, published around 1828. The latter work also argued strongly against birds-nesting. Some authors adopted a religious tone, as did Susanna Watts in *The Animal's Friend,* arguing that humanity to animals is a religious duty. Others wrote pseudo-autobiographical pleas for kindness from horses, dogs, mice or donkeys, as in *The Adventures of a Donkey* (1815) and *Further Adventures of Jemmy Donkey* by Arabella Argus; *The Life and Perambulations of a Mouse, Keeper's Travels in Search of his Master* (1850) and *Tuppy* (1860). Most famous of such books was to be Anna Sewell's humanitarian classic *Black Beauty,* published in 1877. In the anonymous *The Escapes, Wanderings and Preservation of a Hare,* published about 1820, and *The Hare, or Hunting Incompatible with Humanity* of 1799, hares recount to their human rescuers the hunting and deaths of members of their families. These were perhaps the first books devoted entirely to attacking bloodsports. A famous series which ran to numerous editions throughout the second half of the nineteenth century was entitled *A*

Mother's Lessons on Kindness to Animals and published by S. W. Partridge. The chapter headings exemplify the typical themes of the period: 'Don't Whip them, Coachee', 'A Boy Reproved by a Bird', 'Sagacity of a Horse', 'Birds and their Nests', and 'The Progress of Unrestrained Cruelty'. Another popular work was *Our Duty to Animals* (c.1870) by Mrs Charles Bray, who, although opposed to killing for sport, explicitly condoned meat-eating on the grounds that it is natural and that unless the dead carcasses of animals were consumed disease would become rampant. This is essentially the same line as had been taken by Mrs Trimmer nearly a century earlier, when she had accepted that 'The world we live in seems to have been principally designed for the use and comfort of mankind, who by the Divine appointment, have dominion over the inferior creatures', and that:

Some creatures have nothing to give us but their own bodies; these have been expressly destined by the Supreme Governor as food for mankind, and He has appointed an extraordinary increase of them for this very purpose; such an increase as would be very injurious to us if all were suffered to live. These we have an undoubtful right to kill; but should make their short lives as comfortable as we can, and let their deaths be attended with as little pain as possible.[10]

The other eighteenth-century work of note is *Pity's Gift: A Collection of Interesting Tales to Excite the Compassion of Youth for the Animal Creation*. Its tales of Kind-Hearted Henry and Tender Amelia are said to have been selected by an anonymous lady from the writings of a Mr Pratt. In her Preface she writes:

Everyone must have noticed, in most children, a tyrannical, sometimes a cruel, propensity to torment animals within their power, such as – persecuting flies, torturing birds, cats, dogs, etc. Some friends of mine joined me in thinking that a collection of humane facts, and arguments, in favour of these suffering creatures, might be of considerable use if brought into view, not only to our own offspring, but if made public, to youth in general.[11]

It has been claimed that these early educationalists were concerned not about the welfare of animals but for the character of the children. This is debatable. Admittedly, a concern for the reader's character is often expressed, but in most cases this seems to be offered by way of justification, being intended to persuade the more speciesist parent or teacher that kindness to animals is indeed a subject fit for serious concern.

The reforming streak found in some earlier educational works had all but vanished by late Victorian times. Kindness to favoured animals, even sentimentality, by then had become so much a part of polite society that the sense of urgency had almost disappeared from the educational literature.

THE NATURALISTS

As we have seen, during the late seventeenth and throughout the eighteenth centuries the naturalists had been moving away from the Renaissance anthropocentric view of nature. It began to be clear to them that animals were *not* made solely for the service of mankind. Thomas Bewick (1753–1828) wrote about nature fondly and fairly, putting the human race into a context with the other creatures, and the Reverend Gilbert White (1720–93), showing a similar respect and sensitivity for all living beings, planted four lime trees at Selbourne to block his view of the butcher's yard opposite. White's *Natural History of Selbourne* remained a favourite for over a hundred years.

Nor did the old division of animals into benevolent and malevolent seem to be quite so clear-cut. Creatures like toads and snakes, previously regarded as repulsively ugly, came to be treated more rationally by the early 1800s. People also began to realize that some animals, in the past considered to be dangerous, could be quite unthreatening unless provoked; even the wolf, renowned in folklore for its wickedness, began to receive kinder portrayals.[12]   Keith Thomas cites John Ray, writing in the seventeenth century, as being the first English naturalist to break away from the Aesop and bestiary traditions which had portrayed nonhuman animals emblematically, describing them in terms of imagined virtues, vices or other symbols of alleged significance to humankind.[13] Certainly, by the nineteenth century there is, among naturalists, a general respect for the animal kingdom *per se* which sometimes becomes distinctly humanitarian, especially in books for children such as *Gleanings in Natural History* by Edward Jesse, published in 1861; the popular writings of the Reverend J. G. Wood in the 1870s and Mrs Brightwen's *Wild Nature Won by Kindness* of 1893. All these are aimed at the older child and are far more concerned to 'excite kindly feelings' in the reader than are similar biological textbooks from about 1900 onwards, which too often reek of the arrogance of science.

Even insects are shown respect, as, for example, in *Insects and their Habitations,* which was published in 1833 under the aegis of the Society for Promoting Christian Knowledge. Although this book still harks back to an earlier generation of texts in its tendency to urge the reader to 'reflect upon the lessons of wisdom and virtue which they [insects] teach', it also enjoins kindness:

It is a sin against that God who created both them and you, to inflict unnecessary suffering upon any of His creatures. Ask yourselves too, how you would like such treatment, from one stronger than yourself. If you meet a beetle or a caterpillar, step aside, and do not wantonly crush it. And should you see a poor earth-worm, lying in the dusty path, parched with the sun, and too much exhausted to regain his home, extend a kind hand to help him, and place him on the nearest cool and moist ground. He is a harmless little creature, though not pleasing to the eye or agreeable, but he is God's workmanship; and while you are thankful for being endowed with reason, and with an immortal soul, let the inferior creatures enjoy their little lives while they may.[14]

VEGETARIANISM ESTABLISHED

As we have seen, a few exceptional people have questioned the slaughter of animals for food over the centuries. Some, like Leonardo, kept their views private, while others have spoken out, like Richard of Wyche (1197–1253), Bishop of Chichester, when he observed animals being killed for food: 'you, who are innocent, what have you done worthy of death?'[15] Joseph Ritson, the antiquarian, was one of the first to devote a whole book in English to vegetarianism. *His Essay on Abstinence from Animal Food as a Moral Duty* was published in London in 1802. In it, Ritson argued against meat-eating on the grounds that it is unnatural, unnecessary, unhealthy and immoral. He repeated the notion that meat 'is the cause of cruelty and ferocity' among those who devour it, and drew attention to the widespread existence of vegetarian cultures. He quoted the eighteenth-century zoologist, William Smellie, who wrote:

Of all rapacious animals, man is the most universal destroyer. The destruction of quadrupeds, birds and insects is, in general, limited to particular kinds: but the rapacity of man has hardly any limitation. His empire over the other animals which inhabit this globe is almost universal.[16]

Medieval prohibitions on the consumption of useful animals such as oxen continued in some Mediterranean countries until the seventeenth century. But by this time Europe had become far more carnivorous than most of the rest of the world and England probably had a greater density of food animals than any other country save the Netherlands. By 1700 oxen were no longer regarded as draft animals in England and the country became notorious for its ravenous consumption of beef. Strangely, the decline in the agricultural use of horses and dogs in the present century has not led to a corresponding increase in their consumption, presumably because of their enhanced sentimental status.

Around 1790 an American sect in Vermont, the Dorrilites, prohibited the wearing of clothes derived from animals and the eating of meat, and in 1809 William Cowherd in England made vegetarianism obligatory in his Bible Christian Church based near Manchester. This was the start of the organized modern vegetarian movement. One of Cowherd's followers, William Metcalfe, emigrated to Philadelphia and became a founder of vegetarianism in America.

From about 1812, Percy Bysshe Shelley advocated vegetarianism and, during the ninetèenth century, abstinence from animal flesh gradually became established among a minority of the middle class. Slaughtering and slaughter houses began to be concealed from public view, and the animal origin of meat dishes became obscured, as recognizable carcasses were less frequently served at table. The word 'vegetarian' appeared in 1842 and came into widespread use after the establishment of the Vegetarian Society in England in 1847 by secular followers of Metcalfe.[17] At the end of the century the cause received a considerable boost from Howard William's *The Ethics of Diet* (1883) and from the writings of Henry Salt, himself inspired in part by advocates of vegetarianism such as Shelley and Henry Thoreau (see pp. 125−8).

Perhaps some children have always disliked meat; it may be this is especially true among those who realize the connection between meat and animals before they are addicted to flesh-eating. One may speculate on the use of Norman words for meat derived from animals who are called by their Saxon names. By calling cow-meat 'beef' and pig-meat 'pork', many an infantile eater is deceived. Words like 'chicken' and 'lamb' can, however, suddenly give the game away. It was in the first half of the nineteenth century that vegetarianism, thanks to the influence of Gompertz, Ritson, Shelley, Cowherd, and others, first became an established minority fashion in Britain. Today young children who refuse meat spontaneously are being allowed this dietary freedom by more permissive twentieth-century parents: they like animals and therefore, quite logically, decline to eat them.

7 Victorian Consolidation

The Victorian era was a period of active consolidation for animal welfare in Britain, and the reign saw numerous campaigns to reduce the miseries of food animals being driven to slaughter through the streets of London and other cities, to improve the methods of slaughter, to stop the export of worn-out old horses to Belgian abbatoirs, to protect performing animal in circuses and to outlaw the use of dogs for the drawing of carts. Some of these agitations only bore fruit in the following century — such as the ban on the export of live horses for slaughter in 1914, and the effective prohibition of the cruel bearing-rein for horses under the restrictions of the major Protection of Animals Act of 1911. The legislation of 1835 had outlawed cockfighting and dog-fighting, but this encouraged rat-fighting, which continued until it was also made illegal under the 1911 Act.

These campaigns have already been well written about[1] and will not be discussed here in detail. By far the two most controversial welfare issues of the era, however, were the killing of birds for sport and millinery, and the use of nonhumans in vivisection. A closer examination of these cases illustrates the degree to which the ideals of animal welfare had become part of British culture by the end of the nineteenth century, and how this had occurred through two principal channels — nursery education and the influence of the aristocracy.

THE ELEVATION OF THE RSPCA

The aristocracy had, no doubt, noticed the example set by the young Princess Victoria, who had honoured the SPCA with her patronage in 1835 and, after she became Queen, with the royal prefix in 1840. These were momentous developments, for they put the cause of animal welfare on the way to the international and fashionable respectability which would guarantee its progress.

Who planned this ennoblement of the RSPCA? It may have followed quite naturally from the involvement of Victoria, but little is known about how she became involved. The only record is of Robert Batson, one of four members of the SPCA committee attending its monthly meeting on 6 July 1835,[2] reporting that 'at the suggestion of several Ladies he had presented a Report of the Society and a letter to their Royal Highnesses the Duchess of Kent and the Princess Victoria with a request that they would honor [sic] the Society by becoming Ladies Patronesses.'[3] Sir John Conroy, the Duchess of Kent's close friend, had presented the request of 2 July to the Duchess and her daughter, and had replied two days later to Batson that 'Her Royal Highness very readily acceded to your request that her name and that of the Princess Victoria be placed on the List of Lady Patronesses.' The Committee resolved that Batson write letters of thanks to their Royal Highnesses and to Conroy.

Who the 'several ladies' were remains unknown. But to them and Robert Batson much credit is due for this initiative, which did much to further the cause of animal welfare. It was certainly very timely; once she had become Queen in 1837, it might have been too late to expect Victoria's involvement as a Patroness. The Earl of Carnarvon had consented to be the SPCA's president in 1834, and from then on until the next century the society's president and vice-presidents tended to be titled. In 1850 it was the turn of the Duke of Beaufort to be president, in 1854 the Marquess of Westminster, in 1861 the Earl of Harrowby, in 1878 Lord Aberdare, in 1893 HRH the Duke of York (the future King George V), in 1910 the Marquess of Cambridge and in 1918 the Prince of Wales. By 1887 the society could boast no less than twenty royal and four ducal patrons, and thirty-four titled vice-presidents (including Field Marshall Lord Wolseley). The Church connection was maintained by an archbishop, five bishops and Cardinal Manning as vice-presidents.

When, after the First World War, royalty and aristocracy drifted away from the RSPCA, its prestige and effectiveness declined. Traditional aristocracy was, for several decades, replaced not by the 'modern aristocracy' of bankers, industrialists and intellectuals but by people of little influence.

In the Victorian era, however, the endorsement of animal welfare by the Crown and aristocracy in an upward-looking and class-conscious society had the undoubtedly beneficial effect of making the cause fashionable and effective. The emulation of the upper classes, after all, was a central preoccupation in the lives of thousands of Victorians. But there were disadvantages. Certain aristocratic exceptions and inconsistencies had to be accepted. The aristocratic pastimes of hunting and shooting animals, for example, could not be included in the campaign for reform, their importance in the web of British upper-class ritual being too great. Some of the cruelties associated with horse-racing, game-fishing, meat-eating and agriculture also had to be tolerated. Predominantly working-class cruelties were, however, to be fair game and the RSPCA played an important part in the suppression of bull-baiting and cockfighting. Indeed, in 1838 the society's then secretary, Henry Thomas, and two inspectors of the society, visited Hanworth in Middlesex after hearing of a proposed cock-fight. There they were set upon by the cock-fighters and badly injured. Shortly afterwards one of the inspectors, James Piper, died in St Thomas's Hospital, although the post-mortem stated that the cause of death had been tuberculosis.

This double-mindedness in the RSPCA, a willingness to attack working-class cruelty while condoning that of the upper crust, provoked some objections. John Stuart Mill, for example, wrote to the society's secretary on 26 July 1868 declining any closer association with the society 'while it is thought necessary or advisable to limit the Society's operations to the offences committed by the uninfluential classes of society.'[5] He cited pigeon-shooting exhibitions as an example of a cruel sport which ought to be opposed. In retrospect it appears most unfortunate that Mill, one of the greatest of political philosophers, should have been alienated in this way. Following the Bentham line, he had strongly argued that nonhumans should be included in efforts for reform. Writing in *The Principles of Political Economy* in 1848, Mill had made this quite clear:

The reasons for legal intervention in favour of children apply not less strongly to the case of those unfortunate slaves and victims of the most brutal part of mankind — the lower animals. It is by the grossest misunderstanding of the principle of liberty that the infliction of exemplary punishment on ruffianism practised towards these defenceless creatures has been treated as a meddling by government in things beyond its province; an interference with domestic life. The domestic life of domestic tyrants is one of the things which it is the most imperative on the law to interfere with.

The RSPCA had certainly played a part in promoting legal changes, building on the pioneering work of Martin's 1822 Act. That Act was amended after the passing of a Bill put forward by Joseph Pease MP (himself a member of the RSPCA committee) in 1835 to prevent 'fighting or baiting any bull, bear, badger, dog, cock or other kind of animal, whether of domestic or wild nature'; in 1854 legislation was passed prohibiting the use of carts drawn by dogs; in 1869 wild birds received some protection. In 1876 it was the turn of laboratory animals; in 1878 animals in transit; and in 1900 even wild animals were legislated for to a very limited degree. By the end of the century the RSPCA's handbook listed a score of such statutes.

PROPAGANDA AND PROSECUTION

Within the RSPCA there was a debate as to whether to emphasize education or prosecution as the society's chief instrument of reform. But from 1857 onwards, with the co-option of two government school inspectors to the society's staff, and with the appointment of John Colam in 1860 as secretary of the society (a post he held until 1905), it was education which was paramount. Early RSPCA tracts dealt with cruelty to donkeys, post-horses, race-horses and dogs and were religious and rather patronizing in tone:

> A man of kindness to his beast is kind,
> But brutal actions show a brutal mind;
> Remember he who made thee made the brute;
> Who gave thee speech and reason, formed him mute.
> He can't complain – but God's all-seeing eye
> Beholds thy cruelty – he hears his cry.
> He was designed thy servant, not thy drudge:
> And know that his creator is thy judge.[6]

Quotations from the Bible, especially the Old Testament, were used profusely: 'A righteous man regardeth the life of the beast' is frequently found, as is 'God delighteth in mercy.' Cruelty to animals was depicted as 'unnatural and abhorrent to the original constitution of human nature' and as 'the direct road to cruelty to our fellow [human] creatures and to its final reward – the gallows'. In its educative drive the RSPCA exhorted donkey-drivers to withold 'the merciless whip', butchers to show 'humanity', schoolboys to desist from birds-nesting, cabmen to remember that 'fair play is an Englishman's motto', and drovers to show 'kindness' to their sheep and cattle:

Remember the extreme agonies they endure from hunger and thirst, cold and heat, want of rest, stiffened limbs, bleeding feet, wounds from blows and dogs; never forget the heart-sickening, unnumbered cruelties awaiting them at those places of dreadful torture, THE MARKETS AND SLAUGHTER HOUSES.[7]

In 1860 the RSPCA published *The History of William Brown, or Cruelty to Animals Punished,* which relates how William graduates from torturing flies and worms to dropping a kitten from high places and thence to bull-baiting. When whipping a horse one day, he misses, and so severely injures his own leg that it has to be amputated without anaesthetic. In contrast, another pamphlet relates how the kindly Charles Jones makes friends with a mouse who obligingly wakes him when the house catches fire; Charles saves his employer's family and is duly rewarded.

The publication and use of numerous educational works on animals continued until the First World War. Broadly, these taught that it is wrong to inflict cruelty wantonly and that it is right to put wounded or diseased creatures out of their miseries by killing them humanely.

As an extra spur to influence their readers the RSPCA often included in their pamphlets detailed reports of the convictions they had obtained. Despite the emphasis upon education, prosecutions continued to increase, approximately doubling in each decade between 1830 and 1900. Probably this was a reflection not of increasing cruelty but of growth in the number of inspectors (or 'constables') employed by the society. In 1832 there had been two; by 1855 there were eight, by 1878 forty-eight and by 1897 one hundred and twenty.

From 1856 onwards the inspectors were invariably uniformed. Antedating the establishment of the police by a few years, the society's inspectors in England found that the police tended to regard the enforcement of the cruelty laws as chiefly the concern of the society, rather than their own. In the late twentieth century such an expectation of a charity seems somewhat anomalous, but it continues, encouraged by a cost-conscious state, and inspectors and police are in some respects still mutually dependent. In the nineteenth century the society often recruited ex-policemen, and the police themselves occasionally would solicit assistance from RSPCA inspectors in the enforcement of law and order unrelated to the treatment of animals. Inspectors were based in London, but would travel around the country attending to complaints and information received. They were expected to be respectable and disciplined, although Colam was entirely opposed to 'the autocratic military style' which became more prominent after his retirement in 1905.

John Colam's greatest achievement seems to have been to preserve the society's social eminence while at the same time maintaining its campaigning vigour. 'Wily he certainly was', said the author Henry Salt (see chapter 8), but Colam's prudence was combined with strict adherence to principle, as, for example, in his steadfast objection to any infliction of pain in animal experiments. He could also show personal bravery and was sometimes in direct and vigorous action, as when he stopped a Spanish bull-fight staged in London in 1870 by personally jumping into the ring.

Colam not only edited the RSPCA's journal *Animal World*, he often conducted the society's prosecutions himself, and with great skill. Under his guidance, the RSPCA established a special relationship with government, giving advice which was usually heeded, and using its very high-level contacts to influence the introduction and implementation of legislation. Only when such tactics failed would the society use publicity as a means of pressure, but when it felt this was necessary it did not shrink from doing so.

Many radicals, then as now, called upon the RSPCA to take a more extreme line. But instead of treating them as enemies, Colam helped and encouraged them with their work and sometimes prompted them to establish independent organizations. Even Frances Power Cobbe, the formidable leader of the anti-vivisectionists (see below), has nothing but praise for Colam in her autobiography.

Perhaps the main criticism to be made of the RSPCA under Colam is that it failed to join forces with the new wave of thinkers on the subject. Nor did Colam's RSPCA attract the great social reformers as it had done earlier in the century, when it had received support from men like T. F. Buxton, Lord Ashley (later Shaftesbury) and even Jeremy Bentham (who had donated to it in 1831). As we have seen, the philosopher J. S. Mill, who had given money before Colam's appointment, also became alienated. By the end of the century the remarkable union of Utilitarian and Evangelical which had characterized its foundation had been lost; the more intellectual, and even more intelligent, among the animal reformers now chose to remain independent of the RSPCA.

The radical John Bright, although he signed several anti-vivisection 'memorials' and described humanity to animals as a 'great point'[8] had no real connection with the society. Lord Shaftesbury became disillusioned with it and so did Frances Power Cobbe. Charles Dickens, although opposed to animal experiments, never became actively involved with the RSPCA. Not even the campaigning Duchess of Hamilton (see chapter 8) in the Edwardian era was to support it, nor her colleague Louise Lind-af-Hageby. Towards the end of the century, few of the literary figures who sympathized with animals − Shaw, Salt, Galsworthy, Carroll, Browning or Ruskin, for example, were involved in any way with the RSPCA. Perhaps some of these writers were considered by the RSPCA to be too extreme; what Victorian worthy, after all, could take the poet Christina Rossetti (1830−94) seriously when she claimed:

> The tiniest living thing
> That soars on feathered wing,
> Or crawls among the long grass out of sight
> Has just as good a right
> To its appointed portion of delight
> As any King.[9]

Rossetti was not an activist in the movement, but, like so many other poets and writers of the age, she so easily might have been if the RSPCA had sought to enlist her services. Although the RSPCA owed much of influence to its aristocratic support and, above all, to the Queen, its preoccupation with established respectability caused it to lose touch with the more progressive and inspirational elements in the animal welfare movement.

For a time, this division among campaigners did not undermine the promotion of reform, but, when Lord Aberdare took over from Lord Harrowby as the society's president in 1878 and began to water down the RSPCA's opposition to vivisection, the split between the 'radicals' and the 'traditionalists' widened.

VIVISECTION

After the seventeenth-century fad for experimentation on living animals had died down, the practice had continued among a small fraternity of scientists. After William Harvey (see chapter 4) and the surgeon John Hunter came nineteenth-century physiologists like Charles Bell and Marshall Hall, who practised this approach. France, to a large extent, became the centre of vivisection, François Magendie (1783–1855) Claude Bernard (1813–78) and Louis Pasteur (1812–95) being three of its most prolific proponents. Magendie was, according to Claude Bernard, the founder of experimental physiology. He was, however, an experimenter in the hit-and-miss sense of the world, lacking the modern concern for precision and the control of variables. John Elliotson, afterwards professor of medicine at the University of London, attended some of his demonstrations in Paris and was appalled at the clumsy savagery of 'Dr Magendie, who cut living animals here and there with no definite object, but just to see what would happen'.[10] Magendie used huge numbers of animal subjects, including some old army horses who had survived Waterloo. An eye-witness account of one of Magendie's demonstrations brings home the unpleasantness of such work:

Magendie, alas! performed experiments in public, and sadly too often at the Collège de France. I remember once, amongst other instances, the case of a poor dog, the roots of whose spinal nerves he was about to expose. Twice did the dog, all bloody and mutilated, escape from his implacable knife; and twice did I see him put his forepaws around Magendie's neck and lick his face. I confess – laugh vivisectors if you please – that I could not bear this sight.[11]

There is no doubt that Magendie's callousness was outstanding even for the age he lived in, and shocked some of his contemporary physiologists. Even Hooke and Boyle had shrunk from experimenting upon the same animal twice 'because of the torture of the creature'.[12] John Elliotson wrote that 'In one of his [Magendie's] barbarous experiments, which, I am ashamed to say I witnessed, he began by coolly cutting out a large round piece from the back of a beautiful little puppy as he would from an apple dumpling.'[13]

All of Magendie's experiments, and nearly all of those carried out by his successors, including Claude Bernard, were of course without any form of anaesthesia or analgesia. Moreover, each of these experiments and demonstrations went on for some time and the agonies of the subjects must have been both intense and prolonged. We know from Claude Bernard that dogs were cut open in preparation 'an hour or more' before the actual demonstrations took place. We also know that they were not destroyed immediately afterwards, but if still alive were available for further operations by students.

Twenty years after Magendie's death Dr Francis Sibson (Consultant Physician at St Mary's Hospital) testified to the first royal commission investigating vivisection in 1876 that 'Magendie might have made his experiments with much greater consideration for his animals...I do not think that the idea entered his mind that he had a suffering being under him.' Another witness before the commission was Dr William Sharpey, who had also seen Magendie at work. 'He put the animals to death in a very painful way. The consequence was that I never went back to that course of demonstrations.'[14]

When Magendie died in 1855 he was succeeded in the chair of Experimental Physiology by Claude Bernard. Bernard had begun his medical studies in 1834, taking his degree in 1843. During these nine years he had studied under Magendie and in 1841 took up his first appoinment, as *préparateur* in Magendie's laboratory at the Collège de France. From an early stage in his training as a scientist, Bernard rejected the view common in France at the beginning of the century that the functioning of living organisms is determined in an entirely different way to that which determines inanimate matter: 'We therefore conclude, without hesitation, that the dualism between brute matter and living bodies, which is affirmed by the vitalist school, is entirely contrary to science itself. Throughout the whole domain of science, unity reigns.'[15] Bernard would not, like Descartes, have separated the human organism from the rest of creation. He was, however, entirely determined to ignore the sufferings of his subjects. He had no interest in the practice of medicine, in the healing of the sick or the comforting of the dying. For Bernard, a hospital training was a necessary step towards the medical laboratory, no more; research, and not the patient, was the priority. Indeed, he felt a slight contempt for the medical practitioner and the healer. Bernard's famous remark about biology suggests an extraordinary sense of purpose: 'If I were to look for a simile that would express my feelings about biological science, I should say that it was a superb salon resplendently lit, into which one may only enter by passing through a long and horrible kitchen.'[16]

If Bernard had ever had any feelings of compassion they had been soon dispelled:

The physiologist is not an ordinary man: he is a scientist, possessed and absorbed by the scientific idea that he pursues. He doesn't hear the cries of the animals, he does not see their flowing blood, he sees nothing but his idea, and is aware of nothing but organisms which conceal from him the problems he is wishing to resolve.

Dr George Hoggan worked under Bernard, and subsequently wrote to the *Morning Post* (2 February 1875):

We sacrificed daily from one to three dogs, besides rabbits and other animals, and after four years' experience I am of the opinion that not one of those experiments on animals was justified or necessary. The idea of the good of humanity was simply out of the question, and would be laughed at, the great aim being to keep up with, or get ahead of, one's contemporaries in science, even at the price of an incalculable amount of torture needlessly and iniquitously inflicted on the poor animals...I think the saddest sight I ever witnessed was when the dogs were brought up from the cellar to the laboratory...they seemed seized with horror as soon as they smelt the air of the place, divining, apparently their approaching fate. They would make friendly advances to each of the three or four persons present, and as far as eyes, ears and tail could make a mute appeal for mercy eloquent, they tried it in vain.

Like Descartes's wife, Bernard's, too, was fond of animals and detested her husband's work. After years of dissension she left him. During his last years, however, Bernard gained the fame and admiration he had always yearned for, and his example encouraged the setting up of animal research laboratories all over Europe.

The other outstanding Frenchman whose work contributed to France's reputation as the country of vivisection was Louis Pasteur (1822−95), whose life-long advocacy of germ-theory led him to experiment upon many animals, infecting them with various fevers, anthrax and rabies. His work on rabies was the subject of constant attack by anti-vivisectionists in the 1880s,[17] not only on grounds of cruelty but because it was claimed that his rabies vaccine was a danger to his patients. Indeed opposition to vaccination became closely associated with the anti-vivisection movement from this time until the First World War.

German scientists were also contributing to the new experimental physiology, but it was these three Frenchmen, François Magendie, Claude Bernard and Louis Pasteur, who were mainly responsible during the first eighty years of the last century for turning vivisection into an everyday scientific practice throughout much of Europe and America. They also ensured that it would become the outstanding animal welfare issue of the second half of the century.

ANTI-VIVISECTION AND FRANCES COBBE

In 1824, Magendie had visited London and provoked a considerable outcry after public demonstrations of his physiological experiments on rabbits, frogs, dogs and cats. A few months later, pioneering legislator Richard Martin raised the subject in the House of Commons (24 Feb-

ruary and 11 March, 1825) on hearing that Magendie was planning a
return visit. Magendie, although defended by Sir Robert Peel, seems to
have had second thoughts about his lecture tour.

In 1846 the Reverend David Davis had petitioned the French authorities to suppress the practice of vivisection at the veterinary college at
Alfort near Paris, but in 1857 reports reached the RSPCA that horrendous cruelties were being continued there and the society petitioned
for an audience with the French emperor, which eventually took place
in April 1861. The experiments, however, persisted. *The Times* of
8 August 1863 reported that 'At the Veterinary College of Alfort a
wretched horse is periodically given up to a group of students to
experimentalise upon. They tie him down and torture him for hours, the
operations being graduated in such a manner that sixty and even more
may be performed before death ensues.' These operations included dissection of eyes and viscera and the removal of hooves. British veterinary
surgeons signed a mass protest and sections of the French press joined in
the campaign for reform. Even the *British Medical Journal* attacked the
French vivisectors. Indeed it went much further: 'It has never appeared
clear to us that we are justified in destroying animals for mere experimental research under any circumstances; but now that we possess the
means of removing sensation during experiments, the man who puts an
animal to torture ought, in our opinion, to be prosecuted.'[18]

Among those members of the British public who felt revulsion at the
Alfort revelations was the writer and welfare-worker, Frances Cobbe,
destined to become the most doughty and effective anti-vivisectionist of
the nineteenth century. Frances Power Cobbe (1822–1904) was born in
the year that Richard Martin's Act was passed. The daughter of wealthy
Anglo-Irish parents, at an early age she showed an independence of
spirit by questioning and, for a time, rejecting the Evangelical religious
conventions in which she had been instructed. In their place she developed her own personal brand of Christianity, addressing her prayers to
the Unknown God and even to the 'possibility of God'. In 1855 she
published a treatise on Kantian ethics entitled *Essay on the Theory of
Infinitive Morals*. For a while she joined Mary Carpenter, the pioneer
social worker, teaching children in the slums of Bristol. An injury to her
ankle, however, put an end to this work after three years, and while
temporarily crippled, Frances again took up writing.

Public opinion in Britain was profoundly shocked by the Alfort
revelations. Frances Cobbe's contribution to the debate was an article
'The Rights of Man and the Claims of Brutes', published in the November
issue of *Fraser's Magazine* (which was reprinted in *Studies Ethical and
Social* two years later). The purpose of this essay was, she said, to find 'a
definition of the limits of human rights over animals'. Although animals
are 'subordinated' to mankind, Cobbe argued, we nevertheless have a
duty to consider their pains and pleasures.

10 Frances Power Cobbe (1822–1904). By the end of the nineteenth century most leaders in the animal welfare world were
women. Cobbe was the outstanding anti-vivisectionist of the period
and, quite typically, also a leading feminist.
(BBC Hulton Picture Library)

During the month that the article was published, Frances Cobbe
travelled to Florence and there happened to hear of the activities of the
physiologist Moritz Schiff. In particular she was impressed by the evidence of a Dr Appleton from Harvard University who 'told us that he

himself had gone over Professor Schiff's laboratory, and had seen dogs, pigeons, and other animals in a frightfully mangled and suffering state'.[19] Those in the neighbourhood of Schiff's laboratory had begun to complain about the disturbance caused by the 'cries and moans of the victims'. Frances Cobbe decided to channel this feeling into a 'Memorial' addressed to the professor, urging him to spare his animals as much pain as possible. The memorial was signed by 783 people, including many eminent and aristocratic Florentines. Among the English signatures was that of the author, Walter Savage Landor, who, according to Frances Cobbe, 'added some words so violent that I was obliged to suppress them'.[20] This document probably constitutes the first instance of organized opposition to the cruelty of vivisection. Although it had little immediate effect upon Schiff, it started a tradition of opposition to his laboratory which led ten years later to the formation of the Florentine Society for the Protection of Animals by Contessa Baldelli. The activity of this society and the continuing lawsuits and complaints against Schiff contributed to his eventual departure to Geneva in 1877.

Frances Cobbe had returned to her life as a professional and successful journalist in London. For another ten years after the Alfort affair and the memorial to Schiff, her main concern continued to be with the rights of human beings rather than animals. One cause on which she often wrote was that of women's rights; in 1862 she was scoffed at for advocating university places for women.

In response to the Alfort affair, the RSPCA offered a £50 prize for the best essay received on the subject of vivisection, with special reference to the question of its necessity. Two essayists, Dr Markham, physician to St Mary's Hospital, London, and Mr Fleming, veterinary surgeon to the Third Hussars, won prizes, and their essays recommending the use of anaesthetics in experiments, were published by the RSPCA in 1866.

Four years later, the British Association for the Advancement of Science published four recommended rules by which vivisection should be controlled: experiments should not be performed for the mere purpose of obtaining greater operative skill; they should always be performed by qualified experts properly equipped; they should be under the influence of anaesthetic wherever possible; and no demonstrations to an audience should ever involve the suffering of pain.

In 1874 the habits of French vivisectors once again caused an outcry in Britain. At a Congress of the British Medical Association held at Norwich, Eugène Magnan, an erstwhile pupil of Magendie, shocked some of his British medical colleagues by publicly operating on some dogs in order to demonstrate the effects of alcohol and absinthe which he injected into them. The meeting was abandoned after strenuous objections from two Irish scientists, Samuel Haughton and Jolliffe Tufnell. The RSPCA instituted proceedings against Magnan, and Sir William

Fergusson (Sergeant-Surgeon to the Queen), called as a witness, described the 'ghastly scene', the 'groaning of the dogs' and 'their writhing agony'.

The action brought by the RSPCA was under the amended form of Richard Martin's Act of 1822. Magnan swiftly withdrew to his own country and the prosecution failed. Nevertheless these events caused some important publicity, and it was in the ensuing public agitation that Frances Cobbe was once more drawn into the issue, on this occasion by personal contact with Mrs Luther Holden, the wife of a surgeon at St Bartholomew's Hospital in London. Frances Cobbe drew up another 'memorial' expressing general concern over the increasing number of experiments being performed in Britain, alluding to the Magnan affair in particular. This memorial was signed by seventy-eight medical practitioners, by many peers and bishops, and by such illustrious Victorians as Cardinal Manning, Lord Shaftesbury, W. E. H. Lecky, the Reverend B. Jowett, John Bright, Major-General Sir Garnet Wolseley, Thomas Carlyle, Alfred Tennyson, John Ruskin and Robert Browning. 'This I know', wrote the latter, 'I would rather submit to the worst of deaths as far as pain goes, than have a single dog or cat tortured on the pretence of sparing me a twinge or two.'[21]

It was while Frances Cobbe was working on her memorial, in June 1874, that the president of the RSPCA, Dudley Ryder, the second Earl of Harrowby, received a letter from Queen Victoria's private secretary expressing the Queen's concern over the treatment of animals in science and enclosing a donation to the society's funds. If the society needed any further encouragement, then here it was. This influential letter was a further indication of the Queen's heartfelt concern.

This was not to be the only occasion upon which the Queen recorded her disquiet on the issue of vivisection. Although unable, for constitutional reasons, openly to patronize a reform movement, she made sure that eminent scientists and her ministers knew her views on the subject. In 1875 she wrote to Joseph Lister, the eminent surgeon, asking him to oppose vivisection, and in March 1876 she urged her prime minister, an initially apathetic Disraeli, to legislate against it. In April of 1881 her secretary wrote to Gladstone, then prime minister:

The Queen has seen with pleasure that Mr. Gladstone takes an interest in that dreadful subject of vivisection, in which she has done all she could, and she earnestly hopes that Mr. Gladstone will take an opportunity of speaking strongly against a practice which is a disgrace to humanity and Christianity.[22]

It was probably such pressure from the Queen that persuaded home secretaries to administer the 1876 Act particularly vigorously in its early years.

The opinion of the ruler of the empire having been made known to the RSPCA, it was hardly surprising that the society was fairly well disposed to receive the advances made by Frances Cobbe and her friends. In January 1875 their memorial was presented to the council of the RSPCA under the chairmanship first of Prince Lucien Buonaparte, nephew of Napoleon, and subsequently of Lord Harrowby. A sub-committee was immediately appointed and the diligent John Colam set about collecting extensive evidence of painful experiments from accounts published in scientific journals. It was at this point that the letter from Claude Bernard's old student, Dr George Hoggan, appeared in the *Morning Post* of 1 February 1875 (see above, p. 107), making a further profound impact upon public opinion. When it came to decisive action, however, the RSPCA dithered. Richard Hutton, editor of the *Spectator*, accused the society of dragging its feet.[25] Prepared to delay no longer, Frances Cobbe joined forces with Hoggan and, with support from various parliamentarians and others, among them Robert Lowe (Home Secretary 1873−4) and Lord Chief Justice Coleridge, and with the approval of the government, a Bill for Regulating the Practice of Vivisection was introduced into the House of Lords by Lord Henniker on 4 May 1875.

On the 12th of the same month, however, a weaker Bill was read in the House of Commons by Dr Lyon Playfair MP, instigated by scientists such as John Burdon Sanderson and T. H. Huxley, who wished to maintain almost complete freedom of research.

Because the two Bills were contradictory, the government decided to appoint a Royal Commission of Enquiry in June 1875 under the chairmanship of a vice-president of the RSPCA, Edward Cardwell. Another RSPCA vice-president who was appointed to the commission was W. E. Forster MP, and at least one of the other commissioners, the journalist Richard Hutton, also was known to be sympathetic to the animals. The scientific community was represented by Professors Eric Erichsen and T. H. Huxley.

Among the witnesses who testified before this commission were several eminent men of science, and, although some attempted to justify vivisection, it is striking that most seem to have expressed general concern over the unnecessary cruelties being perpetrated in animal laboratories. For example, Professor Henry Acland, FRS (Regius Professor of Medicine at Oxford University), spoke of 'experiments of a revolting and grave nature'. Sir William Fergusson, FRS (Sergeant-Surgeon to the Queen) was not impressed by the value of many experiments being performed; Dr Alfred Taylor, MD, FRS, cited 'purposeless cruelty'; Professor George Rolleston (Linacre Professor of Anatomy and Physiology at Oxford) warned that 'vivisection has special and distinctive liabilities and amenabilities to abuse; for it does act on our emotiono-motor nature in a particular way.' This last witness maintained, in effect, that vivisection can sometimes liberate a blood-lust or a sadistic impulse, just as 'soldiers will tell you that the sight of blood upon the gauntlet, that white glove which Dragoon regiments wear, to use their plain language, "wakes up all the devil in them".'[24]

Even staunch supporters of the vivisection *status quo* in England were ready to admit in their evidence that things had gone too far in France. Professor J. Burdon-Sanderson, FRS (Professor of Human Physiology at University College, London), said that 'there are certain things done in connection with research, which ought not to be done on humanitarian grounds, if I may be excused for using the word'; and Dr John Anthony testified that some experimenters gave no thought for animals as sentient beings: 'the continual sight of animals being acted upon, particularly if the observer has any enthusiasm for the pursuit, in a very short time blinds the man's sense of humanity.'

The staunch supporters of experimentation did not do their cause much good. The honest answers of Dr Emanuel Klein, lecturer in histology at St Bartholomew's Hospital, disgusted even Huxley, and convinced the commissioners that there was indeed a strong case for legislation:

Question: When you say that you use [anaesthetics] for convenience's sake, do you mean that you have no regard at all for the suffering of the animals?

Klein: No regard at all.

Question: You are prepared to establish that as a principle which you approve?

Klein: I think that with regard to an experimenter, a man who conducts special research and performs an experiment, he has no time, so to speak, for thinking what will the animal feel or suffer. His only purpose is to perform the experiment, to learn as much as possible and to do it as quickly as possible.

Question: Then for your purpose you disregard entirely the question of the suffering of the animal in performing a painful experiment?

Klein: I do.[25]

This dulling exchange has reverberated down the decades, being frequently quoted as an example of scientific callousness, most recently in the House of Lords by the Earl of Selkirk a century later, during a debate on the Animals (Scientific Procedures) Bill on 12 December 1985. Klein went on to state that British physiologists had the same attitude as those on the Continent towards the suffering of animals, but that there was 'a great deal of difference' in the attitude of the British public compared with abroad.[26]

The commission duly reported (with a short minority report from Richard Hutton seeking to prohibit experiments on dogs and cats entirely) that a total ban on vivisection would be unreasonable, since such research sometimes mitigates human suffering and, furthermore, it would result in scientists emigrating to Europe, so producing no real benefit to animals. Nevertheless they found a case for state licensing both for original research and for teaching demonstrations. After the publication of the report, on 8 January 1876, both sides of the argument set about drafting new Bills.

Frances Cobbe, disappointed by the RSPCA's ineffectual response, had in the meanwhile founded, in November 1875, together with Dr George Hoggan and Richard Hutton (editor of the *Spectator*), her own anti-vivisection society. Originally named the Victoria Street Society, it eventually became the National Anti-Vivisection Society. Hutton shared Cobbe's disgust with the RSPCA, writing in the *Spectator*: 'If they do not show a little more courage and a little more zeal, some other Society will grow up in their place which, by boldly doing the work from which they shrink, will succeed in their popularity and influence.'[27] By 1884, the Victoria Street Society boasted more than a score of titled vice-presidents, including a duke, a duchess and three marquesses. It also had the support of nine bishops, several privy counsellors and MPs, Lord Chief Justice Coleridge, Cardinal Manning, Tennyson and Browning. The president of the new society was Anthony Ashley Cooper (1801–85), seventh Earl of Shaftesbury, the outstanding philanthropist of the age who had earlier been, for a short time, a supporter of Dr Playfair's rather pro-vivisection Bill. After a life-time spent in the service of his fellow humans, in old age he had, like Wilberforce before him, turned his attention to the welfare of dumb animals. By the time he became actively involved in the anti-vivisection cause he had already made major contributions to reforming the legislation dealing with the treatment of the insane, the conditions of the workers in mills and factories, the employment of children in mines and as chimney-sweeps, to measures to improve the housing and education of the poor. He wrote of vivisection: 'the thought of this diabolical system disturbs me night and day.' There is little doubt that his timely intervention in the cause did much to hasten the legislation controlling vivisection.

Shaftesbury several times chaired the meetings of the Victoria Street Society, and he led an important delegation from the society to see the Home Secretary on 20 March 1876. This deputation, which included Cardinal Manning, was favourably received and invited to submit suggestions for legislation. These were swiftly drafted into a Bill which was introduced into the Lords by the Colonial Secretary, the Earl of Carnarvon, and received its second reading on 22 May. Frances Cobbe wrote of this Bill:

No experiment whatever under any circumstances was permitted on a dog, cat, horse, ass or mule; nor any on any other animal except under conditions of complete anaesthesia, from beginning to end. The Bill included licences, but no certificates dispensing with the above provisions.[28]

11 The seventh Earl of Shaftesbury is a notable example of the universality of compassion. The two outstanding human social reformers of the nineteenth century, Shaftesbury and William Wilberforce, both became involved as animal welfare campaigners in their later years, and it was animal welfarists in Britain and America who pioneered legal action against child abuse.
(The Mansell Collection)

The Bill received support from the RSPCA and had a good reception in the press. It proposed to implement all the recommendations of the royal commission (except that proposing an appeal procedure against the revocation of licences) and went further in several respects, including incorporating Hutton's minority report's recommendations. Unfortunately Lord Carnarvon was, at this juncture, called away from London because of his mother's serious illness (she died on 26 May). Despite a letter of condolence from the Queen referring to 'horrible, disgraceful and un-Christian vivisection' and urging Carnarvon to continue his work, Carnarvon was absent long enough to give the scientists an opportunity which they seized.[29]

THE CRUELTY TO ANIMALS ACT, 1876

The General Medical Council, armed with the signatures of some 3,000 members of the medical profession, hurriedly made representations to the Home Secretary, Richard Assheton Cross, petitioning him to modify the Bill. Lord Salisbury, later Prime Minister, gave his support to Professor Burdon-Sanderson and his allies, who now included Ernest Hart, editor of the *British Medical Journal*. The British Medical Association also supported the experimenters' lobby. Apparently this 'active maliginity of the scientific men', as Shaftesbury subsequently described it in a letter to Frances Cobbe, persuaded the hard-pressed Home Secretary to give way, despite a counter-deputation from the RSPCA led by its President, Lord Harrowby, and including the Bishop of Gloucester and Cardinal Manning. Harrowby, in uncharacteristically bellicose style, threatened that if the Bill was thrown out the RSPCA would 'kindle a flame of indignation against vivisection even in the remotest hamlets in this kingdom'.[30]

On 10 August Cross, the Home Secretary, introduced the new Bill, which received the royal assent only five days later. So was born the Cruelty to Animals Act of 1876 which, while making numerous worthy restrictions on animal experimentation, allowed nearly all those restrictions to be annulled by means of special certificates issued to experimenters by the Home Office. Its clumsy and inadequate form suggests, as Sir George Kekewich MP pointed out thirty years later, a rush-job hurried through an ill-attended Parliament at the end of a session. The reformers felt they had been cheated by this Act and with some cause, for it allowed the vivisector, now armed with licence and certificates, to continue to inflict severe pain upon his experimental animals.

The RSPCA, alternately blowing hot and cold, and by now thoroughly unpopular with the anti-vivisectionists in the Victoria Street Society, weakly criticized the new law as being a protection rather more for the scientist than for the animal and describing it as 'very unsatisfactory as a means for the discovery of offences'. In 1881, Cardinal Manning stated that the reformers had realized too late that they had been 'hoodwinked' by the Bill.

Further vain attempts were made to introduce more stringent legislation in every subsequent year till 1884 but, although no further reforms were achieved, the opposition to vivisection continued, not least in the old universities.

SCIENCE AND RELIGION

In some quarters science was viewed with suspicion in the nineteenth century. In literature, Dr Frankenstein had made a monster and Dr Jekyll had liberated the evil Mr Hyde.[31] Richard French has rightly asserted that the great controversy over vivisection was not only about cruelty to animals; it also reflected the tensions surrounding the roles of medicine and science in Victorian society: 'Victorian England was profoundly shaken by the emergence of science as a major influence and a leading institution. The concern was multidimensional: what was the appropriate cultural role for science, what were its religious implications and its institutional perquisites?'[32] French concludes that the Victorian anti-vivisection movement, half unconsciously, was protesting about the declining humanity of the medical profession and 'the cold, barren, alienation of a future dominated by the imperatives of techniques and expertise.'[33] This is surely true, but it should in no way detract from the role played by the spontaneous sense of compassion for the animals in the movement, which explains not only its fervour but the striking social heterogeneity of its membership.

If there is a political point to be made in considering the events of 1876 it is, as French puts it, that the politicians revealed an 'awe of science' and a deference towards it which resulted in 'a measure ultimately administered to protect experimental medicine rather than restrict it, under which research upon living animals prospered as never before.'[34]

Socially, it was a skirmish between the forces of science and religion. But it was also, to an extent, a battle between the old and the new elites; between, on one hand, the aristocracy and the Church, as the old leaders of society, and, on the other, the upstarts of science. The experimental approach in physiology, which came quite late to Britain, was to bring medicine into line with science. This was one of the aims of T. H. Huxley, James Paget and other leading pro-vivisectors. Their colleagues in France and Germany not only saw science as progress but as part of the new order challenging the traditional land-owning ruling class.

CONTROVERSY IN OXFORD

At Oxford, Charles Dodgson (Lewis Carroll) had joined in the controversy in 1875 by publishing an attack on vivisection in the *Fortnightly Review* which he entitled 'Some Popular Fallacies about Vivisection'. His biographer S. D. Collingwood records that:

Mr Dodgson had a peculiar horror of vivisection. I was once walking in Oxford with him when a certain well-known professor passed us. 'I am afraid that man vivisects' he said, in his gravest tone. Every year he used to get a friend to recommend him a list of suitable charities to which he should subscribe. Once the name of some Lost Dogs' Home appeared in this list. Before Mr. Dodgson sent his guinea he wrote to the secretary to ask whether the manager of the Home was in the habit of sending dogs that had to be killed to physiological laboratories for vivisection. The answer was in the negative, so the institution got the cheque. He did not, however, advocate the total abolition of vivisection — what reasonable man could ? — but he would have liked to see it much more carefully restricted by law.[35]

We will never know for certain who was the well-known professor that Dodgson passed in an Oxford street, but it may have been Burdon-Sanderson, who had been appointed Waynflete Professor of Physiology at Oxford in 1882. Burdon-Sanderson had been a keen supporter of vivisection when it was opposed in the Convocation of the University of London in 1874. Furthermore he was the editor of a *Handbook of the Physiological Laboratory* which had been discussed in some detail by the royal commission in 1875. It was admitted before the commission that the book contained descriptions of painful experiments and John Colam, secretary of the RSPCA, had pointed out that the Preface stated that the book was aimed at instructing beginners in research. The chairman of the commission had read from its descriptions of experiments on animals paralysed with curare: 'Rabbits...die before the end of the first day. Dogs live longer; often two or three days.' Burdon-Sanderson had been forced to confess to the commission that the use of anaesthetics whenever possible 'ought to have been stated much more distinctly at the beginning of his book'.

Burdon-Sanderson's appoinment of 1882 began a series of protests and arguments among Oxford scholars. The two chief supporters of the new professor were Sir Henry Acland, Regius Professor of Medicine from 1857 till 1894, and the Very Reverend Henry George Liddell, the Dean of Christ Church. The leading opponents of vivisection in Oxford became Charles Dodgson, John Ruskin and H. P. Liddon, the Bishop of Oxford, aided, later, by Bodley's Librarian E. B. Nicholson and Professor E. A. Freeman.

Charles Dodgson (1832—98) was not only the famous author of *Alice's Adventures in Wonderland* and *Through the Looking Glass*; he was also a mathematician, and it was on logical, rational grounds that he attacked vivisection. Collingwood records a letter he received from Dodgson dated 29 December 1891, in which Dodgson criticized an attempt by Collingwood to justify 'killing animals for the purpose of scientific recreations', not by commenting on his conclusions, but by shooting holes in the logic of the 'poor little essay'.[36] Earlier Dodgson had written to the *Pall Mall Gazette* on the subject: 'Is the anatomist, who can contemplate unmoved the agonies he is inflicting for no higher purpose than to gratify a scientific curiosity, or to illustrate some well-established truth, a being higher or lower in the scale of humanity, than the ignorant boor whose very soul would sicken at the horrid sight?' In 1875 Dodgson expressed his fear that a new breed of scientist was coming to the fore: 'a new and more hideous Frankenstein − a soulless being to whom science shall be all in all'.[37]

The interest that the subject aroused in Oxford can, perhaps, be gauged by the attendance at successive Convocations where grants were to be voted for the new professor. In 1883 the vivisectors were 88 against the anti-vivisectors' 85. In 1884 it was 188 to 147. Three years after Burdon-Sanderson had got his chair the arguments about granting funds for vivisection reached a climax. Dodgson noted in his diary for 10 March 1885: 'A great Convocation assembled in the theatre, about a proposed grant for physiology, opposed by many (I was one) who wished restrictions to be enacted as to the practice of vivisection for research. Liddon made an excellent speech against the grant, but it was carried by 412 to 244.' This result precipitated the most dramatic of all the anti-vivisection protests at Oxford: John Ruskin's resignation as Professor of Art.

Ruskin had been apointed Slade Professor of Art at Oxford University in 1869. On 9 December 1884, Bishop Liddon held a meeting of the new Oxford branch of the Victoria Street Society at which Professor Ruskin attacked vivisection. For him, he declared, the object of education was the teaching of gentleness to the students: 'their noblest efforts and energies should be set upon protecting the weak and informing the ignorant of things which might lead them to happiness, peace and light, and above all other things the relation existing between them and the lower creation in this life.' On 17 March 1885, a week after the university had voted further funds for the setting up and equipping of the physiology laboratory, Ruskin wrote in his diary: 'A lovely and delightful day, yesterday, getting Lilias' and Goodwin's sketches and doing quantities of good work myself, but put in a passion by Acland's speech on vivisection after dinner and slept ill, waking at two to think whether I would resign professorship on it.'[38] Five days later, on 22 March, the melancholic Ruskin resigned his chair. In his opinion vivisection experiments 'were all carried on in defiance of what had hitherto been held to be compassion and pity and of the great link which bound together the whole creation from its Maker to the lowest creature'.

It has been alleged that the Vice-Chancellor declined to read Ruskin's letter of resignation to Convocation as Ruskin had asked him to do, that the *University Gazette* refused to publish the reasons for his resignation and the rumour was deliberately put about that Ruskin had resigned on account of age.[39] It is clear that feelings were running high at Oxford over the vivisection issue. The principal antagonists had known each other for years and most had connections with the same college — Christ Church — where Dean Liddell's influence had for so long been paramount. Charles Dodgson's friendship with Liddell's daughter Alice had been part of the inspiration for his famous stories.[40]

THE REPERCUSSIONS OF THE 1876 ACT

One of the remarkable developments after the passage of the 1876 Act was the firmness of control exercised by the first two home secretaries responsible for its administration. The Conservative Richard Cross refused to license seven established scientists in three years, while the Liberal William Harcourt refused six in his first twelve months. They also refused certificates. Indeed the overall refusal rate was approximately 15 per cent of all applications, and was chiefly on two grounds — either that the proposed research involved too much pain or that it lacked 'utility'.[41] Yet prosecutions under the new Act proved difficult.

In 1881, the Victoria Street Society prosecuted Professor David Ferrier for allegedly experimenting upon the brains of two monkeys without a licence. In his defence, Ferrier successfully claimed that the operations were in fact carried out by a licensee, Professor Gerald Yeo, despite reports to the contrary in academic journals. The case brought together several scientists concerned to protect their right to vivisect, and in 1882 Yeo, Burdon-Sanderson, Sir William Gull, Sir James Paget, Joseph Lister, Sir William Jenner and others formed the Association for the Advancement of Medicine by Research. From 1882, when the Home Secretary, Sir William Harcourt, wrote to Jenner offering to avail himself of their advice, until 1913, the AAMR entered into a clandestine liaison with the Home Office which in effect allowed the scientists themselves to control the administration of the Act.[42] So began a long tradition of co-operation between government and vested interest which today is practically universal in this field. In America, too, the battalions of science united to block any further attempts by humanitarians to restrict their activities by legislation. Conscious and successful attempts were made to promote the image of the scientist as a heroic, even messianic figure. Governments, as well as many of the lay public, came to accept the view that the 'scientists knew best.'

THE PROTECTION OF BIRDS

Anti-vivisection, of course, was not the only great campaign of the animal welfare movement during Victoria's reign, although it created by far the greatest and most prolonged controversy. Some other campaigns resulted in measures to protect animals which seem to have slipped through almost without effort and with relatively little comment: examples are the general consolidating Prevention of Cruelty Act of 1849 and, much later, the Wild Animals in Captivity Protection Act of 1900. But an issue which was both prolonged and controversial was the crusade to protect birds, which began in mid-century, at a time when the bird populations all over Europe were coming under increasing attack from gun, lime and net. Slaughter had reached a new order of magnitude, so that sometimes the distinction between sportsman and poulterer became blurred. One such, the Marquess of Ripon, shot over half a million creatures in his life-time, including 112,598 partridge, 79,320 grouse and 222,976 pheasant. In England song-birds were being devoured by gourmets, and fashion designers decreed that ladies should be clad in feathers. Schoolboys robbed birds' nests, weekenders shot seagulls at the seaside and gamekeepers, anxious to destroy any threats to their employers' pheasants, killed almost anything that fluttered.

In the 1860s the shooting of sea birds for sport reached such proportions that sailors approaching the shores of Britain began complaining that they were no longer receiving their accustomed warnings of approaching land. Evidence that shipwrecks were on the increase was used to support such contentions, and in 1869 Christopher Sykes, MP for the East Riding, persuaded Parliament to pass the Sea Bird Protection Act, which protected sea birds during the nesting season but did not stem their mass slaughter at other times. Indeed the feather trade grew during the 1880s and 1890s, and the European and American millinery markets demanded the deaths of millions of birds worldwide – humming-birds, parrots, kingfishers, birds of paradise, herons, canaries and egrets. Ladies of fashion appeared in dresses covered entirely with plumage and on occasions, and much to the disgust of Bernard Shaw whose night at the opera was once ruined by it, wearing whole birds in their hair. Some three hundred million dead birds were imported into Europe each year in the 1880s, and about twenty-five million of them into Britain.

In 1889 Mrs W. Williamson of Didsbury founded the society which was to become the Royal Society for the Protection of Birds. One of its aims was to curb the trade in song-birds, and another was to stop the escalating destruction of birds caused by the proliferation of breech-loading and double-barrelled shotguns.

John Ruskin was among those who objected: 'Very earnestly I ask you, have English gentlemen, as a class, any other real object in their whole existence than killing birds?'[43] He was not alone in claiming that average 'experts' maimed almost as many birds as they killed. When Lord Walsingham in 1888 dispatched 1,070 grouse in fourteen hours and eighteen minutes, he used 1,510 cartridges. Could such a marksman have entirely missed with the unaccounted for 440 shots? After a shoot organized by the flashy Lord Burnham at Hall Barn in 1913, in which 4,000 pheasant were left in twitching heaps on the ground, King

12 Gustave Courbet's horrific *Hallali du Cerf* of 1867 is a celebration of Man's 'dominion' over the other animals. Today, this
dominion is causing human beings to crowd and pollute and
exterminate the other species of the planet.
(Photographie Giraudon)

George V remarked to the Duke of Windsor: 'Perhaps we went a little
too far today, David.'

Pigeon-shooting from traps had also become a popular sport in mid-
century and consisted of shooting at half-tame and sometimes blinded
pigeons released from boxes. In parks all over London, and especially at
Hurlingham, guns blazed as bets were made and well-dressed ladies
looked on admiringly. Under attack from *The Times* and lukewarm
disapproval from the RSPCA, this so-called sport flourished, despite a
Bill introduced by George Anderson MP in 1883. With the support of
Lord Randolph Churchill, who described the sport as 'the most horrible
and repulsive sight possible to imagine', the Bill passed the Commons
but failed in the Lords. It was only with the persistent opposition of
Queen Alexandra that the pigeon massacres at Hurlingham were eventually stopped in 1906.[44]

WILD ANIMALS

Despite the great agitations to protect birds and laboratory and farm animals, wild animals remained largely untouched by Victorian reforms. Old ideas about the countryside and the unending war between 'man' and 'beast' persisted, tied up as they were with the ownership of land and the seemingly unassailable rights of the landed gentry to treat 'their' wildlife as they saw fit. It has been claimed that during the nineteenth century hostility to hunting was based mostly upon class envy,[45] but this was hardly true of E. A. Freeman, Professor of History at Oxford, whose articles in the *Fortnightly Review* in 1869 and 1870 on 'The Morality of Field Sports'[46] put the case very clearly. Freeman attacked the inconsistent attitudes, current then as now: 'To chase a calf or a donkey either till it is torn in pieces or till it sinks from weariness, would be scouted as a cruel act. Do the same to a deer and it is a noble and royal sport.' Freeman saw fox-hunting as no better than, and probably a little worse than, bull-baiting, asserting that it is wrong 'to inflict and to seek pleasure in inflicting, needless suffering'.

Far from fox-hunting fading away during the nineteenth century, the introduction of the railways and the popular tendency to emulate the gentry had helped to keep it very much alive. Organized opposition appears to have begun only when Henry Salt and Howard Williams founded the Humanitarian League in 1891 (see chapter 8).[47]

During the Victorian era the idea that humans had a duty of kindness towards nonhumans became generally established. Birds, farm animals and laboratory sentients had all benefited to a degree by the end of the century, and the growing exploitation of nonhumans had begun to be restricted by a small amount of red tape. The climate of opinion had changed decisively, albeit selectively, and much progress remained to be made.

8 Edwardian Vigour and Post-War Apathy, 1900–1960

The end of the nineteenth century and the succeeding Edwardian era in Britain was a time of intense activity by animal welfarists. Indeed the forty years up to 1914 represent the most vigorous period in the movement's history until then, comparable with the periods of about 1770–98 and 1822–54. All three periods were interrupted by wars which broke the momentum for a while. In general, influential writings heralded the practical and legislative advances. In the twentieth century, the Second World War succeeded the First World War before the movement could re-establish itself and, as we shall see in part II, it was only from about 1969 that it fully regained its momentum.

An analysis of Henry Salt's bibliography of 1894, for example, shows two major clusters of serious publications about animals rights: one in the last quarter of the eighteenth century preceding the Napoleonic wars, and the other at the end of the nineteenth century. The latter was to be extended by Salt's own writings, eight of which appeared before the end of the First World War. There is even a lesser cluster of publications between 1824 and 1846, just before the Crimean War. After outbreaks of war there are clear-cut gaps from 1798 to 1824 and from 1846 to 1873.[1]

The Edwardian phase of the movement was notable for the intellectual calibre of Henry Salt and his friends George Bernard Shaw and Sir George Greenwood. This was matched by the political enthusiasm of the first mass campaigning of the movement, organized in London by the Swedish ladies Louise Lind-af-Hageby and Leisa Schartau, supported by their British colleagues the Hon. Stephen Coleridge and Nina, Duchess of Hamilton.

THE INTELLECTUAL CONTRIBUTION: HENRY SALT AND FRIENDS

Henry Salt was an influential thinker and leading campaigner for animal rights; it is worth looking into the background and lives of such people in order to round out our picture of the period's developments. Henry was the son of an austere Indian Army Officer whom he rarely saw, and was reared largely in England by his mother and her relatives in Shrewsbury. He grew up as an outgoing and sensitive boy who enjoyed his sojourn at Eton and went on to take a First Class degree in Classics at Cambridge. He then returned to Eton as a master, but left after his advocacy of the poetry and philosophy of Percy Bysshe Shelley began to raise the eyebrows of the orthodox. After marrying Kate Joynes, the daughter of his old tutor at Eton, Henry decided to give up conventional upper-class life and to settle in rustic simplicity at Tilford in Surrey. Here the Salts proceeded to scratch a living from their vegetable garden and from Henry's writings.

Kate and Henry had become socialists, but, more importantly for them, they also developed their own philosophy of trying to live in harmony with nature, showing respect and compassion for all sentient creatures. Among their sources of inspiration were Henry Thoreau and Edward Carpenter. The latter, known affectionately as the 'Noble Savage', had abandoned an academic career to live the life of a shoemaker, overtly confessing his homosexuality. He became both friend and frequent visitor.

George Bernard Shaw was another early associate and shared with Kate a love of music; he wrote passionately against vivisection, bloodsports and meat-eating, describing the latter to Ellen Terry in the summer of 1900 as 'cannibalism'. In a society heavy with moral rectitude and hypocrisy, the Salts and their circle became an oasis of openmindedness, rarely discussing politics, preferring to practise and communicate their ideals rather than campaigning to have them translated into legislation. Shaw wrote shortly before his death: 'We were Shelleyans and Humanitarians...my pastime has been writing sermons in plays, sermons preaching what Salt practised.'[2]

Among Salt's many friends and admirers were George Meredith, John Galsworthy, G. K. Chesterton, Ralph Hodgson, W. H. Hudson, Ramsay Macdonald, Havelock Ellis, William Morris and Bertram Lloyd. For Carpenter's seventieth birthday in 1914, Salt composed a statement of humanitarian principles which was signed by, among others, Rabindranath Tagore, Bertrand Russell, H. G. Wells, G. M. Trevelyan, Prince Kropotkin, W. B. Yeats and Sidney and Beatrice Webb. This intellectual circle was widely influential in the development of modern social thought.

Socialism for Salt was not an end but a means, a way to 'love, beauty and humanity in our daily lives'. He lived to be disillusioned with the British Labour Party which, when in power, showed little interest in the humanitarian reforms that he yearned for. Salt's life was to a large extent a reaction against the pretensions and stoicism of Victorian society. He was part of an intellectual group which attacked the contemporary convention which equated compassion with weakness: 'The longer I live', said Galsworthy (referring to solitary confinement), 'the more constantly I notice that hatred of suffering, abhorrence of cruelty, is called sentiment by those who have never fathomed or truly envisaged the nature of that particular suffering or cruelty.'[3] Yet Salt undoubtedly had an influence upon events. For example, in 1890 he published *The Life of Henry David Thoreau* and in 1917 *David Henry Thoreau: A Centenary Essay*. Years later, Gandhi wrote to Salt from prison to tell him that he came to his policy of peaceful non-cooperation by reading these books. Salt may have played a part in persuading Ramsay Macdonald to invite Gandhi to England for the Round Table Conference in 1931, and Salt and Gandhi certainly met at this time and at Gandhi's suggestion.

Salt was a prolific author, although never a best-seller. Of some forty-six titles including revisions, four were poetry, two advocated vegetarianism, one was about socialism, two were classical, two were on wild flowers, six were on Shelley and ten were to do with the rights of animals. Indeed, animal rights was the subject on which Salt concentrated the largest number of his published works, although this fact has been rather overlooked by his biographers. He founded the Humanitarian League in 1891, yet Salt was not closely allied with most animal welfare campaigners of his era. Although of different generations, Cobbe and Salt were of the same social class, but incompatible politically; Cobbe does not mention him in her autobiography, nor do the two secretaries of the RSPCA who published accounts of animal welfare covering this period. As Salt noted sadly, zoophilists and socialists too often feared one another, and it would be another half-century before the political Left became fully part of the animal protection world.

The four members of the Humanitarian League who were most active politically in the animal rights cause were the Liberal MP George Greenwood, Ernest Bell the publisher, Edward Carpenter and the mystic Edward Maitland. For Salt, the word 'humanitarian' was defined to mean respect and kindness towards all sentient life. Humanitarianism, was not to be confused with philanthropy (love of mankind) nor with zoophily (kindness to animals). It embraced both. Salt fought and debunked the speciesist clichés of his age — the allegation against animal defenders that they were 'sentimental' and the claim that the 'instincts' of animals were entirely different from the 'reason' of men. He proclaimed 'the kinship of all sentient life', and in his sarcastically entitled autobiography, *Seventy Years Among Savages*, he castigated as barbarous and ignorant the attitude of his fellow men and women towards their nonhuman kin, reminding them in a jingle that:

> The motive that you'll find most strong,
> The simple rule, the short-and-long,
> For doing animals no wrong,
> Is this, *that you are one.*

For Salt, the 'creed of kinship' was the greatest religion, and he acknowledged Thoreau, Shelley and Bentham as its recent prophets and before them Seneca, Porphyry and Plutarch. In his major work, *Animals' Rights Considered in Relation to Social Progress*, published in 1894,[4] Salt cites such diverse authors as Humphry Primatt, the Reverend J. G. Wood and Schopenhauer. Salt approved the latter's horror at the English habit of referring to nonhuman animals as 'it', as if they were inanimate objects, and he politely chided Frances Cobbe for asserting that animals have 'no moral purpose'. Such ideas, said Salt, were purely arbitrary; sentience and individuality are what matter. This book was reprinted several times, sometimes with revisions, for the last time during Salt's life on the centenary of Martin's Act in 1922. This edition includes a letter from Thomas Hardy, dated 1910:

Few people seem to perceive fully as yet that the most far-reaching consequence of the establishment of the common origin of all species is ethical; that it logically involves a readjustment of altruistic morals, by enlarging, as a necessity of rightness, the application of what has been called 'The Golden Rule' from the area of mere mankind to that of the whole animal kingdom... While man was deemed to be a creation apart from all other creations, a secondary or tertiary morality was considered good enough to practise towards the 'inferior' races; but no person who reasons nowadays can escape the trying conclusion that this is not maintainable.

LITERARY TRENDS

The enthusiastic attitude of the 1890s is epitomized by the adventure stories of Ernest Seton-Thompson, in which the heroic content is combined with a serious concern for the many animal personalities who fill his pages. Writing in New York on the last day of the old century, Seton-Thompson had proclaimed his commitment to the underlying ethic:

A moral it would have been called in the last century. No doubt each different mind will find a moral to its taste, but I hope some will herein find emphasised a moral as old as Scripture — we and the beasts are kin. Man has nothing that the animals have not at least a vestige of, the animals have nothing that man does not in some degree share. Since, then, the animals are creatures with wants and feelings differing in degree only from our own, they surely have their rights. This fact, now beginning to be recognised by the Caucasian world, was first proclaimed by Moses and was emphasised by the Buddhist over 2,000 years ago.[5]

The literary co-operation between the British and American humane movements had reached a peak towards the end of the century. Ernest

Bell and Edith Carrington published in London in 1895 the stories written for the American Humane Education Society by Harriet Beecher Stowe and Mrs Fairchild Allen, under the title *The Animals on Strike*. Although the tone of the Humanitarian League's publications was indeed sometimes sentimental and anthropomorphic, the commitment to the animal rights ideal was strong and explicit.

Bell, who later became president of the Vegetarian Society, published several animal rights books of his own, among them *Fair Treatment for Animals* and *The Wider Sympathy*. He also published *The Animals' Friend*, a series of pamphlets for the Animals' Friend Society, many written by himself and some by other authors including Sir George Greenwood, Professor E. A. Freeman (a reprint of his famous essay *The Morality of Field Sport*), Jerome K. Jerome (*The Cruel Steel Trap*), Andrew Lang (*On Otter Hunting*) and John Galsworthy (*For Love of Beasts* and *Treatment of Animals*).

Beatrix Potter's anthropomorphic little stories at the start of the century rapidly became classics. Later in the century moralistic writers such as C. S. Lewis continued to use nonhuman animal characters to make their point (such as the lion, Aslan, in his Narnia stories). Hugh Lofting in *The Story of Dr Doolittle* of 1922 shows his hero as someone who not only can communicate with his nonhuman friends but who sets about righting the wrongs done to them. Later again, nonhumans would be depicted as morally superior to the humans, as in Erich Kästner's *Animal Conference* of 1955 and Robert O'Brien's *Mrs Frisby and the Rats of NIMH* of 1971.

Some of the most famous writers of their times are on record as concerned for the relationship between nonhumans and humans. D. H. Lawrence castigated himself for throwing a log at a snake: 'Immediately I regretted it. I thought how paltry, how vulgar, what a mean act! I despised myself and the voices of my accursed human education', and Albert Schweitzer wrote in 1923: 'until we have drawn the animal into our circle of happiness, there can be no world peace.' In discussing his motives for writing *Animal Farm*, George Orwell stated: 'Men exploit animals in much the same way as the rich exploit the proletariat.'[6]

The illustrated monthly magazine, *The Animals' Friend*, was started in 1894 under the aegis of Frances Cobbe's Victoria Street Society; its editor was Sidney Trist, who also edited a paper called *The Animals' Guardian* and, in 1913, a book of essays on animal cruelties entitled *The Under Dog*, to which he contributed the chapters on wounded war horses, pit ponies, vivisection and trapping. Trist repeatedly quoted John Ruskin's words drafted as a rule for the Society of St George: 'I will not kill nor hurt any living creature needlessly, nor destroy any beautiful thing; but will strive to save and comfort all gentle life, and perfect all natural beauty upon the earth.' Trist was a close colleague of Stephen Coleridge,[7] and it was Coleridge's two works, *Vivisection*

published in 1917 and *Great Testimony* in 1918, which mark, together
with Salt's last works, the end of the era.[8] While the horrors of the war
turned the survivors' attention to rebuilding human society, the animal
welfare movement sometimes made itself appear trivial. For example,
a popular contemporary book for children, *The Law of Kindness*,
addressed itself in mincing tones to the members of 'Dumb Animals'
Leagues and Dicky-Bird Societies'. Adam and Charles Black brought out
a series of 'animal autobiographies' in 1904 which continued in vogue
during the war years; written by several authors, they told the life
stories of a dog, a cat, a rat and several other animals, all narrated in the
first person. C. H. Claudy's *Tell me Why Stories about Animals*, published in 1915, carried the whimsy to its extreme. The mud and blood of
Flanders could not have been further removed from precious tales such
as these. The stark contrast of reality at its most hellish with the cosy
world of Edwardian nursery stories was, sadly, to leave the latter looking
discredited. Many serious people could no longer take the subject
seriously.

The RSPCA somewhat changed its public face during this period. Its
monthly magazine, *Animal World,* so dignified in the 1880s and 1890s,
gradually altered during the Edwardian years, growing smaller and less
formal. The embossed portrait of the Queen on the cover gave way first
to a Cecil Aldin picture of two puppies and then to a Harry Rountree
one of a dozen ducklings, as the society's contingent of eighteen royal
patrons of 1901 dwindled over the next generation until it had halved by
the 1920s.

SIR GEORGE GREENWOOD AND THE 1911 ACT

Whether the criterion used is the number of new societies formed, the
number of books published or the number of actions taken for libel, the
Edwardian era was clearly a heyday for animal welfare. Its crowning
achievement in England was the passage in 1911 of the Protection of
Animals Act. From 1822 to 1835 British legislative attention had centred
on baiting, from 1839 to 1854 on banning dogs used for draught, in the
1870s on the protection of birds and vivisection, and in 1887 it had been
the turn of pit-ponies to receive very limited protection. From the end
of the century onwards the pace had accelerated, with legislation being
passed to protect captive wild animals in 1900, to ban the pole trap in
1904, to give some protection to stray dogs in 1908 (prohibiting their
transfer by the police to laboratories), to stop the hooking of birds in
1908, and to restrict the transportation of horses in 1910 (strengthened
in 1914).

Sir George Greenwood MP deserves the credit for the passage of the
major legislation of 1911. Greenwood, a friend of Salt, was Liberal MP
for Peterborough from 1906 till 1918, and the Bill was drafted by him

and the Reverend W. E. Bowen. The latter was not opposed to hunting, and in order to avoid too much opposition to the Bill, its drafters exempted any ban on bloodsports. The Liberal Party had a majority in the House, a fact that aided the passage of the Bill.[9]

The Bill was introduced by Greenwood on 15 February 1911, and received its Second Reading without debate on 8 March. On 30 June Greenwood put forward, and the House approved, a number of amendments at its Third Reading, and the Act became law on 18 August. Besides raising the maximum fines for cruelty, the new Act consolidated the previous legislation, repealing the Cruelty to Animals Acts of 1849 and 1854, and defined 'animal' as 'any bird, beast, reptile or fish'. This rendered illegal the use of living fish as bait, the gutting of live eels and the scaling of live fish, as additional offences to those already on the statute book.

The desirability of all-party support for such measures led Greenwood to obtain assistance from Sir Frederick Banbury MP and Colonel Mark Lockwood MP (later Lord Lambourne), who were Conservatives, and from George Lansbury, the Labour MP, when in the same year he vainly attempted to legislate to improve slaughtering conditions. He was more successful, also in 1911, when, with the support of Keir Hardie MP and Harry Lauder, the famous comedian, he secured regulations under the Coal Mines Act to give greater protection to pit-ponies.

As early as 1906 Greenwood had tried unsuccessfuly to restrict the export of live horses to Belgium, and in 1910 he had introduced the Diseases of Animals Bill which achieved some control over the trade. This was after the well-publicized arrival at Antwerp from Hull of a ship which had encountered heavy storms on the way and in which thirty horses had died or had to have their throats cut at sea.

In the years 1912 and 1913, Greenwood, by this time a member of the RSPCA council, sought to widen the Geneva Convention to cover veterinary surgeons, in order to promote better care for wounded horses on the battlefield. He was also particularly concerned about animal experimentation and, besides supporting Louise Lind-af-Hageby's campaigns, he actively participated in the RSPCA's prosecution of Dr Warrington Yorke in 1913 for cruelty to a donkey left in a field in a suffering and 'mangled' state after experimental surgery. The charge was dismissed on the grounds that Dr Yorke was an experimenter licensed under the 1876 Act.

Greenwood was also responsible for a steady stream of Parliamentary questions on animal welfare, and he put the Home Office on its toes over the administration of the 1876 Act when, in 1915, he revealed that it had been delaying publication of the returns until the statutory six-month period for prosecutions had elapsed.

Throughout the First World War good work was done by the RSPCA and other societies to protect, as far as possible, the thousands of horses being used by the Allied armies. Special shelters and horse ambulances were supplied by the RSPCA and in 1915 the society's chief secretary, Captain E. G. Fairholme, received a temporary commission in the Royal Army Veterinary Corps. In France alone, 725,216 horses were treated by the corps during the course of the war.

BIG GAME AND LITTLE GAME

In 1914 the Humanitarian League published a collection of essays critical of bloodsports entitled *Killing for Sport,* edited by Salt and assisted by George Greenwood. In his preface, Shaw wrote provocatively:

I know many sportsmen; and none of them are ferocious. I know several humanitarians; and they are all ferocious. No book of sport breathes such a wrathful spirit as this book of humanity. No sportsman wants to kill the fox or the pheasant as I want to kill him when I see him doing it...Bloodsport affects me much as the murder of a human would affect me rather more than less; for just as the murder of a child is more shocking than the murder of an adult (because, I suppose, the child is so helpless and the breach of social faith therefore so unconscionable), the murder of an animal is an abuse of man's advantage over animals...[10]

It seemed to Shaw that the plea of the humanitarian had become a plea for widening the range of fellow feeling:

The time will come when a gentleman found amusing himself with a gun will feel as compromised as he does now when found amusing himself with a whip at the expense of a child...Surely the broad outlook and deepened consciousness which admits all living things to the commonwealth of fellow-feeling, and the appetite for fruitful activity and generous life which come with it, are better than this foolish doing of unamiable deeds by people who are not in the least unamiable.

Amusing himself with his gun was precisely what R. Gordon Cummings did in 1850 when he described wounding a large elephant in Africa. Instead of killing it at once, he proceeded to 'light a fire and make a cup of coffee. Having admired the stricken elephant for a considerable time he proceeded to 'make experiments'; that is to say he took pot shots at the wounded giant, observing the effects in a leisurely kind of way until the poor creature, with 'large tears' trickling from his eyes, eventually rolled over and died.[11]

The popularity of big-game hunting had increased during the nineteenth century and into the next. Yet the memoirs of big-game hunters began to reveal an ambivalence about their actions: on the one hand the burning desire to conquer and on the other their growing qualms of conscience – the eternal conflict between the lust for power and the equally innate twinges of compassion.

As I have suggested elsewhere, the motivation for hunting and shooting is both learned and innate. That some of its several components are almost certainly instinctive is hardly surprising for, until the last few thousand years, nearly all humankind has depended to a greater or lesser extent on such activities. But in modern times so many other factors also contribute to their popularity: the pleasures of adventure, of exercising a skill, of observing a tradition, of open-air exercise, and of congenial company. Yet most of these are pleasures which today can be found in alternative modern sports from rock-climbing to hang-gliding. Snobbery, too, can be indulged in other, less harmful ways. Yet there are three other more peculiar motives which lurk just below the surface. These are power, sex and machismo; one or several of these are often present as motives in bloodsports. By 'power' I mean natural self-assertiveness and aggressiveness, especially in the male which, when it is exaggerated by the *culture* so as to become a cult, I call 'machismo'. Anger is, of course, not the same, being an emotional reaction to frustration or insult which nevertheless makes it another common motive for violence towards nonhumans. Sadism, another but far more furtive motive for cruelty, is something different again, being the linking of the infliction of pain or dominance with sexual excitement. Maureen Duffy, controversially, has described the sexual parallels of the hunt in some detail; it has, she writes, 'like masturbation fantasies, two parts: the hunt and the kill; the build up and the orgasm'.[12] Hinting at some partly conscious sadistic feeling, Sir Henry Seton-Karr asked in 1904: 'Why is it, by the by, that the size and beauty of wild stags and other big game arouse in certain individuals this lust to kill?'[13] The same author, in *In Praise of Bloodsports* (1906), suggested that, anxious to cleanse himself of unmanly weakness, the hunter would find his sport 'a healthy natural antidote to the enervating refinements of modern life'. Captain J. T. Newall in his *Hog-Hunting in the East* (1867) revealed, in unguarded and pre-Freudian innocence: 'that was the first pig I ever dipped steel into, and I felt elated at flashing my maiden spear, though I had yet to learn the triumphant delight and rapture of taking a first one' (i.e. literally being the first hunter to draw blood).

Certainly, the language of love and that of hunting had for centuries been partly interchangeable, and lovers frequently might use hunting metaphors: 'Some Cupid kills with arrows, some with traps.'[14] It is also true that hunting and shooting boomed during a period of sexual repression in European society, and it is highly likely that these sports served, in many cases, as releases of libidinous tension. Yet sexual motivation, sadistic or more simple, is surely only one of several which account for the fascination of bloodsports.

At the turn of the century, the fierce discipline in British private schools was followed by a highly structured way of life for those born into the upper classes; not only was the sexual drive likely to be frustrated, so also was general self-assertion. Young Victorians and Edwardians, entering upon their careers, would have felt inhibited in many ways, and the one certain result of this frustration was anger – an anger which could not always be vented with gentlemanly propriety against one's own species. There is little doubt that this thwarted and displaced anger was sometimes discharged down the barrel of the big-game rifle or shotgun. Sir Robert Baden-Powell, the founder of the Boy Scouts, unashamedly illustrated this aggressive component in his *Pig-Sticking or Hog-Hunting* (1889), when he eulogized the sport as 'manly and tip-top', and offering 'a task of the brutal and most primitive of all hunts – namely the pursuit, with a good weapon in your hand, of an enemy whom you want to kill. . .you rush for blood with all the ecstasy of a fight to the death.' The death was, of course, only rarely the hunter's. Less passionately, bloodsports were also (and still are) motiv-ated by the Victorian cult of machismo, by which I mean the high cultural evaluation of the so-called 'manly virtues'. Professor A. E. Freeman, writing in 1869, criticized this in the following terms:

the risk of these sports, and the supposed manliness of facing that risk, is generally put forth as one of their merits. Now I may be very blind and very mean-spirited, but the manly sport of foxhunting seems to me not to be manly at all, but to be at once cowardly and fool-hardy. It is cowardly as regards the cruelty practised on a victim which cannot defend himself by tormentors who, as far as the victim is concerned, are perfectly safe. It is fool-hardy as risking men's lives for no adequate cause. It is manly, it is something much better than manly, when a man sacrifices or risks his life in a good cause. But I can see nothing manly, nothing in any way praise-worthy, in a man risking his life in a bad cause or in no cause at all.[15]

Trophy-hunting also became an important component of blood-sports, and taxidermists were called upon to stuff especially large fish, notably 'gallant' foxes, or the heads of deer and moose. Tiger skins bedecked many a Victorian drawing room, and elephant's feet acted as umbrella-stands in the hall. A Victorian gentleman decorated his house with bits of slaughtered animals in much the same way that a latter-day athlete crowds his or her mantlepiece with cups and medals. Even favourite pets and horses were transformed post mortem into ashtrays, waste-paper bins, piano-covers or hat-racks, perhaps as part of the Victorian fascination with death. In many ways the camera was eventually to replace the gun in 'capturing' moments of the past and as a way to record achievements and adventures.

Henry Salt's Humanitarian League, founded in 1891, made the Royal Buck Hounds one of its early targets. This was an organization which hunted half-tame 'carted' deer and was ridiculed not only because its ribbon-bedecked quarry would sometimes wander into barns and railway stations, but also because of its following of obvious social climbers; hunting then, as now, attracted more than its fair share of those who imagined that such antics lent credibility to their social pretensions. According to Lord Randolph Churchill, the Royal Buck Hounds consisted of 'the counter-jumpers of London'.

In reply to a letter from the Reverend J. Stratton in 1891, Buckingham Palace replied that 'the Queen has been strongly opposed to stag-hunting for many years past.' It was not, however, until after her death that the Royal Buck Hounds were actually disbanded by King Edward VII.[16] Even then, the hunting of carted deer continued in other parts of the country.

The Humanitarian League also turned its attention to the hunting of hares with beagles, in particular to the beagles of Henry Salt's old school, Eton. The campaign was scarcely assisted by the RSPCA, whose ranks had been joined by the Headmaster and Provost of the school, both keen supporters of the sport. The Suffragettes, however, rushed to the hares' defence, protesting vehemently on hearing that quarries were sometimes pregnant. Twenty-four women, including Christabel Pankhurst, wrote to the headmaster in 1906:

It seems that the hunting of a creature so timorous and defenceless as the hare is at best but little calculated to foster those qualities of manliness and courage which it is so desirable to develop in the youth of our nation; but to hunt the female hare at a time when she is handicapped by the burden which Nature imposes on her would seem to be not merely contrary to the spirit of true sportsmanship but positively demoralising and degrading to all who consciously participate in it.

The RSPCA's record was one of inaction. In 1891 the Reverend J. Stratton complained that the RSPCA had never made a persistent stand against bloodsports, and in 1908 a motion passed at the society's AGM to campaign for the abolition of otter-hunting produced no further action. By 1926 the society had become so cautious that it actually refused a bequest of £10,000 which had been made conditional on its opposition to vivisection and bloodsports.

In 1924 two RSPCA rebels, Henry Amos and Ernest Bell, founded the League for the Prohibition of Cruel Sports (later to become the League Against Cruel Sports), and by 1927 some 500 members had joined. According to author Richard Thomas these were mostly 'disgruntled RSPCA supporters' dissatisfied by the RSPCA's failure to take a stand against the cruel sports of the upper classes. The League's early opposition was the *Shooting Times*, which extolled bloodsports as a bulwark against decadence. In 1930, after six years of propaganda from the League, worried bloodsportsmen joined together to set up the British Field Sports Society.

During the 1930s several up-and-coming Labour MPs voiced their support for the League's campaigns; Chuter Ede and Tom Williams were among them. When Labour came to power in 1945, however, despite the pleadings of Labour MP Anthony Greenwood, a fear of losing rural votes caused the Labour front bench to change its mind and in 1949 both Williams, then Minister of Agriculture, and Ede, then Home Secretary, voted against a Bill to ban hare-coursing and stag-hunting. This 'defection' by Labour MPs was a repetition of what had occurred in the case of vivisection twenty years before, and was to be repeated in 1986.

After an internal row, all too typical of the animal welfare scene, Bell, together with the League's president, the Hon. Stephen Coleridge, had resigned from the League in 1932 and set up the National Society for the Abolition of Cruel Sports. But neither organization achieved much progress. After the failure of the 1949 Bill and the disappointing recommendations of the Committee of Enquiry chaired by J. Scott-Henderson KC, which reported in favour of permitting coursing and hunting in 1951, both societies went through a lean decade.

The National Society for the Abolition of Cruel Sports enjoyed the support of distinguished people such as Bertrand Russell, J. B. Priestley and H. G. Wells in the 1930s and of Patrick Moore, Lord Soper and Iris Murdoch later. But, despite its respectability, it achieved little after the publication in 1965 of Patrick Moore's widely reviewed *Against Hunting*.[17]

ANIMALS FOR AMUSEMENT

One particular Edwardian anxiety was the condition of animals kept in zoos and circuses. Earlier, Charles Dickens had criticized the public feeding of live creatures to zoo animals – once a favourite spectator sport at the Tower menagerie and a practice which continued surreptitiously in the Regent's Park zoo which opened in 1829. By the end of the century, voices were being raised about the grim conditions of incarceration in traditional zoos and circuses.

Teaching animals to perform tricks had undergone a boom in the nineteenth century, owing largely to the growing public fascination with the 'sagacity' of animals. Unscrupulous showmen cynically cashed in on this friendly curiosity not with kindness but with hidden cruelty. Based on the age-old idea that wild animals, and especially dangerous ones, could only be trained by being 'broken', the circuses became schools of sadism, where animals were bound and beaten not only as punishment but merely to reduce them to psychological pulp. One of the most outstanding exponents of these techniques was the American lion-tamer Isaac van Amburgh, whose tools included the iron crowbar and the red-hot ramrod. Tigers, bears, monkeys, elephants and hyenas all succumbed to van Amburgh's persuasive methods. Any that would not cower with fear were dispatched. In his defence, van Amburgh quoted Genesis – man had been given dominion. 'The subduing of wild beasts, as men have learned from van Amburgh, is merely the result of merciless thrashing when they are young', stated *The Times* of 24 August 1869.

Towards the end of the century, trainers such as Carl Hagenbeck reacted against such cruel techniques and showed that the laborious use of rewards and kindness were, in skilful hands, just as effective. A campaign to give legal protection to performing animals gained some success in 1900 when the Cruelty to Wild Animals in Captivity Act was passed; this measure outlawed in Britain the abusing, infuriating and teasing of captive animals.

Conjurors also came under suspicion in the early part of the century. Rabbits and doves appeared and disappeared mysteriously, leading to understandable fears about their well-being. A Parliamentary Select Committee discovered that special collapsible canary cages were being sold which disappeared up the conjuror's sleeve when he waved his wand, unfortunately crushing the cannary in the process. The Performing Animals Defence League was founded in 1914, and in 1925 the Performing Animals (Regulation) Act was passed, which required the registration of circus trainers and gave access into training areas for local authorities, but failed to prohibit the use of cruel appliances.

The RSPCA, as too often in its history, was hampered by individuals in its upper echelons who had a vested interest, in this case in the person of Lord Lonsdale, the president of Mills Circus, and the society was widely accused of dithering ineffectually on the side-lines on this issue.

A new form of entertainment using animals arrived after the First World War, namely the cinema. Early silent films showed confined crocodiles being slaughtered by gunfire, horses plunging over precipices or being felled by tripwires at full gallop, and lions and tigers in mortal combat. It is certainly easier to stop new abuses than to end established ones, and the RSPCA in this case did well to approach the newly appointed film censor in 1913.[18] After a long campaign Sir Robert Gower MP, the RSPCA chairman, enhanced the society's record by shepherding through Parliament in 1937 the Cinematograph Films (Animals) Act, prohibiting the production or exhibition of films involving cruelty to animals.

HUMANE SLAUGHTER

Seeking improvements in slaughter-house conditions was another great objective for humane campaigners. As we have seen, as early as 1835 Joseph Pease MP, a member of the RSPCA committee, had introduced the first humane controls over slaughter houses. These had had to be licensed since 1785, but after 1835 the licence could be revoked on evidence of cruelty and all horses and cattle had to be slaughtered within three days of arrival, being fed and watered in the interim period.

In 1901 a competition offering prizes for the invention of humane killers was announced in Germany, and a prize was awarded in 1903 to Hugo Heiss, who predicted the development of the 'captive bolt pistol'. The following year an Admiralty committee under the chairman-ship of Arthur Lee MP recommended that all animals for slaughter should be stunned before blood was drawn. In 1906 Major Derriman, the new RSPCA secretary, designed a successful long-handled humane killer which fired a large-calibre soft-nosed bullet, and in 1911 this was followed by the introduction of German-made captive-bolt pistols which fired a steel bolt. A year later Christopher Cash and J. G. Accles improved the captive-bolt design and the RSPCA stepped up its long campaign to persuade reluctant slaughtermen to adopt these new techni-ques. The society was assisted by two eminent authors, John Galsworthy and Thomas Hardy, who wrote in support of the cause. Finally, in 1933, owing largely to the efforts of Sir Thomas Moore MP, the Slaughter of Animals Act was passed, requiring the pre-stunning of cattle. This protection would be completed when the Earl of Selkirk finally 'per-suaded the House of Lords to include pigs in the pre-stunning require-ment of the Slaughter of Animals (Scotland) Act in 1949 and when, in 1954, the Slaughter Houses Act would extend protection to include animals slaughtered elsewhere than in a licensed slaughter house. With the major exception of ritual slaughter, which is still exempted from these humane requirements, animals slaughtered in Britain after this date have all, in theory, been rendered unconscious before being bled, although the findings of the government's Farm Animal Welfare Council in the 1980s would cast serious doubt on the efficacy of some of the techniques in use.

Why was there so much resistance to such an obvious reform? Why did it take half a century before slaughtermen on both sides of the Atlantic would accept the ways of mercy with good grace? The economic arguments surely were little more than pretexts. Was it not also that men inured to bloodshed can become curiously addicted to it – 'bloodied' and therefore an elite? Was inhumane slaughter not another instance of cruelty being confused with manliness?

VIVISECTION AGAIN

Lind-af-Hageby

In 1897 Frances Power Cobbe had approved the appointment of Stephen Coleridge as secretary of her National Anti-Vivisection Society. A driving character and the son of a Lord Chief Justice, Coleridge began to take a more moderate line than Cobbe's, calling for legislation that did not seek immediate prohibition. At a council meeting on 9 February

1898, Cobbe and her friends were defeated, and sadly left the society which they had founded. Later the same year Cobbe started a new body, the British Union for the Abolition of Vivisection. After she died in 1904 the union was to become dominated by a highly qualified medical man, Dr Walter Hadwen, who maintained its pure abolitionist stance.

Cobbe had never married and had shared forty years of her life with her close friend, the Welsh sculptress Mary Charlotte Lloyd. Shortly before Cobb died, she was visited by two young ladies from Sweden. Louise Lind-af-Hageby and Leisa Schartau had met at a ball in Stockholm where they had begun their life-long friendship; in so many ways, among them the intensity of their relationship with someone of the same sex, these two women were to carry on the lives of Cobbe and Lloyd.

In the year 1900 Schartau and Lind-af-Hageby had innocently visited the Pasteur Institute in Paris and been appalled by the ways in which animals were being used there. Back in Sweden, they had contacted the Swedish Anti-Vivisection League which had been founded by Adolf Nordvall and Princess Eugenie in 1882. They then resolved to register as medical students in England in order to prepare themselves for work as anti-vivisectionists, and for two years they attended lectures and demonstrations at King's and University Colleges in London. In 1903 they published a book, *The Shambles of Science*, giving details of what they had seen. It was a bombshell, receiving widespread attention and acclaim, including more than two hundred reviews in four months, and running to five editions before the First World War.

In the first edition of the book, Schartau and Lind-af-Hageby described the case of a brown dog who had been used for four separate procedures at University College, London, over several months in the years 1902 to 1903. An early reader of this description was Stephen Coleridge, who referred to the dog at a meeting in St James Hall in May 1903; in consequence, a libel action was brought against him by Dr W. M. Bayliss, one of the experimenters mentioned. Although it was admitted in court that regulations had been broken, the jury found Coleridge guilty of defamation and Bayliss was awarded £2,000 damages. Nevertheless, Coleridge's ordeal served to turn the spotlight once again upon vivisection, and press and public opinion veered to his support and that of the Swedish women.

Eighteen months later, in 1906, Lind-af-Hageby founded her own organization, the Animal Defence and Anti-Vivisection Society, and in the same year, the International Anti-Vivisection Council, with the consent of Battersea Council, erected a bronze statue of a dog in Battersea Park, with the following inscription:

In memory of the brown Terrier Dog done to death in the laboratories of University College in February 1903 after having endured vivisection extending over more than two months and having been handed over from one vivisector to another till death came to his release. Also in memory of the 232 dogs vivisected in the same place during the year 1902. Men and women of England: How long shall these things be?[19]

A year after it had been unveiled by the Mayor of Battersea, the bronze statue of the brown dog was damaged by medical students of University College. Summonses, angry meetings and further disturbances ensued. Pressure was brought on the Battersea Borough Council to have the statue removed or the inscription deleted; stalwartly they refused to do either.

Demonstrations were large and violent. On 10 December 1907 about a hundred medical students attempted to remove the memorial, and from five o'clock in the afternoon until midnight they were opposed by growing numbers of local citizens who successfully defended their statue. Finally, a large body of mounted police managed to disperse the mob, arresting ten demonstrators who were fined £5 each on the following day. Two days later a mob of about a thousand students and their supporters surged along the Strand shouting slogans in support of Professor Starling, the brown dog's chief tormentor. Medical students were joined by veterinary students in pro-vivisection demonstrations over the ensuing weeks, and some violently invaded a women's suffrage meeting in Paddington held by Millicent Fawcett, the leading Suffragette, as well as a meeting held by Miss Lind-af-Hageby in Acton. Although the London students failed to enlist much support from colleagues at Oxford and Cambridge, they continued to cause trouble for the hundreds of police detailed to guard the statue. Parliament, the Battersea Borough Council, and public opinion generally, sided with the brown dog.

Suddenly, in the spring of 1910, the statue disappeared, never to be seen again. A protest meeting in Trafalgar Square was attended by several thousand people including representatives of five trade unions, and was addressed by Lind-af-Hageby.[20] To some extent it had been a battle between the sexes and, more particularly, between machismo and feminism. Although the brown dog had gone, in the seven years since its death it had become a martyr and had gained more publicity for the humane anti-vivisection point of view than had ever been previously received. The speeches and meetings and the riots stimulated considerable discussion in the press, and the widespread popular reaction demonstrated once again that whenever the issue is clearly presented to the public, majority British opinion is overwhelmingly opposed to the infliction of unnecessary suffering in the name of science.

While all this was happening, and perhaps influenced by the widespread sympathy shown for the little brown dog, the second Royal Commission on Vivisection (1906–12) was sitting to consider the practice, and the administration of the law relating to it. The commission's main recommendations led to the attachment to licences of a 'pain condition' as well as the establishment of the Home Office's advisory committee on the administration of the 1876 Act.

The royal commission had heard some startling evidence from the Hon. Stephen Coleridge, who charged Home Office officials with 'having placed themselves in improper confidential relations with a private society composed of supporters of vivisection'. The society to which he alluded was the Association for the Advancement of Medicine by Research, founded in 1882 to protect the interests of vivisectors (see p. 120). Under cross-examination by the commission, the Home Office Chief Inspector, Mr Byrne, admitted that his department had been in continuous consultation with this organization, from which it had regularly accepted advice 'in regard to applicants for licences and certificates'. Stephen Coleridge had done some good detective work.

In 1909 two large international congresses were held in England; the first under the auspices of Lind-af-Hageby's society and the second organized by the World League Against Vivisection. The former advocated the gradualist approach supported by, among others, Sir George Kekewich, Stephen Coleridge, the theosophist and social reformer Annie Besant, the leading suffragette Charlotte Despard, the two women from Sweden and Henry Salt. The latter congress, notably under the influence of Dr Hadwen of the British Union for the Abolition of Vivisection, proposed nothing short of total and immediate abolition. This rift in the anti-vivisection movement sapped much of its energies until the outbreak of the Second World War, and may have been responsible for alienating some people from the cause.

Lind-af-Hageby's Animal Defence and Anti-Vivisection Society had maintained the aristocratic image; no fewer than 48 titled persons were vice-presidents of her society, in addition to half a dozen foreign princesses. The church appeared to be less involved, although over 50 MPs, including George Greenwood, were enlisted, and 175 members of the French Chamber of Deputies had pledged their support. The society was founded 'on the principle that the cause of humanity to animals is not a side-issue but a vital part of civilisation and social development', and was given considerable financial and moral support by Nina, Duchess of Hamilton. The Duke, for many years an invalid, was the premier peer of Scotland and both he and the Hamiltons' close friend, Admiral Lord Fisher, gave rather cautious public backing to the Duchess in her humanitarian efforts.

During the First World War the Animal Defence and Anti-Vivisection Society (later abbreviating its title to the Animal Defence Society) set up three veterinary hospitals for wounded and sick horses, and campaigned against chicken batteries, fur-trapping, cruelty to performing animals, bloodsports, the transportation of live animals and the use of pit-ponies in the coal mines. In 1909, and again in 1927, the society organized large and successful congresses in London, and for the 1927 one erected a £40,000 model abattoir at Letchworth to demonstrate humane slaughter

techniques based in part on those they had observed in operation in
Berne in 1922. In 1926 the three ladies tried to introduce humane killers
into abattoirs in France. In 1928 the society held an exhibition in
Geneva, which was attended by George Bernard Shaw. Later, the Duchess,
together with Lind-af-Hageby and Schartau, established the Ferne Animal
Sanctuary in Somerset at a country house belonging to the Hamilton
family. All these activities were in addition to their main drive against
vivisection. Throughout its history the majority of the society's active
members were female, and by the early 1920s only one male, the
vegetarian Howard Williams, remained on its executive council. Far
from being embarrassed by this imbalance of the sexes, the society's
journal on occasion emphasized it.[21]

Eminent Supporters

As we have seen, the cause of anti-vivisection has always been well
supported by some of the most eminent men and women. In later
nineteenth-century Britain, Tennyson and Carlyle (who were both vice-
presidents of the National Anti-Vivisection Society), Browning, Bright,
Ruskin, Cardinals Manning and Newman, as well as Shaftesbury, were
all involved. In the early years of the twentieth century, writers as
different from one another as John Galsworthy, Ouida, Thomas Hardy,
Sarah Grand, Marie Corelli and Colette expressed their conviction that
kindness to others should mean kindness to all sentient creatures, not
only to our fellow men and women. Artists and actors such as Sir
Edward Burne-Jones and Sir Henry Irving concurred, and Walter Crane
designed and presented to Hageby's society a dramatic frontispiece for
its journal depicting a knight in armour, shield emblazoned with the
words 'The Rights of Animals', defending some frightened dogs from
the grasping hand of a cloven-hooved vivisector, which was used from
1912 onwards.

A few medical people, such as Walter Hadwen, dared to follow Dr
George Hoggan in voicing open criticisms of the system; yet to do so at
that time was to court censure from the profession. Even Sir William
Fergusson, FRS, Sergeant-Surgeon to Queen Victoria and president of
the British Medical Association, had been posthumously denigrated for
questioning the validity of much of the animal research that was being
performed a generation earlier.[22] One surgeon who had continued to
support Fergusson's point of view was Robert Lawson Tait (1845–99),
a well-known specialist of his day, a pioneer of aseptic methods and
several new and successful techniques in abdominal surgery.[23] His
independence of mind enabled him to question contemporary orthodoxies and he was closely associated with the movement to allow women
admission to the medical profession on equal terms with men. He
outspokenly opposed vivisection on four grounds – moral, political,
religious and scientific.[24] He respected the moral view 'that we have no

right to inflict sufferings on others that we ourselves may benefit'. After the turn of the century one voice in particular joined in eloquently on the side of the laboratory animals. Shaw, in his *May Lectures,* in the preface to his play *The Doctor's Dilemma,* and in his *The Adventures of the Black Girl in Her Search for God* puts the humanitarian argument very strongly. His earliest brush with the vivisectionists appears to have been when, with jocular gallantry, he attacked Professor Sir Victor Horsley for calling Frances Cobbe a liar: 'I at once took the field against Horsley. "The question at issue", I said, "is not whether Miss Cobbe is a liar, but whether you as a vivisector are a scoundrel." Horsley's breath was taken away. He refused to debate what seemed to him a monstrous insult.'[25]

In 1927 Shaw's old friend H. G. Wells wrote a defence of vivisection in the *Sunday Express.* Wells, to his eternal discredit, put forward the old cliché that because vivisection was not, in his opinion, the greatest cruelty inflicted by mankind, it was thus justified − the 'two-wrongs-can-make-a-right' argument. Shaw replied in the *Sunday Express* of 27 August 1927:

But Mr Wells has another shot in his locker...'There is a residuum of admittedly painful cases, but it is an amount of suffering infinitesimal in comparison with the gross aggregate of pain inflicted day by day upon sentient creatures by mankind.'

This defence fits every possible crime from pitch-and-toss to manslaughter. Its disadvantage is that it is not plausible enough to impose on the simplest village constable. Even Landru, and the husband of the brides in the bath, though in desperate peril of the guillotine and gallows, had not the effrontery to say: 'It is true that we made our livelihood by marrying women and burning them in the stove or drowning them in the bath when we had spent their money; and we admit frankly and handsomely that the process may have involved some pain and disillusionment for them; but their sufferings (if any) were infinitesimal in comparison with the gross aggregate of pain inflicted day by day upon sentient creatures by mankind.' Landru and Smith knew what Wells forgot: that scoundrels who have no better defence than that have no defence at all...

Between the wars, other men of letters were to join Shaw in attacking the practice of experimenting on animals. Prominent among these was John Cowper Powys, who made the subject central to his novel *Morwyn or The Vengeance of God.*

The Changing Social Climate: Feminism, Socialism and Sentiment

Stephen Coleridge's doughtiest adversary was Stephen Paget, the secretary of the Association for the Advancement of Medicine by Research.

13 George Bernard Shaw (1856–1950) wrote passionately in defence of nonhumans, attacking hunting, vivisection and meat-eating – preaching sermons, he said, based upon the humane life-style of his friend Henry Salt. Seldom have great writers remained unmoved by cruelty and many have been active animal welfare campaigners, a fact sometimes played down by their biographers.

(BBC Hulton Picture Library)

Since the publication of Paget's *Experiments on Animals* in 1900, the vivisectors had appeared increasingly the more rational in comparison with their opponents. Gradually the image of science had improved, as knowledge derived from animal experimentation was accumulated and applied.

Since the 1880s scientists had tried to smear the anti-vivisection movement, and eventually the mud began to stick.[26] Paget denounced the anti-vivisectionists as quarrelsome and ineffective, while portraying the scientists as serious and high-minded.

The Victoria Street Society had long dominated the anti-vivisection movement; while Frances Cobbe was in command she had taken pains to keep out extremists like the visionary Anna Kingsford (see p. 168–9) and had been overtly hostile towards vegetarianism. Just as Martin's and Erskine's robust personalities had given the campaign credibility many years earlier, so had Cobbe's at the end of the century. Futhermore, Cobbe's formidable character had also prevented the infiltration of the Victoria Street Society by vivisectors – a fate which had befallen French and German animal protection societies in the 1880s. Whereas in Germany scientists were venerated in the late nineteenth century, in Britain the aristocracy were still the leaders of society and it was they who had decorated the letterheads of Victorian and Edwardian anti-vivisectionism.

The emergence of socialism in Britain after the 1914–18 war was to be a further disappointment to anti-vivisection and to animal protection generally. Although Salt, Shaw and Carpenter saw animal protection and socialism as part of the same humanitarian movement, the leaders of the new Labour party, once in power, were not interested. Carpenter in 1895 could portray animal experimentation 'as the irrelevant and cruel means by which capitalists sought to cure diseases resulting from their own firms' pollution and disruption of the human environment'.[27] In 1909 Sir George Kekewich could enthuse: 'A new party, the Labour Party, has arisen in Parliament; and every member of that party is on our side.' Indeed, four future Labour cabinet ministers – Ramsay Macdonald, Philip Snowden, Arthur Henderson and J. R. Clynes had attended the World League Against Vivisection Congress in the same year. But when these men came to office twenty years later in the first Labour government, they did nothing to honour their pledge to help nonhuman animals. The British working class had not yet taken animal protection to its bosom, and far from seeing nonhumans as an exploited proletariat they tended to view them as a preoccupation of the sentimental rich. This situation was only to change in Britain in the 1970s.

Another feature of the late Victorian and Edwardian scene was that animal protection had become associated in the public mind with the campaigns of women rather than men; after the departures of men like Shaftesbury and Colam the public stage had been left chiefly to the female sex. Five of the major 'stars' of the movement were Cobbe,

Kingsford, Lind-af-Hageby, Schartau and the Duchess of Hamilton; only one of the principal parts was played by a male – Stephen Coleridge. For Cobbe and Kingsford the anti-vivisection campaign was consciously recognized as having the subsidiary aim of improving the social and political position of women, but by cleverly associating her feminism with an aura of respectability and moral conservatism, Cobbe had made it harder for her opponents to discredit her. After she was gone it was easier to play upon male prejudice and to portray the concern for animal welfare as being womanly. The French physiologist Elie de Cyon had gone further in insinuating that involvement in animal welfare was an outlet for frustrated 'old maids'; in Catholic countries such spinsters took to convents, he said, but in Protestant societies they directed their 'disordered minds' towards anti-vivisection. In the first few decades of the century, the divisions within the now predominantly female movement had given it a reputation for 'hysteria', and the cause lacked intellectual and practical leaders to refute the contemporary charge of 'sentimentality'.

While anti-vivisection was the most public and publicized element of the animal protection cause, other elements had made quieter but more solid progress. Trist's book on cruelties to animals of 1913, one of the first to be assisted by the use of horrific photographs, could recount undeniable achievements in the campaigns against the feather trade, the export of worn-out horses, the use of the bearing-rein and the treatment of pit-ponies.

STAGNATION: THE MID-TWENTIETH CENTURY

After the carnage of the First World War the movement seemed to stagnate. In the stunned silence following the last barrage of the war, survivors turned their attention to the welfare of their own species. The animal welfare organizations, dominated by middle-class women, continued their good work, but without the mass support which they had enjoyed before the war. To some of those who had endured the Somme they began to appear faintly ridiculous. The few effective campaigners who remained took great pains to appear moderate and sensible, striving to restrict rather than to prohibit the cruelties they opposed. The Second World War was a further setback and it seems that the period from the mid-1920s until the 1960s represents a gap in the progress of the movement.

In 1926 Major C. W. Hume MC founded the University of London Animal Welfare Society, which later became, more simply, the Universities Federation for Animal Welfare. It was a product typical of the post-war era in its almost fanatical determination not to be fanatical. Hume wrote: 'UFAW helps to compensate the harm done to the cause of animal welfare by animal-lovers of the unbalanced kind, and to form an intelligently humane body of public opinion.'[28] So anxious was he to appear reasonable that on occasions the federation seemed more cerebral than practical. Membership of the Universities Federation for Animal Welfare was limited to those with a university training, and any discussion of animal experimentation was prohibited at its meetings. It was decreed that its approach had to be 'with a maximum of sympathy but a minimum of sentimentality': instead of seeking to ban whaling it initiated scientific experiments with the aim of making whaling more humane; instead of trying to outlaw the fur trade it issued a 'white list' of furs obtained by allegedly ethical means; it researched into less painful methods of killing unwanted domestic pets; and instead of urging a ban on experiments it published a detailed handbook on the care of laboratory animals.

The federation's greatest achievement, however, was its thirty-year campaign to prohibit the use of the leghold gin trap in Britain. In 1935 Viscount Tredegar introduced a Bill to ban steel-toothed leghold traps of this type, reminding the House of Lords that such devices for catching human beings had been banned in 1827. The federation estimated that 1,800,000 birds, 124,000 cats and 35,000,000 rabbits were being caught annually in gin traps, as well as other animals including farm livestock. The Bill was, however, successfully opposed by the British Field Sports Society, and another world war intervened before the Parliamentary Scott-Henderson Committee of 1949, describing it as 'a diabolical instrument which causes an incalculable amount of suffering', encouraged the gin trap's eventual demise under a 1958 amendment to the Pests Act of 1954.

Although much credit must go to Hume for this achievement, and to his colleagues such as Dr Jean Vinter, their argument that the best way to abolish gins was through the promotion of poison gas and other methods as alternative ways of killing rabbits, was unheeded at the time and strikes the modern campaigner as repugnant. At the same time as the federation's members were advocating such tactics, other university scientists in Britain were perfecting the rabbit plague, myxomatosis, which was deliberately introduced in Australia and Europe in the early 1950s, causing horrifying deaths for countless millions of animals. Sightless, swollen and almost hairless, rabbits battered themselves against walls, and corpses littered the roads and fields all over England. With the approval of Winston Churchill, the government agreed to Dr Horace King's demand that the deliberate spreading of this disease be outlawed and the Pests Act was duly amended.

Bodies similar to the Universities Federation for Animal Welfare were established in Germany by Dr Wiema von During and in America by Dr Robert Gesell. Throughout the Western world, however, the forty years after 1918 were a barren period in the evolution of the animal rights ethic; basic speciesism was accepted as common-sense necessity and dissent was dismissed as eccentricity. In Britain, the RSPCA ticked over inoffensively, rescuing, homing and killing thousands of unwanted animals each year, raising money to pay the salaries of two hundred or so uniformed inspectors, cautiously prosecuting only the most flagrant cases of cruelty, and avoiding controversy. Gradually the society had lost its sense of urgency and settled for the status quo. After John Colam retired in 1905, he was followed by stalwarts such as Captain Edward Fairholme and Arthur Moss; loyal dependable men but lacking the drive and initiative of the true reformer. Although as late as 1924 Edward Fairholme and Wellesley Pain's historical account of the society was graced with a foreword from Edward, Prince of Wales, the link with royalty had faded away gradually after Queen Victoria's death in 1901. At the same time the large numbers of aristocrats on the RSPCA council, conservative but often sophisticated in outlook, had slowly given way to the even more conservative middle classes whose less secure social positions sometimes made them even less prepared than the upper classes to criticize the cruel habits of professionals or gentry. With a few exceptions, such as its pre-war chairman Lord Lambourne (Colonel Mark Lockwood), who died in 1928, and Sir Robert Gower MP, the RSPCA came to lack figures of stature. Gower's successful introduction of a Bill banning rodeos in 1934 and the Cinematograph Films (Animals) Act of 1937, prohibiting cruelty to animals in filming, were among the society's few innovative achievements of the period. The RSPCA maintained its position as a household word, but it was no longer peopled by those in positions of great influence; what potential for reform it retained remained under-utilized and, for some, its un-doubted respectability had become an end in itself.

Not only the RSPCA but the whole animal welfare campaign had become bureaucratized; this gave it some durability but restricted its movement forward. What few sparks of inspiration there were came from independent individuals rather than from the organizations: Dr Harry Lillie of Dundee, for example, studiously avoided committees of any sort and, working on his own, used modern technology in the form of a motion picture camera to bring to restricted audiences in the 1950s and 1960s horrific evidence of the cruelties inherent in whaling, trapping, the killing of seals in Canada and the use of animals in research. Lillie's pioneering work sowed the seeds for the rejuvenated campaigns of the 1970s. Through his agency hundreds, rather than a handful, saw the protracted sufferings of whales impaled by explosive harpoons, the clubbing of baby Harp seals and the agonized day-long deaths of animals trapped in the fur trade.

Air Chief Marshall Lord Dowding, too, continued doggedly through-out the apathetic 1950s and early 1960s to plead the animals' cause in speech after speech on twenty-seven separate occasions in the House of Lords. As the man whose policies had saved the country in the Battle of

Britain in 1940 he was given a hearing but little more. His interest in spiritualism unfairly helped his opponents to stereotype him as an eccentric. As we shall see in later chapters, his wife, Muriel, made significant progress in these unsympathetic years by setting up the Beauty Without Cruelty organization and in her direction of the National Anti-Vivisection Society.

What a strange era it was; moving from the sense of progress and confidence of the late Victorian and Edwardian periods through the First World War to stagnation beyond the Second. As far as humankind's attitude towards nonhumans was concerned it saw a transition in Northern Europe from strong sentiment and idealism to excessive caution, practicality and a decline in serious interest.

9 Why Britain? Pain, Evolution and Security

Why did the Victorians lead the way in restraining humankind's exploitation of the other species? Why did the pressure for reform happen when it did?

This chapter considers various possible answers to these questions, looking at the changing attitudes towards pain, the increasing sense of kinship culminating in the theory of evolution, and in social changes which may have given humans the confidence to be magnanimous towards nonhumans. We shall also consider the development of scientific psychology at the end of the century.

THE INDUSTRIAL REVOLUTION

One idea put forward, for example by James Turner, is that Britain's 'urbanisation and industrialisation in some way helped to generate the new concern for beasts'.[1] Up to a point this may be true, for both processes (in which Britain led the rest of the world) certainly removed humans, to an extent, from direct and visible economic dependence upon nonhumans and allowed people to mature in the absence of the sort of desensitizing subculture typical of a rural community which is committed to speciesist exploitation; subcultures which surely train most children to suppress their natural sympathies for nonhumans. Yet it must be remembered that some of the worst cruelties towards nonhumans in Victorian Britain were inflicted by urban-dwellers in the pursuit of objects that were neither agricultural nor sporting: vivisection, the fashion industry and the daily abuse of horses are three major examples. Furthermore, although the animal welfare movement in America was largely an urban phenomenon, in Britain this was not so true; many of the movement's leaders, for instance, were country clergymen or landowners (admittedly often with business in London) such as Martin, Shaftesbury and Lawrence; indeed the industrial middle class played little part in the British animal welfare crusade.

Turner, even more contentiously, argues that it was the incompatibility of bloodsports with the new system of regular and longer working days in the factory that determined the change in attitudes. Certainly there were some mill-owners and other employers who disapproved of sports such as bull-baiting because they could 'affect the regular progress of working and carrying on the Mines and Manufactures of the county',[2] but the importance of this factor was not paramount, nor was the loss of some large open spaces suitable for bull-baiting of any real significance, as Turner alleges was the case,[3] for many other spaces remained available.

QUEEN VICTORIA

It has often been said that the Englishman's dream is to be a country gentleman, and it is certainly true that by the early twentieth century, caricatures of the English would include three features explicable in terms of such an aspiration − a love of gardening, an obsession with the weather and an enthusiasm for keeping animals. Paradoxically, whereas some cruelties (such as bloodsports) were encouraged by this dream, others (such as vivisection) almost certainly were not, and it is still common to find fox-hunters and factory-farmers who are passionately opposed to animal experiments. But above all it was the role played by the RSPCA, and the Queen's patronage from the 1830s onwards, which influenced the attitudes of the established and aspiring upper classes in Britain. Increased wealth meant that more were looking to their social superiors for models of behaviour, and among these they found the new sense of duty towards animals. Unlike France, where revolutionary changes had undermined the influence of royalty, nobility and Church, Britain was still an upward-looking society in which academics were not the unchallenged leaders of opinion.[4]

Indeed, it can be said that animal welfare had become a British upper-class preoccupation by mid-century. As well as commanding some respect from all sections of society, this gave animal welfarists access to the political establishment. Were the upper classes merely emulating the Queen? Probably to a large extent they were. It was known that she had written to scientists and statesmen condemning vivisection (see p. 111), and in her Jubilee address of 1887, in commenting on the spread of enlightenment among her subjects, she noted in particular 'with real pleasure, the growth of more humane feelings towards the lower animals'.[5] This was not mere lip-service − it was real commitment on her part.

But was not the growing interest in animal protection also an effect of the increasing stability of society and the extension of affluence? Never before had so many felt economically and socially secure. They could afford to show some compassion for the underprivileged, both human and nonhuman. Moreover, there was no longer the feeling that they ought to prove their superiority over the brute creation, for the latter

14 Queen Victoria played a highly significant role in promoting the social respectability of animal welfare in the nineteenth century and in making Britain the leading country of reform in this field. Her opposition to cruelty was sincere and passionate. She is pictured here with her dog Sharp at Balmoral in 1867.

(BBC Hulton Picture Library)

was no longer intuitively considered, as it sometimes had been in medieval times, a part of the same social hierarchy. Furthermore, for a hundred years after Waterloo, Britain was not threatened by war. In the previous century the country had, on several occasions, felt threatened by France. In the seventeenth century it had been riven by civil war and in the sixteenth the threat of invasion had come from Spain. For nearly a century after 1815 however, the civilian British felt fairly safe from armed attack. The Queen herself, on the throne from 1837 till 1901, became a symbol of that security. Perhaps this unprecedented affluence and security gave many the chance to reflect upon the condition of the less fortunate. And at the same time attitudes towards pain were changing.

PAIN AND STOICISM

In 1799 Humphrey Davy had described the anaesthetic properties of nitrous oxide; in 1842 Crawford Long used ether to produce surgical anaesthesia; and William Morton publicly demonstrated its use in 1846. In 1832 chloroform was produced, and in 1847 it was first used as an anaesthetic by Sir James Simpson in Edinburgh. In 1899 aspirin was discovered.

In some quarters there was resistance to the use of such anaesthetics and pain-killers on religious grounds. This resistance was strongest against their use in childbirth: 'In sorrow thou shalt bring forth children' (Genesis 3:16) was the much-quoted text. But the opposition declined after chloroform was administered by John Snow to Queen Victoria during labour in 1853. After mid-century, civilized men and women knew that pain, at least theoretically, could be controlled.

Among Victorians, the fear of pain became somewhat more open. Earlier generations, without effective anaesthetics and pain-killers, had been more stoical; pain which could scarcely be avoided had to be endured and the less said the better. Nevertheless it was the pronounced horror of pain in others, including nonhuman sentients, that was the common factor shared by most outstanding reformers; this explains why they came from non-religious backgrounds as well as from every religious sect and from all shades of political opinion. Opposition to pain, and not religious scruple or political doctrine, was their principal motive.

Perhaps it was those who were particularly prone to pain who led the campaigns against it. Wilberforce was not the only humanitarian of the nineteenth century who continuously took opium to dull the aches and pains of living; indeed he advised his friend the first Earl of Harrowby to do likewise for his headaches.[6] Shaftesbury, too, to use his own word, felt 'tortured' by the thought of suffering.[7]

The Victorians were, of course, more accepting of death. The conventional attitude towards nonhumans therefore became one of tolerance of killing, provided trouble was taken to make it 'a clean kill'. In the later twentieth century, as will be discussed in later chapters, at a time when death had become almost a taboo, the animal rights movement would argue as strongly against killing as against inflicting pain.

Paradoxically, in England and Germany in the nineteenth century there was also a strong stoical streak, perhaps typical of imperialistic cultures, which glorified the endurance of pain. In British public schools boys of twelve and over were deliberately subjected to harsh regimes of exhausting physical exercise, rough sports and corporal punishment. They were taught to disregard injury and to make light of pain. To make a fuss was to court the contempt of other boys and teachers alike.

Is it a coincidence that Britain and Germany, two of the most stoical cultures of the period, should also have been the most advanced in social reform and humane attitudes to animals? Those who suffer are often hardened into apparent callousness, but there are others who emerge from suffering as pain's deadliest foes.

Science, however, as it developed, became linked with stoicism and the idea that the head ought to rule the heart. For many years the British were taught that their feelings had to be kept under control, and in this period displays of affection and even compassion could be taken to be indications of weakness or effeminacy. The British macho image was colder and less swaggering than the Latin original, but just as important for the national character. The unflinching *infliction* of pain upon others, provided it was done in the line of duty, was considered no less admirable than the equally unflinching *suffering* of pain; both qualities were regarded as manly and desirable in an Empire-building master race. So, vivisection, a practice which expanded very rapidly during the final decades of Victoria's reign, became a symbol, not only of material progress but also of masculine hard-headedness. Science proudly proclaimed itself to be the antithesis to sentimentality, effeminate emotion and superstition.

Writers like Primatt towards the end of the eighteenth century had already isolated pain as the great evil and the Utilitarians under Bentham formalized this concern by making pain and pleasure the main criteria of morality; if an event increased the total sum of happiness (animal as well as human, Bentham argued) then it was good; if it reduced happiness (or increased pain) it was bad. The mathematics of Bentham's 'calculus of happiness ' pose many problems, but the elevation of the importance of pleasure and pain as motives and as moral criteria remains valid. This was to some extent a revival of the ideas of Epicurus and other altruistic hedonistic classical thinkers, and such criteria went on to form cornerstones of both Freudian theory and experimental psychology. In the former, the 'pleasure principle' is seen as the basic human motivation, just as in modern scientific psychology the concepts of reward and punishment, applied to human and nonhuman alike, are regarded as the fundamental determinants of learned behaviour.

There is little doubt that the avoidance of pain and the seeking of pleasure (defined widely) are the main objects common to all sentient creatures. Pain and pleasure can be 'mental' as well as physical, and each act may be determined by complex combinations of pains and pleasures. Bentham's extension of this biological fact into an ethical theory brought together nature as it is and as it ought to be, and despite the obvious difficulty (although not impossibility) of quantifying such concepts, the main ethical problem is Bentham's proposal to calculate the goodness or badness of an act by adding the pains and pleasures of *all* the individuals affected by it. That it makes no sense to do such a sum across the boundaries of sentience between individuals did not seem to bother Bentham.

Bentham's significance for our subject, as I have already argued, is twofold: first, he had brought animals into the moral fold, and secondly he had put the spotlight on what really mattered: 'the question is not can they *reason*? Nor, can they *talk*? But can they *suffer*?'

The growing movement for the protection of nonhumans can be seen as part of a general trend in nineteenth-century Britain, against pain and suffering. Prison inspectors were introduced in 1835 and the pillory done away with in 1837. The slave trade had been abolished in 1807 and slavery in the British Empire in 1833. Help for the deaf and blind, and Shaftesbury's great reforms for lunatics, factory children, working women and chimney-boys ensued. In 1832 and 1837 the number of capital offences was drastically reduced; death sentences (mostly commuted) fell from 1,549 in 1831 to 116 in 1838.

As we have seen, in many cases the same people who were involved in helping human beings were also active in the humane movement to protect nonhumans from suffering. William Wilberforce and Lord Shaftesbury were the two most striking examples; but there were also T. F. Buxton (the anti-slaver) and 'Humanity Dick' Martin. There was Angela, Baroness Burdett-Coutts, who established a home for 'fallen women', battled for sanitary reforms, pioneered model housing and numerous other humanitarian ventures and was also an active member of the RSPCA from 1839 almost until her death in 1906. Frances Power Cobbe herself had worked as an early social worker.

The anti-vivisection campaigners, Dr Lawson-Tait and Lord Chief Justice Coleridge (the father of Stephen) were also noted feminists, and Charlotte Despard and Annie Besant, campaigners for the rights of women, were also supporters of the anti-vivisection movement. Lewis Gompertz was also a feminist, as was John Stuart Mill. Later, Maria Dickin, the pioneer social worker, turned her attention to animals and founded the People's Dispensary for Sick Animals of the Poor in 1917.

One psychological factor common to bull-baiting, vivisection and indeed all forms of cruelty to animals is that they teach people to overcome their natural scruples against inflicting pain and drawing blood; a useful qualification in fighting men. Such a process was sometimes acclaimed as an advantage and the idea was used, for example, by Windham when defending the 'old English character' as displayed in 'manly sports' such as baiting. The scientist's oft-voiced castigations of anti-vivisectionists as 'emotional' and 'sentimental' have similar connotations, in that they imply that overcoming a natural reluctance to inflict pain is a sign of rationality and manliness. Lord Coleridge had to protest that anti-vivisectionists were 'surely not weak or effeminate',[8] and a twentieth-century scientist, Professor Miriam Rothschild, has far more recently stated: 'I know several zoologists who have admitted that they suffered from the fear of being dubbed 'unmanly' and struggled to overcome their dislike of causing animals pain, or killing them.'[9]

As long ago as 1675 Benedictus de Spinoza had remarked that a concern over killing animals was based upon 'womanish pity',[10] and this irrational argument has been used for centuries to dismiss the seriousness of the reformers' case. It is similar to the claim that because opposition to cruelty is sometimes 'emotional' it is therefore invalid: as if opposition to Nazi atrocities, for example, should not have been accompanied by anger or pity. Emotion should imply neither ignorance nor wrongness; on the contrary, its absence in the context of cruelty could well be a sign of personality disorder. (This point is discussed further in the final chapter.)

The nineteenth-century conflict between vivisectors and anti-vivisectors took on the aspect of a conflict between an old and a new religion; the latter, powerful but amoral, and making sense of the world in a new way. This conflict slotted conveniently into the battle which already raged between religion and science, and between the theories of creation and evolution.

If the three basic psychological ingredients of a religion are its moral code, the meaning it gives to life and the 'magical' power it bestows, then science qualified brilliantly on the last two. But strangely, and terrifyingly for the Victorian moralists, it offered no moral code; morality was dismissed as just another form of behaviour which had evolved through natural selection. Science's only moral code appeared to consist of a narcissistic and arrogant self-worship; whatever promoted scientific progress was right, whatever opposed it wrong. So science meant power without principle, and for this reason remained suspect in the eyes of many Victorians; in so many ways it was itself the monster irresponsibly created by that symbolic nineteenth-century figure Dr Frankenstein – the blasphemy of man playing God.

Paradoxically, although science stood for a hard-headed attitude towards nonhumans, its discoveries about the reduction of pain had encouraged a less fatalistic attitude towards the sufferings of humans and nonhumans alike. As we have seen, lay people began to feel that something could now be done about it. But to what extent did British science, through its promulgation of the idea of evolution, inadvertently encourage the bridging of the gap between Homo Sapiens and the other animals?

EVOLUTION

The theories and attitudes of Charles Darwin have such an important bearing upon the human−nonhuman relationship that they will be looked at in some detail. In November 1859 Darwin published his great work *On the Origin of Species*; this was followed in 1871 by *The Descent of Man*, which demonstrated the evolutionary kinship of all animals. Yet, strangely, Darwinism had very little immediate effect on the way in which humans treated their newly discovered relatives. Darwin himself remained weak and ambivalent on the question of kindness to nonhuman animals and, in particular, on the morality of vivisection. His natural compassion and concern over pain would often prompt him to make a sympathetic statement, but this would be followed by an apparent contradiction, probably motivated by his reluctance to upset his scientific colleagues, particularly T. H. Huxley.

As we have seen, Darwin had dropped out of medical school because he hated dissection; the operating theatre horrified him. Yet, although his squeamishness and sensitivity about pain may have been intense, he did not, like Wilberforce or Shaftesbury, devote his life to reducing suffering. Instead, or so it seems, he tried to discount such sensitivity. His uncharacteristically shrill attack on the anti-vivisectionist Richard Hutton as 'a kind of female Miss Cobbe' may be a clue that Darwin saw his own concern about pain as effeminate.[11] Yet on occasions it could get the better of him and, according to his son Francis, his anger at cruelty would break through.[12]

Darwin argued that humans and nonhumans were not just physically, but also mentally similar:

We have seen that the senses and intuitions, the various emotions and faculties, such as love, memory, attention and curiosity, imitation, reason etc., of which man boasts, may be found in an incipient, or even sometimes in a well-developed condition, in the lower animals...There is no fundamental difference between man and the higher mammals in their mental faculties...The difference in mind between man and the higher animals, great as it is, certainly is one of degree and not of kind.[13]

There is some evidence that the scientific advocates of vivisection successfully manipulated Darwin to their political advantage. When testifying before the royal commission in 1876 he was confronted with some leading questions suggesting that he had participated in the pro-vivisection initiative of the British Association in 1871, and in the preparation of the Scientists' Bill presented to Parliament by Dr Lyon Playfair. Darwin denied that he had participated in preparing the British Association resolution:

Darwin: No, I had nothing to do with that.

Then he qualified this by saying that nevertheless he approved of the resolution. As to Dr Playfair's Bill, he agreed that he had helped in its preparation, but added mysteriously:

Darwin: But the Bill itself did not exactly express the conclusions at which after consultation with several physiologists we arrived; I apprehend that it was accidentally altered.

Question: But in the main you were an approving party?

Darwin: In the main.

Darwin went on to confirm that he had never been directly or indirectly connected with the performing of experiments upon living animals. However, although not a physiologist, he believed that experiments on animals were necessary for physiology and that physiology in the future would 'confer the highest benefits on mankind'. Nevertheless it was his belief that most experiments could be performed while the animal was insensible to pain, and should be so performed. The minutes of evidence conclude with a final question and answer:

Question: Now with regard to trying a painful experiment without an-aesthetics, when the same experiment could be made with an-aesthetics, or, in short, inflicting any pain that was not absolutely necessary upon any animal, what would be your view on that subject?

Darwin: It deserves detestation and abhorrence.[14]

In these exchanges Darwin's position remains ambiguous, partly, one feels, because of the complex and loaded questions from the royal commission's chairman, but also, perhaps, because of his own conflicting feelings – the clash between his love of science and his anger at cruelty. Nevertheless, his general detestation of pain emerges clearly. Darwin says he does not understand the objection (except when held by a Hindu) to killing an animal, but he abhors inflicting pain upon it. One gains the impression that Darwin is uneasy in giving his evidence;

perhaps this was because he was in the presence of scientific friends, including Huxley, who were far more fanatical than he in their devotion to the vivisector's cause. In public he felt obliged to give support. In his private notebooks, however, can be found statements indicating that he linked the exploitation of nonhumans with slavery: 'Animals – whom we have made our slaves we do not like to consider our equals. Do not slave holders wish to make the black man other kind?'[15]

Darwin is, perhaps, the prime example of humankind's inconsistency in relation to nonhumans. He spotted the kinship with them, but, like his pupil George Romanes, continued to shoot them for sport. Unfortunately, Darwin's co-discoverer of evolution, Dr Alfred Russell Wallace, was not summoned as a witness. His views are unequivocal:

I have for some years come to the conclusion that nothing but *Total Abolition* will meet the case of vivisection. I am quite disgusted at the frequency of the most horrible experiments to determine the most trivial facts. . . evidently carried on for the interest of the 'research' and the *reputation* it gives. . .[16]

The *Origin of Species* had made an immediate impact, the whole first edition being sold out on the day of issue. Controversy ensued, reaching a climax with a famous debate in Oxford in 1860 between Bishop Samuel Wilberforce and Huxley as the champion of Darwinism. Darwin believed that morality itself is the result of evolution, and he was disturbed by 'the horribly cruel works of nature', rejecting the idea of any divine purpose in the arrangements of the universe. Such views only intensified the conflict between his theories and conventional religion.

For the intelligent lay person, however, Darwinism had three implications of fundamental importance for the relationship between human and other animals.

First, Darwinism appeared to imply (although not necessarily) a lack of divine purpose. In doing so, it tended to undermine the assertion of a special relationship between man and God, as well as the biblical idea that God has given man dominion over the other species for man's benefit. Secondly, and perhaps conflictingly, Darwinism's concept of natural selection suggested that those who are 'fittest' survive best, and this was taken by some to imply that *stronger* individuals, classes and species have a right to dominate and destroy the weaker. Thirdly, and surely most importantly, Darwinism underlined the *kinship* between human and other animals.

The detailed evidence for the last assertion was to accumulate over the final years of the nineteenth century. Yet its moral implication, that what is considered wrong in the treament of human beings ought also to be wrong for the treatment of our nonhuman sentient kin, was not immediately accepted. Although the scales fell from the eyes of some, such were the colossal implications of evolutionary kinship for the day-to-day comforts and convenience of men and women, and for their commercial dealings, that the full message was unacceptable.

By 1870 Darwinism had been generally accepted on both sides of the Atlantic, yet this made little difference to the intensity or content of the animal welfare debate. A few animal welfare writers used the Darwinian idea of kinship, such as E. B. Hamley in *Our Poor Relations* published in Boston in 1872, Bertram Lloyd in *The Great Kinship* of 1921 and Henry Salt, particularly in his late works *The Creed of Kinship* (1935) and *The Story of my Cousins* (1923); but others, such as Frances Power Cobbe, were alarmed at Huxley's and Darwin's agnosticism and their view of morality . So in general evolution had remarkably little effect on the campaign and, paradoxically perhaps, Huxley became a key advocate of speciesism.

The view that nonhuman animals were quite like humans had been gaining ground for many years before the *Origin of Species.* Indeed, tales of the sagacity of brutes, their loyalty, altruism and parental devotion were as old as the hills, and had again been popularized throughout the first half of the nineteenth century. The corollary, that people were sometimes quite brutish, had also been supported during the preceding two centuries by the increasing volume of travellers' tales of wild and primitive savages in newly explored lands. Were all these creatures, some allegedly ape-like in appearance, truly human, or were some the missing links between men and monkeys? These questions were re-inforced rather than answered by the earliest anthropologists.

Darwinism was thus unveiled at a moment when some human beings had already begun to close the conceptual gap between the species. Nevertheless, bursting as it did upon the highly mannered life-style of the mid-Victorian era, where perceived differences even between social classes were huge and highly exaggerated through modes of dress, speech and etiquette, the idea of kinship with animals was certain to ruffle a few feelings and upset well-bred sensibilities; indeed, there may have been a larger number of people living in Victorian London than at any other time before or since who genuinely found it hard to conceive of themselves as a species of animal.

Furthermore, the sexually repressed and over-controlled middle-class culture of the time caused many to feel alienated from their own 'animal instincts'. For many, the word 'animal' still rang alarm bells about their own unacceptable sexual feelings and excretory and other bodily functions. If Darwin had published *Origin of Species* before Victoria's time, or after Freud's, then its reception might have been less explosive.

It is clear from Huxley that the popular reaction of indignation to Darwinism was based on the assumption that it 'degraded' the human being. In 1863 Huxley wrote:

On all sides I shall hear the cry — 'We are men and women, not a mere better sort of ape, a little longer in the leg, more compact in the foot, and bigger in brain than your brutal Chimpanzees and Gorillas. The power of knowledge — the conscience of good and evil — the pitiful tenderness of human affections, raise us out of all real fellowhip with the brutes, however closely they may seem to approximate us.

To this he replied:

I have endeavoured to show that no absolute structural line of demarcation, wider than that between the animals which immediately succeed us in the scale, can be drawn between the animal world and ourselves; and I may add the expression of my belief that the attempt to draw a psychical distinction is equally futile, and that even the highest faculties of feeling and of intellect begin to germinate in lower forms of life.[17]

Yet, while denying that Darwinism would in any way reduce 'our reverence for the nobility of manhood', Huxley did not say that evolutionary theory logically should extend this sense of reverence to the other species. Instead, he went on to stress that: 'No-one is more strongly convinced than I am of the vastness of the gulf between civilised man and the brutes; or is more certain that whether from them or not, he is assuredly not of them.' Such an inconsistent view indicates that Huxley could not or would not face up to the full implications of Darwin's theory. He went so far as to refer to man as 'The only consciously intelligent denizen of this world'.

Such sentiment singles out Huxley from other students of Darwin such as George Romanes and the banker-scientist Sir John Lubbock and even from his master, Darwin. Of far sterner stuff, for example, was the Darwinian Dr Lauder Lindsay, who wrote in 1879:

In truth, the psychical difference between certain animals and certain men is much less obvious than between different individuals, classes and races of man himself. Thus the difference is not more striking between different ages, sexes, and other conditions of man than between the lowest savage races of man and the anthropoid apes, the dog, or even the ant...Man's claim to pre-eminence on the ground of uniqueness of his mental constitution is as absurb and puerile, therefore, as it is fallacious. His overweening pride or vanity has led to his futile contention with the evidence of facts. He has trusted to a series of gratuitous assumptions.[18]

Lindsay, a medical man, claimed that nonhumans are capable of reason as well as religious and moral sense, and went on to argue that since the lower animals 'are unquestionably our fellow-creatures and fellow-mortals' then man is bound to show them kindness: 'In general terms, the treatment of the lower animals by man is to be conducted on the same principles as that of his fellow man, or of the child by his parent or instructor. This is the only rational system or mode of treatment.' This was more in line with Darwin himself, who had argued in *Descent of Man* that the history of man's moral development has been a continual extension in the objects of his 'social instincts and sympathies'. Originally each man had regard only for himself and those of a very narrow circle about him; later, he came to regard more and more 'not only the welfare, but the happiness of all his fellow men'; then 'his sympathies became more tender and widely diffused, extending to men of all races, to the imbecile, maimed, and other useless members of society, and finally to the lower animals...'[19]

The paradox, that scientists simultaneously wanted, for their own experimental convenience, to put nonhumans outside the moral pale while also affirming their physical similarity with human beings, was already a matter for comment. A. Armitt wrote in 1885:

It is, indeed, the scientists themselves who have proved to us the close relationship existing between man and animals, and their probable development from the same origin. It is they who instruct us to cast aside the old theology which makes men differ from the beasts of the field, inasmuch as he was created in 'the image of God', and yet would arbitrarily keep, for their own convenience, the line of division which such a belief marked out between man and animals.'[20]

Later, Sir John Lubbock warned against treating animals 'too much like mere machines'. For Lubbock, even ants had minds – 'all our recent observations tend to confirm the opinion that their mental powers differ from those of men, not so much in kind as in degree.'[21]

MODERN PSYCHOLOGY

It is in the 1890s, however, that modern experimental psychology was born, and with it the more rigorous scientific view that psychologists should not attribute unnecessary 'human' qualities to the behaviour of animals. If ants crowded together on a pebble and touched one another with their antennae, asked Wilhelm Wundt in 1892, why should the observer assume that they 'sported' or were 'saluting their queen?' Such descriptions, said Wundt, were 'due to the imagination of the observer'.[22]

So began the hardening of the psychologist's attitude which led to a widespread contempt for so-called 'anthropomorphism', a word previously reserved to describe the attribution of human characteristics to the deity. During the twentieth century the pendulum would swing so far in the other direction that it became fashionable for scientific psychologists to ignore almost any subjective experience.

Scientific psychologists of the American and British schools, embarrassed by the popular appeal of the unprovable and (in their opinion) improbable theories of Freud, Adler and Jung, became absurdly objective and quantitative in their approach to behaviour, tending to ignore consciousness not only in nonhuman but also in human subjects. The view that animals are living machines tended to cause some scientists to behave as though living creatures could not be both mechanical (in the sense that they followed observable regularities of behaviour which depended upon the physical state of their nervous systems) and also, at the same time, conscious.

The words 'anthropomorphism' and 'sentimentality', both widely used in twentieth-century Britain to disparage those who treated nonhuman animals in ways considered to be only appropriate to humans, were unheard in this context until after Darwin's day. Is it too fanciful to suggest that they were the animal exploiter's defences against the logical implications of Darwinism? If they were, they were certainly effective, casting doubts, as they did, on both the manliness and the intellectual calibre of those they were used against.

Edward Thorndike and J. B. Watson in America and Romanes's student, C. Lloyd Morgan in Britain followed Wundt in condemning the anthropomorphic approach to the study of animals. Together they steered psychology away from the study of the mind and to the objective aspects of behaviour. Inevitably this led to the increasingly cold-blooded study of laboratory animals under more and more rigorous scientific conditions. In 1894 Lloyd Morgan enunciated his famous canon: 'In no case may we interpret an action as the outcome of the exercise of a higher psychical faculty, if it can be interpreted as the outcome of one which stands lower in the psychological scale.'[23] In 1927, Ivan Pavlov went further. Animals should be studied as 'physiological facts, without any need to resort to fantastic speculations as to the existence of any possible subjective states'.

All this was really a version of the philosophers' 'principle of parsimony', which states that when several explanations are equally satisfactory then the simplest should be used. But where behaviourists, and others fanatically opposed to 'anthropomorphism', have gone wrong is that by ignoring the great *similarities* between human and other animals they have used theories which are *less* explanatory than valuable and valid human analogies would have been. Their reasons for making this mistake may lie in their guilt over the misuse of nonhumans and in their reluctance to face up to the fact that most laboratory species feel fear and pain much as they do.

Unlike so many hundreds of his followers who were to inflict terrible sufferings upon nonhumans in their psychological experiments, Lloyd

Morgan, however, had some feeling for them. As early as 1891 he had counselled: 'Sympathy is one of the great and beautiful bonds of life to life. Without sympathy you cannot study even a humble-bee aright.'[25]

CONCLUSIONS

In conclusion it has to be admitted that the theory of evolution played suprisingly little part in the quickening of anti-speciesism in nineteenth-century Britain. It should have done so, but it did not. Perhaps this was because the animal welfarists of the time saw evolution as an invention of the enemy: science. Some of the arch-vivisectors, after all, were keen exponents of evolutionary theory. It would be only in the following century that the moral implications of evolution would help to inspire the cause of animal liberation.

As for the industrial revolution, it increased affluence and created a large middle class; it may have liberated some minds to ponder the plight of nonhumans. But surely this tendency was augmented by the fact that Britain in the nineteenth century enjoyed an almost unprecedented period of peace which stretched, interrupted only by the Crimean and colonial campaigns (which never, of course, produced any fear of invasion) from 1815 till the end of the century. After the 1830s the upper and middle classes felt relatively safe; few external threats distracted them from considering the sufferings of others. Pain, too, had come out into the open as a fashionable preoccupation, and the discovery of anaesthetics created in some minds the optimistic view that pain had been conquered and could, if only anaesthetics were used, be easily banished from the vivisection laboratory.

The power of Queen Victoria's example should not be underestimated as a cause of Britain becoming the leading animal welfare nation in the nineteenth and early twentieth centuries. The aristocracy followed her lead by supporting the RSPCA, and some of their number, such as Shaftesbury and the Duchess of Hamilton, became leaders of the movement. The affluence and security of the Victorian upper classes, their new conviction that something now could and should be done about pain, and the example of genuine concern which they emulated in their Queen, had all played their parts.

10 The International Movement, 1700–1960

Of necessity, this book has so far concentrated on developments in Britain, but it is worth briefly looking at what was happening elsewhere. In the late twentieth century, international cooperation and action has become widespread – indeed necessary, in view of global threats to wildlife and the increasingly international nature of the exploitation of nonhumans. But the development of organizations concerned for the welfare of nonhumans has been very patchy, and legislation slow to come. This chapter does not attempt to cover all these developments, but merely to give some principal examples of the growing interest around the world, their apparently disparate characters often linked by their common Protestant and European cultural origins.

CONTINENTAL EUROPE AND SCANDINAVIA: BEFORE 1900

Although Britain had been first with formal legislation, many German states were not far behind. As early as 1766 a postilion in Leipzig had been sent to prison for twelve weeks for riding a horse to death at a time when such an act would have escaped unpunished in England, and laws against cruelty were passed in Saxony in 1830, in Prussia in 1838 and in Württemburg in 1839. Pastor Albert Knapp founded the first German animal welfare society in 1837 in Stuttgart; Nürnberg and Dresden followed in 1839, Berlin, Hamburg and Frankfurt in 1841, Munich in 1842 and Hanover in 1844. Earlier still, benevolent German kings had protected animals in their realms; Frederick the Great, a friend of the poor and a great lover of animals, is credited with the remark: 'Since I know men, I have learned to love animals', and Kaiser Joseph II in 1789 had stopped the baiting of animals for sport – forty-six years before it was ended in England.

In Switzerland, animal protection societies were formed in Berne in 1844 and in Basle in 1849, and Pastor Philip Wolff founded the Zurich Society in 1856. The first Swiss legislation was in 1842.

Not only Germany and Switzerland, however, produced pioneers in the humane movement. The Scandinavian countries were also in the forefront. The first Norwegian animal welfare society was founded in Oslo in 1859 by David Graah, apparently inspired by the British RSPCA, and the first Norwegian animal protection legislation was in 1842. In Sweden, too, the first animal protection law of 1857 preceded the foundation of formal animal welfare bodies in Gothenborg in 1869 and in Strängnäs in 1870; the latter begun by the anti-vivisectionist philosopher Adolf Nordvall. In Denmark, the first protective legislation was also passed in 1857.

In the Latin countries of Europe, however, no real legislative progress was made during the nineteenth century. What was it about the Protestant North of Europe that put it ahead of the Catholic South? Was it a different interpretation of the idea of 'dominion', or disillusionment with the notion that earthly pain was part of God's purpose? Or was it not its Protestanism so much as the affluence and urbanization of the North which affected the issue?

Although the Catholic Church had adhered more to Aquinas's view of animals than did Evangelicalism, it seems that social factors in addition to religious ones account for the difference. Where poverty and insecurity lingered, as in the South of Europe, humans were too preoccupied with their own survival to have time or compassion to spare for nonhumans.

Vivisection

In Paris, the world's capital of vivisection, a young English woman, Anna Kingsford, had managed to qualify in medicine without the abuse of animals. This achievement took her six years of study, from 1874 till 1880, and she had to fight every inch of the way. Her professors considered vivisection to be a necessary ingredient in the training of any medical student; Anna Kingsford demonstrated that they were wrong.

A few years after she finished her training, in 1883, the Société Française Contre la Vivisection was formed. It is not clear what part Anna played in its foundation, but her example was probably influential. The first president of this new French anti-vivisection society was the great poet and novelist Victor Hugo. When invited to accept the presidency he remarked: 'My name is nothing. It is in the name of the whole human race that you make your appeal. Your society is one that will reflect honour on the nineteenth century. Vivisection is a crime; the human race will repudiate these barbarities.'[1] Hugo warned that human cruelty to animals might one day 'rebound upon our heads like Nero's cruelties'. He was genuinely appalled at humankind's treatment of nonhuman animals and he went out of his way to attack all forms of cruelty. In reference to the shooting of game birds for sport, Hugo remarked: 'Dieu qui fait des oiseaux ne fait pas le gibier' ('God made birds, not game').

The French society had no success equivalent to that of its British counterpart and the laws of France remained unaltered for many years. Perhaps if Anna Kingsford had not died in the same year as its foundation, her neurotic energies might have driven it forward to achieve greater things. As it was, she claimed she had succeeded in killing Claude Bernard and Paul Bert by magic.

In 1882, the Scandinavian League Against Scientific Cruelty was formed in Stockholm under the patronage of Princess Eugenie of Sweden. In the same year, in Germany, the Anglophile Baron Ernst von Weber had founded an anti-vivisection society in Dresden. It is reported that Bismarck lent a sympathetic ear to the pronouncements of its other leading lights, both friends of Frances Cobbe, Dr Ernst Grysanowski and Marie-Espérance von Schwartz. One of the staunchest supporters of this society was Richard Wagner, who wrote of vivisected animals in an open letter to von Weber in 1879: 'The thought of their suffering penetrates with horror and dismay into my bone; and in the sympathy evoked I recognise the strongest impulse of my moral being, and also the probable source of all my art...'[2] Indeed Wagner, referring often to Schopenhauer, wrote at length against vivisection and in support of vegetarianism, basing his argument on logic as well as 'pure compassion' and quoting Plutarch and Pythagoras. It is strange how Wagner's memorable attacks upon 'the sovereign human beast of prey' and his appeals to Christian love have been forgotten:

Everyone who revolts at the sight of an animal's torment, is prompted solely by compassion, and he who joins with others to protect dumb animals, is moved by naught save pity, of its very nature entirely indifferent to all calculations of utility or the reverse. BUT, THAT WE HAVE NOT THE COURAGE TO SET THIS MOTIVE OF PITY IN THE FOREFRONT OF OUR APPEALS AND ADMONITIONS TO THE FOLK, IS THE CURSE OF OUR CIVILISATION.[3]

In Switzerland, too, there was an anti-vivisection movement in the late 1870s, led by Jules Scholl and Anton von Steiger.[4]

But, compared to the British achievements, legislation was slow to come in these countries. Perhaps the relative lack of success of the French, Swiss, and German movements can be explained by von Weber's comment that in France and Germany a 'superstitious reverence for science' prevailed. Furthermore, in England the anti-vivisection movement was backed by the Queen, leading churchmen and members of an aristocracy which was still very influential.

As we have seen, the British Victorian aristocracy was still the apex of society to whom the middle classes looked for leadership on most matters of importance, and the Church was, to a large extent, the cadet branch of this ruling class. They felt little compunction about putting down scientists, many of whom they considered not to be their social equal or who were, even more contemptibly, foreigners like Klein. In other European countries it was not so easy to see vivisectors as social interlopers or upstarts. Yet members of their upper classes, no longer so obviously dependent upon nonhuman animals as their rural forebears had been, had joined the ranks of those who saw kindness to nonhumans as being an attribute of civilization. Furthermore, it was the same class, the aristocracy, which played a leading reform role in these countries – in the case of von Weber in Germany, for example, and Anton von Steiger in Switzerland. In most cases such figures were internationalists, aware of developments in other countries, and especially Britain. In Sweden, too, the royal family gave support to the anti-vivisection movement which was led by upper-class figures such as Adolf Nordvall, Professor Count Georg von Rosen and the Countess Adele Rudenschold. The Scandinavian countries kept in touch with each other and with Britain through a network which included J. K. Lembke in Denmark and Constance Ullner in Finland. Later, 'Lizzy' Lind-af-Hageby and Leisa Schartau, although living in England, maintained contact with the Scandinavian movement and especially with Christian and Elna Tenow who succeeded Nordvall as the principal figures in Sweden a few years after his death in 1892.[5] Close links were developed with Hageby's Animal Defence Society which was run from London.

Nordvall's writings remained influential in the Scandinavian movement, which also translated those of the British surgeon Lawson Tait and the Anglo-French romantic author Ouida (Marie-Louise de la Ramée, 1839–1908), who had attacked vivisection in her booklet *The New Priesthood*.

The Twentieth Century: Before 1960

In the 1930s, under Hitler, German animal welfare legislation was improved, and the Führer himself showed some sympathy for the subject. Mussolini ordained that no birds should be killed on the island of Capri. But the other Fascist dictator of the period, General Franco of Spain, actively suppressed the humane movement in his country. The Society for the Protection of Animals and Plants had been founded in Cadiz in 1872, and by 1888 a score of Spanish humane societies were in existence. In 1925 the Spanish royal family had helped to establish a federation of these societies as a sub-department of the Ministry of the Interior, and in 1929 a Central Board (presided over by the Minister of the Interior, no less) was set up, together with over four thousand local animal and plant protection committees. Between 1925 and 1933 the Spanish government passed protective legislation affecting pit-ponies, birds, horses used in bull-fights, the pollution of the sea, and animals in general. Furthermore, a widespread humane movement had been started among Spanish schoolchildren.

After some five years these remarkable developments were opposed by the Cardinal Primate of the Roman Catholic Church in Spain and came to an abrupt halt with the Spanish Civil War in 1936. Dictator and Church together condemned animal welfare as 'foreign ideas and Protestant influence'. Only in the 1970s, under the veteran leadership of Dolores Marsans Comas, would the Spanish humane movement begin to revive with the return of democracy in that country and its entry into the European Community.

AMERICAN PIONEERS

In America, similar social forces were at work. Urbanization and industrialization followed the English example, and so did growing concern over the treatment of animals. In 1828 New York made cruelty to horses, sheep and cattle a misdemeanour. Massachusetts legislated similarly in 1835, and Connecticut and Wisconsin followed in 1838. These laws were rarely enforced and seem to have arisen not out of an active reform movement but from the general consolidation and modernization of state codes which still relied on British precedent.

In Boston in 1837 the Reverend Charles Lowell preached a sermon against cruelty to animals, and various individuals began to make efforts to protect birds and horses during the 1840s and 1850s. In 1860 S. Morris Waln, a rich Philadelphian, wrote to the RSPCA in London asking for information to assist in setting up a similar organization. Unfortunately the civil war intervened, and it was not until 1867 that Waln again became active in this endeavour.

In 1865 Henry Bergh, a wealthy New Yorker, attended the annual meeting of the RSPCA in England, where he met Lord Harrowby, the society's president. An aloof and sensitive man, Bergh had been appalled by the treatment of horses he had witnessed the previous year in St Petersburg. Now he saw the way forward. He would emulate the RSPCA by inviting the cream of New York society to help him to establish a similar organization. With some influential colleagues, he petitioned the state legislature for an Act of Incorporation and on 22 April 1866 the American Society for the Prevention of Cruelty to Animals was formally launched.

Later that year, Bergh was visited by Caroline Earl White of Philadelphia, the daughter of a well-known Quaker slavery abolitionist, who proceeded to canvass support from the wealthy elite of her city. In 1867 she united with Morris Waln and Richard Muckle, who had been working independently along similar lines, and on 21 June 1867 the Pennsylvania SPCA was formed. Two years later, White founded the Women's Branch of the society, of which she became president.

Almost at the same time as the PSPCA was established, Bergh was approaching Emily Appleton in Boston, who at once adopted the tactics which Bergh and White had already used. On 25 February 1868 she read

15 Henry Bergh (1813–88) founded the American Society for the Prevention of Cruelty to Animals in New York in 1866. Following British precedent he deliberately enlisted upper-class support in order to give the movement credibility. American campaigns against speciesism intensified in the decade of the 1980s. (Reproduced by kind permission of the American Society for the Prevention of Cruelty to Animals, New York)

a letter in the *Boston Daily Advertiser* from a wealthy Bostonian lawyer, the slavery abolitionist George Angell, expostulating against a recent case of cruelty to race-horses. She at once contacted Angell and on 31 March they formed the Massachussetts SPCA, Angell drafting new anti-cruelty state legislation which became law almost immediately. Such was

Angell's influence that he was allowed to use the services of seventeen Boston policemen to canvass the whole city for funds and membership and to distribute copies of the society's new journal *Our Dumb Animals.* Unlike all the other leaders in the American movement, Angell did not come from a wealthy family; he had made his own fortune as a successful lawyer. Like Bergh, however, he was an Anglophile and an admirer of hereditary wealth and status. Both continued, therefore, to look to London for guidance, although their influence over their state legislatures achieved results with a rapidity unknown in England.

Within ten years almost every large city in the North East of America had an SPCA, and the first on the West coast, in San Francisco, had been started in 1868. Education and prosecution were their main endeavours. Following the example of the RSPCA they consciously chose to make animal welfare an upper-class and fashionable cause. There were campaigns against the bearing-rein, the beating of horses and the horrors of the long-distance transportation of live food animals.

During the 1870s Bergh tried in vain to achieve legislation against vivisection. The cause was assisted later by Dr Alfred Leffingwell, who advocated a moderate approach; as a physiologist he had watched Claude Bernard at work and became the leading American proponent of reform over the last twenty years of the century. Leffingwell was not entirely alone as an academic in criticizing vivisection. As in England in the 1860s and 1870s, some distinguished medical figures of the old school regretted the loss of humane sensitivity engendered by vivisection. In a memorable statement, quoted by Leffingwell, Henry Bigelow, a professor of medicine at Harvard wrote: 'Watch the students at a vivisection. It is the blood and suffering, not the science, that rivets their breathless attention. If hospital service makes young students less tender of suffering, vivisection deadens their humanity and begets indifference to it.'[6] Elsewhere he had written: 'There will come a time when the world will look back to modern vivisection in the name of Science, as they do now to burning at the stake in the name of Religion.'[7]

In 1877 the American societies federated as the American Humane Association (AHA), with the particular aim of dealing with the abuses associated with the long-distance transportation of livestock across state boundaries. Conditions on the railways were terrible and thousands of animals died en route to the slaughter houses of the Mid-West, unprotected from climatic extremes, and often unfed and unwatered.

America lacked a titled aristocracy identical with that which led the humane movement in Europe, but its leaders in America were almost all from the equivalent classes – not only the wealthy elite typified by figures such as Bergh but also other society leaders such as the singer Emma Eames and the actress Minnie Maddern Fiske. Even the eminent psychologist William James had indicated his mild approval of the humane effect of anti-vivisection in a letter published in 1909.[8]

As in Britain, by 1890 the movement was predominantly female in membership and, as in Europe, it declined in influence seriously after 1918. After Bergh's death in 1888 his ASPCA gradually ossified. In 1892 it unwisely took over the statutory duty of caring for the stray dogs and cats of New York and spent the next eighty years preoccupied with this problem. Although its inspectors had police powers throughout the state of New York, these were not used as effectively as they might have been to curb the development of the commercialized cruelties of the modern era. Indeed the parallels with the British RSPCA are striking.[9]

The AHA reached its peak under Dr William Stillman in the early twentieth century and its educational influence spread across the American continent and overseas. Stillman's AHA placed an equal emphasis on preventing cruelty to children and animals, and encouraged a universal spirit of humanitarianism of which Henry Salt must have approved. Stillman also founded the Red Star, to aid army animals in a manner parallel to that of the Red Cross for humans. In the nineteenth century, in America as in Britain, philanthropists were often active in both human and nonhuman welfare work. Samuel Gidly Howe, educator of the blind and deaf, became a director of the Massachusetts SPCA, and anti-slavery writers Lydia Maria Child and Harriet Beecher Stowe also wrote on behalf of nonhuman animals.

In 1884 Henry Bergh had been asked to assist 'a little animal' suffering torment at the hands of a woman. When he discovered that the little animal was a child, he rose to the challenge, persevering with a successful prosecution of the woman concerned. Other similar cases followed, and Bergh went on to help form the New York Society for the Prevention of Cruelty to Children. Through Bergh's association with the RSPCA this idea came back to London, where Colam and the RSPCA committee set about establishing a similar organization in Britain; later the same year the National Society for the Prevention of Cruelty to Children was formed. Shaftesbury and Cardinal Manning were involved in this venture and so was Dr Barnardo. In 1886 the NSPCC was given the use of the RSPCA's boardroom at Jermyn Street in London for their meetings, and for some years John Colam was an active member of the NSPCC's committee. The Reverend Benjamin Waugh, usually regarded as the founder of the NSPCC, acknowledged his debt to the RSPCA when he said 'Your Society, the RSPCA, has given birth to a kindred institution whose object is the protection of defenceless children'. The close connection between the two societies is yet another example of the association of humanity to nonhumans with humanity to humans.

If the RSPCA had somewhat stagnated between the wars, then by 1940 the American Humane Association was in a similar condition. It understood the desirability of sponsoring humane education for children as well as the need to collect stray dogs and cats in the cities, but the monstrous hidden cruelties of the Chicago slaughter houses, as well as those inflicted upon wildlife and in American laboratories, were not effectively criticized. Even the less secret atrocities of rodeos, zoos and the fur trade escaped effective censure.

After the Second World War some more imaginative members broke away from the AHA to form the Humane Society of the United States; under the leadership of Fred Myers, they began to tackle the cruelties entrenched in the mass exploitation of the nonhuman species, just as in Britain, too, disgruntled members of the RSPCA began to desert the society to set up their own groups to protect those nonhumans whom the RSPCA of the early twentieth century had tended to ignore – farm animals, laboratory animals, and exploited wildlife. One major twentieth-century campaign was against inhumane slaughter-house practices. In America and Canada the meat industry objected vehemently to humane pre-stunning techniques, arguing that they cost them five cents' worth of each steer's brain tissue and were too slow. 'We hadn't the time to be humane', a Canadian MP quipped. It was not until after the Second World War, under the leadership of Senator Hubert Humphrey, that the humanitarians of America finally won the day.

MEMSAHIBS AND PUKKA WALLAHS

One of the last successful expansionary moves of the early twentieth-century animal movement was the foundation, as late as 1917, of the People's Dispensary for Sick Animals, by the slum social worker Maria Dickin. Miss Dickin's aim was to provide treatment for the animals of the poor, and in subsequent years her workers extended their operations to other countries in Europe and in North Africa.

The expansion of the British empire had already served to spread its ruling class's concern for animal welfare. In India, Africa, Asia, Australia and Canada societies were founded to care for favoured species. Puzzled natives watched as memsahibs swooned and sweated to help beaten donkeys and starved dogs while their topeed spouses inflicted more deliberate cruelty upon the country's wildlife.

In Montreal the Canadian SPCA was started in 1869 and in 1873 the Ontario SPCA was founded in Toronto. Ottawa followed suit in 1882. In Africa the Cape of Good Hope SPCA was launched in 1872, and India could boast a society founded in Calcutta by Colesworthy Grant as early as 1861, with the support of the Viceroy, Lord Elgin. Bombay followed in 1873. Abroad, the English-speakers continued to proselytize well into the twentieth century. Americans joined with British in funding the Japan Animal Welfare Society, which set about the huge task of trying to ensure the humane destruction of thousands of unwanted dogs and cats in Tokyo, as well as those which had been used for research in Japanese universities. In Italy, the English helped to lead the way with the foundation of the Anglo-Italian Society for the Protection of Animals.

In Greece, Queen Sophia had started their animal welfare movement in 1916, but once again it was British money which supplied the means for humane killing and the building of shelters. In 1959 Eleanor Close set up the Greek Animal Welfare Fund.

Almost everywhere British tourists travelled they were shocked by the condition of the nonhuman animals they saw. In 1921 two British women, Mrs Frances Hosali and her daughter Nina, had visited North Africa and seen donkeys being beaten, dogs being smoked to death and cats being thrown alive into fires. Two years later the Hosalis established the Society for the Protection of Animals in North Africa (SPANA), and by 1939 they had set up some twenty free treatment centres in Algeria and Tunisia. In 1944 Mrs Hosali died of malaria working for the animals in Marrakesh. Other Britons living overseas continue in this tradition.[10]

In Egypt, too, it was the British who provided the impetus and the finance to provide elementary care. Mrs Dorothy Brooke, wife of a British cavalry general, in 1930 established hospitals for horses and donkeys in Egypt. These survived even the Suez Crisis of 1957 and to this day are known as the Brooke Hospitals for Animals.

The British also exported their own extraordinary ambivalence. Parallel with their establishment of societies and hospitals for the protection of nonhuman animals, just as eagerly they set up hunts throughout the colonies. English foxhounds were brought to Canada by colonists deserting George Washington in the 1780s and the Montreal Hunt was founded in 1826. Hounds were shipped out, usually by British army officers, to Gibraltar in 1812 and to the British communities in Pau in 1814, Rome in 1835, Tasmania in 1848, Ceylon and St Petersburg in the 1880s, Iraq in 1919, Hong Kong in 1924 and the Sudan in 1925. Often they hunted the nonhuman natives – dingos, kangaroos or jackals. But, patriotically, the British still preferred to slaughter their own, and English red foxes were introduced specially for this purpose into America shortly before the Revolution, and into Australia in the 1840s.[11]

INTERNATIONALISM

The latter part of the nineteenth century saw a spate of international conferences.The first of these appears to have been that held in Dresden in 1860. This was followed by the RSPCA's at the Crystal Palace in London in 1862, one at Hamburg in 1863, in Vienna in 1864, in Paris in 1867, in Hamburg again in 1870 and at Baroness Burdett-Coutt's London home in 1874. There was one in Paris in 1877 and another in Brussels in 1880 where links with the temperance societies were encouraged. Further conferences were held in Vienna in 1883, in Berne in 1884 and in Paris in 1900. To mark the RSPCA's centenary an international conference was held in London in 1924, accompanied by the publication of an appalling ode by Thomas Hardy:

> 'Cries still are heard in secret nooks,
> Till hushed with gag or slit or thud;
> And hideous dens whereon none looks
> Are sprayed with spurting blood.
> But here, in battlings, patient, slow,
> Much has been won — more, maybe, than we know
> And on we labour hopeful. 'Ailinon,'
> Outcalls one great of old: 'May good have rule!'
> And 'Blessed are the merciful!'
> Calls yet a greater one.

At another international gathering in The Hague in 1950 Arthur Moss, the RSPCA's chief secretary, proposed the establishment of an international animal welfare body. Objections, chiefly from those animal welfare societies which were reluctant to oppose animal experimentation, were numerous. These organizations considered that the RSPCA's opposition (in principle at least) to all painful experiments was a position too radical for them to support. This reaction is a striking indication of the conservatism of international opinion at that time. In the same year, owing in part to the efforts of Dr H. J. Weichert from Germany (and independent of the RSPCA), the World Federation for the Protection of Animals was formed. The aim of the federation was to develop and coordinate animal welfare internationally.

Nine years later, in 1959, the International Society for the Protection of Animals (ISPA) was set up jointly by the RSPCA and the Massachusetts SPCA and became, during the following two decades, the more pragmatic of the two international societies, involving itself in fieldwork, rescuing wildlife stranded by flood or drought, and educating Third World countries in the techniques of humane slaughter.

The performance of the humane movement in the forty or so years after 1918 had been lacklustre; yet what it lacked in intensity may have been made up for by the continuing gradual dissemination of its ideas worldwide. While the rate of progress in any one country, measured by the reduction of cruelty being inflicted by humans upon nonhumans, was always very slow and, indeed, often in a negative direction, nevertheless the basic proposition that humans owe some elementary consideration to nonhumans continued to spread into new cultures.

Part II
MODERN TIMES

11 The Revival of the Movement after 1960

This chapter describes how Britain led a revival in the animal protection movement in the decades of the 1960s and 1970s. It began with the escalation of protests against the RSPCA's failure to oppose bloodsports and was followed by the formation of the Hunt Saboteurs Association in 1963 and the appearance of groups of young people directly confronting fox- and deer-hunts in the south of England. Ruth Harrrison's attack on factory-farming (1964) and Brigid Brophy's restatement of the animal rights ideal (1965) came next, to be followed by the formation of the Oxford Group (1969) (see p. 6). In the 1970s the RSPCA Reform Group forced the society to adopt a modern approach; a major campaign to restrict experiments on nonhuman animals was launched; Peter Singer gave the movement new intellectual leadership (1975); the established British animal welfare organizations were revitalized; the RSPCA successfully extended its influence to the rest of the European Community (1978); and, by the end of the decade, with Lord Houghton's assistance nonhuman animals in Britain were 'put into politics', the major parties for the first time formulating their own official animal protection policies (1979).

But what was the background to these undoubted advances?

After the First World War the animal welfare movement in Britain, almost paralysed by its fear of appearing sentimental or extreme, had become increasingly preoccupied with the day-to-day care of stray dogs, unwanted cats and the declining number of tradesmen's horses. Campaigning against the institutionalized exploitation of animals faded.

Those cruelties in the public eye, such as the abuse of animals in the new film industry, the condition of animals in circuses and zoos, and the steadily increasing number of sea birds being found on the beaches covered in oil, were issues on which the RSPCA took worthwhile action. But the hidden cruelties went almost unchallenged: between 1920 and 1940 licensed animal experiments increased from 70,000 to around one million annually, and factory-farming expanded on a huge scale.

RADICALS AND TRADITIONALISTS: THE RSPCA

In earlier days the split between the RSPCA's progressive and conservative elements, and the society's slowness to come to terms with new cruelties, had been masked by its undoubtedly great achievements in other areas. After 1918, however, the clash between radicals and traditionalists had become public and damaging. Whereas the deliberate social elevation of the RSPCA in the nineteenth century had been highly effective as a means of achieving social and legislative reform, in the present century it became, at best, a mixed blessing. By 1945, the RSPCA council had become composed chiefly of those who had little or no political, social or financial influence. True, there was Sir Robert Gower MP, who was chairman in the 1920s and 1930s, but he was an exception. Senior RSPCA staff, such as Arthur Moss in the 1950s, had felt held back and frustrated by the lack of drive and imagination of their council.[1]

The RSPCA, however, remained by far the most prestigious animal welfare organization in Britain and, probably, in the world. As a charity, its many thousands of members elect an unpaid council which determines its policies and appoints its senior paid staff. The society's large income, mostly derived from legacies, allows it to employ many hundreds of people, which makes it the largest of all professional animal welfare bodies. It receives no funding from the state, but is widely, although wrongly, regarded as a government agency. Several hundred animal welfare organizations around the world are affiliated to the RSPCA, and it is increasingly international in its operations, being especially influential in Europe and in the nations of the Commonwealth.[2]

As we have seen in chapter 8, during the stagnation of the post-war years the pattern, all too often repeated, was that the critics expostulated for a year or two against the RSPCA's failures before being intolerantly expelled from the society by a complacent council, dropping out to form their own independent organizations or giving up the fight entirely in a mood of bitter disillusionment. By 1970, at least a hundred animal welfare bodies existed in Britain, some active and some not, but the majority in principle committed to greater change than the RSPCA appeared to favour. Only in the late 1960s were the radicals to show the persistence necessary to achieve a significant change in the RSPCA itself. It was in this decade that the whole movement began to regain its intellectual power.

THE WIND OF CHANGE

The development in the 1960s and 1970s of the philosophical concern with the status and treatment of nonhuman animals, and the more general public concern has been described in the Introduction. There were other contributions to the debate. In 1964 Ruth Harrison published her book *Animal Machines*, an important attack on the cruelties inherent in certain forms of 'factory farming'. She called for new legislation to ban battery-hen cages and to prohibit the keeping of veal calves permanently tethered or in darkness or on deficiency diets. The book was widely acknowledged and helped alter permanently the public perception of intensive husbandry.

The following year Brigid Brophy's article in the *Sunday Times* caused much interest.[3] Probably not since the First World War had a serious paper given so much space to this all-but-forgotten subject. Brophy, influenced by the writings of Bernard Shaw, had been a vegetarian for ten years and thought it was time she told people 'without apology or embarrassment'. Her motivation was 'revulsion from cruelty, distaste for hypocrisy and double think'.[4] She had not been aware of any significant animal welfare movement during the 1950s and certainly was not part of it.

In 1970 two other authors, Monica Hutchings and Mavis Caver, published *Man's Dominion* – a devastating catalogue of human cruelty which argued the moral case strongly but in the language of the past.[5] This book failed to gain the publicity it deserved and was not, I believe, widely read by the new young activists just emerging. Nevertheless it made a deep impression upon some of the older generation.

BLOODSPORTS

Since Henry Salt drafted his Bill in 1893 attempts to curtail bloodsports have led to Bills being introduced into the British Parliament on more than thirty occasions. Latterly, many were successfully defeated by Conservative MP Marcus Kimball's use of parliamentary tactics, the basic one being to talk at length on the parliamentary business preceding the antihunting Bill so that when the Bill was debated, it failed through lack of time. (The official curtailment of filibusters is considered acceptable only on Bills which are part of a government's published programme.[6])

Nevertheless one Bill passed all its stages in the Commons in 1970, but it did not proceed through the Lords because a general election supervened. The 1975 Bill came even closer to success, but the British Field Sports Society (BFSS) on the advice of Lord Denham, managed to ensure that the Bill was sent to a specially set up select committee which persuaded the House of Lords not to proceed with it. This select committee was assisted not only by a scientist who argued that prey-species may not dislike being coursed, but also by advice received from an eminent law lord, the late Lord Diplock, to the effect that the Bill would be impracticable and difficult to enforce. Diplock did not reveal to the select committee at the time that he was a life-long supporter of bloodsports, nor that he was closely in touch with the BFSS and had written articles for the society in the 1930s.[7] Four out of the seven members of the committee were Conservatives, and these were the four who voted that the Bill should not proceed.[8]

A survey conducted by Richard Thomas in 1977 found that whereas 45 per cent of Masters of Foxhounds actually belonged to the Conservative party (20 per cent being activists) and 81 per cent said they would vote Conservative in the general election, only one MFH said he would vote for the Liberals, and none chose Labour.[9] In contrast, politics were not found to be a central part of the lives of members of the Hunt Saboteurs Association, only 7 per cent saying they were members of the Liberal party, 5 per cent of the Conservative party and 3 per cent of the Labour party; 29 per cent said they would vote Liberal, 23 per cent Labour and 18 per cent Conservative. Thomas, in his excellent study, summed up the two groups:

The evidence from the questionnaires shows that MFHs are a relatively homogeneous group of mainly middle-aged and middle or upper class country dwellers. Hunt saboteurs on the other hand are much more heterogeneous, being a more equal mixture of classes and age groups. They are also more evenly divided between the sexes and between urban and rural dwellers. From the evidence of this study, it is apparent that MFHs are essentially tough-minded conservatives and that saboteurs are radicals, although some are tough- and some are tender-minded.

He concludes that the two groups share almost no common ground: 'The HSA is firmly on the side of freedom and the MFH is strongly on the side of order.' There is also evidence that whereas MFHs were very often following in a family tradition, saboteurs were not. Indeed the latter were sometimes departing from their usual life-styles through their activities in defence of animals – driven very often, it seems, by an overwhelming sense of indignation and compassion.

More than any other aspect of animal welfare, the bloodsports issue in Britain had become party political by 1970. In general, the Conservative party supported these sports, the Labour party opposed them and the Liberals occupied the middle ground. As early as 1967 Eric Heffer had introduced a Bill against bloodsports and by the 1980s the anti-bloodsports campaign in Parliament had become part of the programme of the extreme Left. In his 1982 book *The Hunt and the Anti-Hunt*, Philip Windeatt quoted several well-known public figures of the Left: Tony Benn – 'bloodsports degrade us all'; Arthur Scargill– 'how anyone can inflict unnecessary pain on innocent and defenceless animals is beyond my understanding'; and Dennis Skinner – 'it is unjustified murder'. Yet it is doubtful whether, twenty years earlier, all such pillars of socialism would have expressed this conviction. The change in attitude was probably due partly to the effect the Hunt Saboteurs Association had had upon the image of animal welfare generally.

Direct Action

In 1963 the new chairman of the League Against Cruel Sports, Raymond Rowley, had begun to steer it away from confrontational protest at a time when some members wanted to step it up. These people proceeded to form the autonomous Hunt Saboteurs Association, the aims of which were 'to save the lives of hunted animals by legal, nonviolent, direct means and to bring to the attention of People and Parliament the barbaric cruelties involved in the hunting of animals until such time as these practices are banned by law'. The nonviolent approach was endorsed in the Rules of the Association.[10]

John Prestige, a Devon journalist, appalled when he found himself working on the story of a pregnant hind who had been driven into a village and killed by the Devon and Somerset staghounds, said to a colleague that 'someone ought to sabotage the hunt.' So, with a group of friends, Ken Wanstall, Leo Lewis and members of the Cebo family among them, he fed meat to the South Devon Foxhounds in order to sabotage their meet in Torquay on Boxing Day 1963. His motives, he says, were 'disgust' and 'a feeling that nothing was being done to stop it – the League Against Cruel Sports was ineffective at the time.' He has denied any party political element in his thinking.[11]

Retaliation was brutal. On 2 May 1964 'nearly 300' members of the Culmstock otter-hunt surrounded a car-load of saboteurs, whipped the car, turned it over, dragged Leo Lewis out of it and broke his jaw with an otter-hunting stave. Axminster magistrates in due course imposed small fines upon four hunters and bound over Lewis and Prestige to keep the peace.

Undeterred, Prestige and his friends continued a campaign of weekly sabotage against stag-, otter- and fox-hunting which lasted for three or four years, centred upon Somerset and Devon and using aniseed and hunting horns to divert the pack. They were shortly followed by a London group which began to confront fox-hunts in South and East England.

Using his contacts in the media, Prestige gained a great deal of sympathetic publicity in the years 1964 to 1967. Then, 'disillusioned by the strength of the entrenched system' which he was fighting and because of his dislike of the minority who, he says, wanted to demonstrate chiefly because they were 'anti-establishment', Prestige gave up. The Hunt Saboteurs Association underwent a temporary decline before being revived under the new London-based leadership of David Wetton in 1969.

I had confronted the Bucks and Courtenay Tracy Otterhounds on the family estate around Wytch Farm in Dorset in the summer of 1969, and, although never a member of the Hunt Saboteurs Association, with the support of Wetton and friends from the Oxford area I proceeded to wage a five-year campaign against otter-hunting in the South and West of England which received widespread local and national publicity. The objections to the sport were that it was cruel and that otters were an endangered species in English rivers. I then continued the campaign at the political level until otters became legally protected in England and Wales in 1978.[12]

During the early 1970s Hunt Saboteurs Association members rapidly increased and by 1977 the Association claimed a membership of nearly 3,000, mostly in and around university towns. By 1982 the association's mailing list had grown to around 4,000. Thomas's survey of 1977 showed that members were mostly male and youthful, 46 per cent being under the age of twenty-five. Highly significantly, however, they came from all socio-economic classes, not overwhelmingly from the middle class; for the first time in the history of the animal rights movement, a large number of the working-class young had publicly declared their support. No less than 38 per cent had incomes of less than £1,500 a year. Many were, however, well educated, 19 per cent of the HSA members being students and 59 per cent having had tertiary education.

On some occasions indignant hunting people, some of whom appeared to find it hard to believe that compassion alone could motivate the interruption of their sport, accused the protesters of being professional troublemakers hired by mysterious political godfathers. Lord Houghton, as chairman of the League Against Cruel Sports, angrily rebutted one such 'rent-a-mob' accusation:

If Princess Anne wants to know who is paying the demonstrators of Hunt Saboteurs Association the answer is – no one. They are dedicated young people who risk insult and injury from brutal huntsmen because they are passionately opposed to hunting foxes with hounds for pleasure. And so am I.

The crowd of several thousands of young people who demonstrated in Trafalgar Square against the appalling slaughter of baby seals in Canada at this time of year were not being paid either.

It is a hopeful sign for the future of mankind that so many young people now reject inhuman and unenlightened attitudes and practices towards animals which have become ingrained in society by centuries of greed, vanity and sport.

It is an impertinence for Princess Anne to ask them 'who's paying you?' We may well remind her of who's paying her![13]

The methods of the association in its earlier years were both peaceful and legal. Dave Wetton's anti-violent and good-humoured approach pervaded the organization as he strove, primarily, to protect the quarry rather than to antagonize the hunter. On some occasions, however, his skilful use of the hunting horn would lure the pack in entirely the wrong direction across a river, leaving apoplectic whippers-in trumpeting impotently on the other bank while the quarry made good his or her escape. Other tactics included scaring away the quarry in advance of the hunt or spoiling the scent. Aniseed having proved disappointing, our Oxford clique had introduced the use of 'anti-mate' bitch sprays in 1970, and with some success. Oxford University chemists had suggested methyl mercaptan as one of the strongest smells known to man but, after tests on the Berkshire Downs, this substance, although not known to be illegal or toxic, was abandoned in case it might prove to have detrimental effects on humans, hounds, wildlife or the environment generally. Rotten herring, on the other hand, proved irresistibly diverting to otter-hounds and terriers alike, although somewhat philosophically inconsistent and highly unpleasant to use.

Hardly surprisingly, the reactions of huntsmen and coursers to such pungent opposition was sometimes violent. Their sports were often more to them than mere pastimes, being in some cases a central part of their lives and an important element in their sense of identity. To interfere with such sports struck deep. If, in addition, protests stirred uneasy consciences, then the emotional reaction was compounded.

The infiltration of hunts by anti-hunting protesters requires some courage. Nevertheless, Michael Huskisson in the late 1970s masqueraded as a hunt supporter for two years, obtaining film in the process, and subsequently publishing his observations amid passionate condemnation of his conduct from genuine hunters.

The behaviour of magistrates, too, sometimes reflected an emotional quality, and at the expense of justice. In 1977, for example, Mrs Valerie Waters was called by the police as a prosecution witness in a case concerning alleged violence by some supporters of the Atherstone Hunt.[14] When the huntsmen had been bound over, the magistrates proceeded to bind over Mrs Waters although she had only been a witness, on the grounds that she was a well-known member of the Hunt Saboteurs Association. When Waters refused to be bound over, she was sent to prison for a month where she was treated as a criminal. The fines of the guilty huntsmen having been paid for them by the British Field Sports Society, the Master of the Hunt declared: 'I'm very glad she's in prison. She was a bloody nuisance.' In the same year thirty-one saboteurs were bound over for protesting against a coursing meeting. The Association's request for legal aid was refused even though some defendants were students or unemployed. The judge who refused their application for legal aid did not reveal at the time that he was a member of the British Field Sports Society, with one son a former MFH and another a local hunt secretary. When the Association eventually succeeded in appealing to another judge, the case was dismissed.[15]

Such waywardness in the legal process embittered many in the animal rights movement and helped to escalate the levels of violence. Justice too often had not been seen to be done. The network of apparent interest between hunters, lawyers and government appeared to many to be oppressive and conspiratorial. Their traditional alliance with farmers, however, began to crumble. With fewer free-range hens, farmers by the 1970s had begun to realize that the fox, far from being a pest, was probably doing them a service by keeping down rats, rabbits and slugs; at least it was quite obvious that the fox did less damage to crops than a lot of jodphured gents on horseback. Tensions grew between hunts and farmers and there were some nasty incidents, as when, for example, a Devon farmer shot five hounds of the South Devon Hunt at Christmas 1986.[16]

Undoubtedly, all sides on occasions have been provocative. Violence has provoked counter-violence and injustice has provoked extremism. The desecration of the graves of two well-known huntsmen, John Peel and the Duke of Beaufort, have been bizarre instances of this extremism; the attempted disinterment of the corpses by the self-styled Hunt Retribution Squad in 1977 struck most members of the public as a revolting anachronism, and did much to discredit the whole movement.

REFORM OF THE RSPCA

It was in an anti-hunting context that ginger-group activity emerged within the ranks of the RSPCA. One of the main areas of disagreement within the society, and the one seized upon to the exclusion of almost all others by the media, was this question of bloodsports. The British Field Sports Society had long dreaded the outright opposition of the RSPCA to fox-, stag- and otter-hunting, hare-coursing, deer-stalking and other country sports. Paradoxically, the RSPCA's notorious conservatism meant that its opposition was even more to be feared.

The RSPCA certainly had supporters of bloodsports among its members. But such infiltration was not always deliberate, for the classes that led the RSPCA had many animal-lovers among their ranks, who nevertheless hunted or shot for sport, or who, although not participants themselves, had friends, relatives or acquaintances who were. Furthermore, fox-hunting had the same 'snob' appeal as the RSPCA itself, and so those who joined the RSPCA wholly or partly, consciously or barely consciously, in order to enhance their social standing, might equally admire the world of fieldsports and for similar reasons.

In Victorian times, for those with social aspirations, it had been possible to see vivisecting scientists as threats to the old order in society or to look down on them as foreigners or anti-religious intellectuals. Conceivably, it had been possible to view agricultural and other forms of cruelty as being 'tainted by commerce' or springing from peasant ignorance. But to attack bloodsports, and fox-hunting in particular, struck at the core of the British class system and the nation's traditional fantasies about country life. For nearly two hundred years the English middle classes had dreamt of being country gentry and believed that fox-hunting was one of its principal qualifications. The fact that many established country gentlemen and aristocrats never hunted, and that some regarded the hunt as bourgeois, boorish and a damned nuisance, did not register in the public mind. When, therefore, in the 1960s, some members of the RSPCA challenged fox-hunting head-on, it was an occasion for much publicity.

On 8 April 1960, an extraordinary general meeting of the RSPCA was called by three anti-hunting members of the society, Patrick Moore (the distinguished astronomer), Howard Johnson (Conservative MP for Kemp Town, Brighton) and Gwendoline Barter. But their anti-hunting motion failed to attain the necessary three-fifths majority. Similar motions were put and defeated at the AGM in June and at a further EGM in 1961. On each occasion opposition came from senior members of the RSPCA council and, later that year, Howard Johnson and Gwendoline Barter were expelled from the society.

In 1960 Captain Robert Churchward, a former joint Master of the South Shropshire Hunt, after thirty years in the saddle, published an outspoken attack upon the hidden cruelties of fox-hunting, revealing that it was, in his view, 'specifically designed to maintain the present artificially high level of the fox population'.[17] Churchward's book motivated an RSPCA member, Vera Sheppard, to stage a number of solitary protests against fox-hunts and to raise the question of bloodsports at RSPCA meetings in 1962 and 1963, supported by Patrick Moore. At its meeting in 1965, together with Richard Chapman, she proposed a motion that the society 'deplores the killing of wild animals in the name of sport and calls upon the responsible Hunt authorities to substitute drag hunting instead'. In the relevant issue of *Horse and Hound* the editor of the huntsmen's journal advised his readers to attend the RSPCA's meeting 'to see that the proposed motion is soundly defeated'. Hunters arrived in force, among them the Duke of Beaufort, who was then president of the British Field Sports Society, and Marcus Kimball MP its chairman. The meeting was chaotic; at it, three anti-hunting members of the RSPCA council, Rose and Charles Birkett and Edward Whitley, alleged that at least four fellow members of the council supported live hare-coursing and that several supported both hunting and vivisection. The motion was emasculated by an amendment, and approximately two hundred hunting sympathizers immediately left the meeting in triumphant mood.

In 1967 bloodsports were again debated in Parliament, and an attempt was made by William Price, Eric Heffer and other MPs to outlaw hare-coursing. But, under opposition from RSPCA member Marcus Kimball, the Bill was talked out. At the ensuing RSPCA AGM, Sheppard, Whitley, the Birketts and other anti-hunters attempted to pass a motion to expel Kimball from membership of the society. The RSPCA had been prepared a few years earlier to expel the two members who had attacked the society's equivocation on bloodsports; it showed a reluctance to act likewise against Kimball.

Nevertheless, the society's chairman, Lieutenant-Colonel J. C. Lockwood, and the society's council, shifted their position significantly at this time, and public statements were made indicating that the RSPCA did at least consider that cruelty to wildlife was within its remit and that the hunting of otters was a matter for concern. Senior officers of the British Field Sports Society lunched with Lockwood in an attempt to persuade him to recant. They failed, and subsequently instructed some of their members to attend the 1968 RSPCA meeting, where the RSPCA's annual report was tactically rejected and a motion against hunting was rowdily defeated by 448 votes to 197. This contrasted with a postal ballot of the RSPCA membership at this time which showed a majority of four to one opposed to bloodsports.

One reason for this disparity was undoubtedly the RSPCA's practice of holding its annual meetings on a weekday, thus making it harder for ordinary working people to attend. When this situation was reversed in 1970, so that meetings were held on Saturdays, it became the turn of the traditionalist faction to complain, albeit less logically, that the meetings disproportionately favoured the radicals.

During 1969 supporters of hunting continued their pressure. In a letter to *Horse and Hound* published on 17 January, Sir Robert Grant-Ferris MP urged friends of hunting to join the RSPCA and to support leading council-member John Hobhouse.

The annual RSPCA council elections became highly charged. Conservative MP Harold Gurden publicly lobbied against candidates who were known to be opposed to hunting. After a particularly acrimonious AGM, the council ousted its chairman, who was replaced by John Hobhouse, and co-opted, as vice-chairman, Frederick Burden, a Conservative MP who was also president of the Kent Wildfowlers Association. At the subsequent annual meeting in 1970 Sheppard, Whitley and the other anti-hunters were effectively silenced when microphones were switched off, and the meeting itself ended in uproar as protesters were forcibly removed from the platform.[18]

The RSPCA Reform Group

In the same year, a new ginger-group was formed. RSPCA members who were opposed to hunting and dedicated to trying to modernize the society came together as the RSPCA Reform Group. Their leaders were Brian Seager (no relation of Major Ronald Seager, the society's chief officer – then styled secretary but later executive director), Stanley Cover and John Bryant. One of its first actions was to protest in January 1971 against a fox-hunt for children in Warwickshire, organized by someone who was both a huntsman and a member of the RSPCA. A few days later Vera Sheppard was summonsed to appear before the RSPCA council to face expulsion on a charge that by her protests against hunting she had behaved in a manner 'prejudicial to the interests of the Society'. When she arrived at the society's Jermyn Street headquarters accompanied by Edward Whitley, she was met by a crowd of supporters waving placards carrying statements such as 'The RSPCA has *never* expelled a Blood Sportsman.'

In her defence Sheppard alleged a long-standing conspiracy by bloodsportsmen to control the RSPCA, quoting letters published in the sporting press to support her allegation.[19]

In the event, the RSPCA council decided not to expel Vera Sheppard. The RSPCA Reform Group felt that the major reason for the decision was fear of further adverse publicity. History, however, would certainly repeat itself and many others who criticized have found themselves faced with expulsion merely because they *have* criticized the society; indeed a pattern emerged in which outstanding reformers have been expelled, often by those within the society whose contribution to the movement has been negligible.

By 1969 some pro-hunting members had discovered a new weapon. They threatened that if the RSPCA did not cease all campaigning against bloodsports a complaint would be made to the Charity Commissioners arguing that the RSPCA should lose its charitable status because it had become 'too political'. Such a loss of status would mean the loss of tax exemptions, and cost the society many thousands of pounds a year. This threat, believed by many and cynically exploited by a few, severely hampered reform of the society for most of the ensuing decade, making the radicals' task even harder.[20]

The following year, the Reform Group supported a number of sympathetic candidates for the annual RSPCA council elections, five of whom, including Bryant and myself, were elected. Nevertheless, the dominant factor on the forty-six-strong council fought back vigorously and in early 1973 it even attempted to expel from the society the tenacious Reform Group chairman, Brian Seager. Once again the attempt failed when the national publicity surrounding the affair began to escalate.

Concerned about the general running of the society, the Reform Group then mounted a campaign for an extraordinary general meeting to examine the state of its administration. As a counter-move the council proposed, and the Annual General Meeting in June 1973 passed, a resolution to set up an independent inquiry to report on the society's constitution, rules, conduct and management. The three-man inquiry, under the chairmanship of Charles Sparrow QC, started work in August

1973 and reported the following year, after months of lurid publicity as allegations, some wild and some accurate, were aired in its public hearings of witnesses.

The first of Sparrow's thirty-eight recommendations was that the society must have a new chairman. The report also recommended halving the size of the council and urged the need for more council members with expert knowledge; co-option to the council should only be for 'true cases of persons with special qualifications'; the value of the inspectorate was emphasized and the council was reminded that its own function should be limited to 'questions of principle and policy', leaving routine administration to the paid staff. At the council meeting on 21 November 1974, I proposed that the report's recommendations (except that affecting the chairman) should be accepted. Against considerable opposition, but with the support of Lord Houghton, a recent Labour cabinet minister who was, for a short period, a member of the council, this motion was eventually carried, and the whole RSPCA council voluntarily resigned.

Reform Group candidates did well again in the following postal elections to the smaller council of twenty-three, and under its new chairman Michael Kay, an accountant from Leeds, the RSPCA began its slow and belated journey into the modern era. Kay, however, failed to be re-elected in the 1975 council elections and was succeeded as chairman by Roy Crisp, a Suffolk antiquarian.

Neither Crisp nor Kay, both moderates, had been Reform Group members, yet, although the old supporters of the now disbanded Reform Group were still in a minority on the new council and still deeply mistrusted in some quarters, their policies gradually became acceptable to some older members. Indeed, although the Sparrow report had been highly critical of the Reform Group, some of the report's recommendations and most of its consequences were in line with the Reform Group's long-published ideas. Although almost every reform proposed was fiercely resisted by the old guard, enough of the middle ground on the council changed its mind in the succeeding years to allow my election as vice-chairman in 1976 and chairman in 1977.

SOME CHANGES IN THE RSPCA: THE 1970S

The eight years from 1972 to the end of the decade were a period of rapid changes within the RSPCA, initiated by its reforming minority on the council. The first surprise for the new members who joined the council in 1972 had been the discovery that the RSPCA had no written policies. Such as it was, policy consisted solely of half-recalled council resolutions and the *ad hoc* pronouncements of senior officers. A huge staff, some five hundred strong, lacked the basic guidelines that a written policy could provide. Often confused and insecure in the midst of the society's then tumultuous affairs, with policy at the whim of one faction or another, staff understandably played safe. Afraid to take new initiatives which might provoke criticism from council members, they preferred to be cautious. This situation aggravated the society's already powerful inclination toward inertia and blandness.

While many of the branches of the RSPCA had carried on vigorously with routine welfare work, mostly involving domestic pets and strays, certain areas of cruelty and exploitation had received scant attention from the national body for some fifty years. Intensive farming had been allowed to expand and develop with minimal opposition from the one organization prestigious enough to have checked it. Laboratory animals and wildlife had been neglected and their exploitation and abuse had escalated. It seemed that the RSPCA was at this time actually lagging behind public opinion rather than leading it on cruelty issues. It seemed completely out of touch with the philosophical revival and mass protest against animal experimentation and the exploitation of wildlife of the 1970s (see chapters 12 and 13).

Under RSPCA Reform Group influence the council began reform in 1972 by setting up expert advisory committees on cruelty in animal experimentation and farming. The former committee, under the secretaryship of Bill Jordan and chaired by Dr Kit Pedler (one of the creators of the television series *Dr Who* and *Doomwatch*, the latter being a dramatized attack on pollution and the dangers of uncontrolled science), fast established itself as a radical and effective committee. The farming committee on the other hand, tightly controlled by the RSPCA's then chief veterinarian (considered by some, rightly or wrongly, to be a covert friend of the farming industry), initially did little more than postpone firm action by commissioning research.

Under its new chairmen (the term of office for this position was, after 1975, limited to two years), the council set about formulating policies across the board. Some forty areas of cruelty were considered and the society's basic policy upon each was decided, based usually upon wordings drafted by the society's education officer, David Paterson, and myself. An analysis of the council's minutes in these years will show that nearly all the new thinking came from the Reform Group minority, and that it was consistently opposed by the votes of traditionalists led by Sir Frederick Burden MP. As part of this programme of policymaking, the contentious issue of hunting came up and, remarkably, in a meeting on 25 February 1976, the council of the RSPCA voted without opposition that the society should 'oppose all hunting with hounds'. After fifteen years of bitter wrangling, the supporters of bloodsports within the society had quietly accepted defeat. Strangely, when the policy was restated nine years later, in 1985, it provoked a strong reaction from the hunting community: *Horse and Hound*, ignoring the fact that by this time more traditional figures were once again in control of the society, announced that the policy was due to 'entryism by extremists' whose real aim was 'social change, not animal welfare' (3 January 1986). The *Daily Telegraph* reiterated such inaccuracies and the British Field Sports Society retaliated with leaflets using the RSPCA logo. (In July 1986 they were forced in the High Court to destroy all these leaflets and to pay the RSPCA's legal costs.)

The next step taken by the reformers in the late 1970s was to insist that *priorities* should be decided.[21] Within the wide spectrum of the policies it was resolved that the four major areas – the treatment of farm animals, wildlife, domestic animals, and laboratory animals – would be given equal priority. This move represented a major step away from the society's almost total preoccupation with stray and unwanted pets, which had taken up most of its resources for at least fifty years.

In a complete reorganization of the council's committee structure in 1975, the number of committees was drastically reduced. A council subcommittee continued to deal with the management of domestic animal matters, while the expert advisory committees (now numbering three, after the formation of a Wild Animals Advisory Committee) offered technical advice on the other priority areas.

Trying to alter the direction of the RSPCA was like trying to turn around a huge ship: it took time. By November 1976 little change in the society's animal welfare performance was noticeable to John Bryant. In exasperation he circulated a satirical document to fellow council members ('With the Greatest Respect and So On, while 400,000,000 Animals Suffer') describing what he saw as typical RSPCA council meetings at that time, with lengthy discussions of minor issues, fierce arguments between the factions, the failure to make changes, to face up to facts, to take firm decisions or to use the society's huge resources effectively. Bryant went on to reiterate the view that the society's role should be changed to tackle the mass modern cruelties through education and campaigning. At the most generous estimate, he wrote, the society could not have helped more than two million animals that year, although 'in terms of our own policies, there are in any one year in this country, 400,000,000 animals suffering cruelty. These include 370,000,000 victims of 'over-intensive' farming and 5,500,000 victims of vivisection.' In other words, so Bryant claimed, the RSPCA was squandering its resources on being 'part of the state law enforcement machine' and was helping only half of one per cent of the animals in need – 'What about the other 99½ per cent?' he asked. Looking at the society's account, he reckoned that 87 per cent of the money (over £2 million annually at that time) was spent on the half of one per cent of animals, including the cost of destroying annually over 100,000 unwanted *healthy* dogs and cats.

Traditionally, the RSPCA had destroyed colonies of feral cats. But the so-called radicals at this time backed Celia Hammond's alternative plan to neuter such cats and return them to site. After long resistance from the RSPCA establishment this approach eventually proved practicable and became RSPCA policy.[22]

Over the following two years, against constant opposition, the reforming group on the council did manage to achieve some redistribution of the society's effort and expenditure to cover the neglected areas, and, before the end of my term of office as chairman, the society had established for the first time full-time staff departments to campaign in each of the three new priority areas (cruelty to wildlife, laboratory and farm animals) and to service the recently established expert advisory committees.

Collaboration with Other Agencies

Although the RSPCA, in the mid-twentieth century, had been reluctant to collaborate with other animal welfare organizations, the new council members successfully urged RSPCA co-operation with three joint committees that were established during the 1970s. The first, JACOPIS (the Joint Advisory Committee on Pets in Society), set up by the veterinarian Peter Mann and sponsored largely by the pet food industry, brought together the veterinary profession and the welfarists.[23] It quickly adopted the proposal of Ruth Plant and myself that the country's huge unwanted dog problem (and dog pollution problem) should be dealt with by raising the dog licence fee (for more than a century fixed at 37½p) and funding a statutory nationwide service of dog wardens trained to enforce the law and to educate the irresponsible dog-owner. JACOPIS, initially under the chairmanship of Lord Houghton and later Lord Listowel, was not a charity and so had the advantage of being able to act totally unfettered as a pressure group on the government. Houghton pressurized government direct and we had meetings with senior government ministers on several occasions, vainly urging our reforms.

The RSPCA also gave support to the Farm Animal Welfare Coordinating Executive (FAWCE) and the Committee for the Reform of Animal Experimentation (CRAE), both formed in 1977.[24] The latter, established by Lord Houghton, Clive Hollands and myself, had frequent meetings with officials and ministers (including Home Secretaries Merlyn Rees and William Whitelaw) in pursuit of our intention to reform the law controlling animal experimentation. For a few years, until the end of the decade, these three joint committees involved most of the leading campaigners and the major animal protection organizations in the country.

In other ways, too, the RSPCA reformers sought to make the society collaborate with other organizations and individuals travelling in the same direction. It gradually became a little more gracious towards other campaigners. Although the RSPCA had always been generous with awards to its own senior personnel, it had nothing to give to independent animal welfare workers. We managed to rectify this by creating two new top awards for this purpose in 1978 — the Richard Martin and Lord Erskine Awards — Lord Houghton becoming the first recipient of the former. We also created an RSPCA media award to recognize those reporters and television directors who had helped the cause.

Publicity and Pressure Group Activity

Having established policies, priorities, specific legislative goals, and the corresponding new committees and departments, the RSPCA reformers saw that it was necessary to help the society change gear, so that the new machinery could begin to work properly. This meant a creative use of the media, a revival of the society's nineteenth-century role as a proselytizing pressure group and, under David Paterson, the vigorous deployment and expansion of the society's Education Department. The reformers were also quick to initiate a 'consumerist' approach and Paterson was instructed to draw up a list of cruelty-free cosmetics which was made available to members.

The society's very bad publicity throughout the 1960s and early 1970s had compounded the council's natural fear of the media. By the time that Reform Group members arrived on the council in 1972 they found that the shutters were down; the council was attempting to keep all its deliberations secret. Almost every council document was labelled 'Strictly Confidential' and meetings were held in an aura of conspiratorial self-importance.

It was indeed difficult to persuade the society to regard the media not as the enemy but as potential allies in the campaign against cruelty. The appointment of creative press officers and the setting up of an appropriate committee were clearly necessary steps. Later, a staff Campaigns Department was established, and for a short while showed that a positive attitude towards publicity was far better than a purely defensive one.

Another major problem encountered by the more radical RSPCA council members was that many members of the council and staff opposed any approaches to government in the pursuit of legislative reform. Since the 1940s the society's role as a service charity, prosecuting cruelty cases and dealing with the nation's unwanted dogs and cats, had expanded, while its original role as political pressure group had fallen away to near zero. An ill-defined middle-class dislike of 'politics' was aggravated by the recent deliberately raised fear that the society's charitable status was at risk. In consequence, when I, as newly elected chairman, asked the council to approve my proposals that the society should lobby government in pursuit of its policies, I found it sometimes extremely difficult to carry the majority of the council; even correspondence with ministers was considered to be unacceptable.

The society continued to be cautious to an almost unbelievable degree.

Nevertheless, expansion of the legal staff (hitherto preoccupied with matters such as conveyancing of property) and the appointment of two staff to deal with parliamentary affairs and to lobby Parliament on the society's behalf, were eventually agreed, and, although still hotly opposed, the elementary principle was re-established that the RSPCA should strive for improved legislation. Expert legal and political committees were also set up to encourage a more imaginative prosecution policy and to help plan strategy in the political sphere; in January 1979 the RSPCA staff was persuaded to produce a list of specific legislative reforms sought by the RSPCA. This list cited some thirty amendments to existing legislation in addition to proposals for entirely new law. No doubt, if the reforming element had remained in control, an effective team could have been established to push forward these legislative proposals with greater urgency. But the ground had at least been prepared.

In 1976 we set up an inquiry into shooting and angling under the independent chairmanship of Lord Medway, the distinguished zoologist. His committee reviewed the latest evidence on the transmission of pain and concluded that it was reasonable to assume that all classes of vertebrate, including fish, were capable of suffering. This straightforward scientific finding helped to provide a firm foundation for the campaigns which followed.

The RSPCA was also pushed by the radical minority on its council into organizing an Animal Rights Conference at Trinity College, Cambridge, in 1977, which was attended by nearly all the key figures in the movement of that period, except Peter Singer, who compensated for his absence by writing a foreword to the published proceedings.[25]

The two-day meeting concluded when the Declaration Against Speciesism, which I had written, was signed by 150 people.[26] The Declaration went as follows:

A Declaration Against Speciesism

Inasmuch as we believe that there is ample evidence that many other species are capable of feeling, we condemn totally the infliction of suffering upon our brother and sister animals, and the curtailment of their enjoyment, unless it be necessary for their own individual benefit.

We do not accept that a difference in species alone (any more than a difference in race) can justify wanton exploitation or oppression in the name of science or sport, or for food, commercial profit or other human gain.

We believe in the evolutionary and moral kinship of all animals and we declare our belief that all sentient creatures have rights to life, liberty and the quest for happiness.

We call for the protection of these rights.

This declaration, youthful and idealistic in tone, became the basis for many subsequent charters ratified by local authorities in Britain.

The conference, instigated largely by Andrew Linzey and myself, was not only a novelty for the RSPCA, it was also the first serious conference ever held anywhere which was devoted entirely to the subject of animal rights, and I hope, the last such occasion at which meat was offered to those staying for lunch! RSPCA conferences followed shortly on animal experimentation (in London) and farm animal welfare (in Armsterdam).[27]

In 1978 another extraordinary event occurred. The council decided to stage an RSPCA march through Dover in protest against the cruel export of live food animals from British ports. This was probably the RSPCA's first, and so far only, official mass protest march, and involved over a thousand members of the society.

Our so-called SELFA campaign (Stop the Export of Live Food Animals) had started in 1974, and sought to replace the 'on the hoof' trade with one that was entirely 'on the hook'; it failed to achieve this end, but led to a tightening up of the rules under which animals were transported across Europe.

We met officials at the Ministry of Agriculture and with John Silkin himself, the Minister for Agriculture, in trying to achieve reform. But the power of the industry and its friends within the ministry proved too great, aided by the fact that the RSPCA's publicity campaign was vitiated by constant blimpish attacks from some of the society's own senior staff and council, who continued to feel that publicity and 'embroilment in politics' were somehow beneath the society's dignity. Furthermore, they failed to understand that the minister himself needed (and had privately requested) public pressure in order to overcome the resistance of his own officials; instead, some of our own staff publicly attacked me for unfairly pressurizing him!

The European Sphere

Another highly important step initiated by myself and the RSPCA reformers was the decision to enter the European arena. In 1978 'Mike' Seymour-Rouse was appointed the RSPCA's Director of European Liaison, and in an attempt to coordinate the principal welfare organizations within the EEC we formed a new federation under the title Eurogroup for Animal Welfare – later abbreviated simply to Eurogroup. Almost at once the constructive attitude of EEC officials in Brussels and the growing enthusiasm of members of the European Parliament in Strasbourg were evident, in welcome contrast to the negativity and red tape of Whitehall (see chapter 16). By the 1980s the European Commission was showing as much (or more) interest in animal welfare as in conservation.

International Co-operation

The RSPCA's contribution to the campaign against the killing of seals in Canada was also novel. After an approach from Brian Davies, the founder of the International Fund for Animal Welfare (IFAW), I had arranged in 1977 for the RSPCA to join the campaign on both sides of the Atlantic. In Canada, an RSPCA team comprising Richard Adams, Bill Jordan and Mike Seymour-Rouse undertook a gruelling lecture tour in oppositon to the hunt, and in Europe the RSPCA assisted the Fund in bringing pressure to bear on governments, culminating eventually in the ban of baby seal imports into the EEC in 1983 and its extension in 1985 (see chapter 12). Such an RSPCA campaign would have been unthinkable a few years earlier, demanding, as it did, co-operation with other bodies such as IFAW and Greenpeace, an international and political approach, and a concern for wild animals.

Scottish Seals

One of the most satisfactory campaigns of this period was that initiated by Greenpeace in 1978, when they sent a ship to oppose the killing of grey and common seals by Norwegian sealers off the coast of Scotland. This move created massive publicity during the summer period when news was scarce. Greenpeace, by positioning its personnel near the seals, forced the British government to order the Norwegians to delay the use of their rifles.

The next moves were made by IFAW and the RSPCA. The former placed whole-page advertisements in the British national newspapers depicting a young seal, and carrying the simple injunction 'Write to the Prime Minister'. The result was that James Callaghan received in one week some 17,000 letters opposing the seal hunt — more than any British prime minister had ever received before on a single topic.

Meanwhile, I took an RSPCA delegation to the Secretary of State for Scotland. At this meeting Bill Jordan, then the RSPCA's first Chief Wildlife Officer, produced scientific evidence which cast doubt on the government's estimates on the amount of fish predation by seals.

These three separate tactics were well timed. Shortly afterwards the government announced that the seal hunt had been called off. For another decade the British government refused to license a similar man-oeuvre, and since the government's own research by the Sea Mammal Research Unit eventually supported the RSPCA's view that seals were not responsible for declining fish stocks, the seals were left in relative peace for some years.

This operation usefully illustrates the mechanics of a successful cam-paign for which no single individual or organization can take total credit. Greenpeace had created the headline publicity; IFAW had mobil-ized its supporters to bombard the prime minister with letters; and the RSPCA had negotiated with the government directly, providing a science-based face-saver which allowed the minister off the hook. Surely, whenever ordinary diplomatic pressures fail to produce results, a good campaign requires these elements: co-operation among campaigning groups, publicity, the channelling of public opinion and negotiation at a high level. This was how the so-called RSPCA 'radicals' had always hoped to see the animal welfare movement operating.

The RSPCA's role was also significant as the parent society for numerous smaller, and on the whole rather conservatively minded, societies all over the world. In 1960 there had been 47 such affiliated societies overseas which, while remaining autonomous in terms of policies and finance, looked towards the RSPCA in England for support. By 1986 this number had grown to 128. Liaison of a less formal sort was maintained between RSPCA headquarters and some 300 other organizations. In addition, the RSPCA could claim three overseas branches, in Hong Kong, St Helena and Gibraltar.

The RSPCA, however, was to play little part in assisting Georges Heuse's unsuccessful efforts to create a United Nations convention in 1977 or in Bill Clark's International Committee for the Convention for the Protection of Animals which met in Geneva in July 1986; as far as Britain was concerned the main effort for this enterprise was left to John Alexander-Sinclair.

Putting Animals into Politics

The successful campaign to 'put animals into politics' (in Lord Houghton's words) aimed to persuade the major political parties in Britain, for the first time, to commit themselves in official policy to the welfare of animals. This idea was formulated by Houghton, Clive Hollands and myself in 1977 and grew out of our disillusionment with the tradition in British politics of leaving legislative reform in this field to the almost invariably frustrated efforts of individual back-bench MPs. Private members' Bills rarely achieved results, and we felt we had to upgrade the issue so that legislation would be introduced by governments themselves. We had had enough of the specious argument that such 'matters of conscience' should be shunned by government. Had politics sunk so low that British administrations no longer wished to concern themselves with moral issues?

Early in 1978 we set up a joint committee with this aim, entitled the General Election Co-ordinating Committee for Animal Protection (GECCAP). This venture followed the limited success of Animal Welfare Year in 1976; this had been organized by Clive Hollands, who had found it difficult to secure co-operation between the many animal welfare bodies he involved. After many resignations it fell to Hollands and myself to do a speaking tour of Britain in which some increase in public awareness of the major issues may have been achieved.

One of the hardest battles the radicals fought at this time was to persuade RSPCA council colleagues to agree the funding of the General Election Co-ordinating Committee for Animal Protection (GECCAP).

Once again the threat of loss of charitable status was raised by Frederick Burden MP, and the Charity Commissioners were contacted by those who feared this more politically effective animal welfare approach. In their annual report the following year, the Commissioners went so far as to name the RSPCA and to object to its funding of the GECCAP campaign; but by then the role and efficiency of the Charity Commission itself was under scrunity. Furthermore, the right of charities to pursue political action, provided it was relevant to their objectives but subsidiary to their main functions, was being widely advocated.

In the event, the GECCAP campaign was a success. We persuaded the Labour party to produce a policy background leaflet in July 1978 entitled 'Killing without Cruelty'. The Liberals took matters a step further by passing actual policy resolutions proposed by ex-party president, Basil Goldstone, and after approaches from Hollands and myself, the Scottish Nationalists also pledged their interest. Only the Conservative party hung back, and I was assigned the task of persuading them to join the rest; after approaches to William Whitelaw and the party's chairman, Lord Thorneycroft, assistance from the Earl of Selkirk, and a meeting with Conservative party officials, the Conservative Research Department promised to write a leaflet. This was not published, however, until September 1979 – six months after the general election.[28]

In April 1979 all the major parties – Liberal, Conservative and Labour – mentioned animal welfare in their election manifestos for the first time. GECCAP had asked the parties for policy under six headings reflecting the interests of the main constituent bodies on the joint committee – the protection of horses (especially in the meat trade), radical reforms in intensive animal husbandry (affecting pigs, veal calves, and battery chickens), the welfare of dogs (especially as regards the need for dog wardens), experiments on animals (such as the need to control the infliction of suffering, improve training and to restrict the use of animals for non-medical purposes), the protection of wildlife[29] (for example the banning of hare-coursing and otter-hunting), and the substitution of live food animal exports with a carcass-only trade. Although the response of the parties was rather piecemeal, both the Liberal and Labour parties endorsed the GECCAP suggestion that there should be a new permanent statutory animal protection body to monitor and co-ordinate the whole field and advise government on new legislation.[30]

After this, all the major parties continued to include animal protection in their official thinking, although Richard Sayer, the RSPCA Parliamentary Officer, was reporting by 1985 that the greatest grass-roots interest, as gauged by attendance at party conference meetings, was being shown by members of the Alliance parties (Liberal and SDP).[31] The Alliance too went ahead with detailed proposals from the SDP's Katya Lester on how to draw together the administration and enforcement of animal protection legislation under a united Animal Protection Commission rather like the Health and Safety Executive.[32]

REACTION: 1980–1983

Shortly before the 1979 election, the Prime Minister, James Callaghan, had written to me confirming his plan to set up a Council for Animal Welfare; after her victory, Mrs Thatcher, the new Prime Minister, sent a letter reassuring me of her intention to honour her party's manifesto pledges. Almost at once, in 1979, the Thatcher government announced the establishment of a Farm Animal Welfare Council (FAWC) to investigate and advise the Minister of Agriculture. The composition of this committee, however, immediately created alarm among the more go-ahead element on the RSPCA council because it contained a preponderance of those with commercial intersts in farming and the meat trade, one of whom was the director of a company recently convicted of cruelty. What had been hoped for was a committee reflecting a balanced composition between agricultural and welfare points of view. A section of the agricultural press was clearly delighted by 'the skilful way' in which the minister had 'spiked the welfarists' guns'.[33]

When the government proceeded to appoint two of the then top officials from the RSPCA, Julian Hopkins and Philip Brown (one of whom, Brown, accurately or not was suspected by some of having sympathetic connections with the agricultural industry) without even the knowledge, let alone approval, of the RSPCA council, a major row erupted. A narrow majority of the RSPCA council voted against allowing the officials to take their place on FAWC. Certain society members, some deliberately misinformed of the true nature of the dispute, reacted angrily, summoned an extraordinary general meeting early in 1980, and tried to expel from the society the eleven dissenters (who included two recent chairmen – Michael Kay and myself). Tempers were lost at the meeting in Central Hall which was attended by 1,600 members.[34] Two announced that they were factory farmers and proud of it, several proclaimed their membership of the National Farmers' Union and others, without any awareness of their absurdity, accused the dissenters of 'disrespect to one of Her Majesty's Ministers'.

The motion failed after a fierce debate.[35] Nevertheless, this meeting marked the commencement of another unhappy period in the society's history after five years of relative peace. The meeting had been advertised in hunting circles and readers of *Horse and Hound* had been urged to give up a day's hunting to rid the RSPCA of its 'anti element and political opportunists of the extreme left'.[36] Furthermore, most of the members attending this meeting were only partially informed of the facts; some had been carefully primed and organized by traditionalist members of the society's staff and few knew, for example, of Brown's threat to testify against the society if it proceeded in a case involving cruelty to zoo animals, or that following his clumsy and unauthorized killing of scores of cats rescued by the society from OLAC (a laboratory breeding business in Wales), the council was actually in the process of considering his dismissal as the society's Chief Veterinary Officer. Revealingly, perhaps, sections of the farming press[37] as well as that of the veterinary profession[38] continued to support Brown against the so-called 'militant' RSPCA council.

To many it appeared extraordinary that Peter Walker, then Agriculture Minister, could have appointed two members of the RSPCA staff to this committee without seeking the approval of the RSPCA's board, or that Hopkins and Brown could have accepted his offer without asking for such approval; both, in the event, ceased to be society employees within three years, one through ill health. Without any publicity, however, the government gradually improved the composition of FAWC over the ensuing months, and it went on to produce a succession of sensible proposals for reform, before having its composition again changed in the mid-1980s.

The reaction against the RSPCA reformers came principally from a handful of branch workers who feared that the rapid changes within the society would threaten its standing. Wild rumours were circulated, sometimes deliberately, to the effect that the younger group on the council was seeking to dismantle both the society's inspectorate and the branch system itself. In fact neither of these objectives ever had been considered and both would have been strongly opposed by most of the reformers. Some widening of the role of the inspectorate to cover the society's new priority areas had been discussed, and the much-maligned 'radicals', after consultations between myself and Mike Seymour-Rouse, had instigated in 1977 the 'plain clothes' undercover arm of the inspectorate, the Special Investigation Unit, which over the years was to do valuable work. But there had never been any wish to do away with inspectors, only to improve their training and to modernize their role. Nor had the disbandment of the branches ever been contemplated, only a development of the role of branch member to allow those who wanted to campaign to do so with the informal co-ordination and briefing of paid staff.

By 1979 the so-called 'radicals' could see that they had shaken the RSPCA from its slumbers. We had created written policies for the society and selected the priorities within them. We had set up expert committees within the new areas of priority and established new staff departments to service them. We had then sharpened the society's campaigning edge so as to put the new policies into effect through the use of political pressure, prosecution, increased educative effort and creative publicity. Furthermore, we had extended our range of operations into Europe and included an undercover element in our inspectorate. We had tried to build bridges, and if we had not always succeeded, at least channels of communication had been opened with government, with other campaigning bodies, and with the conservation movement, both nationally and internationally. All this had been achieved in the context of improved finance and growing membership.[39] Those who opposed us wished the society to continue its role as the nation's principal homer and destroyer of unwanted cats and dogs. Frequently they alluded to the past as support for their opposition to change, apparently ignorant of the society's original role as a reforming and proselytizing body and unaware that in the nineteenth century the RSPCA had shown very little interest in the fate of pet animals compared with its concern for the treatment of farm and laboratory species and wildlife.

In introducing considerable 'glasnost' and 'perestroika' into the society, we had ruffled too many feathers. Two editorials in the *Daily Telegraph*, a leading conservative national newspaper, outrageously asserted that the RSPCA had been deliberately infiltrated by extreme left-wing conspirators intent on using the society's prestige and funds for ulterior political purposes: 'Hunting, the fur trade and almost any sphere of activity related to animals can be used as a stick with which to beat the free society.'[40] The charge of 'Marxist infiltration' into animal welfare circles was repeated in a further editorial later in the month;[41] despite the editor's admission that the original leader has been 'opinionated' and the hysteria about 'reds under the bed' − a charge frequently flung at anyone who tried to change almost anything in post-war Britain − continued. Indeed an RSPCA council member on the BBC's major *Panorama* programme about the society went as far as to say that she thought some of the RSPCA reformers were part of a 'Communist' conspiracy![43] The old slur was resurrected that the reformers were not interested in nonhuman animals but in human revolutionary politics.

Financial Problems

In this sadly paranoid atmosphere, evidence began to come to light in 1980 that, under the new executive director (Major Ronald Seager had retired on health grounds in 1978 and his successor had been appointed shortly before Christmas of that year), the society's finances were deteriorating seriously. In 1978 and 1979 the society had enjoyed surpluses of approximately £1 million each year, but after 1980 these were turned into large deficits caused chiefly by the employment (unauthorized by the society's council) of an additional 200 staff, taken on between the autumn of 1979 and the end of 1980.

It was the much-maligned 'radicals' who had been the first to spot the trouble and to attempt to put it right. We had called for a special finance committee to be established early in 1980 and, when this had been blocked by traditionalists, we had proposed in April an independent investigation. This too had been overruled. On 21 September 1980 the *Sunday Telegraph* broke the news to the public − and to most shocked members of the RSPCA council as well − that the RSPCA was indeed

£1 million in the red. At about the same time allegations began to be circulated within the RSPCA council insinuating extravagance or worse on the part of one or two of the senior staff. Calls by the 'radicals' on the council to have these allegations independently and confidentially investigated were, however, angrily rejected.

Other channels were tried, and deputations of 'radicals' and concerned senior members vainly approached both the Charity Commissioners and the society's auditors for help. Not only were those who were trying to regularize the society's financial affairs repeatedly rebuffed; they were subjected to lawyers' letters threatening libel action on behalf of senior staff and by official moves, in some cases successful, to have them expelled from the society. Indeed, the pilloried would-be saviours of the society's finances were obliged to employ the services of the distinguished lawyer Sir David Napley to defend their positions.[44] The dismal row rumbled on until March 1982, when the results of investigations by the society's able new treasurer, Rachel Smith, were announced to the council, and the society's executive director and finance controller immediately left the society's employment.

One of the sad aspects of this affair is that had the warnings of the radicals been heeded when they had first been raised, the society could have avoided over two years of bad publicity and saved itself many hundreds of thousands of pounds. Instead, two out of four of the key 'whistle-blowers' in this row were ignominiously forced out of the society. Even after they were proved to have been absolutely right about the mismanagement of the society's finances, they received neither apology nor thanks. On 29 September 1982, Richard Adams had been forced to resign as the society's president, supported by the vice-presidents Lord Houghton, Lady Dowding and Clive Hollands who issued a public statement critical of the society's 'institutional lethargy' and of its unfriendliness 'towards the increasing number of younger members who demand more vigorous action against the growing commercial exploitation of animals'; all had supported the reformers' call for an investigation of the society's finances.

It was perhaps because the row over finances had been seen as a clash between radicals and traditionalists that it had taken an unnecessarily long time to resolve. If the so-called traditionalists themselves had called for the inquiries in the first place the matter might have been over in a few weeks.

Not until Rachel Smith became council chairman in June 1983 did the grievous wounds within the society begin to heal and the factions within its council begin to blur. Although not one of the 'radicals', Smith could see the merit in some of their concerns. Late in the day, the finances at last were overhauled, and gradually the society was put back on the more progressive course it had been on since the mid-1970s. This process was very much assisted by the appointment of Frank Dixon Ward as the society's temporary executive director late in the summer of 1982. A recently retired chief executive in local government, Dixon Ward proved a sound administrator and one who took for granted the reformers' hard-fought-for redefinition of the society's role as being, in part, that of a campaigning pressure group seeking new and improved legislation.

COMING TOGETHER AGAIN: 1983–1989

To what extent was the 'Great RSPCA Row' of 1980–3 of any real significance? In some respects – incompetent management, almost incredible resistance to change, unionization, over-manning and bureaucratic lethargy – the society had been a microcosm of some of the problems of British society in general.

In the event, the society's large deficits had forced the axing of its new Campaigns Department, the reduction of its newly appointed parliamentary staff to one, and the decimation of its once-vigorous Education Department. As usual in such situations it was the new small departments which suffered proportionately more than the old and inflated ones. By the end of 1982 over 170 jobs had gone and the RSPCA's inspectorate training college was up for sale. Under Rachel Smith such necessary cuts were not used to return the society to its uninspiring role of the 1940s and 1950s. Gradually, the more modern aspects were reinstated and, although the few remaining 'radicals' were firmly kept out of office, their theories of the late 1970s were reapplied. They had, in effect, lost the battle of personalities but won the war of ideas, and had succeeded in dragging the RSPCA, yelping and caterwauling, into the twentieth century.

In general, subsequent events proved the reformers right on all issues of substance, but we had made serious mistakes of style and tactics. Sometimes we had appeared arrogant and confrontational, and we had not explained sufficiently to branch members what it was that we were trying to do. Acting under the constraint of a two-year limit to my term of office as chairman, I had tried to go too far too fast, stirring up resentment among the traditional and unsettling many with the literally scores of innovative motions put before council. Furthermore, the reformers had agreed to several unfortunate appointments among senior staff, including those of the two senior staff members who subsequently had to leave.

The crippling internecine warfare within the RSPCA must have delighted many exploiters of animals who, a year or two earlier, had been worried by the society's more incisive approach. Despite all its bad publicity in the 1960s, early 1970s and early 1980s, however, the RSPCA would emerge in the mid-1980s as still the most potentially influential animal welfare society in the world, with over 600 employees, substantial liquid assets and an income of over £18 million in 1987.[46]

Although recovering its performance under Smith and Dixon Ward, the society sometimes continued at odds, however, with the wishes of members attending its AGMs, most of whom wanted a still more vigorous approach. Furthermore, they could point to the fact that, despite the redefinition of the role of the society, still only about 2 per cent of its expenditure was earmarked specifically for the welfare of the hundreds of millions of farm, laboratory and wild animals – three out of four of its main areas of concern. Nevertheless a series of BBC documentaries about the inspectorate, entitled *Animal Squad* and shown in 1986 and 1987, helped considerably to raise public awareness of the superb routine work done by this arm of the RSPCA, and some of the society's younger staff showed themselves to be vigorous and effective campaigners with a modern outlook.[47] Sadly, such able staff rarely continued long enough in the society's employ.

At its annual meeting in 1986 the members threw out an attempt to increase branch representation on the council (which would have reduced still further the influence of the younger and more go-ahead members) and reinstated the reformers' previous council commitment to phasing out the killing of healthy dogs by 1996. Furthermore, the membership reaffirmed its dislike of the government's new Animal (Scientific Procedures) Act.

By 1987 the society was getting to grips with two major issues: the need to extend the law to cover psychological suffering as well as physical pain, and the desperate need to begin to extend protection against cruelty to animals in the wild. These were among its aims published before the general election of 1987. Others included improving the availability of search warrants, increased fines for dog-fighting and baiting of all sorts, the power to remove any cruelly treated animal from its owner on first conviction, the financing of a national dog warden service, universally effective pre-stunning of all animals in slaughter – including ritual slaughter – the banning of pig stalls, veal crates and hen batteries, the banning of live export of food animals across the sea, and of cruel horse-tethering and the use of snares.

The council's chairman from 1986 to 1988, Joan Felthouse, brought tremendous energy to the job, and the society's new executive director, Andrew Richmond, set about the improvement of its regional structure. Together they began to expand its effectiveness not only as a modern service charity but also as a campaigning organization in accordance with the original vision of its vigorous founders over 160 years before. These improvements continued to be marred, however, by occasional disturbances, as when, for example, in November 1988, a majority of the council ordered the expulsion of five active members of the society on the grounds that they had circulated criticisms of the society's work. This self-styled RSPCA Watchdog group, whose avowed aim was to improve the RSPCA's performance, comprised Margaret House, Richard Farhull, Joan Watson (recently elected to the society's council by the membership), and the two outstanding animal welfare campaigners David Wetton and Angela Walder. These expulsions created bad publicity for the society and illustrated once again the society's failure to deal with criticism in a constructive and democratic way.[48]

VETERINARY INVOLVEMENT

One of the saddest aspects of the worldwide campaign for animal protection has been the part played – or not played – by the veterinary profession. Widely seen by members of the public as being interested in the welfare of animals, with a few glorious exceptions vets have been distinguished by their absence from the great campaigns of the last two hundred years.

Attempts to secure the open support of the veterinary authorities in Britain for RSPCA campaigns in the late 1970s were met with prevarication. The president of one august body explained that such were the vested interests of his members that if he publicly criticized bloodsports or cosmetics experiments on animals or factory-farming he would immediately cease to be president.[49] Another distinguished veterinarian explained that, although veterinary students were sometimes 'starry-eyed animal lovers', such 'sentimentality was soon knocked out of them' by their teachers in preparation for their future roles.[50]

In Britain, members of the Royal College of Veterinary Surgeons make a solemn declaration of loyalty to the college, adding: 'I further promise that I will pursue the work of my profession with uprightness of conduct and that my constant endeavour will be to ensure the welfare of animals committed to my care.'[51] Despite this promise cases have arisen in which veterinary surgeons have been closely involved in practices widely disapproved of in animal welfare circles. A member of the Royal College, for example, published a paper describing how he had repeatedly poured weedkiller down the throats of beagle dogs. After passing blood-streaked faeces and vomiting, several dogs died after days of continued poisoning. Post-mortem examination found that the blood was 'dark chocolate brown' and that the mucous membranes had turned blue.

Even if this research, carried out at a commercial testing establishment, had been for the benefit of veterinary medicine (and nowhere in the paper is this claimed), it is a horrific experiment and it is difficult to see how slowly poisoning dogs to death can be consistent with the oath.[52]

It is, perhaps, hardly surprising that, after the appointment of a harecourser as the president of Britain's top veterinary body in 1987,[53] some members of the profession have begun to come in for more criticism. Clive Hollands, addressing a British Veterinary Association Congress at Warwick in September 1987, attacked the lack of protest against cruel experimentation from the veterinary profession, their policy of not reporting clients suspected of being involved in organized dog-fighting, and their ambivalent attitude towards the animal welfare movement.[54] Hollands quoted a veterinarian's letter in the national press: 'We vets view the animal welfare/conservationist lobby as motivated by sinister, political, anti-British organisations'[55] and a statement by a veterinary surgeon attending a meeting with local council officials in 1987 to discuss spaying clinics: 'We are in it to make money not provide a social service.'

Reassuringly, Hollands also cited some positive statements of veterinarians, suggesting a growing criticism of their own profession,[56] such as Professor John Webster's statement that 'It was important for practitioners to question their motivation for practice. Were they achieving the right balance between animal welfare and a desire for an adequate income?'[57] In America, vets Neil Wolff and Ned Buyukmichi went further and founded an Association of Veterinarians for Animal Rights.

In April 1988 the columnist Celia Haddon in the *Sunday Telegraph* (17 April 1988) expressed surprise that although 'On television, vets are handsome, cuddly men with a warm, caring attitude towards animals', yet some in reality cut the tails off dogs, work in factory-farms or block the solution of the unwanted dogs and cats problem. She quoted Bill Jordan, himself a veterinarian, as saying that 'their feelings for animals get devalued by too great an interest in science...as science grows so beauty dwindles.'

Perhaps it was the report in June 1988 that 'canned safaris' in Texas, in which clients can shoot caged lions for 2,500 dollars a time, were being run by an American veterinary surgeon[58] which prompted a tirade from Angela Walder at the RSPCA's AGM a few days later, in which she attacked those vets who commercially breed animals for research, carry out experiments on nonhuman primates, block the setting up of cheap neutering clinics, or who are 'more in love with their bank managers than with their animal clients'.[59]

Many veterinary practitioners are indeed caring and conscientious professionals. But if one applies the 'human test' to the actions of certain other members of the veterinary profession – those who breed laboratory animals, experiment on dogs or course hares, for example – then the results are, to say the least, highly disturbing. Imagine the public reaction if members of the *medical* profession were found similarly exploiting their *human* patients.

GROWING SUPPORT

Writing in the *New Statesman*, Jolyon Jenkins remarked in 1986:

Animal rights have probably entered the popular consciousness. According to the most recent poll (Gallup 1985), nearly 1.5 million people have given up meat, though only half for 'moral' reasons – an increase of 23 per cent over the previous year. More specifically, animal liberation is arguably the youth movement of the 80's. Magazines as diverse as *Just Seventeen* and *Class War* discuss it, and a host of rock stars and youth cult figures have announced that they have become vegetarians for moral reasons. The trend has been most marked in women between 16 and 24, 10 per cent of whom are now vegetarians.[60]

Indeed, the extent of support from the contemporary well-known is itself an interesting feature of the movement.[61]

Film-makers, too, have absorbed and strongly reinforced the animal liberation ethic, notably with Franklin J. Schaffner's *Planet of the Apes* series in the 1960s which showed nonhumans experimenting upon humans, Steven Spielberg's *E.T.* (1983), Hugh Hudson's *Greystoke* (1984) and Alan Bridges' screening of Isobel Colgate's 1980 novel *The Shooting Party* (1985) – all brilliant films in their own distinct ways.[62]

Desmond Morris's *The Naked Ape*, published in 1968, was, I believe, a turning-point. Scientific, creative and exciting, it brought home to many the simple reminder that we are animals. The Darwinian message, almost universally accepted on an intellectual level and almost as universally rejected emotionally, morally and politically, began to be driven home. How far Morris's reminder played a part in the formation of the Oxford Group is hard to say; it was not overt or recognized at the time. Yet *The Naked Ape* helped us to face up to our animality and its moral implications.[63] Richard North's *The Animal Report* (Penguin 1983) and Maureen Duffy's *Men and Beasts* (Paladin 1984) have provided very worthwhile documentary comments upon the movement and helped the subject to gain a permanent intellectual standing.

In the 1970s and 1980s British and American academic works began to appear which took into account the welfare of nonhuman animals,[64] the animal liberation movement spawned its own magazines,[65] and serious programmes on British television and radio devoted a good deal of attention to animal liberation in the period 1975–84;[66] in the late 1980s wildlife programmes showing concern for welfare as well as conservation appeared.

EPILOGUE

This chapter has concentrated on the *political* developments of the 1970s and the revival of the RSPCA – still the colossus which dominates the animal welfare scene in Britain and, to an extent, internationally. Much else happened in the 1970s and early 1980s.[67] The seventies saw the philosophical revival (see chapters 1 and 17); the growth in direct action both legal and illegal[68] (see chapters 12 and 15); far more effective political lobbying (see chapters 12, 13, 16 and 17); and the increasing internationalism of the movement (see chapters 10, 12, 16, and 17), all of great importance to the history of the period. Lively new groups, too, were established; for example Animal Liberation in Australia (see chapter 16) and People for the Ethical Treatment of Animals (PETA) in America (see chapter 16). In the UK existing groups such as the British Union for the Abolition of Vivisection and the National Anti-Vivisection Society were revived (see chapter 13), as were the Scottish Society for the Prevention of Vivisection and the League Against Cruel Sports (see chapters 11 and 12). New bodies were founded, such as Compassion in World Farming (see chapter 14), the Hunt Saboteurs Association, the Animal Liberation Front (see chapter 15), and Coordinating Animal Welfare. One of the most charismatic was Animal Aid, founded by Jean Pink in the 1970s, which captured the imagination of the young and radical and spread the word. By 1986 it could claim some 12,000 members under the leadership of John Bryant and Mark Gold.

The 1970s had been a remarkable decade, but in Britain at least the 1980s started badly. The government of Margaret Thatcher did not show an interest in 'green' issues, and resisted almost all radical proposals for reform in animal protection.[69] Yet as the 1990s approached, an underlying mood of optimism in the movement began to be felt again and the summer of 1988 turned out to be highly significant for the whole 'green' movement. Much publicity was given to the attempts to dump in Britain toxic waste sent from Italy in the ship *Karin B*, to artificially caused floods in Bangladesh, human starvation in the Sudan and the plight of thousands of seals dying of a viral infection in the North Sea. Shortly before the September 1988 conference of the Social and Liberal Democrats and the address from their new leader, one of the 'greenest' of Britain's leading politicians, Paddy Ashdown, the Prime Minister herself announced a complete change in the British government's attitude to the environment generally; Britain would, in the future, she said, strive to protect the planet from pollution.[70] Three weeks later, the predicament of three grey whales trapped by Arctic ice in Alaska brought a pledge of unlimited help from President Reagan,[71] and, under the spotlight of the international media, the rescue of two of them was achieved after a symbolic joint operation by Americans and Russians.

At their conference in March 1989 the Social and Liberal Democrats passed a comprehensive animal rights policy resolution. British media attention to all green issues (especially the problems of air and water pollution, acid rain, the 'greenhouse effect', and threats to rain-forests, the ozone layer and the survival of the African elephant) increased sharply during the year.

12 The Protection of Wildlife

From the mid-nineteenth century, naturalists had joined in the successful campaigns to protect wild birds and other species, and the first international treaty to protect wildlife, which was to protect salmon in the Rhine basin, was signed in 1886 by Germany, Switzerland, the Netherlands, and Luxembourg. This foreshadowed the plethora of national, EEC and international conservation regulations in force a century later. In general, however, wild animals remained unprotected from acts of cruelty, and in Britain they continue to be excluded from the basic anti-cruelty legislation to this day. Any protection that wildlife has gained over the centuries has been derived principally from the desire to preserve species from extinction or to protect local wildlife populations in order to continue their commercial or sporting exploitation.

Undoubtedly the conservation of wildlife has progressed more rapidly than its protection from cruelty; the concern for the species rather than the individual has been dominant. This has led to occasional clashes between conservationists and animal welfarists particularly in America. It is, however, precisely because powerful scientific, agricultural, commercial and sporting interests have backed the conservation movement that progress has been made, often against opposition from the more ruthless and less far-sighted elements of the same interest groups.

By the nineteenth century Western societies could feel that the ancient war against the animal kingdom had been won. Those Europeans who insisted on continuing it took their elephant and tiger guns to India or Africa in pursuit of quarry which was fierce enough to lend conviction to their warrior fantasies. Living up to the St George ideal, the defender of weak humanity against the dragon-like threats of the animal kingdom, remained a powerful dream. But the awareness that in most Western countries the victory had been won long since allowed the conservation movement to flourish.

EARLY CONSERVATION

For centuries there had been glimmerings of interest in conservation. The Pharaoh Akhenaten of Egypt, for example, had set aside land as a nature reserve as early as 1370 BC, and in the third century BC the Emperor Asoka in India had issued a decree prohibiting the killing of 'parrots, mynas, the aruna, ruddy geese, wild geese, the nandimukha, cranes, bats, queen ants, terrapins, boneless fish, rhinoceroses and all quadrupeds which are not useful or edible'.[1]

In Europe, game laws protected certain species against poachers and in England from Norman times strict laws were passed, limiting the killing of game to huntsmen of an elevated social class. From the thirteenth century onwards there had been attempts to establish 'closed' seasons in order to encourage the breeding of game species such as hares, otters, deer, hawks, wildfowl, salmon, and even foxes, and by 1773 the shooting seasons for game birds were established in their modern form. Closed seasons for deer were well established in America by the time of the Revolution.

In England and America most of these early conservation efforts were clearly motivated by human self-interest. They were designed simply to improve sport by creating artificially high populations of game species. Seventeenth-century objections to the draining of the Fens were similarly inspired. True, there had been some seventeenth-century theological concern over whether 'if it were possible for man to do so, it were lawful for him to destroy any one species of God's creatures...'[2] Here again, however, the concern was for God and not for the creature itself.

Early efforts at less selfish conservation in Britain can be found from the late eighteenth century onwards. An example was the preacher Rowland Hill, who built 'a place of retirement' for the toads in his garden, calling it his 'toadery'. Almost at once the conservationists found themselves up against the farmers and sportsmen whose aim it was to destroy creatures competing with their interest, whether 'weeds' or 'pests'. Epitomizing this conflict, the fourth Duke of Marlborough forbade his servants to disturb the birds nesting in his shrubberies at Blenheim, although they might kill them if they flew over the wall into the kitchen garden.[3]

Only gradually did people become aware that humankind itself was responsible for the demise of other species.

EXTINCTION

For centuries humankind has been obliterating species, and since the year 1600 over 350 species and subspecies of birds and mammals have disappeared for ever. Particularly vulnerable have been the huge and the amiable. Friendly birds such as the great awk and giants such as the

Maltese vulture, the elephant bird of Madagascar, the teratorn of North America and the twelve foot-high moa of New Zealand have all been dispatched into oblivion by Homo Sapiens, as have the giant beavers, camels, bisons and sloths.[4] When men and women have populated new areas those creatures, such as some in the Antarctic today, unwise enough not to fear them have soon perished.

At least three fascinating and friendly species of marine mammal have recently become extinct: the sea mink (in about 1880), the Caribbean monk seal (since about 1962) and the Steller's sea cow (since 1768). Steller recorded the huge sea cow as displaying 'signs of a wonderful intelligence, indeed, an uncommon love for one another, which extended so far that when one of them was hooked, all the others were intent upon saving it.'[5] The Caribbean monk seal was noted for its apparent affection for humans, which made it an easy prey; Columbus's crew slaughtered eight of them for food in 1494. The precedents give cause for concern for whales, dolphins, elephants and other amiable giants.

ZOOLOGICAL AND PRESERVATION SOCIETIES

In 1826 Sir Stamford Raffles and Sir Humphrey Davy founded the Zoological Society of London, which led to the opening of the Zoological Gardens in Regent's Park in the following year. But they did so with purely scientific objects in mind. Little hint of conservationism entered into the deliberations of the zoo authorities for another century, until Whipsnade Zoo was opened in 1931. Yet in 1869 an Act to preserve sea birds was passed in Britain and in 1872 the US Congress established the first national park at Yellowstone for the enjoyment of future generations. In 1889 the Society for the Protection of Birds was started, and in 1900 Britain, France, Spain, Portugal, Germany, Italy and the Belgian Congo signed in London the Convention for the Preservation of Animals, Birds and Fish in Africa, to curb the wholesale massacre of African game.

Then, in 1903 the Society for the Preservation of the Wild Fauna of the Empire was founded by Edward North Buxton, later becoming the Fauna Preservation Society, its main aims being to preserve wildlife populations throughout the world, with a particular emphasis on species in danger of extinction. Taking a leaf out of the RSPCA's book, Buxton had invited men of the greatest eminence into his society, including game hunters such as President 'Teddy' Roosevelt; partly as a result of work by the society agreement was reached in 1911 between the USA, Britain, Russia and Japan to restrict the killing of sea otters and certain species of seal.

In 1912 Charles Rothschild founded the Society for the Promotion of Nature Reserves in London. This eventually became the Royal Society for Nature Conservation (1981) and was one of the first bodies to emphasize the importance of preserving habitats for wildlife. In 1977 the

Prince of Wales became the society's first patron and during the 1980s Sir David Attenborough was its chairman.

In 1922, the International Committee for Bird Preservation was founded and, in 1926, the British environmental movement had taken a further step forward with the foundation of the Council for the Preservation of Rural England, although the council was more concerned with beautiful landscape than with wildlife. Indeed this dichotomy between landscape and wildlife, between aesthetic and other criteria, looms large in the British conservation tradition. Nature protection was made the responsibility of the official Nature Conservancy[6] under the National Parks and Access to the Countryside Act 1949, which also gave the Nature Conservancy the power to designate a site 'of Special Scientific Interest' (SSSI) by virtue of its 'flora, fauna, or geological' features. So the test of virtue was clearly whether the fauna were of interest to human science. On the other hand, the responsibility for designating national parks and areas of outstanding natural beauty was given to another agency, the Countryside Commission, set up under the Countryside Act of 1968 to replace the National Parks Commission and to oversee landscape conservation and recreation activities over the whole national countryside.

In the 1930s and 1940s the Universities Federation for Animal Welfare, the British Ecological Society and individuals such as Dr Charles Elton had pressed for government involvement in the conservation of wildlife. This campaign had borne fruit with the establishment of the Nature Conservancy in 1949.[7] The rapid increase in public support for the conservation ethic came after the Second World War, and it accelerated a decade or more earlier than the revolution in attitudes towards animal rights. It also had been, to a large extent, an Anglo-American inspired movement.[8]

In 1946 the International Whaling Commission was set up to advise whaling nations on conservation measures, and forty years later it had all but brought the whaling industry to a halt. In the same year, Peter Scott founded the Wildfowl Trust at Slimbridge to study and conserve the waterfowl of the world, and in 1948 British and Swiss naturalists joined in setting up the International Union for the Protection of Nature; largely the brainchild of Sir Julian Huxley, unlike his grandfather T. H. Huxley a strong advocate of partnership between human and nonhuman; two years later it became the International Union for Conservation of Nature and Natural Resources (IUCN) and was based in Switzerland. IUCN (or the World Conservation Union) has many governmental and non-governmental organizations as members and its Red Data books list plant and animal species under threat.

In its early years the Union languished through lack of funds and, in order to improve its finances, Guy Mountfort, Max Nicholson, Scott, Huxley and others set up the World Wildlife Fund in 1961, with Ian Macphail as its first Campaigns Director. Within a matter of weeks the

Fund had gained public support from Prince Philip and Prince Bernhard of the Netherlands, as part of Scott's deliberate policy to involve the leaders of society.

The launch of the World Wildlife Fund (now named the Worldwide Fund for Nature) received massive publicity and began rapidly to increase public awareness of conservation issues. Of all the conservation bodies established at that period, the Fund proved to be by far the most effective in wooing the international media and in making world opinion conscious for the first time of the threat of extinction. For example Macphail, given an almost free editorial hand by Hugh Cudlipp of the *Daily Mirror*, launched an edition on 9 October 1961 with seven pages devoted entirely to wildlife conservation.

Although the Fund itself remained a 'top people's' organization it managed to communicate quite effectively with the masses. No longer was conservation an idea circulating only among an elite. From the early 1960s wildlife programmes on British television by Armand and Michaela Denis, David Attenborough, Gerald and Jacqui Durrell, Sir Peter Scott and, later, Tony Soper, accelerated the process of dissemination. Kenneth Alsop, too, one of Britain's leading television journalists, took up the cause of wildlife protection in the early 1970s, shortly before his untimely death.

ECOLOGY AND ETHOLOGY

In 1962 Rachel Carson published her powerful book *Silent Spring*, a timely warning of human damage to the environment. Prince Bernhard and Ian Macphail, visiting President J. F. Kennedy the following year, found him influenced by Carson's predictions and prepared to set in train events which led eventually to the Washington Convention and the US Marine Mammal Act of 1972.[9] Environmental disasters, such as the wreck of the oil tanker *Torrey Canyon* in 1967 and the Minamata mercury poisonings in Japan, forced the threat of pollution into public awareness. In 1970 the Council of Europe announced European Conservation Year; in Britain a standing Royal Commission on Environmental Pollution was set up, and a major government department was renamed the Department of the Environment.

Since the Second World War ethology — the study of the behaviour of animals in the wild — had gained popularity through the writings of Konrad Lorenz and Niko Tinbergen. Concepts such as territoriality, imprinting, pecking order and displacement behaviour became common currency in Europe and America and helped to link the behaviour of human and nonhuman animals. Later studies, in the 1960s by Jane Goodall and George Schaller,[10] increased general awareness of the closeness to human behaviour of our primate cousins, the chimpanzee and the gorilla.

Still, however, the emphasis of conservation was upon the saving of species from extinction rather than a campaign to protect individuals from cruelty. The usual justifications for conservation were that the extinction of a species would permanently reduce the richness and variety of the world experience, or that it would have some other knock-on effects deleterious for the human race. Thus the three usual arguments for conservation, that it produces advantages which are commercial, aesthetic or ecological, are all ultimately anthropocentric. Species should be saved for their benefits to science or for the enjoyment of humankind generally — 'for the sake of our children'.

The compassionate motive for conservation, although probably implicit for many decades, has been overtly admitted only in recent years, and logically leads to animal welfare — that is to say a frank concern for the individual's suffering rather than the survival of a whole species. Whereas most of the earlier conservation organizations justified their work in terms of human benefit, later ones, such as The People's Trust for Endangered Species headed by Bill Jordan, as well as the International Fund for Animal Welfare, openly stated their humane premises.

On the twenty-fifth anniversary of the World Wildlife Fund in 1986, Sir Peter Scott portrayed conservation as a way of protecting 'the life support system of the planet'.[11] This was more the language of ecology. Indeed ecologists had for years been interested in this perspective. For them, the survival of individuals, and even species, was more or less incidental to the health of the whole biosphere and to allowing 'Spaceship Earth' a free passage in the universe.

In America the Sierra Club had been founded on these principles, and in Europe the Club of Rome alerted many to the dangers of human over-population and the exploitation of the planet. Typically, those Europeans who wanted action turned to politics and, in Germany, the Green party began an ascent which, under Petra Kelly in the late 1970s, led to the election of 'green' politicians and a strong ecological influence over ensuing German governments.

In Britain, inspired by the writings of Paul Ehrlich and by Edward Goldsmith's *Blueprint for Survival*, Anthony and Lesley Whittaker, together with Michael Benfield and Freda Sanders, founded the British Ecology party in January 1973. Significantly, it was initially named 'People', but became in 1986 the Green party whose leading spokesperson was Jonathon Porritt. By this time, indeed from 1969 onwards, the British Liberal party had evolved its own 'green' policies in some detail, as also, but to a lesser extent, had the Labour party.

Ecologists sometimes saw themselves as taking a more global and long-term view than the conservationists, emphasizing the interconnectedness of biological and physical systems. Their ultimate aim was not always well defined, sometimes stressing the integrity of the planet *per se*, at others seeing this as a means towards human advantage, emphasizing the need to safeguard wildlife for future generations. Neither conservationists nor ecologists typically saw sentience as being of prime importance; it was the quality of human life which was their main concern.

CONSERVATION OR WELFARE

Ian Macphail of the World Wildlife Fund was never of this anthropocentric school, and he opened negotiations with the RSPCA in 1961 with a view to forming a liaison which would embrace not only conservation but also the protection of wildlife for its own sake; encouraging early progress, however, was halted by the death of RSPCA secretary John Hall. For a decade the RSPCA's interest in wildlife subsided and in Britain it was left to the Hunt Saboteurs to lead the fight, albeit on a narrow front, against the unnecessary sufferings of wild creatures. It was not until ten years later that the RSPCA established its Wildlife Advisory Committee and, under the influence of its more radical members, re-opened friendly communications with the World Wildlife Fund and the new, less elitist, conservationists of Friends of the Earth and Greenpeace (see p. 230). Although the emphasis upon animal protection displayed by Greenpeace varied from one country to another, by 1988 Greenpeace's involvement in this field was strong. Nearly one third of British *Greenpeace News* of May 1988, for example, was taken up by animal issues ranging from whales to kangaroos, seals and lizards.

The difference in emphasis between conservation and welfare would still cause occasional comment: 'I would rather that there were no rabbits at all left in the world than that one of them should be subjected to unnecessary cruelty', said Celia Hammond in 1978, and in 1988 the Royal Society for the Protection of Birds and the Nature Conservancy Council publicly clashed with the Hunt Saboteurs Association after members of the latter organization had interfered with the annual massacre of grouse on the 'Glorious Twelfth' of August. If the moors of northern Britain were not managed for shooting purposes, so the conservationists argued, 'their unique habitats would be lost'.[12] The Hunt Saboteurs and the League Against Cruel Sports replied that the moors had been turned into a 'wilderness denuded of most other wildlife' in order to promote 'Britain's snobbiest sport'. Some gamekeepers, they claimed, poisoned and shot any species which threatened the grouse, including foxes, crows, hawks, and even eagles.

Yet, in the same year, Greenpeace and the RSPCA jointly financed and staffed the establishment of a rescue centre to help hundreds of common and grey seals afflicted by a viral epidemic in the North Sea.

CITES AND OTHER LEGISLATION

A major wildlife conservation achievement was the passage of the Convention on International Trade in Endangered Species of Wild Fauna and Flora (CITES) signed in Washington on 6 March 1973, after a campaign in which IUCN played a prominent role. Twenty-one states signed CITES initially and by 1985 the number had risen to eighty-seven. Bill Jordan, the RSPCA's Chief Wildlife Officer, with support from Peter Scott, wrote the important guidelines on the transport of wildlife which were incorporated in the convention despite opposition from the International Air Transport Association. Although couched in conservation terms, these are in reality based on welfare principles.

The convention is probably the best enforced of all conservation treaties and regulates international trade in wild fauna and flora listed in its appendices. Species deemed to be threatened with extinction are listed in Appendix I; species whose survival is not yet threatened, but may become so, are listed in Appendix II. The convention prohibits international trade in all Appendix species except under permit from the state management authorities. The convention is overseen by a Secretariat in Switzerland, and the parties meet every two years to review the implementation of the convention and make recommendations. Of course, widespread breaches of the convention still occur, as for example in the shipment of at least 50,000 prohibited skins into Europe from South America annually; these usually end up in Germany where they are used by the fur trade.

British governments have done reasonably well in keeping up with the internationally rapid progress in conservation, and the export or import of almost any wild animal requires a Department of the Environment licence under the Endangered Species (Import and Export) Act of 1976. Other countries, however, have done very much better. Denmark, for example, under its Conservation of Nature Act of 1969, provides highly effective wildlife and habitat protection. Spain, Portugal, Italy and Greece, on the other hand, have very little legislation and, except in small reservations, run usually by private organizations, wildlife is at the mercy of the human predator. In Italy, for example, there is no national legislation protecting endangered habitats[13] and many southern European states ignore the Berne Convention (see below) to which they are parties. Once again we see the division between the north and south of the continent on matters affecting the relationship between human and nonhuman beings.

A further major achievement by the international conservation lobby was the Convention on the Conservation of European Wildlife and Natural Habitats (the so-called 'Berne Convention') which was drawn up in September of 1979 following an instruction from the Council of Europe's Committee of Ministers. Its aims are to conserve listed wild flora and fauna and their natural habitats. The convention came into force in 1982, and the EEC and thirteen states had signed and ratified it by 1985. Like CITES, the convention is policed by a secretariat (under the Council of Europe), holds regular meetings (annually) and has provisions which are strictly mandatory.

In Britain the Wildlife and Countryside Act was passed in 1981 and gave powers to the Nature Conservancy Council to protect designated habitats. Some of its worst loopholes were plugged by David Clark's amendments of 1985, but the Act still offered no real protection to wild animals. Indeed it is worth noting that all these pieces of legislation had a conservation objective and were not intended to protect wild animals from suffering, although sometimes they had such an effect incidentally which was to be welcomed. Welfare spin-offs were always to be savoured, like crumbs from the table. But where was the legislation purpose-built to save wildlife from cruelty?

Even the Badgers Act of 1973, laboured over by Lord Arran and Peter Hardy MP, did not stop the British Ministry of Agriculture, with powers of compulsory entry on to private land, torturously poisoning to death thousands of badgers in the 1970s and 1980s on the merest suspicion that they might be infected with tuberculosis and on the hunch that badgers spread this condition to cattle; few glimmerings of interest in animal welfare or rights had ever emanated from that mercenary ministry. All over the country individuals like Ruth Murray, Brenda Charlesworth and John Bainbridge strove to protect badgers from their persecutors. People have always sought scapegoats for blighted crops and ailing cattle. Once such ills were blamed upon witches; in the 1970s upon badgers.

The Dangerous Wild Animals Act of 1976 which severely restricted the keeping of large exotic wild animals as pets in Britain is a further example of legislation which does not openly admit any welfare objective. No British government, it seems, dares to admit that it takes the welfare of wild animals in the slightest degree seriously. Yet this Act has saved many animals from miserable lives locked in garages or confined in small cages. Furthermore, it has allowed the RSPCA to put a stop to the use of monkeys by street photographers.

THE ROLE OF THE RSPCA

The RSPCA's role in the protection of wildlife expanded rapidly after the establishment of its Wildlife Department under Bill Jordan.

Jordan, hitherto the Society's Deputy Chief Veterinary Officer, was one of the few in his profession in the 1970s who showed a genuine interest in animals' rights. Indeed, this conviction had caused him trouble with his colleagues when, in 1973, he had criticized cruelty in animal experimentation and agreed to be the first secretary of the RSPCA's new

Animal Experimentation Advisory Committee; in consequence he had been hauled before other members of the British Veterinary Association to explain himself. Later, Jordan had played a prominent role in the whale and seal campaigns. In 1977, he had been sent to the seal hunt in Canada and had returned with evidence that seal pups were sometimes being skinned alive, probably while conscious.

Under his influence as head of the RSPCA's Wildlife Department the society made a number of important moves: it opposed the use of cyanide gas in the killing of badgers; funded research by Dr David Macdonald into the wild fox; set up the important expert committee on pain in shooting and angling chaired by Lord Medway;[14] held a scientific conference on the marking of animals which produced an influential publication;[15] and commenced an ultimately successful campaign to ban the import of tortoises into Britain (concluded by his successor in 1984 under the provisions of the Berne Convention).

In 1980 Jordan, concerned at the moral and financial decline of the RSPCA after the 'radicals' had lost control (see chapter 11), departed to head the recently established People's Trust for Endangered Species. He was succeeded as head of the Wildlife Department by Stefan Ormrod with whom, two years earlier, he had written *The Last Great Wild Beast Show*, a book which had raised again the issue of cruelty to animals in zoos and wildlife parks.

The RSPCA had found itself constantly trying to push the conservation organizations away from the 'numbers game' of trying to determine whether a species was or was not threatened with extinction towards showing some concern for the animals' welfare. Like men afraid to show compassion, conservationists too often declined to be pushed. On the other hand, Ormrod and Jordan sometimes found it hard to persuade their animal rights supporters to show any concern for conservation; often the conservation lobby was suspected of being concerned only with trying to conserve species for sport.

After the success of the joint committees on farm, laboratory and domestic animals, the RSPCA asked Bill Jordan to look into the feasibility of setting up a joint wildlife conservation and welfare group. But the problems were enormous, for there simply were no British bodies dedicated to the *welfare* of wild animals other than the three whose main task was opposition to bloodsports. On the conservation side there were many, and they were well organized, but there was no way that the anti-bloodsports brigade at that time was going to be able to join a federation with representatives of traditional conservation groups and come to amicable and constructive decisions. Eventually this problem was well solved when Joanna Gordon Clark and Richard Fitter asked Lord Melchett to head a new federation after the demise of the Council for Nature. In 1980 Wildlife Link was formed under Melchett's chairmanship and, with Hazel Phillips as secretary, provided a useful liaison between the major welfare and conservation groups.

The reformers on the RSPCA council had long fought the conventional wisdom which decreed that a wild animal was a pest unless proved useful, and that, if so, the only means of control was death by the cheapest means. We urged that the RSPCA advocate a policy of 'minimum violence' towards all nonhumans and encouraged the attitude that all animals are innocent unless proved guilty. Harmless chemical deterrents, better fencing and other modern technological innovations should be sought to protect legitimate human interests and to replace the barbarities of trapping, poisoning and shooting.

In 1979 the following principles were published in the RSPCA's statement of policies:

Where animals are being used by man and common sense indicates that they are suffering as a result, animals, and not their users, must be given the benefit of the doubt.

Where the killing or the imposing of suffering upon animals is claimed to be necessary in order to protect human interests, such claims must be fully substantiated before action is taken since these acts violate the rights of the animals concerned.

For these reasons, the principle of minimal interference must always be applied even where the control of animal populations has (allegedly) been justified. Thus, humane alternatives to killing or causing suffering shall always be chosen first and, should killing be deemed to be necessary, then the most humane method available shall be used.

Economic reasons alone do not justify the infliction of suffering.[16]

CRUELTY

Yet still, in some quarters, the wholesale massacre of vertebrates could be regarded as a crusade − even in Britain. Shortly before the Second World War some coypu (a South American aquatic rodent) escaped from fur farms in England and became established in the wild. Stigmatized as foreign pests over the years with an almost racist intensity, they were attacked for damaging crops and river banks. In 1981 a massive destruction campaign was launched and seven years later government trappers congratulated themselves on having killed over 31,000 coypu, describing their work enthusiastically as 'a great job' and hoping they had wiped out the species in Britain. No one, it seems, shed a tear for these unfortunate yet intelligent creatures, imported involuntarily by human exploiters into a cold and hostile habitat.[17]

Yet since the Second World War, there had been some advances in the protection of wildlife. The gin trap had been outlawed in Britain and the badger (thanks largely to Lord Arran) and the otter had received the protection of the law. But there was still no protection against cruelty to wildlife in general. Not only bloodsports, but cruel practices such as snaring and the use of strychnine to kill moles continued to be legal. The law was that any wild animal was protected from cruelty only when it was 'captive'. In 1986 a case involving a hedgehog horribly highlighted the absurdity of this. The hedgehog had, in effect, been tortured to death for fun. But because it had not, at the time, been captive, in the sense of being tethered or contained in a cage, the defendant was acquitted.[18] The RSPCA, with this case in mind, launched a campaign in 1986 to amend the law to cover cases of this sort. The government, however, fearing protests from the powerful bloodsports lobby, still declined to plug this large loophole in Britain's anti-cruelty legislation.

There appears to have been a general increase in cruelty in the 1980s: the RSPCA investigated just under 30,000 complaints in 1980; by 1985 this had risen to 65,000. Convictions rose from 1,400 to just over 2,000 in the same period. Staged dog-fights and cock-fights, for example,[19] seem to be increasing, but so also does cruelty to children, and British newspapers have reported numerous pitiable cases of children being assaulted and killed by their parents in recent years.

Cruelty to wildlife has also increased. RSPCA figures for prosecutions have reached record levels and there has been a disturbing increase in reported cases of badger-digging and, disgracefully, badger-baiting. Why has this medieval sport, once nearly extinct and for so long outlawed, shown a resurgence in the 1980s? Is it correlated with increasing unemployment? Is it another symptom of Britain's overall moral decline? Does it arise naturally out of the deliberate return to a harsher society modelled, as Mrs Thatcher puts it, on 'Victorian values'? In the case of the organized throwing of cats to dogs to be torn to pieces, a correlation with unemployment has been claimed,[20] and three men convicted of organized dog-fighting in Yorkshire in January 1986 were all unemployed.[21]

Sociologists will have to analyse in depth this disturbing phenomenon, to determine whether and why the Britain of the 1980s is crueller than for many decades. Are people using animals and children as scapegoats and displacing on to them their feelings of frustration in an uncaring society?

ZOOS

Jordan and Ormrod's book *The Last Great Wild Beast Show*,[22] published in 1978, not only highlighted the cramped and boring conditions under which many animals are kept, but also asked the fundamental questions – what is the purpose of a zoo? Is it to entertain, to educate, or to study or to preserve rare species?

Jordan and Ormrod's message was a combination of genuine concern for the humane treatment of the animals and a plea that zoos should play a part in conservation by becoming specialized breeding establishments – an attitude powerfully promoted by Peter Scott and Gerald Durrell a decade earlier. Although Lord Jenner, and later Lord Craigton, had been the prime movers in Parliament, it was in no small measure as a result of this book, and the lobbying done by Jordan and Ormrod, that the Zoo Licensing Act was enacted in 1981, coming into force three years later. Under the Act it became illegal to operate a zoo without a local authority licence. Despite shortcomings, the Act and its inspectorate have led to rising standards of care.

For many people, however, all zoos are wrong in principle, and actress Virginia McKenna, her husband Bill and son William Travers in 1983 set up an organization called Zoo Check, which lobbied for more radical change. When an elderly white rhino, for example, was shipped all the way from London to Czechoslovakia in 1986 for breeding purposes, Zoo Check received support from Ormrod and the RSPCA in condemning this on welfare grounds, Ormrod stressing the need for conservation in the wild rather than in captivity. IUCN and the London Zoo, however, supported the move, an official of the zoo dismissing Zoo Check's attitude as 'ignorant'.

INTERNATIONAL ACTION

Although the English-speaking nations had initiated progress, the Latin states in Europe had gradually become alive to wildlife issues in the 1970s and had responded especially well to IFAW's seal publicity. In France the actress Brigitte Bardot emerged as a leading figure, asking 'Who has given Man (a word which has tragically lost all its humanity) the right to exterminate, to dismember, to cut up, to slaughter, to hunt, to chase, to trap, to lock up, to martyr, to enslave and to torture the animals?'[23]

In Italy, Luigi Maccoschi succeeded in securing a unilateral Italian ban on seal imports in 1979 after his instigation of a national referendum. He then proceeded to harass Italian vivisectors, hauling several before the courts under half-forgotten statutes, boldly defying the experimenters' hostility, and undaunted even after his shop in Florence had been subjected to machine-gun fire.

Even in Africa, where European big-game hunters had, to a large extent, exchanged their rifles for cameras by the 1970s, some organized conservation programmes were set up to oppose the cruel depradations of ivory and rhinoceros-horn poachers. Indeed, in some countries conservation has itself adopted violent methods: in Zimbabwe, for example, government game scouts have shot dead poachers involved in the trade in rhinoceros-horn,[24] twenty-nine being killed in the period 1985–7.[25]

THE INTERNATIONAL FUND FOR ANIMAL WELFARE

Nobody has been more successful in promoting the idea that wild animals need international protection for their own sakes, and not just as part of an anthropocentric conservation movement, than Brian Davies. Davies, born in Wales in 1935, left an insecure home life for Canada as a boy of fourteen. After some time in the Canadian Army, he took a job as an investigator in the New Brunswick Society for the Prevention of Cruelty to Animals. In 1965 Davies was asked by the Canadian government to inspect the annual harp seal hunt in the Gulf of St Lawrence. Instead of introducing a 'whitewash' report, which perhaps had been expected, Davies outspokenly attacked the clubbing to death of the baby seals for their white fur coats. His opposition was on grounds of cruelty and from a general 'aesthetic' revulsion at the barbarous and ugly carnage he witnessed.

In 1969 Davies set up the International Fund for Animal Welfare. He became its executive director, and began the long campaign which culminated in the ban of baby seal imports into the EEC in 1983, and the consequent collapse of the Canadian seal hunt which previously had accounted for the deaths of around a hundred thousand seals annually off the East coast of Canada.

Davies's tools were publicity, the mobilization of public opinion and political pressure. He proved a genius at using all three. He had learned to fly a helicopter in order to ferry the media people of the world on to the treacherous ice-floes of the Gulf of St Lawrence, and in 1977 this massive publicity exercise reached its zenith, with Davies transporting forty-five television and newspaper reporters on to the ice to witness the slaughter. They duly passed on what they saw to millions in America, Canada, Britain, France, Scandinavia, Holland, Germany and Australia, and, for the most part, they did so sympathetically, the main exception being elements in the Canadian media, virtually alone in the English-speaking world in continuing a dogged opposition to the work and ideals of animal protection.

Davies had to contend not only with physical attacks from the seal hunters of Newfoundland but also with the outright hostility of the then Canadian government under Premier Pierre Trudeau. A regulation was passed in 1970 forbidding the flying or landing of helicopters in the vicinity of a seal and Davies was arrested in March 1977 after flying newspeople to the scene of the slaughter. On 14 July, 1980 he was sent to prison for twelve days in Newfoundland. On various other occasions

16 Kent Gavin's well-known 1968 photo for the *Daily Mirror* shows a Canadian sealer about to club to death a seal pup. This picture, which symbolizes the helplessness and beauty of the wild and its merciless exploitation by humankind, aided the successful campaign to ban seal pup imports into the EEC. But the killing continues.

(Syndication International)

he was fined, assaulted and his life threatened; and his helicopters were impounded and wrecked.

In 1970 Davies published his first book *Savage Luxury*, and so inspired articles about the US Marine Mammal Protection Act which banned the importation of baby seal products into America. In 1972 his International Fund presented a million signatures to the Canadian government calling for the end of the seal hunt. Three years later another million signatures were presented to the Norwegian embassy in America and, in 1982, 3,500,000 people were prompted by the International Fund for Animal Welfare to write to the EEC calling for a European prohibition on seal imports.

After much lobbying and working in close alliance with Eurogroup, these efforts led to a two-year ban which came into effect in October 1983, despite fierce opposition from the Canadian government. The ban was extended for another four years in 1985.

During this campaign IFAW and other groups had mobilized considerable support from the US legislature. Congressmen had declared 1 March 1982 as National Day of the Seal, and 55 senators and 129 congressmen had telexed their support for the ban to the EEC the same year. In 1985, 17 senators and 100 congressmen did likewise. In 1982 320 British MPs had supported the ban, and members of the European Parliament had voted 160 to 10 in 1982, and 55 to 0 in 1985, in its favour. In 1983 and 1985 British and Dutch delegates attending conferences of Liberal International, a body composed of liberal groups from many countries, fended off attempts to oppose the ban initiated by the powerful Canadian Liberal government delegation.

During the successful campaign, IFAW had involved celebrities such as Brigitte Bardot, who had flown out to the ice to be an eye-witness of the hunt; had lobbied key officials and politicians in Washington, Ottawa, London, Brussels and Strasbourg; organized massed peaceful demonstrations in the world's capitals; and arranged an effective international boycott on the sale of Canadian fish products. In the process, it had expanded to become an organization with a large income and with a supporters list which reached 500,000 in 1985. But Davies had avoided the pitfalls of over-bureaucratization which bedevilled some other successful bodies. By maintaining a worldwide staff of only about thirty, IFAW continued to be light on its feet and effective in its actions. Like Mohammed Ali, it could float like a butterfly and sting like a bee.

IFAW also had the money to use massive advertising as a weapon. Whole-page advertisements in the British national press had been a key ingredient in exerting pressure upon the British Prime Minister to stop the killing of seals in Scotland in 1978, and in the 1980s a huge anti-seal hunting billboard outside the Canadian High Commission in Trafalgar Square in London had served to maintain the pressure against the harp seal hunt. IFAW's attacks upon the Thatcher government's record were advertised during the 1983 general election in Britain, were controversial, and helped build a perception of the Conservative party as unsympathetic on 'green' issues generally. But, typically, Davies said 'thank you' to Mrs Thatcher in equally large headlines in October 1985 when, under heavy pressure from IFAW, the British government supported the renewed EEC ban on seal imports.

Davies had the wisdom not to turn IFAW into a membership organization. Instead, his computers listed donors and activists, and massive mailings ensured a regular income and caused the dispatch of thousands of letters and pre-printed postcards of protest to selected targets — premiers, presidents and ambassadors. IFAW showed other organizations how to cut corners and avoid getting bogged down in committees and irrelevancies. Davies's aim was to get to the right people in the right place and at the right time. To do so, the best scientific and other experts were employed, as in IFAW's presentations to the Canadian Royal Commission on Seals and the Sealing Industry in 1985, which advocated the compensation of sealers and the humane exploitation of the living seals by the tourist industry as an alternative to their destruction, courses of action which eventually received some political support.

IFAW's scientific witnesses, marshalled before this royal commission, were among the world's experts in their fields — the philosophers Peter Singer and Tom Regan, the marine biologists Sidney Holt and David Lavigne, the international lawyer Maxwell Bruce, the economist William G. Watson and the veterinarian Bill Jordan.

IFAW, in Macphail's words 'a committed commando', could not afford to fight on too wide a front, but, despite leading on the seal issue, it also rescued some eighty Canadian polar bears in 1971 and later campaigned to save birds from extinction, funded research on the Mediteranean monk seal, saved sea otters in Thailand, manatees in Florida, iguanas in Central America, vicunas in Peru and cheetahs in South West Africa; and, in 1982, it persuaded President Marcos of the Philippines to restrict cruelties to dogs and cats being killed for the table. With typical generosity Davies and IFAW helped fund the saving of donkeys in California's Death Valley carried out by Cleveland Amory's Fund for Animals in 1986. Amory, with reciprocated chivalry, praised Davies's 'class act'. At the time of writing, IFAW is campaigning to stop the horrific hanging of dogs and boiling of live cats in Korea, the stoning to death of animals in Spain and the killing of sperm and pilot whales.

With the almost total collapse of the Canadian seal industry in 1985, Brian Davies gave up his role as IFAW's executive director and handed over to Richard Moore, who had for years assisted the anti-seal hunt campaign as a senior *Daily Mirror* reporter.

In Canada, as IFAW had long urged, tourist interests began to move in upon the seals, and cameras began to replace the clubs; seal-watching, like whale-watching on Cape Cod, became a major commercial operation.

A strange ambivalence towards seals could be detected around the world. Early in 1986, some Canadian fishermen continued to kill any seal they encountered, fishermen in East Anglia fought to rescue the life of a seal they found injured in shallow water, and in Alaska, Americans lifted seals out of a glacier-locked fiord into the open sea.

It had taken over eighty years of campaigning to force a massive reduction of the Canadian seal hunt: the Humanitarian League had campaigned against it from the turn of the century and it had been condemned by distinguished Edwardians such as Professor Lloyd-Morgan and Sir George Baden-Powell.[27] The IFAW campaign demonstrated that breakthroughs can only be made by prolonged assault of an intensity sufficient to breech the defences of the status quo; merely scratching the surface of an issue can sometimes stiffen resistance.

GREENPEACE AND FRIENDS OF THE EARTH

Greenpeace, with its far catchier title, had become better known than IFAW, but Greenpeace's leader, David McTaggart, also with a Canadian background, had never seen Greenpeace as an animals' rights organization;[28] Greenpeace's chief interest was to protect the environment, animate or inanimate, from human threats such as pollution. Nevertheless, members of Greenpeace played a powerful part in protecting seals, whales and other wildlife during the 1970s, often risking their own safety by putting themselves between the exploiters' weapons and the prey. With a slightly less formal political style than IFAW's, Greenpeace concentrated skilfully upon the tactics of newsworthy confrontation. Its boat *Rainbow Warrior*, and its other vessels, harried the dumpers of nuclear waste, the industrial polluters and the killers of marine mammals.

Greenpeace had started as a Canadian-based protest against American nuclear tests in the Aleutian Islands in the late summer of 1969.[29] It is of note that this was within weeks of the founding not only of IFAW, but also that of Friends of the Earth in San Francisco by David Brower, the publication of the Council of Europe's Seven Point Plan for animal welfare (see chapter 16), and the beginnings of the unnamed 'Oxford Group' against speciesism (see chapter 1). These beginnings, which would all prove historically interesting in their way, were entirely independent one of another, and it would be years, in some cases, before the leaders of these campaigns would come into (usually friendly) contact or before their different but allied objectives and styles would closely interact: Greeenpeace, adventurous and confrontational; IFAW, courageous and influential; the Council of Europe, advisory and bureaucratic; the 'Oxford Group', philosophical and academic. In 1976 Greenpeace first joined in the anti-sealing campaign in Canada.

Greenpeace would move from a conservation and anti-nuclear position slowly towards a partial animal protection involvement, arguing in 1986, for example, against dolphinaria in Britain entirely on cruelty grounds. IFAW, using a similar style initially, was always concerned with the welfare rather than the conservation of wildlife, and gradually widened its operations to include some contact with domestic and laboratory animals. The 'Oxford Group', philosophically based, produced intellectual leaders like Peter Singer, and in Singer's case and my own, deployed into nearly all areas of animal abuse and suffering, basing our political campaigns on the moral argument.

While Greenpeace's early style had been hippy, IFAW's became jetset. Over the years there was a tendency in Britain for the campaigners to become committee-bound, while in America both Friends of the Earth (FOE) and Greenpeace gradually grew more bureaucratic. When FOE, increasingly interested in lobbying, moved its headquarters from San Francisco to Washington in 1985, its founder, David Brower, parted company. Meanwhile, the International Union for the Conservation of Nature predictably continued to adhere to an old-fashioned 'rational resource exploitation' view of conservation; so also, to a lesser extent, did the World Wildlife Fund. Despite all their efforts, however, by the mid-1980s the situation was little better and some biologists were estimating that each year the number of plant and animal species disappearing was '10,000 and increasing'.[30]

WHALES

An ex-Greenpeace executive, Allan Thornton, became a leader in the campaign to stop the annual massacre of pilot whales in the Faroe Islands. In 1986 his Environmental Investigation Agency filmed the slaughter for international television, and IFAW collaborated in subsequent approaches to the Danish and Faroese authorities.

Ian Macphail, observing the 1986 kill for IFAW, described his immediate reactions into a tape recorder:

It's impossible to find the right words to describe the horror. I cannot believe that what I am witnessing belongs to the twentieth century. Here is a so-called, well not necessarily a civilised society, with all the modern appliances and appurtenances, and there are these poor wretched animals thrashing about, being gaffed, hacked; ropes attached and hauled ashore. The sea is now blood red. But almost as bad as this spectacle is the spectacle of the spectators. Well dressed, leisure clothes, on a day's outing: bring the children to join in the fun: suffer the little children! Nobody seems in any way affected — well, they're moved to laughter, let's put it that way. It's a sort of joyous occasion, a fiesta, a time for dancing about and shouting and encouraging friends.[31]

Ex-wartime fighter-pilot Macphail later mused about the indifference of the Faroese at what they were doing. All seemed to accept the slow chopping to death of scores of terrified and intelligent mammals, and Macphail attributed their equanimity to the Faroese genetic background.

A far simpler explanation is that most people accept what is custom. Even when such a hunt has lost all economic value it continues as a relic of the past, enjoyed partly as a tradition and partly as a satisfaction of men's need to prove their so-called 'manhood'. It is as macho as bull-fighting, football or fast driving. Ironically, it is those who are the first to say 'stop' who show the real courage.

The anti-whaling campaign illustrates clearly the evolution from a purely conservationist origin to an anti-cruelty position. Greenpeace itself had been split in the early 1970s on whether to get involved with wildlife at all; McTaggart had wanted to concentrate on the campaign to stop French nuclear tests in the Pacific. Eventually it was Paul Spong and Robert Hunter in 1973 who started the Greenpeace involvement with wildlife, but they still justified it in anthropocentric terms. In Spong's words:

It seems to me that in time we might be able to learn an awful lot from the whales. But if this generation allows the whales to be wiped out like the dinosaurs, future generations will never have the oppurtunity to make the discoveries that are possible. It will be too late. So we have to do something now. That's all there is to it.[32]

After McTaggart attended a meeting of the International Whaling Commission in 1978, however, he also became keen, and Greenpeace took up the anti-whaling campaign with a new seriousness, aware that it had become a symbol of the struggle for the future of the planet's eco-system.

In 1931 the Convention for the Regulation of Whaling had been signed. It prohibited the commercial killing of right and bowhead whales but was not effective, as five whaling countries refused to observe it – Japan, Chile, Germany, USSR and Argentina. Stocks continued to decline. In 1946 the International Convention for the Regulation of Whaling was signed in Washington. It established the International Whaling Commission which meets annually to fix quotas. In its early years the IWC did little to restrain the expanding industry and by 1960 as many as 64,000 large whales were being killed annually. In the USA alone the industry employed some 70,000 people.

Dr Harry Lillie in the 1950s had done much to raise concern about whaling methods and declining populations by showing films he had made of whaling to selected audiences. In 1959 Dr Sidney Holt, a leading marine mammal biologist, became one of three experts appointed to an IWC committee to investigate the killing quotas; the committee duly recommended widespread reductions in quotas and complete protection for blue whales and humpbacks. The IWC itself still dithered.

The attitude of reformers at this time was one of 'let's make the IWC work', and the overt argument deployed in favour of reduced quotas was a husbandry ethic: whale populations, so it was said, must not be reduced so far as to endanger their capacity to yield a sustainable crop.

About 1970, American conservationists such as David Brower of Friends of the Earth began to increase the pressure on the US administration which led to the passage of the US Marine Mammal Protection Act of 1972. In the same year the United Nations held a conference in Stockholm attended by 113 nations which provided an inspirational impetus to governments around the world. Nevertheless its Declaration on the Human Environment remained entirely people-centered in tone, calling for an improved quality of human life and the protection of the environment 'so that progress may really be put at the service of mankind'.

Following the Stockholm conference's plan for the environment, the USA proposed a ten-year moratorium on commercial whaling. The IWC turned it down. In 1973 the United Nations repeated the suggestion. Still the IWC refused to act. But in the following year it at last adopted new management procedures to conserve certain species. The role of the two new Seychelles delegates, Sidney Holt and Lyall Watson, was to prove extremely influential over the ensuing years.

The cruelty argument had been raised intermittently during the 1950s and 1960s but had never made progress. At first the 'good husbandry' idea had been the only argument to carry weight, but after the Stockholm conference the ground shifted a little and a purer conservation rationale became respectable. In the mid-1970s, however, the cruelty question was again raised with regard to the so-called 'cold' killing of minke whales, using harpoons without explosive heads, which killed the whales even more slowly. The Australian delegates took the lead on this issue and, following the Frost Commission Report, the Australian government under Premier Malcolm Fraser closed down its own whaling industry.

In the IWC, Australia continued to press for stricter quotas, supported by the British, American, New Zealand and Swedish delegations. A ban was eventually adopted on the cold killing of large whales and in 1979 the commission recommended a ban on the cold killing of minke. By 1986 Norway and Japan had adopted explosive harpoons, although Iceland, Greenland and Korea continued their traditional and extremely cruel methods.

In 1982 the IWC reached the historic decision to prohibit commercial whaling from the 1985/6 season in Antarctica and from 1986 elsewhere until it should decide otherwise. The commission pledged itself to view the situation not later than 1990. Nevertheless, Norway, Japan and the

USSR registered objections to the decision and continued whaling. Iceland also continued under the pretence that its whaling operation was purely for scientific research, while Korea continued without even objecting or attempting a justification.[33]

Nevertheless the Russians, although a major whaling nation, had begun to show an interest in conservation. In 1985, for example, Russian ships, at huge costs, rescued white whales from the ice, with no obvious commercial motive.

The Americans had taken a lead in promoting the moratorium until they were put under pressure by Alaskan Eskimos in 1980. Friends of the Earth in America, as committed to the idea of ethnic rights as to the conservation of wildlife, backed down just as Greenpeace would do five years later on the fur issue. Eventually the Eskimo problem was resolved by allowing them a quota of kills, despite the Australian objection that native kills are often more cruel than commercial ones; the Eskimo, using only small harpoons, may take hours to kill a whale. In the EEC the Greenland Eskimo influence was also effective through the agency of Denmark. The German delegation, still adopting a strictly agricultural attitude towards the 'harvesting' of whales, supported the Danes.

Japan, however, as the buyer of nearly all the world's whale meat, continued as the chief opponent of conservation in this field, and used diplomatic and financial pressure to do all it could to undermine the growing 'green' influence on the IWC. Although the Reagan administration showed significantly less interest in conservation than previous governments, American counter-pressure on Japan, and the decisions of its courts during 1985, helped to ease the situation. In July 1986, Iceland accused the USA of intolerable coercion against a NATO ally in trying to force an end of their centuries-old whale hunt, and Premier Hermansson alleged that Washington had threatened Iceland with economic sanctions on fish exports to the USA. Nevertheless Iceland called off its so-called scientific whale hunt.[34] Later in the year, two Iceland whaling ships were sunk in Reykjavik harbour after their main plugs were removed by saboteurs claiming to be connected with the American-based Sea Shepherd group.[35]

By the 1980s the human world was more aware of whales than ever it had been, but still almost as ambivalent in its attitude. As Faroese children waded in a sea of blood and laughed while their fathers hacked pilot whales to pieces, in Western Australia and Scotland children as young as five helped to form human chains to pour water upon stranded whales to keep them alive,[36] and men and women in New Zealand and Massachusetts risked their own lives herding whales back into safer waters.[37]

All major conservation organizations had played a part in protecting the whales. Peter Scott of the World Wide Fund for Nature had exerted influence and McTaggart of Greenpeace had became increasingly involved.

IFAW had quietly sponsored scientific research and financed key campaigners. Holt had helped shift the intellectual centre of gravity from the traditional position of controlled exploitation to a purer conservation ethic. Gradually it shifted further still towards the anti-cruelty position. Partly this was spontaneous and empathetic, encouraged in wildlife circles by campaigners such as Bill Jordan, and partly it was in response to the increasing worldwide public interest in animals' rights which encouraged Greenpeace, dependent upon small donations and subscriptions, to take note. The World Wide Fund for Nature (and hence IUCN), relying more upon large funding from a few major sources, remained less susceptible to this pressure. Indeed, its change of name from World Wildlife Fund in May 1988 indicated as much and reflected its swing in the opposite direction towards more general environmental concerns.

In June 1987, at the International Whaling Commission's annual meeting in Bournemouth, the US delegation tabled a motion to prevent whaling nations from continuing commercial exploitation by claiming that they were killing whales only for scientific research. This resolution was passed, and the three most conservation-minded countries – USA, Australia and the United Kingdom – proceeded to persuade the commission to prohibit the so-called scientific programme being conducted by Korea, Iceland and Japan. Any country defying these restrictions would face punitive action from the USA which is, by federal law, obliged to impose sanctions against any nation acting in a way which diminishes the effectiveness of the IWC. Such sanctions take one of two forms: the denial of fishing rights in US waters (the Packwood-Magnusson Amendment) or trade bans on fish products (the Pelly Amendment). The former was eventually invoked against Japan on 6 April 1988, while Britain continued to protest to Japan through diplomatic channels.[38]

Whether these actions effectively bring to an end the international whaling industry, or whether they provoke nations to withdraw from the commission, remains to be seen. Norway, one of the most backward of all Western nations in its attitudes to wildlife, sees whales as 'pests' and continues to kill minke whales in the North-east Atlantic despite estimates that it has already depleted the whale population to a mere 10 per cent of its pre-exploitation level.[39]

In October 1988 the joint Russian–American rescue of two grey whales mentioned in Chapter 11 raised hopes for a more enlightened future for both whales and humankind, and the success of Heathcote Williams's long poem *Whale Nation* reflected the English-speaking world's abiding concern.[40]

THE FUR TRADE

Over thirty million animals continue to be killed annually for their skins, and Britain imports some three million furs each year from wild animals horribly slain in steel-toothed traps, mostly in America and Canada. In 1984 Greenpeace commenced a campaign against this fur trade which was abandoned a year later after representations were recieved to the effect that a few Canadian and American Indian peoples depended upon furs as a vital source of income, and despite evidence that only 2 per cent of trappers in America are professionals, the remainder doing it mostly as a 'sport'. This decision led to the resignation of British Greenpeace campaigner Mark Glover, who joined forces with the author Richard Adams to continue the anti-fur campaign under the aegis of their new organization entitled Lynx. Adams and Glover toured Britain, often assisted by a volunteer team of models who displayed a collection of fur coats to the accompaniment of Adam's mock coutourier's commentary, and the showing of a film made specially by David Bailey, together with horrific pictures of animals dying slowly in leghold traps. Adams, thumping his walking-stick upon the stage, spared neither his audiences nor himself as he poured forth his impassioned pleas for mercy. Nor was he without humour: hearing that a leading furrier, Mr X, had employed people to 'bug' his talks, Adams proceeded to address some of his most acid comments to 'Mr X and his buggers'.

Independently of Greenpeace, the RSPCA began its own anti-fur campaign in the same year. Its approach was through advertising, and the cries of protest from the British Fur Association suggested that it had an effect. In North America, too, the campaign against the powerful fur trade began to gather momentum. In Canada, the crusade waged by the veteran George Clements was joined by Stephen Best, a film and television producer and vigorous ex-IFAW lobbyist, who galvanized the campaign as executive director of the Toronto Humane Society, one of Canada's largest and wealthiest animal welfare bodies. Earlier Best had played a prominent role in IFAW's successful anti-sealing campaign along with colleagues Donna Hart and Dr Jeremy Tatum of British Columbia.

In South Africa the fur trade took action for libel against Beauty Without Cruelty's use of a David Bailey-inspired poster depicting a woman dragging a fur coat dripping with blood. Much to the delight of anti-fur campaigners around the world, in August 1986 the case was dismissed with costs against the Cape Town furriers who had brought the action. The judge concluded that 'the poster is a hard hitting, dramatic and indeed emotive appeal to people not to wear fur coats', but was no more defamatory to furriers than 'an advertisement admonishing people not to smoke can be said to apply to every vendor of cigarettes or tobacco'.[41] In Britain the fur trade complained that another of David Bailey's brilliant pictures – this one depicting an elderly man holding up a fur coat with the slogan 'How would you like your fur, madam? Gassed, strangled, trapped or electrocuted ?' – was anti-semitic.

The truth was that, until this complaint was made, few of us in the anti-fur lobby had even realized that the fur industry was largely run by Jews, and to accuse us of anti-semitism was itself defamatory and insulting. Later in the same year the anti-fur campaign held its first mass rally, attended by two thousand people in Trafalgar Square and addressed by round-the-world-yachtswoman Clare Francis, Mark Glover, George Clements, myself and others.

The anti-fur campaign had received a boost in 1979 when Fay Funnell had bought an extremely valuable fur coat in a Harrods sale in London and then publicly burned it in the street outside the store. This story went around the world. The campaigns were effective in swaying public opinion.

The Greenpeace and Lynx slogan 'it takes up to forty dumb animals to make a fur coat but only one to wear it' had also caused controversy. Some members of the feminist movement objected. But Richard Adams and Mark Glover persisted unabashed.[42] In the mid-1980s the anti-fur campaign, supported by Compassion in World Farming and many other groups, had become the principal item on the animal rights agenda, boosted by the welcome news from Buckingham Palace that Princess Diana did not wear fur.[43]

In February 1988 the campaign appeared to achieve a significant success when Britain's Trade Minister, Alan Clark, announced his intention to have retailed furs labelled with the words: 'includes fur from animals commonly caught in leg-hold traps'. After pressure from the Canadian government, however, at a time when Britain was anxious to secure the sale of submarines to Canada, the proposal was abandoned in June of the same year. Depite this setback, the anti-fur campaign, based as it was entirely on the question of cruelty and not conservation, had made a promising start. In 1974 members of the RSPCA council and their guests attending a 150th anniversary celebration at the Tower of London had left twenty-three fur coats hanging in the cloakroom. By the end of the decade such as a situation had become unthinkable.

BLOODSPORTS

As we saw in Chapter 11, the campaign against bloodsports in Britain continued, steadily winning over public opinion. But despite Private Members Bills in Parliament no laws were passed.

The League Against Cruel Sports, under the leadership first of Edward Hemingway (who died in 1963) and later of Raymond Rowley, had tried a certain amount of direct protest in the field, and in 1958 Hemingway's followers began to use aniseed in attempts to disrupt hunts by masking the scent of the quarry. When these tactics seemed ineffective, the League adopted the alternative approach of buying small parcels of land in hunting areas, particularly Exmoor, from which the hunts were then barred. The first legal action taken by the League was in 1959 and was against Devon and Somerset Staghounds who had crossed the League's property. More land was purchased and by 1976 the League owned twenty-four lots totalling over 1,500 acres. By 1986 this had grown to more than 2,500 acres.

From 1977, the League for a decade came under the effective control of Richard Course, at first as a committee member and later as director. Lord Soper, the distinguished Methodist leader, who had struggled for so long and sometimes almost single-handedly for better legislative protection of wildlife from the 1940s onwards, was the League's president in 1977 and, together with Course, he prevailed upon ex-Labour Cabinet Minister Lord Houghton to take the chair on Rowley's departure.

As one argument after another in support of bloodsports was demolished, the British Field Sports Society, now ably led by Conservative MP Marcus Kimball, hopped nimbly on to the new ground. The society was, for example, quick to jump on the conservation bandwagon when it began to roll in the 1950s, arguing that hunters maintain a healthy 'balance' and that anglers effectively oppose pollution. By 1963 the society claimed to be 'playing an ever growing part in the conservationist world'.[44]

Throughout the 1960s, as we have seen, the RSPCA was heavily infiltrated by members of the British Field Sports Society and, even as late as 1977, nearly half the Masters of Foxhounds, responding to a questionnaire, admitted that they were also members of the RSPCA. Interestingly, only 25 per cent of Hunt Saboteurs said that they were RSPCA members.[45] But the BFSS also set about the business of making allies among more neutral bodies. Since the 1940s for example, the society had cultivated good relations with the powerful National Farmers' Union, the Ministry of Agriculture and, later, with the Country Landowners' Association. In the 1960s and 1970s as an apparently conservationist body, it also hobnobbed with the Nature Conservancy Council, the Forestry Commission, the Council for Nature, and the Fauna Preservation Society. Such tactics were highly successful, and, until a younger generation of zoologists and university-qualified ecologists took over from the old school of 'huntin' and 'shootin' naturalists in the 1980s, they paid dividends in keeping influential civil service and scientific opinion broadly in the bloodsportmen's camp.

CONCLUSIONS

The twentieth century has seen a gradual change in attitude towards the treatment of wildlife, from a position of total exploitation, to anthropocentric conservation, through to a more genuine concern for the nonhumans themselves.

For many born before the First World War a concern for the careful husbandry of stocks was what made sense. But to those of the next generation the idea of the conservation of species, regardless of their immediate utility for humankind, became the rallying cry. Later, for many of those campaigners born after the Second World War, a desire to spare the suffering of sentient wild creatures for their own sake became an additional ideal.

It can be seen that there are three main differences between traditional conservation and modern wildlife protection. First, the former is for human benefit whereas the latter is for the sake of the wild creatures themselves. Secondly, conservation is concerned with saving species whereas protection includes care for individuals. Thirdly, protection aims to stop suffering as well as to protect life and habitat.

The three great international wildlife issues have been the fights to protect seals and whales and to restrict the fur trade. By 1985 the first two had achieved a large measure of success; the campaigns had been waged on the ice-floes, along the corridors of power and in the minds of ordinary people. Battles had been won but the war had only begun; much remained to be done. In virtually every country in the world it was still perfectly legal to trap, snare, poison or shoot most wild vertebrates, regardless of the suffering inflicted. By the end of the decade the fate of the African rhino and elephant loomed large.

13 In the Laboratory

SOME ARGUMENTS

Scientists frequently justify experiments upon nonhumans in terms of the benefits they may bring to others: 'It is odious for anyone to let futile considerations stop the progress of science...you sacrifice one but may save millions. Can one be subject to doubt when the price is so modest?' Ironically, the argument is used here by Dr Rodin, in the Marquis de Sade's monstrous novel *Justine* (1787), as he prepares to kill his own fifteen-year-old daughter in a cruel surgical experiment.[1] Nazi doctors who experimented on prisoners in concentration camps used similar arguments when being tried for their lives after the war.[2]

No reputable scientist, of course, would for a moment contemplate such experiments upon a child nor indeed on any member of the human species, normal or handicapped. Yet, as Singer reminds us:

whenever an experimenter claims that his experiment is important enough to justify the use of an animal, we should ask him whether he would be prepared to use a retarded human at a similar mental level to the animal he is planning to use. If his reply is negative, we can assume that he is willing to use a non-human animal only because he gives less consideration to the interests of members of other species than he gives to members of his own – and this bias is no more defensible than racism or any other form of arbitrary discrimination.[3]

What is so special about our own species? Especially if we all know, as we now do, that other animals can suffer pain and distress much as we do ourselves. After all, experimenting on humans might well produce far more valid results than do tests on rats. 'If experimenting on retarded, orphaned humans would be wrong', asks Singer: 'why isn't experimenting on non-human animals wrong? What difference is there between the two, except for the mere fact that, biologically, one is a member of our species and the other is not? But that surely is not a morally relevant difference.'[4]

Experimenters are quick to complain about the activities of militants who break into their laboratories to liberate their experimental dogs, cats or rats, condemning them often on the grounds that their violent or illegal means are not justified by their compassionate ends. Yet it is the experimenters themselves who live by this very principle, inflicting often horrific violence upon their nonhuman captives allegedly for human benefit. If ends do not justify means in one case, then they cannot in another.

Moreover, the scientist is often quick to point out that his or her nonhuman subjects are excellent biological models for human beings. Indeed a British surgeon involved in research into transplanting organs from pigs into people recently exclaimed that, physiologically, pigs 'are horizontal men − or men are vertical pigs'.[5] Why then one may ask, if nonhumans are so *physically* similar, do they not share a *moral* similarity with humans? Scientists cannot have it both ways: either nonhumans are poor models for humans or they ought to be treated with similar consideration and respect.

This moral argument − the argument against speciesism − is rarely responded to by scientists, perhaps because there *is* no rational reply.

In the twentieth century the moral argument has carried great weight with public opinion but not, it seems, with governments. The other argument against vivisection − that it is useless, or worse, that it is dangerous to human health, may have carried more weight in the nineteenth century before the human benefits of medicine and surgery were as obvious as they are today. Nevertheless, a revival of this argument has occurred since the passage of the Animals (Scientific Procedures) Act in 1986, as we shall see later.

SOME FIGURES

In Britain alone over three million animals die in research annually. Estimates for the world range between 50 and 150 million. In 1987 in Britain there were 3,631,393 licensed procedures on nonhuman animals recorded under the Animals (Scientific Procedures) Act of 1986. This included the use of 4,935 cats, 5,078 primates and 10,853 dogs. In the toxicity testing of non-medical products 254,002 animals were used, 14,534 in cosmetics testing, 1,256 in tobacco and tobacco substitute testing, 31,973 in procedures causing psychological stress, 24,314 in the application of substances to the eye, 91,934 in radiation experiments, 3,746 in alcohol research, 77,976 involving injections into the brain or spinal cord and 137,322 in procedures causing animals to have cancer[6]. The Ministry of Defence conducts numerous experiments on nonhuman subjects annually, although the figure has recently declined, from 14,400 in 1982 to 6,600 in 1986.[7]

In the USA numbers appear to be steeply increasing. US Department of Agriculture figures released in July 1988 show that the numbers of dogs, primates, guinea-pigs, hamsters, rabbits and wild animals used had increased in the year 1986−7; particularly disturbing was an increase of 25 per cent in the use of nonhuman primates to 61,392, out of a total of approximately 20 million nonhumans experimented on annually in American laboratories.[8]

THE 1960S: SMALL BEGINNINGS AND HUMANE ALTERNATIVES

In 1959, commissioned by the Universities Fund for Animal Welfare, two British scientists, William Russell and Rex Burch, published their book *The Principles of Humane Experimental Techniques*[9] − a well-researched proposal that scientists should take greater pains to replace, reduce and refine their use of laboratory animals. It received scant attention at the time but continued over thirty years to have a gradual beneficial effect in moderate circles.

It was in America that well-organized campaigning against animal experimentation first reappeared after the Second World War. Eleanor Seiling in New York and Christine Stevens in Washington (see chapter 16) both launched into well-prepared campaigns. The blatant cruelty of American laboratories may have given them more ammunition than campaigners were used to having in more secretive Britain, and the greater freedom of information in America undoubtedly helped.

The RSPCA too, albeit cautiously, had let the government of Britain know in 1961 that it wanted some reforms of the administration of the 1876 Cruelty to Animals Act, calling for a veterinary presence in the Home Office inspectorate which was charged with monitoring animal research in the country.[10] The following year, Home Secretary R. A. Butler initiated the process which led to the setting up in 1963 of an official inquiry, under the lawyer Sir Sydney Littlewood, into the workings of the Act. The committee reported two years later, making some eighty-three recommendations for administrative and other reforms. Over the ensuing twenty years a few of these were put into effect during a period of growing public agitation, but in general, like Russell and Burch's book, the Littlewood Report received remarkably little official acknowledgement.

The main emphasis in the British movement during the 1960s was the setting up of small trust funds to promote research into the development and dissemination of humane techniques which were alternatives to using living animals, such as tissue and organ cultures, or the use of films and models in teaching. The first of these funds appears to have been the Lawson Tait Trust started in 1962 by Muriel Dowding, Nora Turnbull and Wilfred Risdon in association with both the National Anti-Vivisection Society and the British Union for the Abolition of

Vivisection in London, and the Scottish Society for the Prevention of Vivisection in Edinburgh. Later, in 1974, the Lawson Tait Trust started the Humane Research Trust, to be run by Pamela and R. MacAlistair Brown.

In 1969 Dorothy Hegarty, with the support of Dr Charles Foister and backed by Lady Kinnoull, launched what was to become the best known of these ventures, which she named the Fund for the Replacement of Animals in Medical Research (FRAME).[11] FRAME actively encouraged the involvement of scientists in its own administration and one, Dr Michael Balls, became an active campaigner in the 1980s.

In 1970 Sidney Hicks, secretary of the British Union for the Abolition of Vivisection, started the Dr Hadwen Trust for Humane Research, later to be run ably by Dr Gill Langley, as a small-scale source of funds for scientists wanting to develop alternative techniques. Shortly afterwards, the National Anti-Vivisection Society established its own body for this purpose – the Air Chief Marshall Lord Dowding Fund which was administered by Bernard Conyers.

This proliferation of organizations, although it did not raise sufficient funds to subsidize a major shift in the direction of British research, nevertheless helped to put the message across. In 1984 the British government for the first time gave financial backing to FRAME (£185,000) and the UFAW (£30,000) to promote alternatives.[12]

THE REVIVAL 1969–1975

It was around 1969, with the formation of FRAME, the emergence of Clive Hollands as a campaigner in Scotland, the appearance of the informal Oxford Group and the changing public mood, that the reform campaign in Britain seemed to change gear. The content of the campaign altered, too, adding several major themes to the drive for alternative techniques, including a new emphasis on the moral argument (see chapter 1), a concentrated attack upon the infliction of pain and distress, a call for greater accountability to the public at large (for whose alleged benefit the research was being conducted and whose tax money often paid for it), and a publicity campaign which singled out for special criticism the widespread use of animals in tests and experiments which were not for strictly medical purposes, such as cosmetics testing.

Most of these themes had been brought out in *Animals, Men and Morals* published in 1971.[13] Part of my own role, as a psychologist who had worked in animal laboratories both in America and in Britain, was to emphasize that much research was *not* for strictly medical purposes. The academic study of animal behaviour (at one time my own field) was a case in point.[14] The more I researched this area the more non-medical examples I found – weapons research, and the testing of weedkillers, soaps, detergents, toiletries, cosmetics and inessential food additives, for example. Armed with this information it was easier for us to erode the then widely accepted view of animal experimentation as a high-minded medical necessity involving little or no suffering for its nonhuman victims.

We realized that the success of our campaign would depend upon the support of the mass media, but at the start of the 1970s Clive Hollands and myself, at that time two of the best-known campaigners in Britain, found the media cynical and apathetic. Despite the campaigns of the hunt saboteurs (see chapter 12) most reporters and editors still had a stereotyped view of animal welfare campaigners as eccentric and senti-mental. The mere fact that we were male, however, somewhat helped to challenge their prejudiced vision that the animal welfare world was peopled entirely by peculiar old ladies in hats. The publications of mem-bers of the Oxford Group assisted in the demolition of such stereotypes.

THE BREAKTHROUGH: 1975

Until 1975, however, every news story had to be worked for. Sarcastic and hostile reporters had to be persuaded that we were serious and sensible and that we knew what we were talking about. It was around 1975 that the mood of the media changed. Newspaper and television editors began to discover that not only were we able to articulate what we wanted but that thousands of readers and viewers agreed with us. Our deliberate campaign to use the media to rouse public indignation against speciesism eventually took off under its own motivation in 1975 after the *Sunday People*'s revelations about beagle dogs being forced to smoke tobacco in the Imperial Chemical Industries (ICI) laboratories in Cheshire.[14]

The pictures of dogs being forced to inhale cigarette smoke were not so awful as to make the squeamish look the other way. Instead, thou-sands of indignant Britons rose in anger, determined to stop this abuse. Joan Latto and Lady Parker, the widow of a previous Chief Justice, were among the leaders of a nationwide protest.[16] We had meetings at the Home Office and with the management of ICI, and it was our first success when the Secretary of State announced that dogs would not again be used in smoking research in Britain.

Two weeks after the *Sunday People* broke the smoking beagles story my book *Victims of Science*, completed two years earlier, was eventually published, and widely reviewd in the national press. More importantly, it provoked a number of television programmes over the ensuing five years in which I found myself able to promote the issue to audiences of millions; a topic previously wrapped in secrecy suddenly became news. Whereas the smoking beagles story engaged one end of the media, the book engaged the more 'serious' end.[17] The movement had really taken

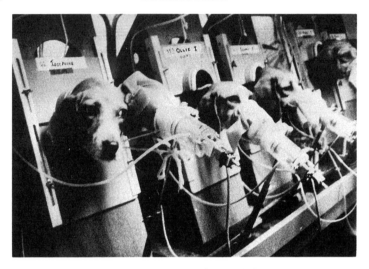

17 Beagle dogs being forced to smoke in a laboratory experiment.
Upsetting, but not so horrifying that readers had to 'switch off'.
This classic anti-cruelty photo was published in February 1975 by
the mass-circulation *Sunday People* newspaper; it caused widespread
protest in Britain, but only minor improvements in the law have
followed.
(Syndication International)

off and would continue at a high level of activity until the early
1980s.

In the twelve month period following the publication I was in correspondence with several thousand people whom I tried to mobilize into a
letter-writing army to badger industry, the media and government press-
ing for reforms. Peaceful demonstrations were organized, newspaper
articles were written,[18] and scores of Parliamentary Questions and several
Early Day Motions in Parliament were composed and tabled, which
ensured that a subject which had, until recently, taken up only part of
the working week of one Home Office official escalated so that by the
end of the 1970s, it was a political hot potato which involved the
attention first of secretaries of state and finally of prime ministers.[19] A
letter in *The Times* calling for extensive reforms was signed, among
others, by Brigid Brophy, David Daiches, Margaret Drabble, Maureen
Duffy, Willis Hall, Philip Larkin, Olivia Manning, Spike Milligan, Iris
Murdoch, Anthony Powell, Arnold Wesker and Lord Willis.[20]

As first steps we called for more inspectors, the reorganization of the
Home Office committee which advised the government, more pressure
on the scientists to develop and use alternative techniques, a prohibition

on the infliction of pain, a ban on trivial tests, and greater detail in the Home Office statistics. As a deliberate ploy to sting the Home Office into action on the latter, I repeatedly claimed (accurately) that, judging by their figures, only one-third of the licensed experiments could be 'seen' to be for medical purposes.[21] This was frequently misrepresented as a firm claim on my part that only one-third *were* actually medical, but those who attacked me on these fallacious grounds only increased the pressure upon the Home Office to provide more information.[22] This tactic worked very well and quite soon the presentation of the statistics was completely changed and far more information made available.

Later in 1975 Singer's classic *Animal Liberation* was published in America,[23] and in Britain in the following year, where it played a crucial role in further altering intellectual opinion. Rapidly it became the 'bible' of anti-speciesism.

The leaders of the two major London anti-vivisection societies were giving the revitalized movement their full support. The National Anti-Vivisection Society, under the guidance of Muriel, Lady Dowding, John Slatter and John Evans (and later of Colin Smith and Brian Gunn), was modernizing its methods, and Sidney Hicks, Alan Whittaker and John Pitt of the British Union were also accelerating their campaigns. But clearly there was a need for a new vehicle, one that could penetrate the defences of an unsympathetic government and a bureaucracy whose instinct, when faced with a call for change, was to close the shutters and put on the brakes.

THE COMMITTEE FOR THE REFORM OF ANIMAL EXPERIMENTATION

Later in 1975, therefore, Houghton, Hollands and I set up the Committee for the Reform of Animal Experimentation (CRAE), partly to evade the restrictions imposed by those who argued that the RSPCA could not take political action (see chapter 11). CRAE, under the chairmanship of Lord Houghton, grew out of the RSPCA's Animal Experimentation Advisory Committee and in due course came to have a very similar membership. Until recently Douglas Houghton had been chairman of the Parliamentary Labour Party; in 1974 he was elevated to the House of Lords, where he proceeded to use the chamber to champion the animals' cause in many a rousing speech.[24]

CRAE quickly attracted to its ranks another outstandingly well-qualified member in the person of Lord Platt, a previous president of the Royal College of Physicians, and outspoken in his criticisms of the manner in which the Home Office had been administering the Cruelty to Animals Act of 1876. In particular, Lord Platt attacked the 'geriatric' composition of the Home Office's Advisory Committee and the rareness of its meetings. To all effects it had become a dead letter, he claimed.

In May 1976, in the centenary year of the Cruelty to Animals Act,

CRAE sent a memorandum to the Home Secretary calling for reforms. The memorandum, written chiefly by Houghton, Hollands and myself, called for controls on pain and stress, restrictions on non-medical uses such as the testing of cosmetics on animals, the greater use of humane alternative techniques, better training, and a wider scope for legislation. All these reforms could come under the control of an improved Home Office committee, provided it was fairly composed so as to balance animal welfare and other interests.

Although the Home Secretary in the Conservative administration in 1975 had been forced to give the assurance to Parliament that dogs would not in future be used in smoking experiments, the response from the new Labour government was less than encouraging. A CRAE delegation in 1976 consisting of Houghton, Platt, Jordan, Hollands, Pedler and myself received a frosty reception from Dr Shirley Summerskill, the Home Office minister.

The following year, however, amid continuing political and media interest in the subject, we had meetings with the new Secretary of State, Merlyn Rees, who promised to 'nudge forward' along the lines that CRAE was advocating. We achieved the following reforms: the amount of information published annually by the Home Office was further expanded, the advisory committee was reorganized, the inspectorate was increased, and licensed experimenters were 'exhorted' by the Secretary of State to use humane alternative techniques whenever possible. Gradually, the total number of experiments licensed in Britain fell from a maximum of 5.6 million in 1970 to 3.3 million in 1985, although the chief reasons for this were probably the increasing cost of animals and declining research funds.

LEGISLATIVE PROPOSALS

Various private members' Bills, none of them entirely acceptable to CRAE, were put forward over the next few years, and one presented in 1979 by Lord Halsbury, the President of the Research Defence Society (RDS), was fundamentally objectionable. Nevertheless it was this Bill which advanced the legislative process by initiating a very searching investigation by a House of Lords select committee under the chairmanship of Lord Ashby.

The Labour government was succeeded by the Conservatives in 1979 after an election in which, as a result of pressure from our General Election Co-ordinating Committee (see chapter 11) they had promised to 'update' the law controlling animal experimentation. CRAE in 1980 met William Whitelaw, the new Secretary of State, and eventually we received assurances that the government would produce its proposals for new legislation.

In the early 1980s, however, CRAE became divided between those, led by Houghton, who sought a working compromise with scientific interests and those who felt that such a compromise was premature and who were prepared, if necessary, to hold out for reform until after the passing of the unsympathetic Thatcher era. After several resignations from CRAE (including my own), Houghton, supported by Hollands, formed a loose alliance with FRAME and the British Veterinary Association, and started negotiations with the almost moribund Research Defence Society. Meanwhile the Lords select committee had reported on 24 April 1980 and their report was, in many respects, as thorough as that of the 1906–12 royal commission or of the Littlewood committee of 1962–5. It proposed that considerable power should be given to the Home Office advisory committee to advise the Home Secretary in the performance of his role. The composition of this committee, however, was to be almost entirely from science and the chemical and pharmaceutical industries; animal welfare representation was noticeably thin. Furthermore, the report took on board the idea that the new legislation should not seek to prohibit objectionable practices outright but should enable the government to control experimentation, at its discretion, through flexible powers.

The two government white papers which followed, outlining their legislative proposals, adopted this 'enabling' principle.

THE RSPCA AND THE ANTI-VIVISECTION GROUPS

All major animal welfare organizations, except the Scottish Society for the Prevention of Vivisection, of which Hollands was secretary, opposed such a flexible approach, arguing that under continuous expert 'inside' pressure from industry and science, governments would tend to bend in the direction of the experimenters. The RSPCA, although engulfed in internal dissension during the early 1980s (see chapter 11), still officially opposed non-medical experiments, urged the development and use of humane alternative techniques, sought greater public accountability and wanted a statutory ban on all painful research.

In 1983 the RSPCA Animal Experimentation Advisory Committee, of which I was chairman, sent to the Home Secretary a bulky report on pain in British experiments, concluding that severe pain was not an unusual occurrence and urging certain reforms, including the training of all licensed experimenters in skills of analgesia, anaesthesia and euthanasia. We reminded the government that the RSPCA was opposed to any experiment which caused pain. This report, however, was almost totally ignored, despite several meetings with the Home Office minister, David Mellor.

The government continued to resist our requests to take steps to eradicate pain in experiments, with the excuse that 'there is and can be no definition of the term [pain]'.[25] My committee was very much assisted in our rebuttal of this argument by the intervention of Professor Patrick Wall of University College, London, one of the world's leading experts on pain. He provided us and the Home Office with succinct definitions for 'pain' and 'severe pain', as follows:

Pain in animals is defined as abnormal behaviour which can be alleviated by analgesic procedures which relieve pain in humans. Severe pain in animals is defined as pain produced by procedures to which normal humans would not voluntarily submit without appropriate analgesia or anaesthesia.

In 1985 the British Union for the Abolition of Vivisection, now controlled by Kim Stallwood and Steve McIvor, took a court action against the Royal College of Surgeons, which was found guilty of cruelty to experimental monkeys and fined £250 by Bromley magistrates. Much of the evidence was based upon photographs and documents removed from an RCS laboratory during a raid by South Eastern Animal Liberation League activists in August 1984. Perhaps most revealing of the experimenters' attitude towards the animals was the name 'Crap' tattooed on the forehead of one of the little monkeys. In 1986 the conviction against the Royal College was quashed, and one of the leading witnesses against the Royal College, the animal rights campaigner Michael Huskisson, was charged with offences connected with the raid and later sent to prison for eighteen months.

In November 1985, in the Queen's Speech, the government announced that it would legislate in the ensuing session, and almost immediately introduced its Animals (Scientific Procedures) Bill, just as the two London anti-vivisection societies, BUAV and NAVS, unveiled on 12 December a replacement statue of the brown dog in Battersea Park (see chapter 8).[26]

It was a good moment for the government. Not only was the RSPCA barely recovered from its troubles, but the British Union for the Abolition of Vivisection, too, had only recently emerged from one of its periodic turbulent upheavals. Two factions of genuine enthusiasts had fought a bitter internecine war, in which Margaret Manzoni and the group surrounding Kim Stallwood (who had been expelled from the RSPCA, and hence from its council, in 1985 for some public criticisms of the society) had gained control of the Union. Rumblings from within the National Anti-Vivisection Society would also have informed the government that the other large pressure group likely to oppose a weak Bill was hardly in a united condition and fit to fight a powerful campaign; early in 1986, as the Bill proceeded through Parliament, the NAVS parted asunder with the resignations of some of its best officers – Brian Gunn, Colin Smith and Dr Robert Sharpe – while the supporters of Prince Alexander Galitzine gained ascendancy, Jan Creamer becoming director. Sharpe moved over to find employment with the BUAV.

All the societies of the movement had, throughout the 1970s been trying to get across the fact that nonhuman experiments in general only produce results that are *partially* valid for the human species; applying results from one species to another does not have 100 per cent validity. On the other hand we never claimed that research was *entirely* invalid. There were, however, some disturbing instances where the relative invalidity of animal experimentation showed up with tragic clarity: the deforming effects of thalidomide, for example, did not manifest themselves in the usual laboratory species in use at the time of its development. On the other hand penicillin would probably never have been produced if its pioneers had chosen to test it, not on mice and rabbits as they did, but upon guinea-pigs; for penicillin is very poisonous to guinea-pigs.

The National Anti-Vivisection Society in 1988 produced a leaflet listing some of the other medicines which show these marked interspecies differences – digitalis, chloroform, morphine, aspirin, eraldin, opren, flosint, osmosin, chloramphenicol and clioquinol. Some of these, when used clinically, had produced deaths or hideous injuries in human patients.[27]

In the middle 1980s a major theme of the British anti-vivisection societies – one not much heard for decades – became the claim that research on animals was of little use scientifically or, worse, that it was positively dangerous. Both NAVS and BUAV produced evidence to assert that the major advances in the reduction of infectious diseases had been made by nineteenth-century improvements in sanitation and not by new vaccines or medicines,[28] and a new society, The Eleventh Hour Group for Animals, which came to the fore at this time, also employed these arguments. Furthermore, several societies gave credence to the startling view that the AIDS virus was the product of American research on animals.[29]

The publication of Dr Robert Sharpe's book *The Cruel Deception* in 1988 was a landmark in the history of this line of argument – that research on animals, in the production of new drugs for example, was often useless and could be dangerously misleading. Sharpe analysed the decline in diseases such as tuberculosis, scarlet fever, whooping cough, measles, diphtheria, smallpox, typhoid fever and poliomyelitis, and concluded that society's control of infectious diseases has resulted not from animal research but primarily from 'efficient public health services and a good standard of living'.[30] This argument was supported by independent historical analysis.[31]

INFILTRATION AND EXFILTRATION

That a section of the American-based laboratory animal breeding industry was boasting in the 1980s that it had infiltrated both the Humane Society of the United States and the RSPCA in Britain in order to block reforms is a fact, as was their claim that some members of the veterinary profession on both sides of the Atlantic were giving them support. Whether or not such claims, printed as they were in promotional literature, should be taken seriously, may depend on whether conspiratorial or 'cock-up' theories of history are favoured. It is, nevertheless, certainly true that several British vets came out in public support of animal experimentation on BBC television on 14 July 1986, and that the British government publicly thanked two veterinarians, both associated with the RSPCA, for their parts in preparing the unsatisfactory legislation of the same year which the RSPCA had opposed.

Admittedly, many scientists in the 1970s and 1980s have, in a sense, 'exfiltrated' and spoken out against aspects of animal experimentation — Alice Heim, Harold Hewitt, Richard Dawkins, Kit Pedler, Lord Platt, Gill Langley, Bill Jordan, Louis Goldman, J. D. Whittall, Stuart Britten, Dallas Pratt, Donald Barnes, Michael Fox, Andrew Rowan, Vernon Coleman, Eliot Slater amd myself have been among them. In 1987 Jane Goodall, the outstanding ethologist, joined the attack by criticizing the growing use of chimpanzees in research.[32] She reported on a visit to a laboratory: 'It was a visit I shall never forget. Room after room was lined with small, bare cages, stacked one above the other, where monkeys circled round and round, where chimpanzees sat huddled, far gone in depression and despair.' Goodall pointed out the close physical and psychological similarities between chimpanzees and ourselves and asked: 'Are we justified in using an animal so close to us — and, moreover, an animal that is highly endangered in its African forest home — as a human substitute for medical experimentation?'

THE ATTITUDES OF GOVERNMENT AND SCIENTISTS

British governments have rarely had the courage to invite into their very closest counsels leading and genuine reformers, and this has been especially true in the field of animal research; when, in 1978 CRAE and the RSPCA, for example, were invited to submit the names of six scientifically qualified persons to become members of the Home Office advisory committee on animal experiments, not one of them was appointed. No reasons were ever given for this extraordinary snub; all six were genuine experts but they were concerned about animals. Instead, British governments have usually opted for supporters of the status quo. Indeed, two-thirds of the old Home Office advisory committee, for instance, were scientists sympathetic to research, many of whom had well-known public records as defenders of nonhuman experimentation. The Animal Procedures Committee appointed after the passage of the new legislation was composed similarly, with twelve of its twenty members having clear connections with science or industry and only five having any sort of record as reformers.

Governments in general, and British ones in particular, have simply been unable to grasp the idea that nonhuman as well as human rights need to be fairly protected by such advisory committees. They have not even been able to grasp the far simpler democratic notion that as a large majority of the public is opposed to certain forms of research on animals (e.g. for cosmetics and weapons testing) then the *public* interest, that is to say their wishes as mature tax-paying individuals, also ought to be represented fairly. Instead, governments have always tacitly sided with the scientists, rather than recognizing a genuine difference of opinions and attempting to produce a properly balanced committee to try to resolve them.

Whitehall has been aided in keeping reformers at bay by the fact that animal welfare is spread across half a dozen goverment departments, including some with a natural interest in maintaining exploitation: the Ministry of Agriculture, Fisheries and Food supposedly safeguarding farm animal welfare, the Home Office that of laboratory animals, the Department of Trade animal imports and so on. In 1986 Katya Lester of the Social Democrats and I for the Liberal party formulated detailed draft Alliance proposals for drawing all animal protection administration under one Animal Protection Commission in order to facilitate coherence, reduce costs and avoid buck-passing.

Neutralizing tactics are a feature of most bureaucracies, but in Britain they have appeared more pronounced than, for example, in the European Community, where the officials of the EEC and the European Parliament have shown a far more open, constructive, prompt and action-oriented approach. Once again the experience of the animal movement is probably only one instance of a more general failing of the British body politic after a period of national decline. Ironically, one of the key figures in the European hierarchy's more positive approach to animal protection is Stanley Johnson, who is himself an Englishman. Johnson, having played a key role (then as a Conservative MEP) in banning the import of seal products into Europe, went on as a Commission official to draft the EEC Directive on the Protection of Animals for Experimental and Other Scientific Purposes (COM (85) 637) which was passed in 1986. This promised to raise standards in some European states, to restrict severe suffering in experiments, and to require specific authority and constant veterinary supervision for procedures causing suffering that is more than momentary.

Scientists have thin skins; they do not like to be criticized. Indeed, the vivisectors' anger and irrationality when criticized by opponents of speciesism are sometimes remarkable. Such signs of guilt usually are not strong enough, however, to overcome most vivisectors' motives for persisting, and once they have been 'blooded' they have a psychological vested interest in continuing their trade: to turn back would be an admission that they are wrong; to continue is to feel part of a select group who have conquered their scruples. It is usually a one-way ticket: like the primitive tribesman who undergoes an ordeal at puberty and then emerges as a 'man', the student scientist conquers his or her initial revulsion at seeing animals cold-bloodedly taken apart and graduates as part of an 'elite'. There is no going back. This psychological initiation process is also akin to the training of members of special armed forces, who emerge having faced great stress, priding themselves in their ability to endure it. Furthermore, in as much as science competes with religion as a source of power and meaning, its qualified exponents take on, whether they like it or not (and many like it) some of the social connotations previously reserved for the priesthood. Sometimes the vivisector appears as a pseudo-high-priest waging a holy war against the compassion of mere 'ignorant' mortals.

Some scientists, too, being no longer truly independent of government or industry, are remarkably conservative. British science in particular has often allowed itself to be used to support the status quo, arguing that nothing should be changed unless there is almost 100 per cent proof that change is absolutely necessary; examples have included the argument over the threats to the environment caused by nuclear and chemical pollution. Scientists have also been reluctant to give up using animals even when satisfactory or superior alternatives have been established. Dr Gill Langley has cited three examples of such inertia − the failure to use human diploid cells in the production of polio vaccine, to use cell cultures for the diagnosis of tuberculosis, and to give up using nonhuman animals for the safety testing of polio vaccine. In each of these three cases, scientists ignored for many years the evidence that new non-animal techniques were available.[33]

THE ANIMALS (SCIENTIFIC PROCEDURES) ACT, 1986

For several years an alliance between the Glasgow and London antivivisection societies and Animal Aid, calling itself Mobilisation for Laboratory Animals, campaigned energetically but vainly for bans on the LD50 and Draize methods of toxicity testing and on weapons, cosmetics, tobacco, alcohol and psychological tests on animals, and for a balanced Home Office committee, as reforms to be included in the new legislation. But in the Animals (Scientific Procedures) Bill, introduced in 1985, the UK government made no concessions to this lobby.

The Labour party, much to the dismay of many, announced its support for the Bill almost as soon as it was published. Once again, when faced with the chance of real reforms or a parody, the Labour party had failed to rise to the challenge. After Neil Kinnock, no doubt impressed by Houghton's acceptance of the government's proposals, had publicly supported the Bill, Labour's official position remained unaltered, despite the strenuous efforts of a few Labour backbenchers such as Harry Cohen MP, and the eloquent proclamation of the animal rights position by the Labour peer Lord Melchett.

Most devastatingly for the reformers, the passage of the Bill was almost entirely ignored by the British media which, during the previous decade, had devoted so much space to the campaign. When it finally bore bitter fruit in the new legislation, newspapers and electronic media displayed extraordinary indifference. After scores of television interviews and a thousand press reports, campaigners suddenly found no interest whatever in what they were saying. How far this was due to 'news management' by the government, or a switching over of coverage to political editors, and how much was due to a general swing away from interest in animal matters by the media, is hard to ascertain. Certainly during the 1970s the movement had been hugely assisted by the keenness of the media in Britain and, later on, in Australia and America. Then, the animal rights campaign had been something new, or at least a new variation on an old and traditionally popular theme.

Only the Liberal/SDP Alliance parties officially opposed the Bill, and a motion to stop it was proposed by the parties' leaders David Steel and Dr David Owen, largely at the instigation of the SDP's Michael Hancock MP. This motion urged that the Bill be denied a Second Reading because it:

fails to prevent a single experiment that takes place at present, does little to encourage, in the long term, the replacement of animals in experimentation, does little to increase the protection for laboratory animals and does not allay public concern for the need to have greater public accountability in the field of animal experimentation.[34]

In the Commons, the Alliance position was firmly put by Michael Hancock. In the Lords, the majority of the proposed amendments were put down by the Liberal peers Lord Beaumont of Whitley and Lord Airedale, but few had the slightest effect upon the ultimate wording of the Act. Of the five major reforms sought by the Liberals — greater restrictions on pain and on the testing of *non-medical* products and weapons, improved public accountability and openness, firm guarantees of animal protection under the Act, and greater incentives to use humane alternative techniques — only the latter ultimately achieved any significant degree of success. The Earl of Selkirk, one of the few Conservative voices critical of the Bill, had no greater effect, and Lords Houghton and Halsbury, previously on opposite sides, both gave the Bill their support.

The Bill's main innovation was the introduction of a 'cost–benefit analysis' to be carried out by the Secretary of State when issuing licences, requiring him or her to balance the pain of the nonhuman subject against the possible human benefits of the research in each case. This represented, perhaps, a step forward in terms of political awareness, but philosophically its statutory enshrinement of the 'ends justify the means' position was unsound, and indeed quite disturbing.

One of the few practical reforms in the legislation was the introduction of fees for the licences required to carry out experiments. This idea was one we had been advocating for over ten years, and may turn out to be an effective means of reducing some unnecessary types of research.

The RSPCA's position of not welcoming the Bill until certain amendments (e.g. on pain, alternative techniques and the training of licencees) were made held steady during the passage of the Bill but was not effectively deployed or driven home. Mass rallies in opposition to the Bill were organized in London, Cambridge and elsewhere by the two London anti-vivisection societies (the NAVS and BUAV) and by the new Laboratory Animal Protection Society and Terry Hunt's Eleventh Hour Group which, departing from the altruistic moral argument, made the deliberate decision to base its campaign on the alleged dangers to human health posed by animal experiments.

Representing the International Fund for Animal Welfare (IFAW), I spoke at these meetings and lobbied Parliament with 'ten reasons why it is a bad bill', proposing twenty-nine detailed amendments to the Bill's wording. Rebecca Hall and Gordon Newman's group Writers for Animals Rights brought together talents as diverse as those of Richard Adams, Bob Geldof, Fay Weldon and Angus Wilson in public defence of nonhumans in laboratories.

Church leaders, too, spoke out against the Bill and, co-ordinated diligently by Ann Dalton, they made a significant contribution to the debate. The Catholic Study Circle for Animal Welfare, through its magazine *The Ark,* maintained its usual high standards of humane and constructive criticism. *The Times,* on 22 February 1986, published a letter attacking the Bill, signed by the Catholic Bishop Agnellus Andrew and five other distinguished religious spokesmen – Bishops Alan C. Clark of East Anglia, Derek Bond of Bradwell, John Baker of Salisbury, Lord Soper the Methodist leader, and Rabbi Lionel Blue. They stated:

There is a strong swell of public opinion about experimentation on live animals and we believe that human beings have grave duties towards their fellow creatures, unable to speak for themselves. As stewards of creation, we feel a moral duty to concern ourselves in this matter and we express a strong hope that the Bill at present before Parliament will be suitably amended.

Until the day comes when experiments on live animals are abandoned we believe it to be our duty to avoid unnecessary duplication, to seek alternative procedures, and to abolish or reduce to a minimum the distress and pain inflicted on animals by scientific experiments.

This ecumenical letter received widespread attention in Church news-papers,[35] and on 26 March was supported in a *Times* letter signed by five reformers with experience of working in animal laboratories — Angela Walder, Dr Harold Hewitt, Dr Gill Langley, Bill Jordan and myself, and listing IFAW's ten reasons why we disliked the Bill; princi-pally that it did not stop pain or non-medical research, that it proposed to increase the secrecy surrounding experiments, that experimenters were not required to be skilled in pain-reduction and that, generally, the Bill contained no firm guarantees of improvement.

On the same day a *Times* letter from the RSPCA council chairman, Anelay Hart, criticized the Bill along similar lines, stating: 'the Society has offered support for the Bill itself only if the changes which we regard as critical are incorporated.' They were not, and the Bill became law a few weeks later with only a few milk-and-water concessions to the reformers' point of view.

A few 'Houghtonite' campaigners disagreed with us and our letters were criticized in one from Clive Hollands and others published in *The Times* on 15 April. But a final letter on 25 April, signed by Rebecca Hall, Susan Marshall, G. F. Newman, Brigid Brophy and other writers also attacked the Bill.

The Bill became law on 20 May 1986, after little or no effective opposition in Parliament. Houghton's support for it, and that of the Labour party, together with the RSPCA's lack of vigour in opposing it, had ensured its safe passage. Houghton later stated that he had felt that he had to seize the opportunity offered by the active involvement of the relevant minister, David Mellor. If this opportunity was missed, Mellor's successor might not have been the person to push it through.[36]

Our campaigns stretching over some fifteen years had undoubtedly caused the legislation to happen, but they had not fashioned its content. Only time will tell whether laboratory nonhumans are better off than they were before under the new British and EEC legislation, or whether the flexibility of the new Act allows even further erosion of their rights.

CURRENT TOPICS

As the decade of the 1980s drew to a close, there were seven areas of special concern in the movement internationally:

1 Pain and distress; their classification, control or prohibition.
2 The use of Ethical (or Care) Committees to monitor experiments at laboratory level.
3 The restriction or prohibition of non-medical experiments (such as cosmetics and weapons testing, and psychological experiments).
4 The development and use of humane alternative techniques.
5 Genetic engineering.

6 The prohibition of toxicity testing (in particular LD50 and Draize tests).
7 The use of nonhuman primates.

The last three issues had become especially topical: genetic engineering
(see p. 7) was an area where those interested in farm animal welfare
joined forces with animal experimentation reformers. The suffering of
transgenic creatures was the central issue. How likely was the mixing of
animal species to produce in-built weaknesses that would cause pain?
The Maryland pigs who contained human genetic material, were a glaring
example: reportedly they were so arthritic that they were reluctant even
to stand. Religious groups, too, began to attack genetic engineering.
Speaking of the mixing of human with nonhuman apes, a Vatican spokesman described the possibility as − 'a Satanic attempt to destroy every
presence of God in the Universe, destroying his likeness, which is
Man'.[37]
Toxicity (poison) testing had long been a bone of contention with
reformers, at least since the end of the 1960s. We had continuously
attacked certain standard procedures for testing the safety of new substances on animals, whether drugs or weedkillers, detergents, cosmetics
or almost any other chemical product, however trivial. These were being
force-fed to tens of thousands of animals (of many species) each year in
crude LD50 procedures, the aim of which was to ascertain what dose of
the test substance would cause 50 per cent of the animals to die within a
fixed period, often fourteen days. Clearly this was causing untold suffering worldwide. As early as 1973, however, some toxicologists were
prepared publicly to attack this barbaric travesty of science. Dr Gerhard
Zbinden went on record as describing the LD50 as 'a ritual mass execution of animals'. Yet it went on as production companies, always in fear
of actions for damages, tried to prove their lack of negligence through
this hideous observance of bureaucratic protocols.[38]
Testing of concentrated soaps and other substances on the eyes of
rabbits (the Draize test) is another form of toxicity testing which has
been, and continues to be, a target of reformers. Towards the end of the
decade slow moves were in hand to alter the bureaucratic regulations
which required toxicity tests of these types.
The use of nonhuman primates (apes and monkeys) in research is
nothing new. Hundreds of thousands were used in the 1960s by American drug and vaccine procedures alone, but it was only in the 1980s,
with actions taken in America by PETA (see chapter 16), the active
involvement of well-known figures such as Dr Jane Goodall and Prince
Sadruddin Aga Khan, and representations made to the British government, that the issue became a priority. Coincidentally, the growing
opposition to the use of our nearest evolutionary relatives for experimentation (chimpanzees share 99 per cent of our genetic material) came
at the same time that governments in America and Europe began

to launch programmes into AIDS research using primates. Conservationists, worried by dwindling stocks of wild apes and appalled at the wasteful killing of as many as ten chimpanzees for every one reaching a laboratory alive, united with animal rightists to urge bans on the export of primates (or, at least, apes) from their countries of origin.

SCIENCE UNDER ATTACK

Public opinion internationally is widely critical of science in the 1980s – of the dangers it poses, for example, through pollution, the use of food additives, genetic engineering and nuclear power.

Some scientists themselves share these doubts. Others argue that at least they should respect the variety of viewpoints expressed by the community at large.[39] After more than half a century's unchallenged sovereignty within Western cultures, science is beginning to show a few signs of humility; among them a growing awareness that using nonhuman subjects in research is a moral issue of considerable magnitude.

Oxford again became a centre for this controversy. The experiments of Dr Colin Blakemore on the eyes of cats and kittens made news over several years, and the well-known historian, Professor Norman Stone, reportedly attacked the demands of Oxford scientists for more money for experiments – 'Research has given Oxford a fabulous infrastructure of revolting concrete buildings where animals are sadistically done to death',[39] he wrote, while the equally known Oxford philosopher, Baroness Mary Warnock, defended the scientists – 'we face the return of a dark age in which rhetoric will take the place of rational thought', she warned.[41] Addressing a conference in Venice, and in reply to the American anti-technology activist Jeremy Rifkin, who had stated that 'we can no longer trust the scientist to determine the course of science', Mary Warnock lamented: 'I fear we are at the beginning of an era of anti-science.'

Coming from the chairman of the Home Office advisory committee helping to control animal experiments – a committee charged with the protection of nonhuman animals as well as scientists – these comments sounded a trifle one-sided.

14 On the Factory-Farm

It has been estimated that, worldwide, some 1,000 million animals, excluding poultry, are slaughtered each year for their meat,[1] and about 100,000 per *day* in Britain alone. This holocaust has provoked increasing concern on three major grounds: first, from those aware of the human health dangers of a diet rich in animal fat and chemical additives; secondly, from those convinced that meat is an extravagant and immoral way to produce protein in a world where a third of the human population is overfed and a third is near to starvation; thirdly, from those worried about the welfare of nonhuman animals who are subjected to cruel slaughter techniques and increasingly intensive systems of production.

THE NONHUMAN ANIMALS

Chickens

The rearing of poultry in confined conditions goes back many centuries in Europe. But such practices increased rapidly after the Second World War and especially after the mid-1950s. In 1954 there were 20 million broilers being reared in Britain, and by 1960 this had risen to 142 million. In the USA at this time the figure was nearly 2 billion. In 1986 approximately 400 million broilers were reared in Britain, 480 million in France, 170 million in Germany, 280 million in Italy and 230 million in the Netherlands.[2] A total of over two *billion* broiler chickens are slaughtered in the EEC each year.

Those birds used in the production of eggs have been even more confined. They are kept in small 'battery' cages, traditionally three or four birds in a cage only fifteen or sixteen inches wide. In America, farmers sometimes put ten birds in cages twenty inches by thirty inches. In this way, each shed can accommodate several thousand birds. When birds become restive and peck their fellow prisoners, the answer is to burn off their beaks.

What is the purpose of this overcrowding? Quite simply it is because it reduces capital costs (i.e. the cost of cages and sheds) as well as labour bills. With battery chickens it became possible in the 1960s for a man and a boy to operate units of 15,000 birds.

Large-scale battery chicken farming appears to have been a joint Anglo-American invention made during the 1920s. In 1930 both countries began the commercial production of battery cages. By 1951 there were three million cages in use in Britain, and ten years later 40 per cent of all layers were in batteries. By 1986 there were at least forty million layers in Britain, of which about 90 per cent were battery birds.[3] In America average flock sizes rose from 20,000 birds per shed in the 1950s to 80,000 birds twenty years later. Today's American battery cage typically holds four or five chickens on a twelve- by eighteen-inch floor. In 1986 the EEC alone produced approximately 82 *billion* eggs.[4]

Veal Calves

The factory-farming of veal calves also expanded after the Second World War. In Holland calves had been immobilized and reared in darkness for centuries in the belief that these conditions produced white meat, which farmers understood was what the housewife wanted. In Britain, farmers frequently bled calves in the equally mistaken belief that this produced pallid flesh.

The outcry against the rearing of calves without straw and in small dark crates, sometimes no more than twenty-two inches wide, really began after the publication of Ruth Harrison's *Animal Machines* in 1964 and with the early efforts of Peter Roberts's persistent pressure group, Compassion in World Farming, which he started in 1967. The media amplified the message, and without the formation of any special 'anti-veal calf' society, without any highly costly campaign or the passage of new legislation, the consumption of veal in Britain declined so steeply that in 1980 the main veal producers, Quantock Veal Ltd, announced that they had abandoned highly intensive methods in favour of straw yards and other less objectionable rearing systems. Furthermore, after publicity from Compassion in World Farming and the *Sunday Mirror* the practice of muzzling veal calves fell into disrepute.

Yet about 40 per cent of the British veal industry continued rearing calves in crates, and in 1984 Mary Rose Barrington, a London solicitor, working in conjunction with Compassion in World Farming, brought a case against the manager of a veal farm at Storrington in Surrey owned by Catholic Canons. Despite evidence from John Douglass of the RSPCA, two veterinarians, several experts and myself, the magistrates found the defendant not guilty, and all costs were awarded against Compassion in World Farming. The concept of mental suffering, although applicable in the cases of children and pets, did not seem appropriate for livestock in the eyes of British law. Nevertheless this veal farm was closed down in 1985.

Pigs

In general, it was the corporate businessman who used the more objectionable methods, while the traditional 'small farmer' often steered clear of factory-farming. The intrusion of a big business approach into agriculture produced intensive methods of rearing other livestock, most worryingly pigs, who, during the 1960s, increasingly were to be found tethered in stalls unable to turn round or crowded into un-cleaned-out 'sweat boxes' without straw. Pigs were kept to make money, an agricultural scientist reassured farmers, and 'the test of a sweat box is whether or not it pays.'[5] In 1986 there was a breeding stock of over 800,000 pigs in Britain, about two-thirds being intensively reared. Over twelve million pigs are slaughtered annually in Britain alone.[6]

Intensive systems almost inevitably produce unnatural and unhygienic conditions in which animals, already weakened by the stress of overcrowding and the frustration of their natural needs for exercise and stimulation, easily succumb to disease. In order to counter this, the veterinary profession is enlisted to medicate the animals with antibiotics and growth-promoting drugs. Scientists, often heavily subsidized by the taxpayer, strive to develop methods of maximizing the quantities of meat produced in the shortest times. Producers are also paid taxpayers' money to produce more and more, almost regardless of the *quality* for the consumer or the *cruelty* to the animals. For three decades an unholy international alliance between government, science and business has governed agriculture in the West, building obscene meat mountains while much of the rest of the world has starved. The nonhuman animals have stood little chance caught between such giants.

THE WELFARE CAMPAIGN

Various small societies were formed in Britain to combat the evils of this situation, such as the Farm and Food Society in 1969, Compassion in World Farming in 1967, the Free Range Egg Association and the Dartmoor Livestock Protection Society. Eileen Bezet of the latter had done a great deal to publicize the transportation of livestock from Britain across continents, another form of cruelty often practised to earn subsidies. Mrs A. M. Allen, Joanne Bower, Hilda Holmes and Barbara Macdonald were other stalwarts in this campaign. In the long term it has been Peter Roberts's Compassion in World Farming which has been the most durable and effective of all the European groups working in this broad field. A more specialized, but equally effective group has been Chickens Lib, founded by Violet Spalding and her daughter Clare Druce in 1971 and run initially from their Oxfordshire home. These two women bought hens from batteries in order to give them a better home, publishing photographs of bedraggled and almost bald specimens which shocked the conscience of the British public, constantly lobbying the worldly Ministry of Agriculture, urging improved regulations and challenging the complacency of the industry. Chickens Lib has maintained the pressure year after year, and their campaign against batteries received support in 1986 from well-known figures ranging from noted campaigners of the 1960s such as Iris Murdoch, Patrick Moore, Lord Soper and the Reverend Edward Carpenter, to later celebrities such as Richard Adams, Catherine Cookson, Bruce Kent, Ken Livingstone, Joanna Lumley, Tony Soper and Desmond Morris.

Ruth Harrison, although wary of 'animal-lovers who anthropomorphise the animal' or put nonhumans before their own species, made clear her hope in her *Animal Machines* of 1964[7] that mankind's attitude towards farm animals would be reassessed. Rachel Carson in her foreword to Harrison's book roundly rejected humankind's right to reduce a nonhuman animal's life to a mere existence, and called for a true reverence for life. Neither, however, expanded upon the subject of suffering or the ethical issues. In 1964 such restraint had been necessary: any emphasis on animal rights would have reduced the impact of Harrison's book. But the need for such caution had gone by 1980 when Peter Singer and Jim Mason published their book *Animal Factories* in America.[8] Europe, and particularly Britain, had once again led the way in calling attention to the need for reform. Equally characteristically, Britain seemed among the least inclined actually to *do* anything to put matters right.

In 1965 the official Brambell Committee, set up after the publication of Ruth Harrison's book, recommended the passage of new legislation to prohibit the debeaking of hens, the docking of pigs' tails, and the close tethering of veal calves and sows, and to lay down maximum stocking densities.[9] But no legislation was ever passed. All that happened was that in 1971 the Ministry of Agriculture established some vaguely worded and purely voluntary codes of practice (revised in 1983) that neither bound the producers nor convinced the reformers. Despite radical reports from the House of Commons Select Committee on Agriculture and from the official Farm Animal Welfare Council[10] during the 1980s, legislative action still had not been taken in Britain by 1987. What *had* happened, however, was that European governments had begun to cut subsidies to the agricultural industry and to impose production quotas in an effort to contain the over-production of certain products in the EEC.

In America, Singer and Mason's book stimulated renewed interest in the fate of farm animals, and major organizations such as the Animal Welfare Institute, the Humane Society of the United States, and the

Food Animal Concerns Trust all stepped up their campaigning, while grassroots organizations such as the Farm Animal Reform Movement initiated peaceful and legal direct action.

The response of agricultural interests in Britain to welfare campaigns had been to call for more research to prove or disprove that batteries and other intensive methods were cruel. This call has helped to slow up reforms considerably: scientific evidence to prove the obvious is not always easy to establish. On the continent of Europe such cynical delaying tactics have not been so popular, but in Britain the RSPCA financed much unnecessary research into the keeping of farm animals during the 1970s. Other than the findings of Dr Marian Stamp Dawkins in Oxford, by 1980 this research had produced very little information of value and had helped to reduce the debate to the level of arguing about what size or shape of cage or crate would produce less stress, instead of seeking radical alternatives to the cages themselves. The RSPCA council, half acknowledging its error, tried to shift the emphasis by laying down that nonhumans should always have the benefit of the doubt. It should be up to the producer, in other words, to prove that intensive and unnatural methods cause *no* suffering, rather than for the campaigner to prove that they do.

Dr Marian Dawkins's book *Animal Suffering: The Science of Animal Welfare*, published in 1980, was a genuine and scientific attempt to determine the preference of nonhumans. Dawkins faced up to the problem of how to decide whether nonhumans are suffering, in the absence of obvious signs of injury or disease, by devising a series of preference tests for chickens, giving to the experimental subjects a number of choices on what sort of environment they wished to be in. Although such an approach has many methodological difficulties, offering the inmates an element of choice as regards temperature, lighting, bedding, companionship and so on opens up a range of new possibilities for captive animals in general. Pigs in particular seemed quick to seize such opportunities, and Dawkins cited one pig who took only five minutes to realize the connection between a switch and a heater. She asserted that 'animals may still suffer despite an external appearance of good health.'[11]

Another important development was initiated by the Council of Europe, which, in its Convention for the Protection of Animals kept for Farming Purposes (see chapter 16), introduced the principle that animals should be housed and cared for in ways 'appropriate to their physiological and ethological needs'. Although vague, this convention has been ratified by the EEC, and had led to an increasing acceptance that nonhumans have needs for space, companionship, exercise and interest, as well as for food, warmth and water, and that such psychological and other needs will vary with each species and, indeed, from individual to individual.

Britain, as usual strong on ideas and weak on action, has produced several other significant books touching on modern husbandry methods, not least Mark Gold's *Assault and Battery* of 1983 and Richard Body's *Agriculture: The Triumph and the Shame* of 1982.[12] Gold attacks five 'myths' used by those who defend factory-farming. The first is the charge levelled at reformers that they are being emotional and anthropomorphic and that only science can provide the answers; the second is that the consumer 'demands' the intensive production of protein; the third is that factory-farming of livestock is a solution to world starvation; the fourth that modern techniques produce a happy human workforce; the fifth that factory-farming is an economic necessity. Gold refutes all these 'tall stories', providing evidence that in several instances they are clearly quite contrary to the facts. In 1984, for example, while thousands of Ethiopian children died of starvation, the UK had imported from the best agricultural land in Ethiopia some £1.5 million worth of seed cake to fatten British cattle.[13]

Sir Richard Body, a Conservative MP, provided some powerful support for the view that factory-farming has hit both the consumer and the taxpayer and has deprived some efficient industries of the capital they have needed for development. Hundreds of millions of pounds have been diverted into intensive agriculture by pension funds and insurance companies, with consequent loss of jobs in other industries, he argued. The British system has encouraged the big agricultural interests at the expense of the small livestock farmer; some 60,000 were driven out of business during the 1970s. Millionaires have benefited from agricultural tax incentives while farm workers have become poorer, about 90,000 losing their jobs entirely over a decade in which they have been replaced by factory-farm machinery. Body deplored the uprooting of woodlands and hedgerows and the draining of wetlands which have been encouraged by government hand-outs of taxpayers' money. He attacked the pollution caused by the excessive use of agricultural chemicals and the impoverishment of the world's poor aggravated by Britain's 'selfish' policies.

Without emphasizing the cruelty aspect of factory farming, Body's book has nevertheless done much to change the direction of official thinking and to hasten the return of the small farmer with a more traditional approach to livestock.

POLITICAL MOVES

During the 1980s, the RSPCA's record on farm animal welfare considerably improved under John Douglass, the head of its Farm Animals Department since its inception in 1979. The first European Conference on the Protection of Farm Animals, organized by Philip Brown of the RSPCA and held in Amsterdam in 1979, hosted almost five hundred delegates from all over the world. It urged appropriate legislation on a Community-wide basis and specifically attacked the close confinement of sows, veal calves and poultry, stressing the need to take into account the birds' 'fundamental behavioural and physiological needs'.

In the same year the Social and Economic Committee of the EEC gave an 'opinion' on the EEC's Directive on the Protection of Animals during International Transport which stressed that animals should 'be killed as near as possible to the point of production' (see chapter 16). This still remains a fundamental objective of reformers and in 1982 a second conference was held in Strasbourg, at which the transportation of food animals was the principal topic discussed.

In 1981 the House of Commons Select Committee on Agriculture published a report which courageously recommended the phasing out of battery cages for hens and a major campaign against crated veal calf production. The report was rejected by the government. Later the same year, after years of urging by its council, the RSPCA at last took an action against a battery farmer for not adhering to the Ministry of Agriculture's codes: the finding was that he had not 'thoroughly inspected' his hens.

In the following year, the ministry revised its codes of practice on the housing of cattle and pigs, and Sainsbury's led the way among the big British supermarkets by deciding to sell free-range eggs in six of their stores. Marks & Spencer, urged on by Chickens Lib, were soon to follow, and so, eventually, did other stores.

In 1984 the British Government's Farm Animal Welfare Council (FAWC) published reports recommending radical changes in the annual slaughter of 480 million poultry and red meat animals in Britain.[14] Disturbingly, it found that humane slaughter techniques were far from universally effective and that many chickens and sheep were having their throats cut while conscious. Pigs, too, were not being effectively stunned by piece-rate slaughtermen too often in a hurry.

In the following year FAWC turned its attention to the ritual slaughter of over four million animals in Britain each year, recommending an end within three years of the Jewish and Muslim exemptions from the legal requirement in Britain that animals should be stunned before slaughter. The RSPCA and Compassion in World Farming took the lead in urguing the adoption of this proposal and the institution of a ban such as those already introduced in Norway, Sweden and Switzerland. This campaign received support from the British Veterinary Association.

The Farm Animal Welfare Council also recommended that farmed deer should be slaughtered in slaughter houses rather than on site. This was the first of the council's reports to cause major dissension among its members, many of whom considered that the timid deer would suffer excessively in transportation and in the strange environment of a slaughter house.

So the early 1980s in Britain were a period not of legislative progress so much as of gradual attitude change on the part of veterinarians, farmers and officials. Both the Farm Animal Welfare Council and the House of Commons select committee had, against the expectations of the radicals but perhaps partly because of their pressure, produced quite far-reaching recommendations. True to form, the government had largely ignored them, as they had ignored so many reports on animal welfare before, such as those of the Brambell and Littlewood committees in 1965. However, in 1987, regulations were introduced prohibiting the keeping of calves in crates in which they are unable to turn round freely or in which they are deprived of the iron and roughage they require for full health and vigour, and, on 27 November 1986, the government announced that it would prohibit crates altogether from the year 1990.

Despite the very respectable composition of the Farm Animal Welfare Council, under its distinguished chairman Professor Sir Richard Harrison, its opinions, in general, have proved too progressive for the died-in-the-wool elements in the ministry. Nevertheless, vets, and even the National Farmers Union, have been forced to take cognizance of the new climate of opinion. Younger members of the farming and veterinary professions are beginning to take an interest in the technical and moral aspects of animal welfare, swayed increasingly by the argument that animals ought to be reared in 'natural' conditions.

In 1985 the British Veterinary Association were instrumental in setting up at Cambridge the first Chair in Animal Welfare in Britain. Unfortunately its first incumbent, Professor Donald Broom, was quick to distance himself from the animal rights ethic, thereby disappointing many activists.

The National Farmers Union, which had for so long had the ear of the ministry, and provided the principal opposition to reform, set up its own Animal Welfare Committee and gradually agreed to dialogue. Increasing scruples on the part of the farmers have meant that by 1986 approximately 30 per cent of British pigs were not being reared intensively,[15] and following the supermarkets' lead smaller producers had discovered that some consumers were indeed prepared to pay more for free-range eggs.

In the EEC, progress often seemed faster than in the UK, although, ironically, the main movers were often British MEPs and the British-sponsored Eurogroup (see chapter 16). The attitude of European officials and parliamentarians to the animal protection lobby was certainly more positive and helpful than the dead hand of Whitehall. Belgian and French MEPs sometimes showed a confidence that they could get things done which contrasted with the resigned air of impotence too often encountered in Westminister.

By 1984 the whole wartime ethos of 'food production at almost any cost' seemed to have run its course. The introduction of agricultural quotas to limit production heralded a revolution which was accelerated in February 1987 by the government's announcement that restrictions on agricultural land for development would be relaxed.

Horses had often continued to be considered as agricultural animals, and John Douglass of the RSPCA's Farm Animals Department played a leading role in 1987 in highlighting the cruelty to tethered ponies in Britain, helping David Amess MP bring in a successful Ten Minute Rule Bill which became the Protection of Animals Act of 1988. This Act amended the Protection of Animals Act (1911) to make cruel tethering of equines an offence.

THE DECLINE IN MEAT-EATING

The 1986 Realeat Survey on Great Britain's changing attitude to meat-eating was conducted and researched by Gallup (Social Services) Ltd and sampled 3,881 adults aged sixteen and over at 200 points across the British Isles. The results of the survey showed a steady decline in meat-eating among higher (but not lower) socio-economic groups, especially in the south of England, over 40 per cent citing health as their principal reason. Students and young women between the ages of sixteen and twenty-four led the way.

The vegetarian movement had also benefited from publications during the 1970s, notably from Jon Wynne-Tyson's *Food for a Future* in 1975. *The Times* commented on Wynne-Tyson: 'perhaps his most subtle achievement is the slow revelation that the arguments for meat-eating are in fact those that are emotional and irrational.' In 1986 Peter Cox published *Why You Don't Need Meat*, in which he claimed that eating pork more than once a week is associated with a doubling of breast cancer and that charcoal-grilled steak weighing one kilogram contains as much carcinogenic benzopyrene as the smoke of 600 cigarettes. Cox stated: 'economists have calculated that if the Western world was to cut its meat consumption by just 50 per cent, each person doing so would release enough grain to keep two more people alive who would otherwise starve.'

In Britain Dr Alan Long has spearheaded the vegetarian movement for some years and furnished it with a strong scientific basis. By the end of the 1970s hundreds of young animal rightists were vegans (eschewing dairy products as well as meat), and thousands more were vegetarians. The Vegetarian Society itself held numerous conferences, but did not always satisfy those who wished to take a more political stance against cruelty.

In America there was an explosion of new books on the subject, beginning with Dudley Giehl's *Vegetarianism: A Way of Life* in 1979.[16] A Gallup poll in America in 1985 revealed that 9 million Americans described themselves as vegetarians and a further 40 million as 'semi-vegetarians'. A survey in Britain in 1987 revealed that 4.3 million people (7.7 per cent of the population) were either full vegetarians or avoiding red meat, and that 11 per cent more adults were full vegetarians than in the preceding year. These figures compare with 11 per cent of children

(1.4 million) under sixteen being said by their parents to be full vegetarians or beginning to avoid red meat. Interestingly, twice as many
women are vegetarians than men.[17]

Greater knowledge of meat production methods such as the administration of antibiotics and hormones, the use of intensive husbandry,
and the injection of the flesh-tenderizing papain enzyme into animals
before stunning, have given the meat industry an increasingly dubious
image, in terms of both human health and cruelty.[18]

As Alan Long remarked: 'It's only the application of massive amounts
of drugs that is propping the whole wretched business up, but, as it is,
disease keeps erupting.' Reports of salmonella in poultry, meningitis in
pigs, BSE (dementia) in cattle, tuberculosis in farmed deer, mastitis in
dairy cows, and of alleged cross-infection to humans in some cases,
supported his warnings.[19]

CONCLUSIONS

The 1970s and 1980s have seen hugely increasing public awareness of the
sufferings of nonhumans in intensive husbandry, transportation and
slaughter, and a swing against meat-eating.

Perhaps the saddest victim of the factory-farm system is the breeding
sow kept for almost her whole life closely confined in a stall, unable to
turn round and scarcely able to move. Professor T. K. Ewer, former
head of the animal husbandry department at Bristol University, backed
Compassion in World Farming in 1986 in condemning the practice as
'cruel and distasteful': their report concluded that sows were severely
distressed by their treatment, developing behaviour which sometimes
resembled chronic psychiatric disorders in humans.[20]

The economics of factory-farming, too, have come under the reformers'
scrutiny. An increasing number of egg producers in Britain found in the
1980s that the consumer *was* prepared to pay more for quality. As Jim
Mason put it:

I believe that the financial benefits of factory farms are exaggerated, and
furthermore, that they produce unhealthy animals and poor-quality products; to offset these effects factory farmers must employ an arsenal of
antibiotics, hormones, drugs, chemical additives, colouring agents and other
substances that may threaten human health. When one considers the potential magnitude of these health problems and the social cost of dealing with
them, the food produced by factory methods may well be too expensive –
regardless of its price at the supermarket.[21]

As the 1980s came to an end, several issues were simmering politically.
In Britain the regulation of farmed deer, the campaign to prohibit the
cruelties inherent in Jewish and Muslim religious slaughter and mounting

concern at the finding that about one-third of battery hens were arriving for slaughter with broken bones were examples. Worldwide, however, the extraordinary ethical aspects of genetic engineering, and its implications for farm animal welfare, became a major subject for debate.[22]

Although the food industry was showing signs of responding slowly to changing public attitudes it was still a force which impeded animal welfare reforms. At the end of the 1980s most farm animals in Britain continued to be kept in unnatural and distressing conditions conducive to disease, often fed upon the processed products of their own excreta and the bodies of other members of their species who had died of disease or injury.

The resignation of the well-known government minister Edwina Currie in December 1988 for publicly stating that most egg production in Britain was affected by salmonella illustrated the immense power of the industry and the collusion of the Ministry of Agriculture. Regardless as to whether she was right or wrong, Mrs Currie was forced to go, and consumer interests were over-ruled by commercial ones. In food quality control the comparison between the performance of the British Ministry of Agriculture – secretive and partisan – with that of the open and independent US Food and Drug Administration, was odious.

In 1965 the Brambell Committee had recommended that every farm animal be allowed five freedoms – 'to be able, without difficulty, to turn round, groom itself, get up, lie down and stretch its limbs.' This was precious little to ask for. Yet, at the end of the 1980s, even these minimal comforts continued to be unenforced and routinely denied to millions of hens, calves, pigs and other sentients.[23]

15 Violence and the Animal Liberation Front

The Animal Liberation Front was started in 1972 by two young men, Ronald Lee and Clifford Goodman, and was initially called the Band of Mercy – the resurrection of a name first used by Catherine Smithies and young supporters of the RSPCA in 1876. Goodman, an engineer from Northampton, and Lee, an articled clerk from Luton, had for some years been associated with the Hunt Saboteurs Association, but began to feel that action should also be taken to save animals in laboratories and factory farms.

In March 1975 Lee and Goodman, arrested at Bicester on 23 August 1974, were convicted at Oxford Crown Court of causing more than £50,000's worth of damage to equipment at various animal laboratories in England and Wales over the two preceding years, and were given sentences of three years' imprisonment. The damage they had caused had included setting fire to buildings in Milton Keynes which they believed had been used in animal experimentation, the damaging of vans at the Huntingdon Research Centre in Cambridgeshire and at Capel Isaac in Wales, and the daubing of slogans such as 'Down with Speciesism' on laboratory walls.[1]

Their associate Robin Howard, a young computer programmer, was the first of the modern militants to be convicted, on 12 February 1975 at Oxford. This was for causing damage to two Lincolnshire sealing boats. Subsequently, he joined the established animal welfare movement and later became a respected council member of the RSPCA.

Released after twelve months in gaol, Goodman set up an animal rescue squad which aimed to work within the law, while Lee continued as spokesman for the Band of Mercy which he renamed the Animal Liberation Front in 1976. Lee, for many years a vegan, had been sceptical of the political approach, believing that powerful commercial interests would successfully resist change. Far from being a strong-armed bully-boy, Lee is in fact physically diminutive and emotionally sensitive, deeply sincere and utterly convinced that nonhumans have moral rights that are everywhere being flagrantly flouted. He wrote in 1975:

We have been at war with the other creatures of this earth ever since the first human hunter set forth with spear into the primeval forest. Human imperialism has everywhere enslaved, oppressed, murdered and mutilated the animal peoples. All around us lie the slave camps we have built for our fellow creatures, factory farms and vivisection laboratories, Dachaus and Buchenwalds for the conquered species. We slaughter animals for our food, force them to perform silly tricks for our delectation, gun them down and stick hooks in them in the name of sport. We have torn up the wild places where once they made their homes. The million-year Reich of the master-species continues. Speciesism is more deeply entrenched within us even than sexism, and that is deep enough.[2]

For years Lee meticulously eschewed violence towards human and non-human, although, after more than a decade of campaigning, some of his followers as well as Lee himself have been on the receiving end of violence from those whose exploitation of nonhumans he has doggedly sought to curb.

He had called for 'Militant action limited only by reverence for life and hatred of violence. Compassion's patience is now exhausted.' His aim was 'To end *all* forms of tyranny and exploitation. To build a society based on love and sharing and reverence for life instead of hate and greed, violence and butchery.'[3]

In 1977 Lee served a further prison sentence for stealing some laboratory mice, and was again imprisoned in 1987 on conspiracy charges. He was clearly reacting with impatience against what he felt was the pusillanimous conservatism of the movement:

The animal welfare movement has been run for far too long by wealthy ladies in hats and retired army majors. It has been far too compromising, and too afraid to offend the Establishment and the forces of 'law and order'. Its failure to use direct action when necessary has been deplorable. But the radical young are slowly beginning to interest themselves in the struggle for animal liberation, and therein lies hope.[4]

During the 1980s sections of the British media began to portray Lee and other activists as thugs of the extreme right or left of politics.[5] Almost certainly, however, the ALF is not the highly organized and centrally controlled organization that some people have claimed, nor is it funded lavishly by sinister or other sources, but quite meagrely and by very ordinary British people. It is, most probably, a collection of individuals acting independently, driven by a sense of outrage and compassion, with no ulterior or party political motive and no particular flair for organization.

The militants participating in protest marches have certainly attracted to their ranks a few of unusual appearance, some of them black-suited and punk-hairstyled, who call themselves anarchists. For many of these, one motive has appeared to be a need to find an identity and a sense of purpose in a society with high levels of unemployment which offered little hope to the young. They may, to an extent, identify with the 'underdogs' they strive to protect. For some, it is a passing phase, but for the others, the majority vegans and vegetarians, it is a passionately felt and rationally argued conviction.

For a few, perhaps, anarchism may take precedence over animal liberation. For them, any protest movement may appear worth infiltrating if it is against 'the system'; and from this quarter violence could one day spring.

The very great amount of damage done to the property of animal exploiters over the years has put up insurance premiums and forced many to think seriously about the economic as well as moral implications of animal abuse. Public sympathy for the Front continues to be widespread in Britain, and some police forces during the 1970s developed a reputation for turning a blind eye to law-breaking by animal militants. But this situation changed during the 1980s, when Scotland Yard was reported to have set up a special Animal Liberation Front unit.

DAMAGE TO PROPERTY

The activities of the Animal Liberation Front as described in the *Sunday Times* in 1986, included no use of weapons, violence or even threats of violence to people, although property has been attacked. Cal McCrystal wrote:

In the past year the ALF has produced a trail of damage across Britain. Targets included a pig farm in Bristol (arson), a butcher's shop in Leighton Buzzard (catapult attack), the Holcombe Hunt in Frodsham (arson and glued door locks), meat lorries in Poole (arson), Leys Egg Farm in High Ongar (hens rescued), a fur shop in Worcester (smashed windows), the John Leggott College in Scunthorpe (24 rats liberated), a dogfight organiser in Lincoln (car damaged), the Cancer Research Campaign in London (paint-daubing), Lynch Hill Farm in Stanton Harcourt (partridges liberated), Kentucky Fried Chicken restaurant and a frozen meat centre in Tyne and Wear (cement poured down the toilets).[6]

In reporting a major operation by the Central Animal Liberation League against the animal supply centre at Oxford University in July 1985, in which thirty-two laboratory dogs were rescued, the *Black Beast* magazine stated that even damage to property was deliberately kept to a minimum: 'At all stages of this operation, CALL had a policy of minimum damage – concentrating instead on liberating animals and highlighting what was going on at UPF and Oxford University. Doors

or windows were only broken when access to a building was needed.'[7]
The magazine went on to assert that many of the dogs rescued had
clearly once been pets.

PROSECUTIONS

In June 1986 twenty-seven militants were sentenced at Leicester Crown
Court to prison sentences totalling forty-five years, after being convicted
of conspiring to burgle Unilever Research Laboratories at Sharpbrook in
Bedfordshire in August 1984, when over a hundred members of the
Eastern Animal Liberation League had removed quantities of files and
research documents.[8] Eight of the sentenced were women. The judge
branded those convicted as 'enemies of society' and 'trained agitators'.
Trained by whom, one wonders?

In March 1986 and, coincidentally or not, at the same time as the
Government's Animals (Scientific Procedures) Bill was passing through
Parliament, more than a score of the best-known ALF members, including Lee, were arrested and remanded in custody, charged with conspiracy
to commit criminal damage. Some were also charged with conspiracy to
steal beagle dogs. Lee was held without trial for over a year. By the
autumn of 1986 activists claimed that thirty-four of their number were
in prison in Britain for ALF-type offences, and on 5 February 1987 ten
were gaoled at Sheffield Crown Court, convicted of conspiracy to
commit arson and criminal damage and conspiring to incite criminal
damage to fur stores, butchers' shops and laboratories. Ronnie Lee,
described as the leader of the ALF, received the stiff sentence of ten
years. Ian Oxley, a fitter from Sheffield, the inventor of an 'ingenious'
incendiary device which had caused more than £200,000's worth of
damage at a fur shop, received four years, as did Vivian Smith, Roger
Yates, Brendan McNally, Kevin Baldwin and Gary Cartwright. Julia
Rodgers, Isobel Facer (aged nineteen) and John Hewson received lesser
sentences. All, except Lee, Hewson and Facer, were said to be in their
twenties.[9]

Using emotive language, which was duly seized upon by the media,
the judge described Lee as a 'fanatic' and a 'dangerous criminal', and
accused him of carrying out 'a campaign of terror'. Indeed, the *The
Times* headline report of the trial was 'Nine Terrorists Jailed After
Campaign of Fire Bombs'.

The ten-year sentence on Lee came in the same week that a man was
gaoled for only three years for a particularly brutal rape in the course
of a robbery, and provoked the widespread criticism that damage to
property appeared to be rated as far more serious than the suffering of
women. A few months later a butcher's son was caught red-handed and
later convicted of breaking the windows of a house belonging to Penny
Goater, a well-known disabled animal rights activist in Somerset. He

was fined only £50.[10] The disparity between the sentences given to animal exploiters and animal liberators no doubt reflects the establishment's fear of those who deliberately and systematically break the law for reasons of conscience.

The day after Lee started his sentence, the ALF defiantly liberated fifty-two hens and four piglets from a laboratory in Cheshire, its new spokesman reiterating that the ALF had no intention of physically harming people,[11] and in July allegedly caused £9 million's worth of damage in the fur departments of three Debenhams stores.[12]

Despite the mass imprisonments of 1987, or because of them, the ALF allegedly launched its most spectacular campaign at Christmas 1988 with a wave of incendiary attacks upon eight firms associated with the fur trade. Incendiary devices were detonated on 19 December at Harrods and Selfridges in London and a House of Fraser shop in Cardiff. In Plymouth, Dingles' department store was wrecked. Parcel bombs — of which at least two were clearly marked 'ALF. Do not open. Telephone the police now' — were delivered to four addresses in Birmingham, London and Cambridge, and a further unexploded incendiary device was found at the House of Fraser store in Oxford Street in London. Nobody was hurt in these incidents but total damage to property was estimated at several million pounds.[13]

In the BUAV's November/December 1988 edition of their magazine *Liberator* Ronnie Lee, writing from prison, had reiterated his disillusionment with political action. Consumerist 'cruelty-free' campaigns are more useful, he argued, but most effective is direct action which damages the property of animal exploiters. Taking a very ecological line, he identified 'increasing human population and industrialization' and their effects upon habitat as the main causes of animal suffering.[14]

Most major raids appear to have been against laboratories, but factory-farms come a close second. The first liberation of battery chickens occurred in Britain in the mid-1970s, and in America in June 1986, when twenty-five hens were released from Sydel's Egg Farm in Hartly, Delaware, by the Farm Freedom Fighters. From 1985 onwards the ALF in Britain began to step up its attacks on fur shops, and although accused of using bombs, claimed that these were small non-explosive incendiary devices or 'sophisticated fireworks' intended to ignite in the fur departments of large stores at times when the stores were empty. They would pose no risk to life or limb, they claimed, but should set off automatic sprinkler systems which would damage the furs on display. Police disagreed and talked of life sentences. In February 1989 high explosive was first used, in an attack on a Bristol University laboratory.[15]

POLITICAL MOTIVATION?

To the 'official' mind the ALF has probably appeared more politically sinister than it is. The ALF has certainly been successful in its aims, but this is because its targets are everywhere, and are (by military standards) poorly defended. The ALF has been hard to stop, but this is probably not because its activities are brilliantly organized but precisely for the opposite reason — they are a disorganized series of largely unconnected manifestations of spontaneous feeling. It seems that when compassion and indignation replace a formal chain of command they constitute a difficult problem for the police to deal with.

Peter Janke has asserted:

Following the establishment of its philosophical foundations in the early 1970's, the movement's politicization is already well under way. The issue will grow as slogans such as 'Every burger means a murder' brings militant vegetarianism into the folds of animal liberation, whose activities will become more radical as the hard core ultra-left sidles up to the sentimentalists. Corporations will need to look at the implications of the animal liberation movement on sales, whilst police and security directors will be confronted by problems of increasingly well planned direct action involving mass trespass, breakage and entry, stealing of documents, harassment of key individuals and actual sabotage. As unemployment grows throughout Europe and leisure time expands, young people will be at risk from pressure groups anxious to recruit and so to promote causes, and willing to push the limits of their activities beyond the law.[16]

The ALF are militant and radical certainly, yet there is little evidence to support the claim that they are 'ultra-left' in the sense of being associated with socialist or Marxist organizations or ideals; indeed, even the extreme right-wing National Front produced some primitive animal rights literature in the early 1980s.[17] Jolyon Jenkins, writing in the *New Statesman*, described how anti-speciesists have clashed with left-wing groups on the issue of ethnic ritual slaughter, and pointed out the irritation of left-wing feminists with Lynx's anti-fur slogan — 'it takes up to forty dumb animals to make a fur coat but only one to wear it'.[18] Yvonne Roberts in *The Times* underlined this lack of clear-cut left- or right-wing character to the movement: 'The Right feels that animal liberation is nothing but a camouflage combat jacket for a group of anarchists more interested in revolution than rodents. The Left, on the whole, believe that the activists in the movement have their priorities wrong and that people should come first.'[19] Nor is there real proof that animal liberationists are directed by a calculating central core seeking to dupe or recruit the idle young.

Admittedly most, although not all, of the protesters appearing at public demonstrations are young; the women appear slightly to outnumber the men. McCrystal reckons that of the 'up to 2000' ALF activists about half are working class and half middle class: 'with a strong presence of lawyers, teachers and civil servants. Unlike many other fringe or outlaw groups, the majority of ALF members currently at large have

It takes up to 40 dumb animals to make a fur coat.

But only one to wear it.

LYNX
Fighting the fur trade

If you don't want animals gassed, electrocuted, trapped or strangled, don't buy a fur coat. P O Box 509 Dunmow, Essex Tel: 0371 2016

18   David Bailey's famous picture of blood cascading from a fur coat created quite a stir. It suggests both the professionalism of the international anti-fur campaign for which it was made and the increasing rejection of speciesism by the young and fashionable of the 1970s and 1980s.
(Reproduced by kind permission of LYNX)

secure jobs.' A BBC television *Brass Tacks* programme in 1986 also investigated the composition of the ALF, and its analysis rather endorsed this view, stating that political anarchists, moderates and right-wingers are all involved. Indeed the most extreme spokesperson on the programme was described as a '*Daily Telegraph*-reader' from 'respectable middle class Conservative voting suburbia'.[20] One leading activist, Mike Nunn, is a retired butcher. None appear to enjoy breaking the law and most are reported to dread going to prison.[21]

Whatever the motives of the members of the ALF and similar organizations (such as the Northern, Central and South East Animal Liberation Leagues), the chronic deafness of governments to the animal rights message has certainly added fuel to the flames of protest.

At Lee's 1987 trial the court was guarded by armed police − a situation extremely unusual in Britain.[22] It seems that in some people's minds the actions of the would-be animal saviours have been equated with terrorism. Yet the rescuing of mice from laboratories and of hens from batteries compares not at all with the methods of the modern madmen with machine-guns. The use of the word 'terrorism' in such a context is, surely, a deliberate slur and a debasement of the meaning of the word.

VIOLENCE INFLICTED

Although most campaigners tend to oppose the breaking of laws in order to save animals from suffering, a growing minority has argued that law-breaking is morally justified in extreme circumstances and to save nonhuman life. Often the analogy with Nazi Germany has been raised, with questions such as – 'If you had had an opportunity to liberate Jews from concentration camps in 1944 would you have done it, taking into account that to do so would have been against the law?' Lee argues:

It seemed to me a perfectly natural and a very moral thing for people to intervene directly to save animals from persecution. Of course, this would often mean breaking the law, but those laws had been made by a selfish and arrogant human species without taking the interests of animals into consideration.[23]

Almost all the leading animal militants have, however, scrupulously drawn the line at violence towards the person, arguing that their mission is to reduce suffering, not to increase it, and the recorded cases of actual injury have been surprisingly few at the time of writing. Ronnie Lee is reported to hold the view that it is 'against ALF policy to injure anybody except in self-defence', and has denied that his brand of animal liberation is 'terrorism'.[24] In the 1986 *Brass Tacks* programme, a militant was recorded as saying that in his opinion it is only a question of time before a vivisector is killed. [25] In the programme it was claimed that between November 1982 and mid-1986 sixteen animal liberation 'bombs' had been planted in Britain, that each year some 2,000 acts of sabotage by militants are causing approximately £6 million worth of damage, and that it has been costing laboratories hundreds of thousands of pounds to protect themselves against attack. Opposition, even to conventional campaigning, has certainly become expensive, as, for example, in Switzerland in 1986, where the major pharmaceutical firms were forced to spend an estimated $9.3 million in their successful advertising campaign against the proposed banning of vivisection in that country.

On 28 November 1982 small letter bombs were received by leaders of the major political parties in Britain – David Steel, Michael Foot and Margaret Thatcher. The one addressed to Mrs Margaret Thatcher exploded at 10 Downing Street, causing minor injury to a letter clerk. In statements to the media a group calling itself the Animal Rights Militia claimed responsibility. This group was unknown to all major activists in the United Kingdom and no arrests have been made.

This outrage obviously provoked public anger and came at such a time that many activists considered that it must have been a deliberate attempt to discredit the animal rights movement, possibly perpetrated by someone connected with the fur trade. Three pieces of evidence were used to support this theory. First, some obscure elements in the fur trade also claimed to have received a letter bomb, although the campaign against the fur trade was at a low priority in animal rights circles at that time. Secondly, the bombs were sent during the final run-up in the campaign to ban the import of seal products into Europe and could have weakened it. Thirdly, the bombs were sent on the eve of Liberal party leader David Steel's advertised speech on animal rights made at Croydon on 30 November – probably the first speech entirely devoted to this topic by any party leader anywhere in the world. Why send such a man a bomb unless it was to dissuade him from speaking on the subject?

Subsequently, according to *Brass Tacks*, the Animal Rights Militia made six minor bomb attacks on scientists' homes in 1985 and planted four car bombs in January 1986, one under the car of a veterinary researcher. These later attacks, none of which caused injury, against targets that would seem appropriate to the militant, and characterized by an intention to scare rather than hurt, appeared genuine.

VIOLENCE SUFFERED

On the other hand, writing in *Liberator* in August 1986, Jill Lockwood stated:

It is revealing that NOT ONE person who exploits animals has ever been seriously injured, yet compare that to the following:
* Anti-bloodsports campaigner Eddie Coulston was severely injured during a demonstration at the notorious Waterloo Cup hare coursing event. He was attacked with a shooting stick by a bloodsports fanatic who later spent four months in prison. Eddie had his skull badly fractured and underwent lengthy brain surgery and almost died. He still now suffers from epileptic fits and has been told that he will never work or drive again. 25 animal rights campaigners have recently been sentenced to a total of 41 years imprisonment for smashing the torture equipment of vivisection, yet the man who almost murdered Eddie Coulston was dealt with lightly.
* Hunt Saboteur Gary Mallard suffered a small skull fracture after being struck with a riding crop by a member of the Cambridgeshire Foxhounds.
* Another Hunt Saboteur had his leg broken when the huntsman of the North Staffordshire Moorland Beagles deliberately drove him down with the hound van. Compensation was settled out of court.
* Circus violence. There are many examples of circus employees attacking demonstrators giving leaflets out to the public. A recent case resulted in two of Gandeys Circus's workers being convicted after they hospitalised one person with cracked ribs and attacked two others. Similar incidents have occurred in Blackpool and Yeovil (the latter involving a broken jaw).
* Hunt Saboteur Mary Jones was demonstrating at a country show when

she had her back broken by a policeman. The court case for this is due this
year.
* Anti-bloodsports campaigner Peter Skinner was attacked by hare coursing
  thugs, again at the Waterloo Cup. He was taken to hospital with a
  suspected back injury and kept in for observation.

Included in this article was a photograph purporting to show a 'Wiltshire
fur farmer' firing a gun at animal rights campaigners. In the same edition
of *Liberator* was a piece by an imprisoned activist, Roger Yates, who
attacked the misrepresentation of the ALF in the media, and added:

the animal rights movement is now subject to much violence, physically and
indirectly. In my prison cell I have had time to tot up the figures of animal
v. human deaths in the current hysterical 'the animal rights movement is
violent' era. Since the Animal Liberation Front has been in existence (about
ten years) TENS OF HUNDREDS OF BILLIONS of animals have been
massacred by human kind, yet not ONE person has ever been seriously
injured by the animal rights movement anywhere in the world. On top of
that I know of at least four animal rights campaigners who have received
broken bones from the opposition, including one broken back and two skull
fractures, one very serious case which involved subsequent brain surgery:
can anyone state similar injuries sustained by an animal exploiter?

These attacks upon animal liberationists are substantiated by four
photographs published in the Hunt Saboteurs Association magazine
Howl in the summer of 1986.[26] These apparently show demonstrators
being physically assaulted and threatened with a pickaxe and a shovel.
Three Hunt Saboteurs were hospitalized after being attacked by hunt
supporters near Horsham in November 1986,[27] and in other incidents it
is the supporters of hunts who have been accused of rowdiness and
'acting like morons'.[28] In January 1988 the prominent wildlife photographer, Eric Ashby, who seven months previously had won an injunction against foxhounds being allowed on to his property in the New
Forest, had to complain to police about shots outside his house at night
and damage to his car and garage.[29] At a peaceful protest at a mink farm
in Hampshire a young girl who had joined the demonstration was
knocked unconscious by a car; strangely it was the demonstrators who
were arrested by the police and not the car-driver.[30] In an incident in
March 1988, a young protester was attacked by a huntsman with a
whip. Once again the police acted very strangely: they arrested the
injured man and not his attacker.[31]
     On 19 October 1965 a young couple were shot dead with a shotgun
near the Canadian home of Mrs and Mr Brian Davies (the founder of
the International Fund for Animal Welfare and the key campaigner
against the killing of seals in Canada). What is remarkable is that the

dead couple were approximately of the same age and general physical description as the Davieses, and that the dead woman was wearing a rather unusual red duffle-coat of the same type as one worn by Mrs Davies. Furthermore, the couple's dog was similar to that owned by the Davieses.[32] No explanation for this double murder has ever been found, and no arrest has been made. Nor was there ever any explanation of the murder in 1974 of Claudia Ross, an American conservationist and reporter for the *Bangkok Post*, who had, just before her death, written three articles attacking the international trade in animals.[33]

In 1978, when I was chairman of the RSPCA council, I arranged for an anti-seal-hunt lecture-tour of Canada and the United States to be conducted under the aegis of the RSPCA by Richard Adams, the well-known author, and by Mike Seymour-Rouse and Bill Jordan, two senior staff members of the RSPCA. After the two latter flew from Toronto via Chicago to Boston, a bomb, apparently intended to explode during the flight, was discovered, by retired army officer Seymour-Rouse, in a suitcase taken from the plane. Despite inquiries by the Boston police, no arrest was ever made. The campaigners returned to Canada and completed their tour without further incident.

In 1985 it was the turn of Greenpeace to experience violence when on 10 July the Greenpeace flagship *Rainbow Warrior* was sunk in Auckland Harbour, New Zealand, by underwater explosive charges. A Dutch photographer and member of her crew, Fernando Pereira, was killed. The boat had been about to set sail to oppose French neutron bomb tests at Muraroa in the Pacific. Over the ensuing months the New Zealand Prime Minister, David Lange, hinted that France was responsible. At first this was denied. Eventually, after leaks to the French media, the French government on 22 September officially admitted that French secret agents had sunk the boat. The head of the DGSE, the French Secret Service, Admiral Pierre Lacoste, and the French Defence Minister M. Charles Hernu, both resigned. For several weeks the scandal seemed near to toppling the government of France.

This episode reveals not only that Western governments can resort to terrorist action, but also that they consider protest groups such as Greenpeace as justifiable targets. Furthermore, it shows that governments will take the trouble to infiltrate organizations of this sort; another DGSE agent, calling herself Mme Frederique Bonlieu, had worked for Greenpeace in New Zealand earlier in the year.

In December 1985 Dian Fossey, the well-known protector of gorillas, was found murdered in Africa, and on 22 December 1988 the leading Brazilian conservationist Chico Mendes was murdered by cattle-ranchers. Again, or so it appears, those wishing to exploit nonhumans resorted to extreme violence to remove their human opposition. Felipe Benevides, the distinguished Peruvian diplomatist and first winner of the Paul Getty Prize for Wildlife Conservation, escaped two assassination attempts in the 1980s. In May 1989 RSPCA inspector Jeremy Goodyer was wounded by a shotgun booby-trap near Peterborough, and an Australian RSPCA colleague, Stuart Fairlie, was killed while investigating cruelty in Victoria.

The death of Fernando Pereira might have been written off as yet another unsolved crime against conservationists and animal protection campaigners, no arrests might have been made and, like the shooting in Fredericton, the murder in Bangkok, the death of Dian Fossey and the bombs at Boston airport and in Peru, it all might have been quickly forgotten if the persistence of the New Zealand government had not forced the truth to emerge.

Although the exploiters have been quick to accuse the animal liberators of moral inconsistency and personal violence, such faults seem to lie far more with them. Even affluent and apparently respectable British hunters are sometimes guilty of such hypocrisy as when, according to the animal-baiting yobs of Liverpool, 'they'll tell you straight to give the antis a battering. Only when the busies (police) arrive they say they don't know who you are, like.'[34] Yet it is precisely such socially elevated exploiters who have perennially accused animal militants — the so-called 'antis' — of being a 'rent-a-crowd' mob which is likely to be violent. The cynical pro-exploiter press has played down, ignored or put twisted interpretations on the violence of exploiters; referring to the fatal sinking of the *Rainbow Warrior*, a contributor to *Fur Age Weekly* tastelessly remarked: 'When enough whales were "saved" and enough hair seals sprayed, Greenpeace officials had to look elsewhere for their salaries and expense accounts.'[35]

As the world has, at one level, become less discriminatory in terms of class, sex and race, while simultaneously witnessing an apparent increase in worldwide political imprisonment, torture, violent crime and war, so also in the area of the interspecies relationship theory has gone one way while practice has gone the other. Whereas in Britain there has been greater and far more widespread public demand for reform than there was, for example, in the nineteenth century, so the modern establishment of the 1980s has been more resistant to change than was its Victorian counterpart. This gap between public opinion and government action, in Britain at least, created a dangerous gap in which the Animal Liberation Front sprang up. Revolutions do not have to be violent, yet sometimes they are provoked into becoming so through the inertia of governments.

Violence against other people by activists in any cause must be condemned. Such condemnations of violence must be even-handed, however, and the growing number of cases of violence *by* environmental and animal exploiters must be deplored equally and not minimized by the forces of law and order, nor the media. Indeed they deserve to be far more seriously taken into account than they have been in the past.

It is fair to say that the majority of the leaders of the animal liberation movement have condemned violence. Writing in the American animal liberation magazine *Animals Agenda* in May 1985, Peter Singer, Michael Fox, Holly Jensen, Patty Mark and Henry Spira, for example, made their position quite clear:

In light of the sensationalistic media coverage given to acts such as bomb threats, poisoning of food and contamination of consumer products — acts said to have been committed by animal movement activists, we believe the time has come to explore the possible repercussions of such tactics.

While our society's present legal structure reflects a relatively narrow speciesist viewpoint which needs to be challenged in forceful ways, there are fundamental moral principles that should not be violated. Respecting the interests and rights of others is foremost among these. We do not place animals before people; all should be given equal and fair consideration. Threatening the lives and health of any human or non-human is an act of unjustified violence and contrary to our basic beliefs.

We are asking people to extend their moral horizons, to accept the notion of fair play: if we violate this we may relinquish our most powerful means of persuasion and thus risk alienating those very people on whom the success of this movement depends. We should follow the lead set by Gandhi and Martin Luther King and not that of international terrorists.

Yet this was not acceptable to some. Replying in September 1985, Bill Mannetti of Connecticut made three claims: first, that feminist and anti-slavery campaigns had needed violence in order to be successful; secondly that the non-violence of Gandhi and Martin Luther King was only effective because it appeared in the context of already violent movements, and thirdly:

As for 'respecting the interests and rights of others' this, in the given context, is so much philosophical blather. After all, it is frequently in the economic interest of animal abusers to do what they do to animals, so it is precisely their interests that we must contravene. And while 'respecting the interests and rights of others' has a nice ring to it, we must remember that most of those who abuse animals believe they have a right to do so.

There is a clash, clearly, between the interests of the nonhumans and those of their exploiters, and although Singer and others are right to say that nonhumans should not be placed *before* people, but on an equal footing, the dilemma is not so easily resolved. If the *only* way to stop a man from experimenting upon and then killing another human being is by violence, would it be wrong to use such means, or would it be wrong *not* to do so?

The best escape from this dilemma is to demonstrate that violence is *not* the only means of stopping speciesism. As someone who has chosen the non-violent and political route to reform, I sometimes despair at the indifference that some governments have displayed. By appearing so insensitive to legal and peaceful pressures they undoubtedly have increased the likelihood that less patient people will be tempted to seek illegal and violent solutions. The hypocrisy of many governments on matters of this sort is shameful. Why cannot they learn the simple psychological truth that if you wish to contain political violence perpetrated in a good cause which has majority support you should reward the *non-violent* campaigns which are trying to forward that cause? By at least meeting with and listening to the young and radical, governments could diffuse many situations that are incipiently violent, and, even better, by meeting as many as possible of the actual demands for reform that are being put, not just by the partially discredited 'moderates' (who often have a foot in both camps) but by the genuinely committed reformers, they might avoid violence altogether and reinstate a faith in democracy as well. Violence is often the product of prolonged frustration. By not recognizing this fact, and acting upon it soon enough, irresponsible governments can become parties to its consequences.

Singer questions the growing militancy of the Animal Liberation Front not so much on moral grounds as on grounds of political effectiveness. Although he concludes that up till 1985, at least, activism had helped the movement, he warns that violence, if it increases, could become counter-productive. Law-breaking is one thing, Singer argues, but violence against people is altogether different:

My concern with these events is not based on any belief that illegal actions are always morally wrong. There are circumstances in which, even in democracy, it is morally right to disobey the law; and the issue of animal liberation provides good examples of such circumstances. If the democratic process is not functioning properly; if repeated opinion polls confirm that an overwhelming majority opposes many types of experimentation, and yet the Government takes no effective action to stop them; if the public is kept largely unaware of what is happening in factory farms and laboratories — then illegal actions may be the only available avenue for assisting animals and obtaining evidence about what is happening.

My concern is not with breaking the law, as such. It is with the prospect of the confrontation becoming violent, and leading to a climate of polarization in which reasoning becomes impossible and the animals themselves end up being the victims.[36]

Singer urges governments to agree on 'major and significant reforms' *before* violence and counter-violence escalate and the initiative on both sides passes to fanatics. On the other hand, he charges animal liberationists to 'set themselves irrevocably against the use of violence' and defines violence as any action which causes direct physical or psychological harm (such as fear) to human or nonhuman. He argues that Gandhi and

Martin Luther King were successful not just because of the justice of their cause but also because their non-violence in the face of provocation 'touched the consciences even of those who had opposed them'.

I concur. Our whole movement is based upon the ethic of reducing suffering, both human and nonhuman. Deliberately to inflict suffering through violence, on the two unproven assumptions that there is no other way to achieve one's aim and that violence will be effective in achieving it, betrays our moral purpose. I cannot accept the aggregative argument that human suffering is justified by benefits to nonhumans, any more than the other way around. Furthermore, on the level of practical politics one must also be aware of the danger that fanaticism can stimulate equally violent opposition.

Although much has been made of the militant tactics of the Animal Liberation Front and other similar groups, at the time of writing (1988), there is no authenticated case of death or serious injury being caused to humans or nonhumans by these militants. Hundreds of thousands of pounds' worth of damage to agricultural and scientific equipment has been done, but damage of any sort to living beings has been remarkably slight. On the other hand, animal campaigners *have* been killed.

THE ROLE OF THE MEDIA

The media, too, but to a lesser extent, have played an inadvertent part in promoting violence. In 1971 a small peaceful demonstration against otter-hunting, involving only eight demonstrators, could attract the front page headlines and photograph of the leading national paper, the *Sunday Times*. Yet by 1978 the British media were already growing bored with peaceful protests, and a painstakingly organized mass demonstration against seal-killing, for example, attended by an unprecedented 5,000 in Trafalgar Square, went almost unreported. Instead, the headlines on the following day were stolen by the violent action of one deranged person, entirely unconnected with the movement, who had shot at and wounded a policeman in south London.

Was violence, then, the only way to revive the media's flagging interest? Such was the dangerous question raised by the media on that weekend. If governments would not listen to peaceful and democratic protest and if the media would only report violence, then the answer seemed simple to some whose frustration had reached breaking point.

Initially, the militant tactics of the ALF received much attention in newspapers and electronic media. Then, after the unpleasant fiasco of the Mars Bar episode in 1984 when animal rightists, as a hoax, announced that they had poisoned chocolate bars in shops as a protest against the experimental use of animals by the Mars Company, the media increasingly ignored the militants or castigated them as terrorists.[37] This may have been an attempt, albeit a belated one, to act responsibly on the part of the press. But in the complex interplay between the media and the movement, the media, unwittingly, had already acted as 'agents provocateurs'.

In *Turning Point — the Animal Rights Magazine*, in the autumn of 1986, there appeared a long complaint about 'the new trend in the national media'. It accused the media of ignoring the activists' reasons for demonstrating, exaggerating any friction between themselves and the police, portraying the Animal Liberal Front as a 'military hierarchy', emphasizing 'punk hairstyles' and attempting to discredit activists generally. *The Times* had printed Bernard Levin's tirade entitled 'The Animal Lovers Lusting for Blood'[38] and the *Daily Telegraph* had published several articles alleging that animal welfare had been taken over by left-wing extremists (see p. 204).

Smears have an unpleasant tendency to become self-fulfilling prophesies when those who are smeared begin to believe in and live up to their reputations.

Was the greater hostility of the media in the 1980s entirely the fault of the extremists? Or had the media simply grown bored after about ten years of giving the subject much helpful attention? Or had the climate of the Thatcherite era shifted the media into a posture of showing less interest in altruistic issues generally? Perhaps there is some truth in all these explanations.

INTERNATIONAL REPERCUSSIONS

Over the course of the years, the Animal Liberation Front in Britain has inspired the foundation of similar groups in America, Canada, Australia, the Netherlands, France, Sweden and Germany. Literally thousands of farm and laboratory animals have been 'liberated' with surprisingly little hard evidence that any have been abandoned or have suffered in consequence, despite claims from experimenters and fur-farmers to the contrary. (In 1975, for example, after the exposure of ICI's 'smoking beagles', a number of dogs were 'liberated' from ICI laboratories in Cheshire. Despite warnings from experimenters that they would die in normal domestic surroundings, most thrived, and at least one, Bonzo, lived a contented life as a family pet for another nine years.)[39]

Probably the first Animal Liberation Front action in America was the hiding of some of the monkeys from Dr Taub's laboratory in Silver Spring, Maryland, in order to prevent their return to the laboratory. This occurred in September 1981. In May 1984 the American ALF raided Dr Gennarelli's head-injury laboratory at the University of Pennsylvania (see chapter 16), and in December 1984 115 animals were liberated from horrendous conditions in the ironically named City of Hope Medical Center in Duarte, California. In April 1985 the Front rescued nearly 1,000 animals from the Psychology Laboratory of the University of California at Riverside.[40]

In Canada, too, militants have been active, removing a monkey and three cats, for example, from a laboratory of the University of Western Ontario on New Year's Day 1985.[41]

CONCLUSIONS

The RSPCA, at least during the 1980s, took great pains to distance itself from the militant groups, frequently condemning them both publicly and privately. Indeed in 1986, the society expelled from its membership Michael Huskisson, one of the leading activists who had been gaoled in 1977 and in 1985 for his involvement in animal liberation activities. There still remained many, however, like Rebecca Hall, who were not prepared to condemn militancy out of hand, but laid some of the blame for non-violent law-breaking on the failure of the law to change:

As I write, a young man is being made ill by confinement in prison because he attempted to rescue some dogs from a laboratory. Must we not ask who is the real criminal? Is it not the society which protects its right to inflict suffering by punishing those who dare to act upon their feelings of compassion? The law will not move until the people push it into action. Parliament will not speak until the people give it a voice.[42]

After years of almost total indifference from British governments it was also true that many of the activists of the 1970s felt exhausted and disillusioned. Only towards the end of the 1980s were they likely to revive.

Yet the issue continued to burn steadily at the grass roots. Hundreds of those under thirty continued to campaign and attend public meetings, many conscientiously buying only cruelty-free cosmetics and following vegetarian diets. Although temporarily out of the limelight, the subject seemed to be penetrating the way of thinking of the younger generation to a greater extent than ever, and the ethic of animal liberation was fast becoming one of the established ingredients of Western culture.

The Animal Liberation Front had certainly made exploiters sit up and think, and although it raised some deeply disturbing ethical questions, it had shattered the old stereotype of animal protection as being the faintly ludicrous prerogative of the proverbial (and much maligned) old ladies in hats; it was now a matter that had to be reckoned with. Yet the new stereotype, too, of the animal militant as a politically motivated left-wing terrorist perpetrating extreme violence against the invariably peace-loving and decent animal exploiter was equally wide of the mark.

16 International Progress

Campaigners in Britain were not alone in their efforts. All over the Western world the animal rights issue was coming to the fore in the 1980s, often following British ideas but sometimes achieving far quicker results. As in chapter 10, only a sketch can be given here to indicate the kind of progress being made.

In 1978 the reformers on the RSPCA council urged the need for a strong animal protection initiative in Europe. The traditional ties with the Commonwealth and the ex-colonies had faded and, despite the United Kingdom having joined the European Community in 1973, British animal welfare had remained almost entirely insular in outlook. Yet the European Community was growing in cohesion and influence and there was little effective machinery for forwarding the interests of nonhumans in Brussels or Strasbourg.

Against the perennial opposition of most of the traditionalists on the RSPCA council at that time, who argued that the then small International Society for the Protection of Animals should do the job, or that the job was not worth doing at all, we appointed Mike Seymour-Rouse to be the society's Director of European Liaison from 1 January 1979, and approved a strategy to create a federal body to lobby the European Parliament and the Commission in Brussels, funded chiefly by the RSPCA.

Seymour-Rouse set about this task by inviting co-operation from representatives of leading organizations in each member state,[1] and, in February 1980, formed Eurogroup for Animal Welfare, with himself as co-ordinator and Michael Kay as chairman. Each organization had two delegates, and initially the RSPCA's executive director and myself were the United Kingdom delegates. As the RSPCA was the principal source of funds for the operation we had the greatest say in how Eurogroup was to be set up, and under Kay and Seymour-Rouse it began to run very smoothly, allying itself harmoniously with the more established groups in each member state.

The World Federation for the Protection of Animals (WFPA), based in Zurich, had already been active in Europe for some years, run largely by Karl Frucht and Dr H. J. Weichert, but its main sphere of operations was within the larger, but purely advisory, Council of Europe, which had established an Expert Committee on the Protection of Animals in 1972. The WFPA used publicity and political pressure to inform and influence legislators and academics, and had observer status at the Council. Under WFPA's influence, the Council of Europe had promulgated a recommendation on the international transport of animals in 1961 which led to the European Convention for the Protection of Animals during International Transport which came into force on 20 February 1971. In December 1976 the RSPCA began financial support of the WFPA, and in 1980 persuaded it to merge with the International Society for the Protection of Animals to form the World Society for the Protection of Animals (WSPA).

In 1969 the Council of Europe published a comprehensive seven-point plan on animal welfare which stated the need to regulate intensive rearing, slaughter, animal experimentation, the protection of birds, the protection of wild animals, the protection of animals abused in sport and show business, and the need to find 'a uniform legal status for animals'.[2] This important seven-point plan marked the beginning of a co-ordinated European approach to animal protection and led to the publication of the Council of Europe's European Convention on the Protection of Animals Kept for Farming Purposes in 1976, and conventions on slaughter and laboratory animals.[3] Karl Frucht, Tony Carding and Hans-Jurgen Weichert of WFPA had made an excellent beginning.

The Council of Europe's pronouncements on animal welfare, however, had no binding effect upon member countries. It was up to Eurogroup to seek influence in the real seats of power, that is to say, in the EEC Commission in Brussels, in the Council of Ministers, the Economic and Social Committee and in the European Parliament in Strasbourg.

The EEC was already very positive in its attitude to the subject and had made good progress in this hitherto virgin field with a series of minor measures in the 1970s. The first binding animal welfare-related agreement had been the EEC's Directive on Stunning of 18 November 1974; this was followed by Directives on the protection of animals during international transport (18 July 1977), on the breeding of cattle (25 July 1977), and on the conservation of wild birds (2 April 1979). In the 1980s far larger and more contentious issues were addressed, leading to the banning of whale imports (25 April 1980) and seal pup imports (28 March 1983), and a directive stipulating minimum cage sizes for battery hens (25 March 1986). In addition the EEC signed and ratified the Berne and CITES Conventions on wildlife (see chapter 12).

Many of these legislative advances were still based upon groundwork done by the Council of Europe. The council's convention on laboratory animals, for example, provided some of the ideas to be found in the EEC's draft directive introduced in January 1986. This had been written by the ex-MEP Stanley Johnson, then a senior official working in the department of Commissioner Stanley Clinton Davis in Brussels. Johnson was lobbied by all sides and produced a draft directive which touched on the main areas of pain, unnecessary duplication, the purpose of experiments and the encouragement of the use of humane alternative techniques. As some of the newer member states of the EEC, such as Spain and Greece, lacked any effective protection for laboratory animals, the EEC draft directive stipulated that basic steps should be taken, such as licensing and inspection, and provided a minimal foundation on which to build more humane protection in the future.

In 1983, the European Parliament set up its own all-party 'Intergroup' on animal welfare and asked Seymour-Rouse and Eurogroup to provide its secretariat. The whole subject of animal protection had caught the imagination of European members of Parliament during the massive lobbying by Eurogroup and the International Fund For Animal Welfare on behalf of the seals in 1982. Members had found themselves the unaccustomed centre of worldwide attention and their mailbags reflected this sudden awareness among thousands of constituents of the role and importance of the European Parliament. Indeed the good progress made in Europe in part can be explained in this way: animal protection became the first issue on which the European Parliament captured the support of a mass public.

Nevertheless, the progress was piecemeal, and, addressing Intergroup in 1985, Commissioner Clinton Davis urged the need for a more co-herent legislative strategy. On this aspect Eurogroup had been a trifle weak, although its Scientific Co-ordinator David Wilkins had produced a good legislative plan in 1983. Seymour-Rouse, through Eurogroup, had set up an excellent machine, but it now required a clearly planned programme. WFPA initially had been stronger on this documentary side, but by the early 1980s, having merged with the International Society for the Protection of Animals (ISPA) to form the World Federa-tion for the Protection of Animals, its role in Europe had faded as its centre of gravity temporarily shifted across the Atlantic with increased backing from American humane societies.

Although initiated, funded and staffed almost entirely by the British (until EEC funds amounting to about £100,000 were made available in 1986), Eurogroup had received support from all member states. The Dutch and the Danes have shown themselves particularly interested in reforms in this field. The German EEC Commissioner Karl-Heinz Narjes has been an outstanding figure, as have Hemmo Muntingh and Hanna Maj-Weggen of the Netherlands and Barbara Castle and Sir Jack Stewart-Clark of the United Kingdom. By the late 1980s, under the influence of Eurogroup's new director, Ian Fergusson, and his assistant Caroline Vodden, a concise legislative plan, with both short- and long-term objectives, had been submitted to Intergroup, whose meetings became among the best attended of all such committees in the European Parliament under its active chairman, Madron Seligman from the United Kingdom.

The importance of the EEC had been grasped quickly by animal welfarists. Since the Treaty of Rome was signed in 1957, the European Community has grown to include twelve member states comprising a block of comparable population and economic power to either the USA or the USSR. Furthermore, since the passage of the Single European Act in 1986, the sovereignty of the Community has been supreme. In the words of Lord Denning, 'community law, as declared by the European Court, is superior over any Act of our Parliament...gone is the concept of national sovereignty, to be replaced by European unity'.[4] In July 1987 the Treaty of Rome was amended to bring in environmental protection as one of the Community's priorities.

Although the revolution in attitude towards nonhumans has undoubtedly been chiefly a phenomenon of the English-speaking world, as has the manifestation of extreme animal liberation behaviour, nevertheless most European countries have also seen a change.

Recently there has been new legislation in Belgium, Sweden, West Germany,[5] the Netherlands and in Switzerland, where Claude Beck has energized the movement and fought a skilful campaign against the fur trade.[6] In both Switzerland and Hesse (West Germany) court actions have threatened to outlaw the use of batteries for hens, and in West Germany campaigners like Petra Deimer have effectively drawn public attention to the abuse of wildlife.

Scandinavian countries have also made progress. Norway, it is true, maintains an exploitative attitude towards wildlife born of many centuries of close involvement in the world's fur, whale and seal industries, despite the brave efforts of activists like Birgitta Råd and Sonia Lochen. But in Sweden, a huge following for animal rights has appeared in recent years and the Nordic Society Against Painful Experiments on Animals, for example, based in Stockholm and headed by Birgitta Carlsson and Birgitta Forsman, has a membership far greater than that of the RSPCA in Britain. Carlsson, a very effective administrator and campaigner, has been quick to disseminate the ideas of the new animal rights movement. In July 1988 Sweden put into effect sweeping new animal welfare legislation requiring the registration of all laboratories using animals, prohibiting the tethering of sows, and phasing out battery cages for hens over a ten-year period.[7] Although Finland has been extremely active,[8] contact between Eastern Europe and the West has been almost entirely non-existent in this field.

More unexpected have been the intermittent but often passionate waves of support for nonhumans shown in France and Italy. On 8 July 1986 the government of the Italian province of South Tirol banned vivisection entirely, and several years earlier Italy had led the way with a ban on seal pup imports.

CANADA, AUSTRALIA AND NEW ZEALAND

In Canada recently there has been much activity by campaigners like Steve Best and Harriet Schleifer of the Quebec Animal Liberation Collective, but it has been opposed by an unsympathetic media, a hostile government and an unhelpful veterinary profession. In Australia, on the other hand, progress has been spectacular, with a most constructive attitude being shown by the authorities to the widely supported animal liberation movement led by outstanding campaigners such as Christine Townend, Peter Singer, Patty Mark, Glennis Oogjes, Lesley King, Jacqui Kent, Dianna Speed, Elizabeth Ahlston, Richard Jones, Mick Fearnside and Graeme McEwen. The Australian RSPCA had started in 1873, but it was not for another hundred years that other major societies began rapidly to spring up all over the country. Project Jonah began in 1975 and the Australian Association for Humane Research was set up in 1976, as was Animal Liberation. The number of animal welfare groups in New South Wales alone has tripled between 1975 and 1986.[9]

During the 1980s the Australian Senate continued a mammoth investigation of the whole field of animal protection, and Australian media coverage of animal rights issues was at a very high level. The export of sheep over huge distances, the cruel 'mulesing' operations performed upon them, the mass slaughter of kangaroos, the trapping of dingos, and animal research remained the outstanding issues.

In the trade from Australia to the Middle East seven million sheep are exported annually. Many die *en route* in appalling conditions: 40,605 perished, for example, when the *Farid Fares* caught fire and sank in December 1980. Those who reach their destinations may meet a cruel end in Middle Eastern abattoirs, sometimes hanging by a leg for hours before being bled to death.

In New Zealand the government has maintained a strangely hostile attitude. In 1973 it was dock workers loading sheep at Napier who had been so shocked at the handling of the animals by Arab seamen that they had protested; sheep had their eyes pushed out with sticks and their throats cut on deck, they said. The New Zealand government was unmoved. The dockers went on strike.

On one journey from New Zealand, 4,450 out of 30,270 sheep died on the nineteen-day ocean journey to Iran. The resultant public outcry, supported by the Waterside Unions and the Meat Workers Related Trade Union, finally led to a suspension of live exports. Yet in September 1985 the New Zealand government lifted this ban.

19 'Meat is murder' became a popular slogan in the 1980s and there was a pronounced swing towards vegetarianism, especially among the young. Although concern about the safety of eating drug-treated, cholesterol-rich, and sometimes bacteria-infected flesh was one main reason, another was the growing reluctance to consume the corpses of one's sentient relatives.
(Photograph Katharina Reifschneider)

The attitude of New Zealand farmers towards their sheep was exemplified when they protested against low meat prices in 1984 by publicly slaughtering several thousand animals. Nowhere, it seems, is a clash between old and new attitudes more clearly seen than in New Zealand.

JAPAN

Most remarkable of all has been recent progress in Japan. Anyone suggesting in the nineteenth century that the time would come when Japan would have Animal Rights candidates standing in their parliamentary elections would not have been easily comprehended, let alone believed. Yet in July 1986 ten Japanese Animal Rights candidates did just that, and polled a total of 181,940 votes.

Japan has had little or no tradition of interest in animal protection, but in early 1985 Ryu Ota founded the Japan Green Foundation. He at once began to receive support, establishing yet another toe-hold for the animal rights ideal that has spread around the world over the last two decades. On 24 October 1985 Japanese Premier Nakasone at the United Nations remarked: 'To us Japanese, Universe and Nature is our own home. We live in harmony with those living things like human beings, animals, trees and grass — we are all brothers and sisters naturally. That is our "fundamental philosophy".'

In 1986 car crash tests, inflicting terrible injuries upon primates at Jikei and Kyoto universities, were attacked by the newly formed Society for the Abolition of Animal Tests in Tokyo.[10] Ryu Ota challenged his compatriots with the basic question: 'It is often said that the Japanese have their tradition, not with such loudness as the nature-conquering Christian civilisation in Europe and USA, but in harmony with nature. But can we really say so in the present situation?'

In 1987 Ryu Ota, with Kiyoshi Osada, formed the Earth Green Federation of Japan, based in Tokyo and Niigata.

INDIA

The phenomenon which originated in modern times in the West has clearly spread to the East. In India, Premier Morarji Desai in 1977 banned the export of monkeys to the research laboratories of the USA after a meeting with Lady Dowding and Jon Evans. A later Premier, Rajiv Gandhi, has identified himself closely with conservation and the campaign to protect the Indian tiger, and, partly on humanitarian grounds, and after a campaign by David Whiting on behalf of Compassion in World Farming, in October 1985 he banned the export of frogs and frogs' legs to the gourmet markets in the West. Hitherto, India had been one of the biggest exporters of frogs' legs (cut from the living animal), exporting some 4,086 tonnes in 1982.

In India, traditional Hindu respect for nonhumans is still widespread. Yet taking positive steps to assist nonhumans, rather than merely maintaining a position of *laissez-faire*, has often been initiated and maintained by Europeans living in India; in recent years most notably by the Englishwoman Crystal Rodgers, who rescues stray dogs.

Bill Aitken, writing in the *Hindustan Times* of New Delhi, urged his readers not to dismiss acts of cruelty with 'the fatalistic oriental shrug or the equally fatalistic "developing nation" excuse'. He reminded them that:

In matters of compassion to animals, Indian civilisation led the field. But that was two thousand years ago. Near where I live in Delhi on a sandstone outcrop there is an Ashokan edict urging his people to live in harmony with all beings. Significantly this edict was only discovered twenty years ago when estate developers opened up the area.

India's constitution makes no mention of animal rights except 'taking steps' towards the prohibition of cow-slaughter and, as an afterthought, 'to safeguard' the country's wildlife. Judging by the spindly bovine skeletons that eke out a miserable existence, the inclusion of the cow was a sop to majority sentiment.

He concluded: 'The fact remains that the ancient Indian ethic of "live and let live" is much less sick than the Judaistic "subdue and have dominion over every living thing"'.[11]

Beauty Without Cruelty made a documentary film about cruelty in India that was extremely well received in the 1980s, and much pioneering photographic work was carried out by David Whiting there, and published to good effect.

Animal experimentation, too, has come under mounting criticism in India. Ram Swarup, writing in the *Times of India*, remarked: 'We are told that the last century discovered "evolution". This should have taught us a deeper kinship or, at least, a greater moral responsibility, but it has not done so'. He attacked research on nonhuman animals because of its scientific unreliability, its threat to primate species, its densensitizing effect upon men and women and its possible significance in deeper religious and survival terms:

What man does in his laboratory, he himself becomes. Something dies in him and he tends to be brutalized through a deadened sensitivity, the doors of a higher life and higher knowledge are closed. Cruelty and torture set up forces of nemesis. According to the Vaishnava, Buddhist and Jain view, the present condition of humanity, on the verge of atomic self-destruction, is probably the result of this retributive justice, this great law of Karma.[12]

INTERNATIONAL CONVENTIONS

All in all, the influence of the animal liberation message can be seen around the world. An attempt to register this new mood at the United Nations was made by Professor Georges Heuse of Paris in the late 1970s. In the 1980s this endeavour has been continued by Bill Clark of Jerusalem, who has proposed an International Convention for the Protection of Animals, drafted by Professor David Favre of Detroit, to cover all aspects of the human-to-nonhuman relationship, and in doing so he has tried to draw in the governments of countries in Africa, Asia and Latin America.

THE REVOLUTION IN AMERICA

The first half of the twentieth century had seen little new federal legislation passed to protect animals in America. In 1906 the '28 Hour Law' had provided minimal controls over the transportation of livestock and in 1948 the US Customs were empowered to enforce shippers to observe humane standards. Only in 1958 was the first federal humane slaughter legislation enacted, and not until 1966 was there federal law to protect laboratory animals. The paucity and weakness of legislation speaks for itself: at federal legislative level the issue was all but dead until the 1960s. As in Britain, the momentum had been lost after 1918.

In America, the modern anti-speciesist revolution in public opinion began a little later than in Britain, with the publication of Singer's *Animal Liberation* in 1975. By this time the British media had already established terms such as 'animal rights' in popular parlance, the Hunt Saboteurs had been active for more than a decade, the seminal philosophical works had been published by individuals in the informal Oxford Group, the Animal Liberation Front had been formed and its first two leaders imprisoned. It was fortunate perhaps that Singer, an Australian, had published his book while holding a temporary university post in New York. American publishers had shown themselves singularly unprepared to publish earlier British works in this field, and without *Animal Liberation* American consciences might have continued to slumber.

Staunch Campaigners

For years there had been an active animal welfare movement in America (see chapter 10) and organizations like the Humane Society of the United States and the American Humane Association had continued to do good work. A handful of campaigners had been struggling bravely against political indifference to the issue throughout the period since the war.

In 1959 Rachel Carson, the author and naturalist, learned from Ann Cottrell Free of the use of beagles in cruel toxicity testing. She became a scientific adviser to the Animal Welfare Institute and from 1962 onwards lobbied Congress for the humane conduct of experiments.[13] Another outstanding figure was the indomitable Eleanor Seiling (who died in 1985), the co-founder in 1967 with Macdonald White of the New York-based United Action for Animals, who had hammered the experimenters bravely throughout the 1960s and 70s, exposing hideous cruelties published in the scientific journals, accusing business interests and the American veterinary profession of excesses unheard of even in British laboratories. But Seiling, elderly and abrasive, could not inspire a youthful mass movement.

Christine Stevens's style was entirely different from Seiling's. Moving in the upper echelons of Washington society in the 1960s and 70s, her carefully documented attacks upon animal experimentation had been listened to uneasily by American politicians. In Hubert Humphrey, the great American Democrat leader, she found an ally who, if he had become president, could have precipitated a revolution in American thinking during the 1960s. Stevens's sophisticated approach was ahead of the times, and without the support of massive public opinion was often successfully opposed by the vested interests on the other side of the debate. Nevertheless, the Animal Welfare Institute of which she is president has become highly influential, and Stevens is also secretary of the Society for Animal Protective Legislation, which has played a highly significant role in securing new federal legislation.

Between the wars Commander Edward Breck had fought a lonely battle against the leghold trap. Forty years later Cleveland Amory became a modern champion of wildlife in America, bringing some unmistakably American pizzaz to the movement. He founded the Fund for Animals Inc., and his book *Mankind? Our Incredible War on Wildlife*, published in 1974, epitomizes his robust approach to the defence of animals trapped, shot, poisoned and exploited often by American males obsessed with the need to prove their 'macho' toughness in this way. In 1986 Amory launched a campaign to stop the hunting of buffalo outside Yellowstone National Park in Montana. With his collaborator, actress Gretchen Wyler, Amory has been a powerful figure in the struggle to change American attitudes towards wildlife. So have figures such as Dexter Cate, who has specialized in saving cetaceans, and the conservationist author Lewis Regenstein.

The highly qualified English-born veterinarian Dr Michael Fox, for many years an American resident, has also been a significant influence. His inspirational writings throughout the 1970s and 1980s, coming from an author with impressive scientific qualifications, have given the movement in America considerable intellectual stimulation. Appointed director of the Institute for the Study of Animal Problems by the Humane Society of the United States in 1976, Fox, along with another English-born scientist Dr Andrew Rowan, helped to bring scientific credibility to the American humane movement as well as humanity to science.

Peter Singer's cool and rational contribution provided even further credibility, and helped to give the subject both the intellectual power and the youthful idealism which it needed. Those who helped the animal rights issue really take off included Helen Jones, a pioneer of the new awareness of animals' rights in America, the writer Ann Cottrell Free, and the Belgian-born Henry Spira. Spira, a teacher in New York, had seen Singer's review of the Oxford Group's pioneering book *Animals, Men and Morals* and attended his course on animal liberation held at New York University's School of Continuing Education in 1974. As a veteran campaigner for human rights, Spira brought an expertise and hard-headed practicality that the movement needed. Spira could be tough, but was always prepared to be reasonable: 'We always begin with discussion rather than political confrontation, although we do not hesitate to play hard ball when warranted.'[14] Over the ensuing years his determination to achieve results led to major advances in the protection of laboratory animals. Owing mainly to his tenacity, the Avon cosmetics company reduced the number of its experiments by 33 per cent in 1982 and by a further 31 per cent in 1983, and replaced toxicity testing using the cruel LD50 technique (see p. 258) by the more humane Limit Method. Revlon also took steps to avoid duplication of testing, developed a cell culture toxicity test, and reduced animal use by 30 per cent.[15] If Singer was the guru, Spira was the great street fighter of New York's animal liberation. His first campaign was launched in June 1976 against sex experiments conducted on cats at the American Museum of Natural History in New York. After numerous street protests and help from Congressman Ed Koch, the funding for the research was stopped and the laboratory was closed down in December 1977.

Scholarly and passionate in approach was British-born Shirley Mc-Greal's International Primate Protection League, which strove effectively to protect nonhuman primates around the world during the 1970s and 1980s. McGreal had founded IPPL while living in Thailand in 1973, and continues it now from her home in South Carolina. In 1975, 1978, 1979, and 1984 IPPL played a major role in securing primate export bans from Thailand, India, Bangladesh and Malaysia respectively. Referring to the fragility of such bans, McGreal gives them continued attention – 'like babies' bottoms they need constant talcum powder', she comments.

A little later came attorney Jim Mason who, with Singer, filled a glaring gap in the movement with his attacks upon American factory-farming, as a founder of the Animal Rights Network and as editor of the *Animals Agenda* – the outstanding American animal liberation magazine.

Alex Pacheco discovered animal liberation in 1978, sailed on the *Sea Shepherd* (a boat purchased largely with funds supplied by the RSPCA in 1978 to investigate the seal hunt in the Atlantic and subsequently used to harass sealers and whalers under the controversial captaincy of Paul Watson), and joined Hunt Saboteurs' outings in Britain. In 1980, with Ingrid Newkirk, he founded People for the Ethical Treatment of Animals (PETA) to fight cruelty to farm and laboratory animals, went on to expose Dr Edward Taub's treatment of animals after working under cover at the Institute for Behavioural Research in Silver Spring, Maryland and in 1985 successfully caused the University of Pennsylvania to suspend its horrendous head-injury research on baboons (see pp. 303–4). Newkirk and Pacheco's organization has been the fastest-growing of all animal rights groups in the USA during the 1980s. In 1986 Kim Stallwood took over as its director.

On 30 May 1977 Kenneth Le Vasseur, an American dolphin-handler, liberated two bottle-nosed dolphins used for research by the University of Hawaii's Institute of Marine Biology. Le Vasseur and his colleague, Steven C. Sipman, go down in history as the first Americans to be convicted for a typical animal liberation offence. They themselves drew the analogy between their action and that of the slavery abolitionists in the America of the 1850s.[16]

There has always been an element of 'whistle-blowing' in animal liberation; that is to say action by insiders who turn against the practices they see around them and emerge as campaigners against their erstwhile colleagues. This was true of some Victorian anti-vivisectionists such as Dr George Hoggan and Lawson Tait, and more recently Dr Harold Hewitt, Angela Walder, Dr Gill Langley and myself in Britain. Peter Roberts is one of the few ex-farmers to dedicate his life to reforming the agricultural system. In Canada the late Ray Elliott was a courageous old sealer who became an outspoken critic of sealing, paying the penalty with imprisonment, harassment and social rejection. In America there has been Dr Donald Barnes, a behavioural psychologist subjecting primates to high levels of radiation for the US Department of Defense from 1966 until 1980, when he resigned and became a leading figure in the American campaigns against animal experimentation. Since Donald Barnes's action, numerous insiders, most of them still anonymous, have provided horrific evidence to the outside world of what is happening inside American laboratories.

Since the publication of *Animal Liberation* the support in academic philosophical circles in America has been strong. Tom Regan, besides being one of the earliest, has certainly been the most prolific contributor, and has also been an active and persuasive campaigner in the field. In 1986, he initiated an imaginative campaign to take 'the message of Animal Rights to the people, where the people already congregate: in churches and synagogues, in classrooms and art galleries, in theatres and movie houses'[17]. Dale Jamieson of Colorado University is another outstanding American philosopher of animal rights, as are Harlan Miller, Charles Magel, and Bernard Rollin. In 1989 Magel's *Keyguide to Information Sources in Animal Rights* provided an authoritative reference to animal rights publications and organizations.

In the United States, as in Britain, humane societies had risked loss of tax exemption if they lobbied too strongly. Until 1977 United States law had laid down that organizations could not retain tax exemption if they spent a 'substantial' amount on lobbying. In consequence some animal protection bodies spent their time, as in Britain, caring for and humanely killing unwanted pets. Henry Bergh's American Society for the Prevention of Cruelty to Animals, after more than eighty years of near-stagnation since his death in 1888 was, like the RSPCA in Britain, stirred by the members of a ginger-group from 1973 onwards. Gretchen Wyler, John Kullberg and others began the long and difficult process of modernizing a large and conservative bureaucracy which had for decades been preoccupied with administering 'kill' shelters for the stray dogs and cats of New York. Gradually, after Kullberg took over as director in 1978, the ASPCA began to be transformed into a campaigning body again.

If, during the 1970s, the American activists sometimes looked to Britain for inspiration, by 1980 the flow of ideas was in both directions. In 1982 the American film director Victor Schonfeld released *The Animals Film,* and it reached its first television audiences when shown in November of that year on the brand new British Channel Four. Most of its interviewees were British, and the commentary was spoken by British actress Julie Christie. The film made a great impression, arguing, as it did, that animal exploitation was analogous to the exploitation of the human working classes in a capitalist society. Nevertheless it marks the end of a period in which American animal rightists looked to Britain for moral and practical guidance. In 1986, for example, Dr Kenneth Shapiro brought American initiative to Britain by advertising for new Psychologists for the Ethical Treatment of Animals members in the *Bulletin of the British Psychological Society* (December 1986).

In 1984 Syndee Brinkman and Kathy Sanborn formed the National Alliance for Animal Legislation based in Washington to act as a co-ordinating group to lobby Congress. Craig van Note had done the same in 1977 when he formed Monitor to co-ordinate the legislative effort of some thirty-five wildlife and other organizations – which it has done with very considerable success.

In 1985 eleven of the most influential organizations in US animal welfare, animal rights and anti-vivisection united in a joint effort to prevent the use of stray and abandoned cats and dogs in American laboratories.[18] Time will tell whether such a coalition will turn out more effective or last longer than similar alliances in Britain.

Achievements

Working about a decade behind the British in the natural unfolding of their modern animal revolution, the Americans have, on the whole, shown themselves more effective as campaigners. How far this is due to better tactics and how much to a greater responsiveness by political and business institutions is a little hard to ascertain. Certainly, in Britain campaigners had gained the impression by 1980 that at the centre of the British establishment lay an immovable core of cold concrete – as deaf to pleas of mercy and as resistant to ideas of reform as the Versailles of 1789. In America, campaigners have also been assisted by freedom of information legislation which has allowed easy access to information about research projects and their funding.

In 1985, the movement in the US scored a particular success when federal officials cut off the funding of experiments on baboons at Dr Thomas Gennarelli's laboratory at the University of Pennsylvania. In May 1984 members of the American version of the Animal Liberation

Front had entered the laboratory and removed sixty hours of videotape showing baboons being subjected to experimental head injuries. People for the Ethical Treatment of Animals had organized protests and released parts of the tapes to television, showing experimenters laughing at their paralysed and mutilated victims. The prestigious *Washington Post* had published an editorial entitled 'Torturing Animals', and the *New York Times* had criticized laboratory standards. Law professor Gary Francione had started a protest group within the same university, and after a PETA sit-in at the National Institute of Health outside Washington in July 1985, the Department of Health and Humane Services announced a suspension of NIH funding to the laboratory.[19]

Unlike the European effort, which was chiefly a matter of either grass-roots protest or the lobbying of governments, the Americans adopted campaigns aimed at institutions. Under Spira and Pacheco they hit at individual laboratories and at major commercial firms. Individuals concentrated upon the professions and, by 1986, there were effective groups with names like Doctors [or Psychologists or Teachers] Against Experimentation. Scientists Concerned for Animal Welfare, and Feminists [or Veterinarians or Attorneys] for Animal Rights are further examples. American religious groups, too, came together in 1986 in the International Network for Religion and Animals. Dr Kenneth Shapiro, a clinical psychologist in Maine, formed the organization Psychologists for the Ethical Treatment of Animals in 1980. PsyETA campaigns intelligently within one of the worst exploiter professions.

In 1984 Attorneys for Animal Rights changed its name to the Animal Legal Defense Fund. It had begun as a small discussion group in San Francisco and by 1986 had over 200 attorney and law student members. With Steven M. Wise as its president and employing Joyce Tischler in San Francisco and Jolene Marion in New York, ALDF has done much to develop judicial interpretations of laws that have been on the statute book for many years. ALDF aims to function as 'the litigation arm' of the American animal rights movement and has succeeded in making new case law in several areas. It has taken on cases affecting the welfare of veal calves, laboratory animals, trapped and other wildlife.[20] Far more than in Britain the movement has known how to use the hidden strengths and weaknesses of statute law skilfully to create new case law in the courts, employing clever and determined lawyers.

It is true that in Britain, the campaign against the smoking beagles led us to a meeting with ICI in 1975 and that, with David Sperlinger, and supported by a few psychologists of an older generation such as Dr Alice Heim and Dr Donald Bannister, we had opposed animal experimentation within the British Psychological Society after a symposium in 1977 at the society's annual conference in Exeter. This had led to the setting up in 1980 of a special committee and the publication in 1985 of its 'Guidelines for the Use of Animals in Research'.[21] But these initiatives were out of the main stream of our campaigns. In Britain we had put most of our effort into pressurizing the legislators in London, Brussels and Strasbourg.

The American emphasis on wildlife protection has been very striking; it erupted in 1969, that *annus mirabilis* of the movement in which IFAW, Friends of the Earth, Greenpeace and the 'Oxford Group' all began. The emphasis, however, was environmental and conservationist (still the emphasis of West coast rather than East coast America), not anti-speciesist, and the new concern for animals' rights in the US only appeared after the publication of Singers' *Animal Liberation* in 1975. Legislation protecting laboratory and farm animals in the USA is still even more primitive than in advanced European states, despite the undoubted American lead in wildlife conservation.

In 1954 an Act was passed prohibiting the poisoning of wild horses and burros and in 1958 the first federal Humane Slaughter Act was passed. In 1966 the Laboratory Animal Welfare Act required the licensing of dealers and the registration of laboratories, as well as minimal standards of care. This Act was renamed the Animal Welfare Act in 1970 and extended to cover all warmblooded species. To Christine Stevens must go much of the credit for many of these remarkable achievements.

It was after 1969, however, that US action in this field began to make major inroads into exploitation. In that year the Endangered Species Act was passed, restricting the importation of listed threatened species. Unlike in Britain, where bloodsports interests have been a negative influence, most of the protective legislation was aimed chiefly at wildlife, and marine mammals in particular. At the UN Stockholm Conference on the Human Environment in 1971 the US delegation successfully pushed through a unanimous proposal for a moratorium on whaling (see chapter 12), and in 1972 the Marine Mammal Act was passed, prohibiting the killing or harassing of any marine mammal without a permit.

The shooting of wildlife from aircraft was also prohibited and, in 1973, CITES, the Convention on International Trade in Endangered Species of Wild Fauna and Flora, was concluded in Washington (see chapter 12). In 1976 the Animal Welfare Act was broadened and strengthened, requiring that dealers and transporters should be regulated and that animals should be handled humanely; it banned dog-fighting and cockfighting (except where state law permits it) and required that all government laboratories should be in compliance with the Act. In 1979 the Packwood-Magnusson Amendment empowered the US to impose fishing sanctions on nations not adhering to conservation requirements, and the Pelly Amendment empowered the president to embargo all wildlife products from any nation breaking wildlife conservation agreements such as CITES. Senator Dole's amendment to the Farm Bill in December 1985 required all US laboratories to appoint animal committees containing at least one independent member charged with representing the community's concern for animal welfare.[22]

In Britain, an enthusiastic public opinion remained thwarted by apathetic government, but in the USA legislators showed themselves far quicker to respond to public pressure. On the other hand the media in Britain could be more powerful than in the USA, being national rather than local. A television programme sympathetic to animal rights in Britain might, for example, reach an audience of six or seven million viewers, and many did so in the 1970s.

The other area in which America leads Britain is in the teaching of animal rights ideas in schools and universities. This rational and philosophical approach to the subject remains rare in European education.

Conclusion

By the mid-1980s American conservation organizations had begun to enter a new phase. Friends of the Earth, Greenpeace, the Sierra Club, the National Audubon Society and the Wilderness Society all saw significant changes in their leadership, as the original volunteer force of visionaries bowed out to make way for a new generation of professional executives hired to administer growing bureaucracies and bulging funds. FOE with a membership of 27,000 in America, hired a new executive director with a business background, and the Sierra Club, with a membership of 350,000 did likewise. Will these changes mark the consolidation of a firm wildlife conservation ethic in the American establishment, or the beginning of its stagnation and demise?

Many campaigners in America, as in Europe, have stuck to the job tenaciously. Others, such as Fay Brisk and Richard Morgan, have shone but briefly. Scientists such as Dr Geza Teleki and Dr Jane Goodall have, perhaps, been more prepared to take a strong line on animal protection in the America of the 1980s than scientists have in Europe. Surveys suggest not only an increasing interest in animal welfare in American scientific circles but also that those who support animal experimentation tend not to be those who have an especially high regard for science, but those groups such as hunters and the American clergy (sadly), who have a negative view of animals' rights.[23]

When an issue moves in America it certainly seems to move faster and to get results far quicker than it does in conservative and cynical Britain, where our ideas have led the way but our achievements have been so limited. Perhaps Americans enjoy change, but the British do not.

Throughout the developed world changes in attitude became noticeable in the 1970s and even more in the 1980s. Only in Third World countries did environmental concerns, and with them a concern for nonhuman life, show little sign of change.

Part III
THE ISSUES

17 Speciesism

We have seen in the first part of this book how humankind's relationship with nonhumans, far from being a peripheral issue, has often been a matter of practical, religious and intellectual importance. Nonhumans have played principal, not supporting, roles in literature, religion, science, folklore and philosophy, as well as in everyday economics. Although the distinction between human and nonhuman was emphasized in Christian countries, especially during the cruel and anthropocentric centuries of the Renaissance period, the way in which nonhuman animals have been treated, for example in their culpability in the eyes of the law during medieval times, suggests that many men and women continued to regard them as being in many respects like themselves.

There has always been a strange ambivalence towards nonhumans; a tendency to exploit them mercilessly combined with a common respect for some, but not all, things natural. Throughout the middle ages some animals were regarded as models of virtue and, later, as examples of God's beneficence to humankind; it was believed that all creatures were made to serve man, either as objects of exploitation or as teachers of goodness.

NATURAL AND UNNATURAL

This ambivalence, encouraged as it probably was by the contradictory human instincts of compassion and dominance, led to some confusion about what was to be considered natural and what unnatural.

Doing what was 'unnatural' was always considered to be wrong, but fashions changed as to how 'unnatural' should be defined. Those, like the Puritans, who saw great differences between human and other animals believed it was unnatural for men to show beast-like behaviour. Those who felt that men *were* animals tended to take a more lenient view. Sexual and aggressive behaviours, in particular, were often regarded as 'animal', and doing what nonhumans did was thus regarded with contempt.[1] Some viewed the whole process of civilization as a concealment of humankind's animal impulses; an idea to be reiterated by Freud in the twentieth century in his assertion that the 'higher' aspects of human civilization are sublimations of thwarted 'animal' instincts. For many, doing sexually that which not even the nonhuman animals were believed to do was considered still more wicked than the mere venting of animal lusts; thus child sexual abuse, masturbation and homosexuality were especially tainted.

Concerns over what was natural and about the connection between natural behaviour and virtue have always been strong, yet the arguments have often been inconsistent.

Although some of the 'natural' impulses of animals have been considered abhorrent, yet it has also been thought natural and quite right for a parent to protect its child, and natural and right for a child to respect its parents; parallels from nature are often used to support the 'rightness' of this idea. Some have also argued that artifice and affectation are to be mistrusted, along with fine clothes and elaborate decoration, in part at least because they are 'unnatural'. Shakespeare glimpsed man as 'a poor bare forked animal' in *King Lear* – a play deeply preoccupied with the intellectual search for the true nature of human beings. The stripping away of the trimmings of royal pomp and luxury is precisely Lear's predicament as, unnaturally rejected by his children, he flounders his storm-racked way between what is right and what is natural.

During the Renaissance period, in particular, witchcraft was associated with breaches of the natural order epitomized by the 'unnatural' intimacy between witch and cat or some other animal 'familiar'; such animals, if apprehended, could be burned alive. Similarly, any cock 'unnaturally' laying an egg was at once killed and the egg destroyed, lest it produce a deadly cockatrice.

Thus, although the naturalness of nonhuman animals was sometimes despised, any unnaturalness on their part was regarded with even greater horror. The Inquisition, for example, was ruthless in its suppression of what it considered unnatural familiarity between man and beast. The sin was to mix the categories. But why was it a sin? Was this attitude provoked by the fear of repressed human sexuality which appeared to be mocked and perhaps stimulated by the animal's brazenness? Or was it motivated by a sort of snobbery: a 'parvenu' need to feel superior?

We have seen that the Judaeo-Christian tradition taught that man was different, and was halfway between the beasts and the angels and made in the image of God; the animals being despised not only for their unbridled lusts of gluttony, lechery and ferocity, but also for their nakedness, dirtiness and hairiness.[2] Even to portray an animal on stage was unacceptable to some seventeenth-century Puritans. Furthermore, there was a tendency for humans to project on to the other animals qualities within themselves of which they were afraid or ashamed. But which came first – the control and concealment of humankind's natural impulses through religious or 'civilizing' pressures which led to the

perceived separation from the other animals, or a basic urge to feel
superior to the (feared) other species, which led to the suppresion of 'the
animal' in man, which in turn led to religious and moral rationalizations
for this control? Or was the reason for emphasizing the gulf between
human and nonhuman chiefly the need to provide an excuse for the
continued exploitation of the nonhuman animals?

Probably all three factors have played a part. By the sixteenth century
at least lust had become almost synonymous with animality,[3] and the
Puritan period, with its emphasis upon sexual restraint, was a bad time
for animals; too often they seemed to remind men and women of their
own sexuality, of which they were ashamed. In consequence, perhaps,
people punished nonhumans for their own sexual weaknesses. But nonhuman animals in England were treated with particular contempt during
the Tudor period, which also happened to be a time of middle-class
advancement, when many felt a need to look down upon nonhumans
much as they did upon the poor and vulgar of their own species. And in
all ages, probably, there was perennial guilt surrounding humankind's
speciesism and a need to alleviate this by arguing that human and
nonhuman were so different that morality did not transcend the species
barriers.

Fear of sex, 'snobbery' and guilt have all contributed to the development of speciesism. A fourth factor, too, has sometimes appeared – the
displacement on to animals of the feelings of resentment against other
humans felt by oppressed individuals in human society; Mary Wollstonecraft noted as much in 1792 when she observed that the lower classes
tyrannized the animals 'to revenge the insults they are obliged to bear
from their superiors'.[4]

This tension between those people who wish to 'rise above' their own
animality and those who want to accept and 'liberate' it is still a fundamental division in modern society, between conservatives and liberals,
obsessionals and hysterics, right and left, classicists and romantics.

In the eighteenth century it had been Rousseau who argued for a
return to a more simple and natural way of life. Later it would be
Thoreau who advocated a closer intimacy with nature. This is a recurrent
theme in Western cultures, extolled sometimes by those who need to
come to terms with their own natures, through greater sexual honesty,
for example, or the abandonment of social pretension.

In the twentieth century the scientific preoccupation with nature
continues not least in the behavioural sciences. The challenge has been
to establish not a moral code but an explanatory theory of behaviour as,
with the coming of Freud, psychology elbowed religion off the centre of
the intellectual stage. Yet, from Wundt, Pavlov and Lloyd Morgan
onwards, the psychologists turned constantly to the nonhuman animals
for their answers, much as the moralists had done before them. After
Freud, educated humankind began to feel that it was right, or at

least healthy, to be true to their own animal natures, and nonhumans were closely observed in order to ascertain what these were like. Sociobiology, too, the science of the biological basis for social behaviour, would become a mid-twentieth century manifestation of this traditional preoccupation.

CIVILIZATION, SADISM AND COMPASSION

Nonhumans probably constituted an important impetus for the growth of human civilization because it was imperative for human creatures to defend their interests against competing species, and it was helpful that many could be eaten, ridden or employed as beasts of burden. Hunting clearly was a case in point. In the 'civilized' world of today it is an unnecessary relic of what was once a vital enterprise. Before effective agriculture, those with a strong propensity to collaborate with others in expeditionary searches for sustenance may have survived lean years better than the stay-at-homes. They were more likely to find food, whether meat or fruits or leaves or grains. So this adventurous spirit was bred selectively into humankind, as into most other animals, and has not been totally lost beneath the far more sedentary agricultural cultures of the last ten thousand years. Searching is thus instinctive, and since the fulfilment of an instinct is itself pleasurable, many hunters today who dislike the killing of the quarry still enjoy the simple pleasures of the preliminary search. Such motives help to explain the popularity of those sports which involve, literally, 'hunting'. The same can be said of many children's games of the 'hide and seek' variety.

Less attractive is the equally innate human desire to dominate and to exercise power over inanimate and animate things, which can all too often be seen in young children, especially boys, from infancy. In its most unpleasant form it is frankly sadistic, and accounts for much of the pleasure obviously experienced by those who bait and torment captive creatures. In most civilizations this power-lust is usually constrained in human relationships except in times of war or intense personal crisis. Against other adult human beings its crude manifestations are partly or totally prohibited, and are permitted only in certain disguised forms in business, politics or games. But, for centuries, nonhumans were regarded as acceptable targets, becoming not only the butt for humankind's lust for power, but also aunt sallies for venting individual frustrations, and particularly those of the more deprived members of the human race.

This continues to be true. It not only affects those engaged in bloodsports but also those being cruel in other ways. I have known a male vivisector discover sadistic pleasure during the 'punishment' of laboratory animals in a psychological experiment, and, in her brilliant *Animals and Man*, Professor Miriam Rothschild recorded the common link between cruelty and sexual arousal:

I was once taken aback by an unusually able assistant of mine suddenly deciding to quit zoology. Apparently she had been given a live, instead of a dead mouse, to feed to a stoat, in which we were studying pelage change. Not having the courage to kill the mouse herself, she hurriedly pushed it into the cage. She watched fascinated while the animal crouched terrified in a corner, facing the tense, bright-eyed stoat preparing for the kill. To the girl's consternation she then experienced a violent orgasm.[5]

I am aware of the unfashionable nature of such words as 'instinct' and 'innate', but I use them deliberately. The human animal, no less than other creatures, is programmed before birth with certain behavioural potentials. These can be channelled and coloured by cultural and other environmental influences, and indeed suppressed entirely. Nevertheless I am saying that in *all* cultures the human animal tends to show two conflicting and instinctual ways of relating to other individuals — the compassionate and the dominating. These two basic impulses — call them what you will — are fundamental to the human predicament generally, and nowhere are they revealed more clearly than in the human-to-nonhuman relationship.

The spectators of baitings, in addition to enjoying vicariously the satisfaction of domination, derived an additional pleasure: the thrill of feeling fear while at the same time knowing that they were safe. This must have been the origin of much of the excitement felt by audiences in the Roman amphitheatre and medieval bear garden, as well as in the bull ring of today. Such people identify with the man who is fighting the allegedly ferocious beast. The fact that many bulls do not want to fight, or indeed that many lions did not seem particularly eager to eat Christians, is unlikely to spoil the viewer's fantasy; such people do not identify with the object of their fear. Men are invariably the 'good guys' while the nonhuman is cast in the role of villain.

As with most human activities, the motivation for cruel sports is multiple. Not all hunters today hunt for the same mixture of reasons; some, as I have said, do so mainly because they enjoy searching, some for the love of outdoor exercise, others for social reasons, and only a few, probably, for the pleasure of the kill. Instinctive drives and culturally acquired ones have become compounded. The macho motive is probably strong in some men but not in others.[6]

In the late medieval mind the indulgence in bloody and sadistic behaviour towards nonhumans was not only unashamed but taken to be a sign of virility. Despite the steady disappearance of really dangerous species in Europe (the lion had gone around AD 80 and the wolf disappeared in England during the sixteenth century), men continued to convince themselves that the pursuit and torture of animals which were often timid and sometimes inedible was nevertheless heroic. The pleasures of bloodsports were largely on the level of unreality. As humans gained ever-greater control over the other animals, so they used this control to enjoy their 'macho' fantasies, while reducing their risks: sports became safer and easier. Deer were kept in parks and rounded up to be presented to the 'sportsman' to be shot at from point-blank range. Bears and bulls were chained safely before being whipped and bullied. It really took very little courage to watch while a pack of large hounds caught a timid and heavily outnumbered quarry, or to squeeze a trigger from a safe distance, yet men did, and still do, regard such activities as evidence of manliness.

The requirements of the state sometimes encouraged such sports, as in Roman times, when they were considered to breed the martial spirit while distracting the people from their social grievances. Certainly the suppression of compassion and habituation to the sight of blood and injury may have been useful training for soldiers and, later, the tricks of horsemanship learned on the hunting field were rated highly as an apprenticeship for the cavalryman, as were the skills of hunting with bow and arrow for the bowman. Indeed, the similarity between some of the techniques of sport and those of war added to their macho appeal. Sport was war without the danger; like today's child with a plastic gun, the bloodsportsmen could enjoy their fantasies of derring-do in relative safety.

Sports were extolled as a means of maintaining physical and mental fitness in an otherwise idle class – a perennial attitude immortalized in the present century by A. P. Herbert in *Tantivy Towers*:

> Well a chap must do something, I always tell chaps.
> For if a chap doesn't a chap will collapse,
> And a chap keeps as fit as a chap could be wishin'
> As long as there's huntin' and shootin' and fishin'.

Yet, surely, all men and women have a spark of compassion within them; it, too, is natural and universal. Was there not always a tendency for some, particularly the children and the more sensitive adults, to extend their sympathies to the nonhuman animals? It was surely this which generated widespread guilt about our treatment of nonhumans – a guilt which had to be reduced through various rationalizations, including the assertions that animals had been created by God for precisely the uses that man found for them, or that animals lacked souls or could feel nothing (see Part I).

We have seen that differences between human and all other forms of creation have often been emphasized. Only men and women could laugh, suggested Aristotle, or could observe religion, said Edmund Burke. The drawing of a firm line between humankind and the other animals helped to satisfy many scruples, and may have been done unconsciously for this reason. But additional arguments were needed to reduce the guilt felt over unnecessary bloodsports and other more recent forms of exploitation. One popular line was to argue that the exploited animal was more of a threat than it really was, or that it displayed morally reprehensible qualities; foxes are an example.

Too often, since Freud, we tend to assume that kindness is a form of behaviour which has to be learned, and that our natural impulses are all aggressive or sexual. Yet in earlier days sympathy was considered to be part of human nature. Even the word 'kind' itself, according to the *Shorter Oxford Dictionary*, denotes in Middle English both 'natural' and 'sympathetic', and kindness meant 'kinship' as well as the 'natural affection arising from this'.

I use the words 'compassion', 'empathy' and 'sympathy' interchangeably, although I recognize that 'compassion' suggests not only fellow feeling but the helpful and protective actions which follow from it. Where, then, does compassion come from? Maybe it is not uniquely human, as anyone who has seen a dog licking a wounded human or canine friend will suspect. Clearly it is as strong an instinct, or collection of behaviours, as any other, and is at its most powerful in the parental role. More than this, it is surely one of those behaviours with high survival value, which helps us and other species to work together effectively in groups. Yet frequently it is suppressed, often by other primitive motivations such as those arising from anger or fear, as in battle. Or, as I shall argue, it may be stifled by cultural factors such as the macho ideal and the consequent fear of ridicule. (The macho motive has much to answer for.) Ambition and any sort of stoical training may inhibit the natural expression of sympathy, just as over-exposure to scenes of suffering may, in some individuals, lead to habituation or de-sensitization.

The psychologist Randall Lockwood described what he calls the 'empathy crisis' in America – 'the problem of insensitivity among doctors, nurses, veterinarians, teachers, psychologists and psychiatrists', and tellingly attributed this to the pressure to conform to the 'scientific model' and the identification of this model 'with the exorcism of emotionality, empathy and compassion'.[7] Science has indeed been given these values by those who see it as being in opposition to human feeling, which it does not have to be. Science is, however, much concerned with the control of nature, and so is, in this sense, the continuation of the age-old story of human conquest. Hence it can all too easily become a bastion of speciesism.

Lockwood traces five paths to feeling compassion towards non-humans: traumatic suffering; a sense of oneness with nature; close familiarity with animals; logical deduction; and a supportive and nurturant family background. Surely Lockwood is right: any or all of these can and do play an important part in the free flowing of compassion. Perhaps, however, a distinction should be made between the emotional and the cognitive aspects of compassion; between the *feeling* and the *objects* of that feeling. Traumatic suffering (or indeed prolonged suffering) may accentuate natural compassion, and an affectionate family background will surely nurture it, and, although compassionate people almost always tend to spread their compassion to nonhuman and human objects alike, the special emphasis upon the nonhuman may be encouraged by Lockwood's other factors – a sense of oneness with nature, close familiarity with animals and logical deduction (i.e. the force of the animal rights argument). One may go further and speculate that a disappointment in human relationships may be an experience which drives some into putting a far greater emphasis upon nonhuman than human objects of compassion. Early experiences are, as usual, probably of special importance here. Certainly, some recently reported survey findings in America confirm the view that a positive attitude towards the idea of animal rights is formed early in a child's life and remains relatively unchanged in adulthood.[8] Children do not seem to feel much difference between themselves and nonhumans; instead, they tend to assume a great deal of similarity. They are probably right. The psychological difference we perceive between ourselves and other animals is due chiefly to the accumulated human knowledge and sophistication which we acquire through learning. Such cultural factors, based largely on language and writing, which tend to obscure the similarities between human and nonhuman, are not present in children to the same degree.

One can distinguish between several types of compassion. First, there is the intellectually held belief that helping others is the 'right' thing to do; second, the emotional urge to give comfort and (parental) protection; third, the 'gut' feeling of hurt at seeing another's hurt. Squeamishness is not the same as compassion, but is very much linked to the latter type of it. Perhaps those who are most compassionate are those who have themselves suffered badly, but whose sufferings have not dulled their sensitivity nor made them bitter.

It is intriguing to speculate whether or not civilization is marked by an underlying greater gentleness, as Lecky suggested, or whether it merely shows a widening of the moral 'in-group'. From the seventeenth century onwards there may have been an average decline in the use of state torture in Western Europe, and the twentieth century advent of the welfare state demonstrates, at least in theory, the increasing power of humanitarian feeling for other humans in times of peace. But beside this general increase in the average humanitarianism of the state there has also been an erosion of the feeling of 'us and them' which, in past centuries, so often led to double standards. Whereas in the seventeenth century an Englishman would feel considerable duties towards and compassion for members of his own family, he might not have extended such scruples to his treatment of, say, foreigners or those of another religious group. In the following century the differentials between family

and others were challenged by the universal thinkers of the Enlightenment, who wrote for *all* human beings. The status of women gradually
improved (after periods of active feminist campaigning) in the succeeding
two centuries, and foreigners, blacks, the lower classes, orphans and the
insane were all more fully admitted into the circle of moral concern in
Europe during the nineteenth century.

Nonhumans, too, began to be admitted. Since Stuart times at least,
people had found it repugnant to eat any pet, and, as Bernard de
Mandeville remarked, some people found it difficult to consume any
creature they had daily seen and become acquainted with. In nineteenth-
century England it was common for families to exchange pigs at slaughtering time so as to avoid eating a pig who had, to some extent, been a
family member.

Was it growing affluence or a further extension of the 'family circle'
that caused English people gradually to cease eating small song-birds
from the seventeenth century onwards? Certainly, by the early Victorian
period it sounded more like the latter, if Mountstuart Elphinstone's
reaction to an Italian dish was typical: 'What! Robins! Our household
birds! I would as soon eat a child!'[9]

Indeed, it is possible to see the growth of animal liberation not so
much in terms of increased overall compassion so much as an *expansion
of the family circle*; the perception of other animals as our 'brothers and
sisters', literally as our evolutionary kin to whom we feel 'kindness'. We
see a similar expansion of the moral circle in twentieth-century internationalism, fostered by the increasing speed of travel and (televised) communication; increased knowledge of others apparently leading to increased
sympathy.

As we have seen, the development of the humane movement has been
erratic. The Renaissance was quite a setback and little progress has been
made during periods of war and insecurity. After the First World War,
for example, the movement in Britain lacked political drive, academic
acceptability and intellectual flair. As the importance of the traditional
upper classes declined, so did animal protection as a moral and political
issue. Many of the new social reformers, mostly socialists, saw animal
welfare at best as a mild absurdity and at worst as an aristocratic and
bourgeois confusion of priorities which had encouraged the disgraceful
neglect of the needs of the human working classes. The decline in the
influence of the Liberal party probably made the situation worse.

In addition, the Victorian emphasis upon associating kindness to
nonhuman animals with nursery education had helped to make the issue
appear sentimental, childish, unworthy of mature intellectual consideration and, in the most prejudiced sense, 'womanly'; an imperial culture
which valued the martial virtues found it difficult to assimilate a concern
for animal welfare with its worship of 'manliness', especially after the
searing experiences of war. It was not until the 1960s and 1970s that the

moral and biological differences between human and nonhuman began to seem less absolute.

The real and awful prospect of interbreeding human and nonhuman in the 1990s becomes daily more probable, as agriculturalists scramble to produce cheaper meat and the American administration decides to permit the patenting of new animal forms created by genetic engineering.[10] Within years, the ancient conceptual gulf between man and beast will be closed by the scientists. Will this lead to increased callousness to humans, or to a sudden dawning that we owe duties towards *all* sentient life?

Two other developments have been important in the growth of the humane movement – the gradual removal of animals as *visible* threats to human safety and the decline in dependence upon them. As a larger proportion of the European population became town-dwellers, they felt their interests less threatened by the depredations of pests than did their country cousins and they decreasingly thought of nonhumans as being a source of real danger to them. It was not itself that they lived in the town or in the country which made people more humane. It was simply that fewer town-dwellers felt directly imperilled by nonhumans or had interests visibly bound up with their exploitation. All these trends made it far easier for men and women to begin to extend the circle of compassion. Indeed, it is tempting to postulate that between any alienated groups, *if fear and exploitation are absent*, then feelings of sympathy seep into the vacuum, and that this process can be rapidly accelerated if close personal contact is maintained. This seems gradually to have happened, in the case of nonhumans in Europe, in the four hundred years since the sixteenth century.

Pet-keeping, too, played an important part in this; nonhumans treated as members of the family naturally became eligible for compassionate treatment. Dogs and cats were widely domesticated in early medieval times, although the cat fell out of favour with the Church in the late fourteenth and fifteenth centuries and became shamefully mistreated – further evidence that cruelty to nonhumans increased during the Renaissance period. By the eighteenth century cats were back in favour at both French and English courts and subsequently became special favourites among artists and writers as well as the aristocracy – precisely those groups which led the animal welfare movement in Europe.[11]

Animal rights pioneers such as Montaigne, Johnson, Bentham and Lawrence were all cat-admirers, and it is interesting to speculate on the role played by cats in the promotion of the cause generally. The relationship between cat and human is, at least in the cat's eyes, more or less one of parity. The cat-lover therefore is more likely to be someone who respects animal equality than the dog-lover, who may enjoy the dominant role which the subservient dog encourages.

Today we can see that pets satisfy our psychological needs in a number of ways, some not especially selfish but others extremely so:

they give us physical tactile comfort; they flatter us and make us feel important; they help us to drop our social façades and to be ourselves; they give us a feeling of companionship and security, especially at night; and they can boost our egos as extensions of ourselves or as compensations for our weaknesses. We can gain satisfaction from showing off our pets to others; they increase our self-confidence by submitting to our authority; and sometimes, alas, they relieve our hostilities by acting as our scapegoats – they pander to the tyrant in us by becoming our slaves. They also play with us and so allow expression of the eternal child inside most adults; in playing with children they allow the child to develop his or her fantasies and thoughts; and they can act as go-betweens in human relationships, often facilitating the flow of emotion between people. Above all, pets allow us to love and to be loved – the experience of feeling loved and needed being the greatest service which they give to us. To each member of a family they can become something different – another child to the mother, a sibling to the child, a grandchild to the elderly. As companions they are particularly supportive – especially for the old and lonely. It is hardly surprising that, provided they are happy, pets can make excellent psychotherapists.

SQUEAMISHNESS

It is strange that we have no other word for this phenomenon; so ashamed have we been to admit that the sight of our own or another's blood or injury may make us feel ill or cause us to become 'medically shocked'. Yet various writers over the centuries have described this reaction, and today it is taken for granted (and widely joked about) in medical circles. Patients, particularly intelligent males, so the folklore avers, are liable to faint or feel nauseated when undergoing blood tests or injections. Anecdotes are told about war heroes who feared inoculations more than the enemy or who collapsed when they saw the wounds of others.

This could be regarded as an abnormality, some sort of phobia. Yet even phobias (such as the fear of insects, snakes and the dark) are probably based upon sound instincts which have good survival value. When so many people seem to be afflicted, it suggests a significant aspect of human behaviour, and probably one that has itself promoted survival by encouraging the avoidance of injury and illness. The lesser squeamishnesses, too, associated with aversions to vomit and excrement, may have the same function. Indeed there seems to be a general mild squeamishness which causes an aversion towards other individuals' bodies generally, their odours for example, which may also help to avoid infectious illness by maintaining separation. Is this why the sexual drive has to be so powerful in humans – to overcome these varieties of squeamishness?

What is particularly strange is that these culturally widespread behaviours have not been seriously studied. They have, instead, been studiously ignored. Yet they are clearly powerful phenomena, and far more powerful than many aspects of behaviour which do receive considerable study. Squeamishness can, after all, make grown men faint, or cause doctors to abandon careers in surgery; it may even have caused Darwin to give up his career in medicine. His biographer reports that Darwin was disgusted by the study of anatomy, and 'found that he was squeamish in the operating theatre: he attended two operations, one on a child, and ran away in the middle. The memory of them haunted him for many years.'[12]

Surgeons and nurses must develop a resistance to squeamishness, but even those most accustomed can continue to flinch. One distinguished pathologist has claimed that even his selectively hardy profession 'universally suffers from bad dreams' as a result of their work.[13]

In 1977 I surveyed a group of schoolgirls in Oxford who had recently started studying biology. One of the items in my questionnaire was about the dissection of dead animals. Although these fifteen-year-olds had chosen to do biology no less than 55 per cent indicated that they 'disliked' dissecting and 33 per cent said such procedures made them feel 'sick or ill'.[14] It appears that before habituation to dissection occurs a large proportion of schoolchildren are deeply moved by it. This is true even, it seems, of those who have self-selected for dissection and even when the nonhumans being dissected are dead.

Boys, it is true, quickly cotton on to the idea that it is 'macho' not to flinch at dissections. To an extent some may overcome, or at least conceal, their squeamishness by employing bombast. But I suspect the tendency is still there.

What does all this mean? It means, surely, that there is something inherently disturbing in seeing another creature injured, impaled, dismantled or killed – particularly if this is done cold-bloodedly; that is to say when the observer is not already aroused by fear, anger or other extreme emotion. Leo Tolstoy saw humankind's aversion to all killing as both strong and natural,[15] and so do I.

The excitement generated by a dissection class is often very noticeable, and seems to touch upon sadism on one hand and pity on the other. Some children are shocked to discover sadism within themselves and others by their teacher's apparent callousness. Teachers, so it seems, can become 'bloodied' by the process, which leads them sometimes to defend it almost irrationally, as if it were an initiation ceremony with valued religious undertones. Yet after many years working with disturbed children, I strongly suspect that persuading a reluctant child to dissect, and thus 'brainwashing' or corrupting him or her into this form of speciesism, can be as damaging to that child as sexual abuse or physical attack. Furthermore, I have noticed that children who profess indifference to dissection tend to score high on the 'P' scale of the Eysenck Personality Inventory — itself often a feature of teenage delinquency.

Putting young adults through ordeals of blood and injury is culturally widespread. Once through the gate of initiation there is no coming back, the intense sense of pride in the conquering of fear and squeamishness is a powerful part of the process of maturity, especially, perhaps, in warlike groups. Yet because of our shame at our squeamishness, because it does not conform with our macho culture's view of what is mature and manly, we try to pretend that it does not exist. But it *does exist*, and surely the lesson we should learn is that instinctively we are not programmed to destroy other living things cold-bloodedly; and that possibly we cause emotional damage when we force ourselves to do so. Above all it suggests we can care *innately*.

D. O. Hebb years ago discovered that nonhuman apes were deeply disturbed by the sight of an isolated ape's head, so perhaps we are not alone in being squeamish.

Why have I been concerned to argue that squeamishness and compassion are innate (although they can also be learned)? I am not saying that this is what therefore makes them a good thing. My reason for rejoicing at this is that it suggests that it is quite easy for human beings to be compassionate and it therefore gives us some hope for a kinder and more gentle future.

MACHISMO

Squeamishness is certainly not encouraged in militaristic cultures. This not only explains why the phenomenon has remained intellectually taboo in the West, but why cruelty towards nonhumans has sometimes been seen as a sign of virility. Bloodsports in particular have tended to fall into this category. Writing in 1853, Harry Hieover saw such sports 'as producing a manliness of mind and hardihood of frame that have (as yet) characterised my countrymen.'[16] Demonstrations of manhood are often culturally defined as including the ability to steel oneself to do things which one's natural sympathies shy away from. The teaching of such macho motivation is, surely, still one of the main causes of speciesism.

Roberta Kalechofsky has argued that male fear of female sexuality produced a new sadistic element in the pornography of the nineteenth century. Vivisection was associated by both men and women, so she argues, with this male hostility towards women. Certainly this very much ties in with my belief in the importance of a compensating 'machismo' motive for the oppression of both women and nonhumans.[17] The whole cult of machismo in nineteenth-century Britain is indeed very pronounced. Dr Arnold at Rugby started the 'muscular Christian' fashion for 'godliness and manliness' which led to the cultivation of dangerous team sports intended to mould the character of the English public-school man.[18] What was produced at the end of this educational procedure? Men who could endure and inflict physical and mental suffering in obedience to authority or out of loyalty to the team – ideal specimens so it happened, for the extension and maintenance of the British empire.

The middle-class trend towards respectability, together with the fear of uncontrolled working-class disorder, helped to motivate the suppression of violent working-class recreations, including bloodsports. Any occasion – such as a prize fight or a cock-fight – which attracted an unruly crowd was an object of middle-class apprehension. One response was to suppress; another, defensively, was to toughen up the middle- or upper-class male and to instil in him an intense class loyalty.

In the twentieth century this learned machismo dynamic is still very strong in the Western world of James Bond and Rambo; boys are still encouraged to be tough and brave and to eschew emotion. Historically, this was helpful for survival and was accentuated, perhaps, by fear of revolution, invasion or attack generally. But whatever the reason in the past, machismo is surely responsible nowadays for much unnecessary violence and loutishness of various sorts, including many instances of human oppression of the other species.

Significantly, many who have been involved in real wars and had to prove their bravery or strength in battle no longer feel the need to maintain a macho image: some outstanding war heroes have not been ashamed to express a tenderness towards nonhuman animals. The Duke of Wellington was kind to a toad, Lord Nelson felt open revulsion at a bull-fight, and Lord Dowding and Douglas Bader attacked vivisection. Winston Churchill, too, angrily declined to attend a bull-fight arranged in his honour when visiting Seville in 1958.[19]

It remains true that one of the surest ways of promoting speciesism is to imply that cruelty is akin to manliness. Geoffrey Gorer pointed out that this link between cruelty and manliness is culturally widespread. In the public torturing of prisoners by the Japanese, 'the torturer is demonstrating his manliness to his companions by showing his ability to inflict pain without flinching', and the situation is similar to the almost universal admiration accorded to those who *endure* pain stoically in initiation ceremonies or in other contexts.[20]

Women, in most cultures, have not been enslaved by this macho imperative. If, with emancipation, they can continue to escape its coils, then the growing female influence in the future may make the world a better place for all sentient beings. Yet, when enslaved by machismo, the individual female victim – as one has seen in the cases of certain vivisectors – can become particularly deadly.

Nonhumans, like children, are often our scapegoats. Humans will avenge themselves upon them for their own misfortunes, and this mechanism may well be behind the apparent increase in cruelty in Britain at a time of poverty and unemployment in the 1980s. Research by the World Society for the Protection of Animals carried out in America has found that aggressive criminals report being cruel to animals far more frequently than do less aggressive criminals. Significantly, three-quarters of the aggressive criminals studied were abused and beaten as children, compared with only 10 per cent of non-criminals. One criminal said; 'I beat on animals to get back for the beatings I got.'[21]

In 1986 there were nearly 19,000 more cases of cruelty reported to the RSPCA than in the previous year, an increase of 75 per cent on 1984. The highest increase in complaints by region was the 42.14 per cent increase over one year reported from the severely depressed north-east of England. In the three-month period May to July 1987, of 277 people in England and Wales disqualified from keeping animals because they were convicted of cruelty, 54 were housewives, 104 were otherwise employed and 119 (including 8 retired people) were unemployed.[22] Was idleness encouraging cruelty?

Andrew Tyler found in 1988 that 'blood sports are now all the rage with the inner-city set. Badgers, domestic cats, rats, pet-shop apes and horses are all fair game'.[23] In a revealing report he quoted one young unemployed animal-baiter as saying that from the early 1980s this trend had been associated with unemployment: 'a street lad with nothing to do would take to ratting.' Furthermore he would treat his own terriers with speciesist contempt, consigning them to travel in the car boot. All the familiar motives are described – the alienated young using non-humans as scapegoats for their anger, the emulation of the rich hunting set, the macho cult – 'all so that these fellas could stand around in boozers all night boasting how hard they were'. Even genuine erotic sadism was admitted by one young yob, describing his reaction to watching ferrets kill forty captive rabbits – 'I couldn't believe it, but I was getting off on it.' Tyler concluded:

It would perhaps be comfortable to think of them as an aberrant strain, a kind of runt city litter. In reality they express, in a heightened way, both a traditional smash-and-grab attitude to the natural world and a peculiarly late Eighties malaise whose symptoms are spite, selfishness and violent nihilism.

The man who keeps a dog, unfortunately, may gain satisfaction from the scapegoat relationship; the need for a 'whipping boy', a creature to dominate, and its constant admiration and undying loyalty – these things flatter the sagging ego, they may make him feel 'a man' partly because here he is in control to a degree that is not true in other areas of his life.

NONHUMAN *VERSUS* NONHUMAN?

The relationhip between species is a neglected field of study. Yet such relationships are not merely those of fight, flight or indifference. Prey species do not always show fear of a predator, they sometimes pester it as smaller birds do a buzzard. Cows, and particularly heifers and bullocks, are fascinated by dogs or cats who enter their field; young chimpanzees make friends with young baboons; even cats and dogs can play together. Such interspecies relationships can be strong and amicable. Similarly, people can sometimes relate more openly to their pets than to their human associates. Does this mean that we should interfere in the behaviour of nonhumans when this causes suffering to other nonhumans? Of course we should unless we are speciesists, or unless such behaviour has immediate survival value (as in, for example, a natural carnivore–prey interaction). I rescue mice who are being tortured by cats because the torture (almost certainly accentuated by human selective breeding over centuries) is unnecessary for the survival of the aggressor, just as I restrain a large dog from attacking a small one.

PAIN, PLEASURE AND CONSCIOUSNESS

At least since Epicurus in the fourth century BC, philosophers have suggested that all creatures seek pleasure and avoid pain. When questioned as to why they consider something to be good or bad most people produce an explanation which ultimately can be boiled down to whether or not it causes pain or pleasure, happiness or unhappiness. Intermediary goals such as liberty or equality or justice are ultimately valued for this reason. The two best-known utilitarian philosophers who identified this truth, Jeremy Bentham and John Stuart Mill, both included nonhuman animals in their calculations of pain and pleasure. For them, as we have seen this widening of the circle of compassion, to which both Einstein and Schweitzer have referred, was already explicit.

It is debatable how far this has ever been the case with the world's major religions. Some sense of it is present in Hinduism and Buddhism, as we have seen (chapter 2), but less so in the others. Yet in almost all is the general proposition that it is right to treat others as you would wish to be treated yourself. This is clear in Christianity,[24] Taoism, Confucianism, Sikhism, Zoroastrianism, Judaism and Islam. The problem comes with the definition of 'others'. Aristotle did not include slaves in his definition. Yet gradually over the centuries the definition has been widened to include those of other tribes, other nations and other faiths. The next great step forward, surely, is to include those of other species. That is what the animal revolution is about.

Gradually, more evidence accrues to suggest that nonhumans are conscious and feel pain. Nonhuman primates show electrical activity in their brains which is characteristic of consciousness in humans[25] and all vertebrate classes contain chemicals in their nervous system which are known to mediate the human experience of pain. Consciousness emerges from the material of the brain as mysteriously as electricity emerges from the copper wires of a dynamo, and the brains of many species are materially similar to those of humans. Although there is no conclusive evidence that any animal or insect lacks consciousness, it may be that consciousness increases with the complexity of the nervous system of the species, and when sufficiently complex machines are made they too may become conscious and need protection from cruelty.

Whatever are the *causes* of consciousness, its moral importance is clearly paramount. It matters not if an animal, whether human or nonhuman, is intelligent or communicative, or has an immortal soul. All that matters is that it is conscious: in particular that it can be conscious of pain and pleasure. This should be the bedrock of our morality. Pain is pain regardless of the species suffering it.

SINGER AND REGAN: INHERENT VALUE OR SUFFERING?

An interesting difference of opinion has appeared between Peter Singer and Tom Regan, the two leading philosophers of the movement. Singer argues, as I do, that sentience, or the capacity for suffering, is at the heart of the matter. It is because nonhumans can suffer that they have interests which must be considered. Regan, on the other hand, argues that nonhumans as well as humans have a certain 'inherent value' which may be independent of the pleasures and pain which they experience. This inherent value is possessed by all 'subjects of a life', that is to say beings with beliefs, desires, perception, memory, a sense of the future, an emotional life, preferences, the ability to initiate action in pursuit of goals, psycho-physical identity over time and an individual welfare in the sense that things can go well or badly for them.[27] Regan concludes that an 'equal right' to respectful treatment is possessed by all things with inherent value.

So Regan is using the term 'rights', whereas Singer is not. Singer prefers to use my word 'speciesism'. Singer is basing his position on 'suffering' (or sentience) and Regan is basing it on 'inherent value'. One of the advantages of Regan's use of the term 'rights' is that he can avoid getting into the argument about whether or not the suffering of one can be justified by the greater advantage or pleasure of another. He is, as I am, against such trade-offs. For Regan, to experiment upon an animal is to violate its rights and therefore it is wrong, regardless of any advantage to others. Singer, on the other hand, believes in aggregative trade-offs, and argues, for example, that it is possible to imagine a situation in which a painful experiment upon an unwilling subject (whether non-human or human) *is* justified by its beneficial consequences. Whereas I agree with Singer on the importance of *suffering* as the bedrock of morality, I tend to agree with Regan that it is *wrong to aggregate across individual sentients*. This is because I believe that in such matters the individual consciousness is everything. It is therefore wrong for me to inflict suffering *unless* it brings greater advantages to the *same* individual, or unless that individual gives consent. Surely, to take the aggregative line is to accept that performing agonizing experiments upon a few infants, for example,would be justified if we could be sure that it would lead to a cure for many others. The ends are said to justify the means. This must be wrong.

Besides, there are so many uncertainties in such a cost–benefit analysis. How many infants can be sacrificed for the benefit of how many others? How much agony is justified by what quantity of benefit? How certain must I be of the success of the experiment in advance? One could lay down certain rules. For example, pains and pleasures which are *certain* to occur could be said to count for more than *uncertain* ones, *deliberately* caused pain more than that accompanying *natural* events such as disease, and so on. But none of this is really satisfactory. Whatever our disagreements, however, most of us are agreed that pain and distress are bad and that the suffering of nonhumans should count equally with the same quantity of suffering in humans.

But how can 'quantities of suffering' be measured and compared? They might, for example, be measured by psychological indices of stress (such as heart rate, blood pressure, cortisol levels, galvanic skin response and so on) or by the individual's choice between two or more situations, one less painful than another.[28] Clearly in practice, however, it is extremely difficult to make valid measurements of this sort. It is psychological *experience* which matters, after all, not the physical magnitude of the painful stimulus itself, and stress can accompany pleasure as well as pain. Although pain can be said to vary along two basic dimensions – intensity and duration – its experience varies greatly between individuals and is dependent upon other circumstances, particularly psychological ones. In the heat of battle, for instance, a soldier may scarcely notice a wound which in 'cold blood' might be agonizing.

But how about painless killing? Why is that bad? The utilitarian answer is that it deprives a sentient creature of future happiness, as well as upsetting friends and family of the victim. Strangely, Singer has hinted that because nonhumans are at a lower 'mental level' than most humans, it may matter less to kill them. He concluded that:

In general, though, the question of when it is wrong to kill (painlessly) an animal is one to which we need give no precise answer. As long as we remember that we should give the same respect to the lives of animals as we give to the lives of those human beings at a similar mental level we shall not go far wrong.[29]

Is Singer here assuming that a higher mental level (and that, for Singer, appears to mean 'self-awareness, intelligence, the capacity for meaningful relations with others and so on') is linked with greater happiness? Surely the connection, and there may well be one, is by no means inevitable. In killing a normal human being one may be depriving him or her, not of future happiness, but of future sorrow. One can rarely be certain of such things; it is difficult to predict the future.

But Singer may be edging towards the view that certain qualities, in addition to the experience of happiness, have value in themselves: I find this hard to accept. Surely all such qualities have moral value only in the pain or pleasure they bring. Where Singer is surely right, however, is in the case of inflicting suffering rather than death. Here he maintains that the greater 'mental capacities' of the average human being can sometimes increase and sometimes reduce suffering compared with the suffering experienced by nonhumans in the same circumstances. For example, knowing that one is about to be tortured could very much *increase* the quantity of suffering in the total experience. But, conversely, knowing that the pain one experiences is in a very good cause could *reduce* the total suffering. Such cognitive factors, absent in most nonhuman cases and in some human cases (such as the severely mentally handicapped and infants), can work either way.

One thing remains certain. As Singer puts it:

Pain and suffering are bad and should be prevented or minimised, irrespective of the race, sex, or species of the being that suffers. How bad a pain is depends on how intense it is and how long it lasts, but pains of the same magnitude are equally bad regardless of species.[30]

Despite the difficulties in the measurement and comparison of pain, it is surely true that in very many areas humankind is inflicting severe suffering upon nonhumans – in slaughter houses, factory-farms and laboratories, for example. The most fundamental rights of nonhumans are being overthrown often merely for the convenience or luxury of our own species. Such discrimination, based as it is only upon the difference of species, is sheer speciesism.

For me Singer is right in his emphasis upon pain and pleasure but Regan is right in isolating the importance of the individual; ends, however glorious, can never justify means if the latter themselves entail suffering. Indeed, a common mistake made by those defending speciesism (e.g. animal experimentation) on the grounds of the benefits it brings (e.g. medical advances) is to then complain about those militant groups who damage laboratories and factory-farms and to attack them on the same grounds – namely that compassionate ends cannot justify violent means. If this is the case, then how can human benefits from research or other exploitation justify the infliction of violence and suffering upon nonhumans?

DUTIES OR RIGHTS? SPECIESISM AND SENTIENTISM

Whereas Singer avoids the use of the word 'rights' for the very best of reasons, I do so principally because it seems to me to be synthetic and unconvincing — whether applied in the human case or otherwise. This is one reason why I coined the word 'speciesism' in 1970. There are interesting differences in the psychological aspects of the terms. The word 'rights' has gained in popularity very considerably during this century taking over from the nineteenth century's favourite term, which was 'duty'.[31] One obvious difference between the two words is that rights are said to reside in the victim, whereas duties are in the perpetrator. Moral instruction used to place the emphasis upon the doer now it emphasizes the done-to. Why is this? Is it not partly because the doers, usually of the ruling classes, used to have real power over others, whereas today morality is a concern for *all* classes including many who feel powerless? Significantly, it is only in the late twentieth century that the welfare of nonhumans has very publicly become the concern of the working class. The Victorians, of course, sometimes appeared more worried about the righteousness of the doer than the suffering of the victim.

Speciesism is, I suppose, a compromise word.[32] It is applied mainly to the doer, but it is not as high-minded as words such as 'duty' or 'responsibility'. It describes the doer's negative attitude and actions, rather than his or her positive qualities. It denotes not merely discrimination but prejudice, and, far more importantly, the exploitation, oppression and cruel injustice which flow from this prejudice.

Perhaps there is some correlation with personality. Maybe the authoritarian or right-winger (who may feel confident in the efficacy of his or her action) talks in terms of responsibilities and duties, whereas the less authoritarian (who feels rather more of a victim) uses concepts like justice, liberty and rights. The basic difference here is with whom the speaker naturally tends to identify — the doer or the victim.

Whereas 'speciesism' is semantically equivalent to 'sexism' (or male chauvinism) and Animal Liberation has an equivalent meaning to Women's Lib, what then is the equivalent of 'feminism', one wonders? Will it be necessary to revive zoophilism, or would 'sentientism' be possible? This is, after all, what we are asserting — the overwhelming importance in moral (and political) terms of the capacity to feel. We are saying that whatever feels pain, whether an animal or some machine of the future, should have moral rights.

Such word-play is not, I think, entirely frivolous. Words condition how we feel and act. So much of the problem in our mistreatment of the other sentients is due to outmoded habits of thought which new words can play a part in breaking. They can expand our awareness and alter attitudes. If we proclaim sentientism, then the puzzlement this initially causes may help some people to stop and think. Furthermore it is a term which is positive rather than negative in tone.

THE NEW HEDONISM

We have seen that pain has been the overriding concern of most of the authors and artists who have contributed to the development of the modern animal liberation ethic, although sometimes there are *additional* reasons why they advocate compassion; the sense of oneness with nature, for instance, expresssed by Rebecca Hall as a regard for: 'the natural order of things; an order, a communion, we have forgotten, which we ignore to the detriment of ourselves and all that lives.'[33] Yet even here, presumably, the 'detriment' mentioned can ultimately be reduced to nonhuman and human suffering.

Is it possible that animal liberation, with its foundation partly in utilitarian philosophy, may have an effect upon wider morality and politics generally? The gradual decline in the overt importance attached to Christian values has left a moral vacuum. What more natural, in a hedonistic society, than to fill this void with an explicit morality that all can understand and accept: that to cause pain is wrong and to give pleasure is good; that virtue lies in giving pleasure to others and evil is the deliberate causing of pain or distress?

We have seen in Britain's Animal (Scientific Procedures) Act of 1986 the introduction of an overt utilitarian principle of a speciesist sort: namely that the pain of nonhumans should be weighed against the benefits to humans, and this same spirit could permeate government decisions entirely affecting people. Perhaps nowhere more clearly is this equation tested than in the decisions that governments have to make on whether or not to make concessions to terrorists in order to effect the release of hostages. The conventional wisdom dictates that governments should not do so because the relief of the hostages' sufferings would be outweighed in the future by the greater sufferings of further hostages being taken. The White House, it seems, sided more with Tom Regan's approach than with Peter Singer's in deciding that the relief of the current sufferings of hostages should not be aggregated against future cases, when it traded arms with Iran in 1986. The rights of the individual in the here and now were considered to be of paramount importance. Present and certain effects were thus deemed to count for more than the uncertain pains and pleasures of the future.

Health and welfare policies, too, are based, however vaguely, on utilitarianism. With the increasing cost of heart transplant surgery and other advanced medical techniques, administrators are being faced with awkward decisions. Should money be channelled into the comfort of the many or saving the lives of a few? One or many? The young or the old? Pain or life? Prevention or cure?

It is also interesting that viewing pain and pleasure (or suffering and happiness) as the bases of morality is a bringing together of what ought to be and what is, for pain and pleasure are the bases also for both Freudian and modern Behaviourist theories of behaviour. Just as Rousseau and Locke had believed that humankind had rights and liberties rooted in nature, so in the twentieth century nature again can be claimed as the foundation of morality. Certainly, natural impulses (especially aggressive ones) will clash with mores, and 'id' will conflict with 'superego', but at least there is widespread agreement that conscious contentment is the common natural goal.

The less discrepancy, perhaps, between a moral code and natural impulses the less psychological tension there will be, and this growing together of a *code* for behaviour with the *theory* of behaviour is epitomized in the case of animal liberation; both the criteria for morality and those for behaviour lie in the consciousness of the individual sentient. Consciousness is central. Certainly our clothing, our language and our technology emphasize the differences between species. But science itself has demystified the human–nonhuman difference and some psychologists now assert that nonhumans can indeed be credited with 'thought'[34] and even with the ability to deceive deliberately.[35] Certainly some clever apes are more intelligent than many mentally handicapped human primates. But what (to paraphrase Bentham) if it was otherwise? Intelligence does not matter in this context. The important thing to remember is that we can all *suffer*.

MODERN DARWINISM

I am aware that my emphasis upon Darwinism as grounds for asserting the *moral* kinship of all animals raises the question – 'But didn't Darwin claim that only the fittest survive, and isn't this an argument in support of human dominion?' Such an attitude, by no means incompatible with the political ethos of Reaganism and Thatcherism, would also seem to encourage the exploitation of weaker sexes, races and individuals. The strongest objection to this argument, however, is that 'fittest' does not necessarily mean strongest or most selfish or ruthless. The Darwinian definition of what is fittest to survive is made by the environment itself, and environments change. In a nuclear age and a polluted one, and one where the human conquest of the other vertebrates is all but complete, 'fittest' takes on a more subtle meaning. It may mean the opposite to aggressive, macho, selfish or destructive of the balance of nature. Darwinists today are by no means unwilling to support the idea of animal liberation. Indeed, one of this century's leading Darwinists shows a major concern for the ethics of the human-to-nonhuman relationship, and has confirmed that speciesism ' has no proper basis in evolutionary biology'.[36] Writing in his *The Blind Watchmaker*, Dr Richard Dawkins stated:

Such is the breathtaking speciesism of our Christian-inspired attitudes, the abortion of a single human zygote (most of them are destined to be spontaneously aborted anyway) can arouse more moral solicitude and righteous indignation than the vivisection of any number of intelligent adult chimpanzees! I have heard decent, liberal scientists, who had no intention of actually cutting up live chimpanzees, nevertheless passionately defending their right to do so if they chose, without interference from the law. Such people are often the first to bristle at the smallest infringement of human rights.[37]

Dawkins points out that speciesism is made easier by the convenient fact that the intermediates between humans and other apes are now extinct but reminds us that we share more than 99 per cent of our genes with chimpanzees.

Arguments about humankind's closeness to the other apes have waxed and waned over the years since Darwin. Today it is known that the composition of human blood and DNA put us closer to the chimpanzee than horses are to donkeys.[38] Yet still scientists and politicians behave as if no moral implications ensue. The scientific evidence accumulates to support the view that nonhumans suffer pain and distress very much like ourselves, yet the same men and women who produce the evidence continue to ignore its message.

Biologists more than any other group are guilty of this inconsistency. They cruelly experiment upon nonhumans very often in order to find information they hope will be relevant to the human condition. They scientifically justify these experiments on the grounds that the research tool is physically and psychologically like the human, but they fail to condemn their own cruelty on the same grounds. Either nonhumans are unlike humans, in which case they can have little value as models for research, or they are like us, in which case they should be shown similar respect.

We have seen that Darwinism, despite establishing the almost universally held belief in the *physical* kinship of men and animals, did not cause most people to take the logical next step of admitting *moral* kinship. The nineteenth century witnessed progress in the humane movement for quite other reasons, principally affluence and peace. Yet now, belatedly, the implications of the Darwinian message are beginning to be realized.

THE FUTURE

The worldwide campaign must continue, in all its aspects, undaunted by the apparent slowness of change. It may take thirty or forty years for a movement such as ours to turn the great ships of commerce and custom. But the up-and-coming generations of legislators and managers will be those who have heard about animal liberation and had time to think about it. They may not accept the whole ethic, but mindful of its *logic*, of public opinion and the twinges of their own consciences, they will turn the rudder by degrees until we have a full revolution.

The campaign must continue to strive to alter attitudes and reform the law. The five main areas of speciesist abuse remain the same: those affecting domestic sentients, and those in laboratories, farms, places of entertainment and in the wild. By mobilizing public compassion, we can persuade governments around the world that the treatment of non-humans is a legitimate political concern and that it is up to them, and not the individual politician, to effect change. Some changes will have revolutionary effects upon our life-styles, but in almost every case we are no longer as dependent upon the other animals as once we were; alternatives exist or can be found.

In the past our economic dependence upon the other animals surely helped to fashion our speciesism. As the highly anthropocentric Karl Marx noted, it was not religion but the coming of a money economy which led Christians to exploit nature in a way in which earlier Jewish society had not done.[39] In an age in which our technology can take us to the moon, is it not now possible to develop humane alternatives to laboratory animals? Why is so little spent on researching delicious and nutritious foods as alternatives to eating the dead bodies of our evolutionary kin? Surely there is commercial potential here. Cannot we create far more exotic textiles than the raped skins of creatures who have died in agony? As for sports — there are already draghunts, bloodhounds and clay-pigeon; and if more ingenious quarry are required then surely it is not beyond our computerized creativity to invent them.

The next step is to face up to the logic of anti-speciesism by bringing the law into line with philosophy. The gulf between human and non-human in the eyes of the law is almost everywhere still as great or greater than that between master and slave. The law must be made to recognize, and progressively, that nonhumans have claims to life, freedom and the pursuit of happiness just as we do; and among the liberties that individual nonhumans should be able to enjoy is the freedom from exploitation by humankind. Animal liberation is an idea that is easy to ridicule but hard to refute. So hard to refute indeed that one of the very few philosophers to have argued against the idea, Dr Michael Allen Fox of Ontario, has had the courage publicly to recant.[40]

Perhaps the advances in the law should initially cover those species assumed to possess a high level of sentience, such as vertebrates, octopuses and squid. On the premise, albeit an unproven one, that sentience fades with descent of the phylogenetic scale, then a graduated scale of legal rights may be the politically expedient way to proceed. Legal protection primarily should be against the infliction of suffering, then the causing of death, and then such considerations as the encroachment on and pollution of habitats.

People should not be required to *like* nonhumans before they show them respect. Observing duties of justice and kindness towards other humans should be regardless of any personal feelings of affection for individuals. Likewise with nonhuman sentients; I should not be required to *like* a boa-constrictor before wishing to safeguard her or his quality of life.

Nature's two fundamental aspects, ferocious and tranquil, have inspired fear and romantic fascination in human beings. Sometimes the response has been to dominate or to sentimentalize; to fear Nature 'red in tooth and claw' or to love her; or, more profoundly, to separate humankind from nature on one hand or to identify romantically or mystically with nature on the other. Gradually, our view of our own species as being above nature and central in the scheme of things has been eroded. The theories of Copernicus, Marx, Darwin and Freud have been four major blows to human pride. We must now continue this process by discarding speciesism along with all our other delusions of grandeur, and accept our natural place in the universe.

The feeling of oneness with the natural cycle is in all of us; the dim awareness of the dialectical process within our minds and the great spirals of history which bear us all along together, whether human or nonhuman. Yet we try to stand against this tide; we still strive to be masters of our own fate and tyrants over the other animals. A child may show this ambivalence by loving nonhuman animals and by bullying them at the same time: this microcosm of good and evil remains within all of us.

The future demands a reappraisal of the relationship between humankind and nature; both ruthlessness and sentimentality must make way for rationality and compassion, based upon our awareness of the common capacity for consciousness among all us animals.

CONCLUSIONS

In summary, what does our survey of the centuries suggest? The motives for speciesist exploitation are multiple. Many have an instinctive quality and all are culturally shaped. Material benefits are obvious and today they are very often commercial – in the production of food, fur, ivory or scientific products, for example. Sometimes they are connected with personal ambition and prestige – as is often the case in nonhuman experimentation. In sport, too, the motives are complex. Our bullying of nonhumans is a hangover from past millennia when we feared them.

The institutionalized subjugation of nonhumans is widely accepted, usually out of habit. People do it because it has been conventional in

Western cultures for centuries. We all tend to accept orthodoxies; just as ordinary and decent men and women once accepted the need for slavery and torture, so today the greatest moral blindspots are in our exploitation of the other animals.

Idiosyncratic cruelty, on the other hand, is differently motivated. It is usually the effect of individual deprivation or frustration, or a displacement of anger and revenge from human targets on to nonhuman – the scapegoat principle. In extreme cases it can be a sign of mental illness. Child and animal abuse have much in common psychologically and often their causes are the same.

The inherent urge to dominate is as widespread as are the natural surges of compassion; sadism and sympathy can co-exist and neither is uncommon. Sadism is usually concealed because it is recognized as being unacceptable in a civilized society. But sympathy, too, is often denied because men have been taught to regard some forms of cruelty as manifestations of manliness, and sympathy as a sign of weakness.

What, on the other hand, are the reasons for anti-speciesism and for the growing campaigns to help the 'Fourth World' of the nonhuman sentients? Those whose minds have shown an independence from their own culture, and who have not accepted the conventions of their age without question, have frequently expressed their sympathy for non-humans; we have seen this in the case of numerous writers and thinkers, and in the lives of the saints. They would, on the whole, be described as intelligent and sensitive individuals, who have not been afraid to speak out against orthodoxy.

That compassion, like squeamishness, is a natural impulse, is an un-fashionable idea. Yet it is accepted that parental feelings of protectiveness are largely inherent, and by caring for nonhuman sentients we may only be extending our sense of family, thus maintaining the traditional link between kindness and kinship. It is this widening of the family circle, caused partly by our increasing contact with other sentients through easier travel and the medium of television, which underlies our revolution in outlook.

As in all human behaviour (and in more nonhuman behaviour, too, than is usually recognized), cultural factors play a part. The liberation of our natural compassion and the inhibition of our sadistic, exploitative and domineering tendencies towards nonhumans can be assisted by a change in attitudes, values and, ultimately, sanctions. This is the revolution in which we are now immersed.

In the Introduction I raised a number of questions. Even if our perusal of the history of humankind's attitudes towards nonhumans has not always provided firm answers, it has, I feel, helped us to provide some provisional ones.

In Europe, overt human sympathy for nonhumans (the widening of the moral circle) has probably increased over the centuries, but has been far from universal or continuous, suffering a setback during the Renaissance. When the great religions were formed all of them treated the human–nonhuman relationship as a matter of importance. With the exception of Christianity, all placed some emphasis upon the rightness of treating nonhuman life with respect, for its own sake. Yet, in almost every case, practitioners of these religions today fail to show an organized concern for nonhumans. Paradoxically, it is those living in countries affected mainly by the Christian tradition who do so.

Affluence, and, to a lesser extent urbanization, seem to have fostered greater sympathy for nonhumans. Feelings of personal security and the increasing awareness of the scientific evidence for our kinship with other animals, and for our shared capacity for suffering, have also been instrumental. The animal welfare movement has been a particular feature of Northern Europe and of the English-speaking nations and appears to have made progress in periods of peace in the seventeenth, eighteenth and nineteenth centuries. Often its pioneers, such as Wilberforce and Shaftesbury, have also been noted for their concern for human welfare.

Typically, the leaders of the movement have been intellectuals, secular just as often as religious, and their followers in the nineteenth century were from the upper rather than the middle or lower classes. Only in the late twentieth century have we seen anti-speciesism receive active support from *all* classes.

Although sympathy for nonhumans can, of course, be encouraged through education and example, the way in which individuals have emerged as champions of reform suggest that the potentials for compassion and aggression are innate. These two instincts can produce conflicting behaviours of care and cruelty, and are probably one of the reasons why humankind's relationship with nonhumans has been so remarkably inconsistent and ambivalent. Sadism, too, a particularly virulent and eroticized form of aggression, although widely suppressed, is far from being uncommon.

Humankind, for thousands of years, has striven to conquer nature, and the domination of nonhumans has been regarded as a mark of manhood. In consequence, the culturally based macho ideal is a major additional source of cruelty; primarily in sport, but also in other areas of speciesist exploitation.

The absurdity and exaggeration of the traditional excuses for speciesism – that nonhumans feel no pain, that God created them for human use, that they have no souls or that the benefits of their exploitation are overwhelmingly necessary – suggest very strongly that humankind often, perhaps always, feels guilt over its speciesism. None of the excuses for speciesism are rationally convincing. Ultimately, the reasons are selfish, and the modern animal liberation movement, which has entered a new phase since the late 1960s, has exposed their weakness with its own, far stronger, rationale; its militancy, much condemned, suggesting a failure of the democratic process. Yet, gradually, politicians have taken on board the public's environmental concerns and animal protection is being seen, increasingly, as a major part of that 'green' movement.

In the late twentieth century we are in an era of extraordinary change and ambivalence — some people baiting badgers while others build tunnels for them under railway lines, and children stabbing whales to death in one advanced country while in another they strive to keep them alive.

People who are cruel to nonhumans are not all wicked; most are just unthinking. Those of us who seek change must not resort to hatred or violence, but press on with our campaigns to educate and legislate. We want people to open their eyes and to see the other animals as they really are — our kindred and our potential friends with whom we share a brief period of consciousness upon this planet.

Notes

CHAPTER 1 INTRODUCTION

1   See, for example, Ruth Harrison, *Animal Machines* (Stuart, 1964); Richard D. Ryder, *Victims of Science: The Use of Animals in Research* (Davis-Poynter, 1975); Peter Singer, *Animal Liberation: A New Ethic for our Treatment of Animals* (New York Review, 1975).

2   W. E. H. Lecky, *The History of European Morals from Augustus to Charlemagne* (Longman, Green, 1869), vol. 2, p. 174.

3   See Harlan B. Miller, 'Introduction', in Miller and William H. Williams (eds), *Ethics and Animals*, (Humana Press, 1983), p. 7.

4   *Sunday Times*, 10 October 1965. See also Brophy's 'In Pursuit of Fantasy' in Stanley and Roslind Godlovitch and John Harris (eds), *Animals, Men and Morals: An Enquiry into the Maltreatment of Non-humans* (Gollancz, 1971); id., 'Amnesty and Animal Rights', *Free Thinker*, June 1978; id., 'The Darwinist's Dilemma' in David Paterson and Richard D. Ryder (eds), *Animals' Rights: A Symposium* (Centaur, 1979).

5   Roslind Godlovitch, 'Animals and Morals', *Philosophy*, October 1978.

6   Richard D. Ryder, 'Rights of Non Human Animals', *Daily Telegraph*, 3 May 1969. My other letters to this newspaper at this time were on 7 April and 20 May.

7   Peter Singer, 'Animal Liberation', *New York Review of Books*, 5 April 1973.

8   Others include: Andrew Linzey, *Animal Rights* (SCM Press, 1976); Tom Regan and Peter Singer (eds), *Animal Rights and Human Obligations* (Prentice-Hall, 1976); Stephen Clark, *The Moral Status of Animals* (Clarendon, 1977); David Paterson and Richard D. Ryder (eds), *Animals' Rights: A Symposium* (Centaur, 1979). For reviews of the latter see: Richard Dawkins, 'Brute Beasts', *New Statesman*, 10 September 1979; Alan Whittaker, 'Revolutionary Ideas', *Nursing Times*, 30 August 1979; J. H. Benson, 'Books', *New Scientist*, 26 July 1979, p. 303; Ruth Lumley-Smith: 'Man and Beast', *Ecologist*, July-Aug. 1979. Robin Page's

'Sportsman's Bookshelf' in *Shooting Times*, 26 July 1979, ridicules the whole movement.

9 For example, see Richard D. Ryder, *Speciesism* (privately printed leaflet, Oxford, 1970); id., *Speciesism: The Ethics of Vivisection* (leaflet, Scottish Society for the Prevention of Vivisection, Edinburgh, 1974); id., *Speciesism: The Ethics of Animal Abuse* (RSPCA, 1979).

10 *The Times*, 13 April 1988.

11 'Report of the Panel of Enquiry into Shooting and Angling (1976–1979)', Chairman: Lord Medway (RSPCA, 1980).

12 Marion Stamp Dawkins, *Animal Suffering* (Chapman and Hall, 1980). See also this author's 'How Should Humans Treat Non-Humans?', *New Scientist*, 25 August 1983.

13 Hansard, 1 March 1799.

14 Hansard, 12 May 1799.

15 Hansard, 22 February 1818.

16 Robin Hanbury-Tenison, personal communication, September 1988.

17 James Serpell, 'Attitudes to Animals', paper read to 'The Status of Animals' Conference, Nottingham, 20 September 1988.

18 'The Role of the Veterinarian', papers presented to 'The Status of Animals' Conference, Nottingham, 20 September 1988.

19 C. S. Lewis, *Vivisection* (leaflet, National Anti-Vivisection Society, *c.* 1950).

CHAPTER 2 THE ANCIENT WORLD

1 Angela P. Thomas, *Egyptian Gods and Myths* (Shire Publications, 1986).

2 Quoted by Kenneth Clark, *Animals and Men: Their Relationship as Reflected in Western Art from Prehistory to the Present Day* (Thames and Hudson, 1977), p. 76.

3 Aristotle, *Politics* (Everyman's Library edition), p. 16.

4 Pliny, *Naturalis Historia*, Books 8, 9.

5 W. E. H. Lecky, *The History of European Morals from Augustus to Charlemagne* (Longman, Green and Co., 1869), pp. 175–6.

6 Cicero, *Ad Familiares*, 7.1.3.

7 Aulus Gellius, *Noctes Atticae*, 5.14.

8 Bukkyo Dendo Kyokai, *The Teaching of Buddha* (Kosaido, Tokyo, 1966).

9 James Serpell, *In the Company of Animals: A Study of Human–Animal Relationships* (Basil Blackwell, 1986), p. 168.

10 Al-Hafiz Basheer Ahmad Masri, *Islamic Concern for Animals* (Athene Trust, 1987).

11 Ibid., p. 18.

12 Ibid., p. 21.

13 Ibid., p. 31.

14 Ibid., p. 29.
15 Authorised Version, *Genesis* 1:26–8.
16 I am indebted to Rabbi Julia Neuberger and the Revd Andrew Linzey for their comments in this subject.
17 Isaiah 1:11.
18 Hosea 2:18.
19 Isaiah 66:3.
20 Genesis 1:29.
21 Genesis 9:3.
22 Exodus 20:10; 23:12.
23 Deuteronomy 14:21.
24 Deuteronomy 22:6–7.
25 Deuteronomy 22:10.
26 Proverbs 12:10.
27 Ecclesiastes 3:19.
28 Leviticus 20:15.
29 Lisa Silcock, 'My Life as a Giant', *Sunday Times Magazine*, 1 November 1987.
30 Serpell, *In the Company of Animals*, p. 142.
31 Ibid., p. 7; and Maureen Duffy, *Men and Beasts: An Animal Rights Handbook* (Paladin, 1984), p. 7.
32 Serpell, *'In the Company of Animals'*, p. 66.

CHAPTER 3 THE CHRISTIAN LEGACY: MEDIEVAL ATTITUDES

1 Luke 12:6.
2 I am indebted to the Revd Peter Sanders for this explanation (personal communication, 1987).
3 W. E. H. Lecky, *The History of European Morals from Augustus to Charlemagne* (Longman, Green and Co., 1869), vol. 1, p. 244.
4 Keith Thomas, *Man and the Natural World: Changing Attitudes in England 1500–1800* (Allen Lane, 1983), p. 24.
5 Aquinas, like Augustine, was of the opinion that only humans had 'rational' souls. Animals had 'sensitive' souls which were not 'rational'.
6 Thomas Aquinas, *Summa Contra Gentiles*, iii. 113.
7 Id., *Summa Theologica* II, i, Q. 102, art. 6.
8 Peter Singer, *Animal Liberation: A New Ethic for our Treatment of Animals* (New York Review, 1975), pp. 214–16.
9 *Dives and Pauper*, ed. Priscilla Heath Barnum (EETS, 1976), 1 (2), pp. 35–6. See also Thomas, *Man and the Natural World*, p. 152.
10 H. R. Hays, *Birds, Beasts and Men* (J. M. Dent, 1973), p. 40.
11 'Homily 39, on the Epistle to the Romans', quoted in C. W. Hume, *The Status of Animals in the Christian Religion* (Universities Federation for Animal Welfare, 1957).

12 Quoted by C. W. Hume, in *Universities Federation for Animal Welfare Theological Bulletin*, 2 (1962), p. 3.
13 Thomas, *Man and the Natural World*, p. 152.
14 Florence H. Suckling, *The Brotherhood of Love* (George Bell and Sons, 1910).
15 Peter Singer, *The Animal Liberation Movement* (Old Hammond Press, 1987), p. 4.
16 Thomas, *Man and the Natural World*, pp. 94–7.
17 John Caius, *Of English Dogges* (1576).
18 John Swain, *Brutes and Beasts* (Noel Douglas, 1933).
19 Nicholas Humphrey, Preface to E. P. Evans, *The Criminal Prosecution and Capital Punishment of Animals* (republished by Faber, 1987).
20 Quoted in E. S. Turner, *All Heaven in a Rage* (Michael Joseph, 1964), p. 24.
21 Wynkyn De Worde, *The Demaundes Joyous* (1511). This collection of medieval riddles was the first to be published in England and was republished in 1971, edited by John Wardroper, by the Gordon Fraser Gallery.
22 Quoted in Turner, *All Heaven in a Rage*, p. 28.
23 Thomas, *Man and the Natural World*, p. 164.
24 Lecky, *History of European Morals*, p. 185.

CHAPTER 4   THE RENAISSANCE AND ITS AFTERMATH

1 C. W. Hume has argued, in *The Status of Animals in the Christian Religion* (Universities Federation for Animal Welfare, 1957), that the Renaissance was a revival of paganism which gave new life to astrology and witchcraft. It was during this period, according to Hume, that neighbourliness towards animals dwindled to a new low.
2 Keith Thomas, *Man and the Natural World: Changing Attitudes in England 1500–1800* (Allen Lane, 1983), p. 164.
3 Ibid., p. 152.
4 Ibid., p. 147. Queen Elizabeth's interest in bloodsports was, for a woman, outstanding even for her time. Was there a sadistic streak in her make-up, or was it merely politically expedient for her to emphasize her 'masculinity' in this way?
5 Paul Hentzner, *Travels in England* (1598).
6 E. S. Turner, *All Heaven in a Rage* (Michael Joseph, 1964), p. 37.
7 Thomas, *Man and the Natural World*, p. 147.
8 Ibid., p. 18.
9 Ibid., pp. 19–20.
10 E. McCurdy, *The Mind of Leonardo da Vinci* (Jonathan Cape, 1928).

11 John Vyvyan, *In Pity and in Anger* (Michael Joseph, 1969), p. 16.

12 *The Utopia of Sir Thomas More*, tr. Ralph Robinson (George Sampson, 1910), book 2, pp. 128–9, 181.

13 William Shakespeare, *Measure for Measure*, III. i; *As You Like It*, II. i. 33–40; *Henry VI Part 2*, III. i. 210–18; *Cymbeline*, I. v. 21–30.

14 Michel de Montaigne, 'Of Crueltie', *Montaigne's Essayes*, tr. Florio (republished 1890), book 2, ch. 11.

15 Id., 'An apologie of Raymond Sebond', *Montaigne's Essayes*, book 2, ch. 12.

16 Philip Stubbes, *Anatomie of Abuses* (1583), pp. 177–9 of Colliers Reprints edition.

17 John Calvin, *Sermons*, tr. Arthur Golding (1583) (republished, edited by John Wardroper, Gordon Fraser Gallery).

18 *The Poems of Sir Philip Sidney*, ed. W. Ringler (Oxford University Press, 1962), p. 103.

19 *Magnum Bullarium Romanum*, vol. 2, p. 260: Bull de Salute Gregis, 1 November 1567.

20 Francis Quarles, *Enchiridion* (1641), Century 2, no. 100.

21 Ibid., Century 3, no. 23.

22 Matthew Hale, *The Counsels of a Father* (reprinted London, 1817).

23 Thomas Tryon, *The Countryman's Companion* (c. 1683) p. 140.

24 Thomas Tryon, *Wisdom's Dictates* (1691), p. 94.

25 Thomas Babington Macaulay, *History of England* (1849), vol. 1.

26 Henry More, *An Antidote Against Atheism* (1655).

27 John Locke, *Thoughts on Education* (1693), republished in *The Works of John Locke: A New Edition* (London, 1823), vol. ix, pp. 112–14.

28 *The Statutes at Large* (Dublin, 1786), ch. 15, pp. 168–9.

29 W. E. H. Lecky, *The History of European Morals from Augustus to Charlemagne* (Longman, Green and Co., 1869), p. 173.

30 See Emily Stewart Leavitt, *Animals and their Legal Rights* (Animal Welfare Institute, Washington 1968); Richard D. Ryder, 'The Struggle Against Speciesism', in *Animal Rights: A Symposium*, edited by David Paterson and Richard D. Ryder (Centaur, 1978), p. 5.

31 Thomas, *Man and the Natural World*, p. 122.

32 W. Howell, *The Spirit of Prophecy* (1679).

33 Turner, *All Heaven in a Rage*, p. 45.

34 Sir James Thornton, *The Principal Claims on Behalf of Vivisection: A Refutation* (National Anti-Vivisection Society, 1901).

35 Vyvyan, *In Pity and in Anger*, pp. 22–4.

36 Peter Singer, *Animal Liberation: A New Ethic for our Treatment of Animals* (New York Review, 1975), p. 204.

37 Ibid., p. 204.

38 Robert Hooke, letter to Robert Boyle, 10 November 1664, in Gunther, *Early Science in Oxford*, vol. 6, pp. 216–18.

39 Quoted in Singer, *Animal Liberation*, p. 205.

40 John Hildrop, *Free Thoughts Upon the Brute Creation* (1742), pp. 8–9.
41 Quoted by Andreas-Holger Maehle and Ulrich Tröhler in 'Animal Experimentation from Antiquity to the End of the Eighteenth Century: Attitudes and Arguments', in Nicolaas A. Rupke (ed.), *Vivisection in Historical Perspective* (Croom Helm, 1987), p. 22.

CHAPTER 5 THE AGE OF ENLIGHTENMENT: THE EIGHTEENTH CENTURY

1 Richard Steele, *Tatler*, no. 134, 14–16 February 1709.
2 Joseph Addison, *Spectator*, no. 120, 18 July 1711.
3 Joseph Addison, *Maxims, Observations and Reflections*.
4 Alexander Pope, *Guardian*, 21 May 1713.
5 This argument between Pope and a vivisector, Dr Stephen Hales, is recorded in *Spence's Anecdotes* (1820).
6 Alexander Pope, *Windsor Forest* (1713).
7 Maurice Dommanget, *Le Curé Meslier* (Paris, 1965), pp. 62–3, 249.
8 Voltaire, *Dictionnaire philosophique* (Paris, 1775), under 'Bêtes'.
9 Voltaire, *Eléments de la Philosophie de Newton* (1733).
10 Jean-Jacques Rousseau, *Discourses on the Origin of Inequality* (1755), Preface.
11 Id., *Émile* (Montmorency, 1762).
12 See Andreas-Holger Maehle and Ulrich Tröhler, 'Animal Experimentation from Antiquity to the End of the Eighteenth Century: Attitudes and Arguments', in Nicolaas A. Rupke (ed.), *Vivisection in Historical Perspective* (Croom Helm, 1987), p. 35.
13 Immanuel Kant, *Lectures on Ethics*, trans. J. Infield (Methuen, 1930), p. 240.
14 Arthur Schopenhauer, *On the Basis of Morality* (1841).
15 Keith Thomas, *Man and the Natural World: Changing Attitudes in England 1500–1800* (Allen Lane, 1983), pp. 288–300.
16 David Hartley, *Observations on Man* (London, 1741), p. 222.
17 William Paley, *Moral Philosophy* (London, 1785), vol. 2, BR 6, p. 599.
18 John Oswald, *The Cry of Nature, or An Appeal to Mercy and Justice on Behalf of the Persecuted Animals* (London, 1791).
19 Oliver Goldsmith, *The Citizen of the World* (Everyman's Library, 1934), p. 38.
20 George Nicholson, *On the Conduct of Man to the Inferior Animals* (Manchester, 1797).
21 Ibid., p. 88.
22 Ibid., p. 89.
23 *Tatler*, no. 134, 14–16 February 1709.
24 *Guardian*, 21 May 1713, p. 7.

25 Lord Kames, *Essay on Morals* (1751).

26 Rousseau, *Émile* (1762).

27 Thomas Young, *An Essay on Humanity to Animals* (2nd edn, 1809), p. 20.

28 Susanna Watts, *The Animals' Friend: A Collection of Observations and Facts Tending to Restrain Cruelty and to Inculcate Kindness towards Animals* (William Darton, n.d.), p. 1.

29 H. V. Morton, *Stranger in Spain* (Methuen, 1955).

30 'A Surprisingly Rational Speech of a Hen', *Gentleman's Magazine*, April 1749, pp. 147–8.

31 *Gentleman's Magazine*, May 1754, p. 255.

32 James Ferguson, *Lectures on Select Subjects in Mechanics, Pneumatics, Hydrostatics and Optics* (1764).

33 David Hume, *Enquiry Concerning the Principles of Morals* (1751), ch. MI.

34 *Idler*, 5 August 1758.

35 Richard Dean, *An Essay on the Future Life of Brutes* (1767).

36 James Granger, *An Apology for the Brute Creation or Abuse of Animals Censured* (T. Davies, London, 1772).

37 Religious Society of Friends, *Christian Faith and Practice in the Experience of the Society of Friends* (1960), paras. 47 and 51.

38 Humphry Primatt, *The Duty of Mercy and the Sin of Cruelty to Brute Animals* (London, 1776; Edinburgh 1834), pp. 14–15.

39 Ibid., pp. 17–18.

40 Ibid., p. 18.

41 G. H. Toulmin, *The Antiquity and Duration of the World* (1780).

42 Primatt, *The Duty of Mercy*, p. 73.

43 James Yorke, *Country Life*, 23 June 1988.

44 Quoted in Lawrence Gowing, *Hogarth* (Tate Gallery, 1971), p. 69.

45 Ibid., p. 69.

46 Young, *Essay on Humanity to Animals* (2nd edn), p. 59.

47 James Thomson, *The Seasons* (1730).

48 William Cowper, *The Task* (1785).

49 Robert Burns, 'On Seeing A Wounded Hare' (1785).

50 Id., 'On Scaring Some Waterfowl in Loch Turit'.

51 Robert Burns, quoted in E. S. Turner, *All Heaven in a Rage* (Michael Joseph, 1964) p. 71 ('To a Mouse on Turning Her up in Her Nest with the Plough').

52 William Wordsworth, *Hart-Leap Well* (1800).

53 Robert Southey, *The Dancing Bear: Recommended to the Advocates for the Slave Trade*, lines 21–30. Quoted in Bertram Lloyd (ed.), *The Great Kinship* (Allen and Unwin, 1921), p. 51.

54 Alfred de Vigny (1797–1863) and D. M. Moir (1798–1851) are examples.

55 'In Memoriam', lines 15–16. Quoted in Frances E. Clarke (ed.),

Poetry's Pleas for Animals (Lothrop, Lee and Shepherd, Boston, 1927).
56 Percy Bysshe Shelley, *On the Vegetable System of Diet*, quoted in Jon Wynne-Tyson (ed.), *The Extended Circle* (Centaur, 1985), p. 333.
57 Shelley, *Queen Mab* (1813).
58 Frances E. Clarke, *Poetry's Plea for Animals* (Boston, 1927), p. 280.
59 Ibid., p. 132.
60 Thomas, *Man and the Natural World* (Allen Lane, 1983), p. 132; Edward Tyson, *Orang-Utang, sive Homo Sylvestris* (1699); Sir Thomas Browne, *Religio Medici* (1643).
61 William Smellie, *Philosophy of Natural History* (Edinburgh, 1790).
62 Lord Monboddo, *Ancient Metaphysics* (Edinburgh, 1779), vol. 2.
63 Edward Long, *History of Jamaica* (1774).
64 Joseph Ritson, *An Essay on Abstinence from Animal Food, As a Moral Duty* (1802), pp. 13–14.
65 Jeremy Bentham, *Introduction to the Principles of Morals and Legislation* (1780), ch. 17.
66 An alternative version of this story gives the cat's name as Sir John Langborn.
67 *The Works of Jeremy Bentham*, ed. John Bowring (1843), vol. 10, p. 17.
68 Ibid., vol. 11, p. 81.
69 Ibid., vol. 10, pp. 549–50.
70 Oswald, *The Cry of Nature*.
71 Soame Jenyns, *Disquisitions on Several Subjects* (1782).
72 Nicholson, *On the Conduct of Man to the Inferior Animals*, pp. 255–6; John Lawrence, *A Philosophical Treatise on Horses, and on the Moral Duties of Man towards the Brute Creation* (2 vols, 1796, 1798), vol. 1, p. 132, tells a similar story.
73 *Gentleman's Magazine*, January 1789, pp. 15–17.
74 Lawrence, *Philosophical Treatise*, vol. 1, p. 131.
75 Ibid., vol. 1, p. 154.
76 Adam Fitz Adam, *World*, no. 190, 19 August 1756, p. 1139.

CHAPTER 6 TIME FOR ACTION

1 Henry Alken, *British Sports* (1821).
2 John Scott (pseudonym), *The Sportsman's Repository* (London 1820), p. 18.
3 *Sporting Magazine*, December 1801.
4 Edward G. Fairholme and Wellesley Pain, *A Century of Work for Animals: The History of the RSPCA 1824–1924* (John Murray, 1924), pp. 32–3.
5 Ibid., pp. 27–8.
6 E. S. Turner, *All Heaven in a Rage* (Michael Joseph, 1964), p. 129.
7 Three histories of the RSPCA have been written. They are: Fairholme and Pain, *A Century of Work for Animals*; Arthur W. Moss, *Valiant*

Crusade: The History of the RSPCA (Cassell, 1961); Antony Brown, *Who Cares for Animals?* (Heinemann, 1974).

8 Margaret Blount, *Animal Land: The Creatures of Children's Fiction* (Hutchinson, 1974).

9 Sarah Trimmer's *The History of the Robins* was first published in 1786 under the title *Fabulous Histories: Designed for Children, Respecting their Treatment of Animals*.

10 Mrs Trimmer, *The History of the Robins* (1786; 9th edn, 1811), p. 165.

11 *Pity's Gift: A Collection of Interesting Tales to Excite the Compassion of Youth for the Animal Creation, Ornamented with Vignettes from the Writings of Mr. Pratt, Selected by a Lady* (5th edn, London, 1810), Preface.

12 For example in *Stories from Natural History* (anon., 1832).

13 Keith Thomas, *Man and the Natural World: Changing Attitudes in England 1500–1800* (Allen Lane, 1983), p. 167.

14 *Insects and Their Habitations: A Book for Children* (Society for Promoting Christian Knowledge, London, 1833), p. 48.

15 Mary R. Capes, *The Life of Richard of Wyche* (Sands & Co., 1913), p. 43.

16 William Smellie, *The Philosophy of Natural History* (1824; 7th edn, William Milner, Halifax, 1845), p. 271.

17 Jon Wynne-Tyson, *Food for a Future* (Thorsons, 1988), Appendix.

CHAPTER 7   VICTORIAN CONSOLIDATION

1 For example: E. S. Turner, *All Heaven in a Rage* (Michael Joseph, 1964); Edward G. Fairholme and Wellesley Pain, *A Century of Work for the Animals: The History of the RSPCA 1824–1924* (John Murray, 1924).

2 Arthur W. Moss, *Valiant Crusade: The History of the RSPCA* (Cassell, 1961). The other members attending this meeting were T. G. Meymott in the chair, Captain Charles Bernard and Thomas Butt.

3 RSPCA minute book, no. 1.

4 I am indebted to Derek Sayce and Olive Martyn of the RSPCA for their assistance.

5 Quoted in Ronald Fletcher (ed.), *John Stuart Mill: A Logical Critique of Sociology* (Michael Joseph, 1971), p. 416.

6 RSPCA Tract, London, c. 1860.

7 Ibid.

8 Quoted in M. R. L. Freshel (ed.), *Selections from Three Essays by Richard Wagner* (Millennium Guild, Rochester, NH, 1933).

9 Christina Rossetti, *To What Purpose this Waste?* (1872).

10 Quoted by John Vyvyan, *In Pity and in Anger* (Michael Joseph, 1969), p. 38.

11 *British Medical Journal*, 22 August 1863, p. 215.

12 Keith Thomas, *Man and the Natural World: Changing Attitudes in England 1500–1800* (Allen Lane, 1983), p. 174.

13 Quoted by Vyvyan, *In Pity and in Anger*, p. 22.

14 *Report of the Royal Commission on the Practice of Subjecting Live Animals to Experiments for Scientific Purposes* (HMSO, 1876), C-1397 p. 23, Q. 444.

15 Claude Bernard, *Introduction to the Study of Experimental Medicine* (Paris, 1865).

16 Ibid., 1926 edition, vol. 1, p. 35.

17 Richard D. French, *Antivivisection and Medical Science in Victorian Society* (Princeton University Press, Princeton, NJ, 1975), p. 260.

18 *British Medical Journal*, 11 May 1861.

19 Quoted by Vyvyan, *In Pity and in Anger*, p. 68.

20 Ibid., p. 69.

21 Frances Power Cobbe, *Life of Frances Power Cobbe* (London, 1894), vol. 2, p. 16.

22 Gladstone Papers, British Museum, quoted by John Vyvyan, *In Pity and in Anger*, p. 162.

23 French, *Antivivisection*, p. 66.

24 Quoted by Vyvyan, *In Pity and in Anger*, p. 86.

25 Royal Commission 1876, p. 183, Q. 3538–41.

26 Ibid., p. 183, Q. 3549–54.

27 Richard Hutton, *Spectator* (1875), 48.

28 Cobbe, *Life of Frances Power Cobbe*, vol. 1, p. 652.

29 Moss, *Valiant Crusade*, p. 163.

30 *Animal World*, 7 (1876), p. 132.

31 Mary Shelley, *Frankenstein or the Modern Prometheus* (1818); R. L. Stevenson, *The Strange Case of Dr. Jekyll and Mr. Hyde* (1886).

32 French, *Antivivisection*, p. 408.

33 Ibid., p. 412.

34 Ibid., p. 409.

35 S. D. Collingwood, *The Life and Letters of Lewis Carroll* (Fisher Unwin, 1898), pp. 165–71.

36 Ibid., p. 299.

37 Lewis Carroll, 'Some Popular Fallacies About Vivisection', *Fortnightly Review*, 23 (1875), p. 854.

38 *The Diaries of John Ruskin* ed. Joan Evans (Oxford University Press, 1959), p. 1102.

39 L. I. Lumsden, *Ruskin as a Moral Teacher* (Scottish Society for the Prevention of Vivisection, Edinburgh c. 1916, undated), pp. 5–7.

40 Ruskin, too, had once had tea with the 'delightful' young Misses Liddell together with the Archbishop of Canterbury (on 24 October 1873) and, indeed, had a perplexing dream the following night that he had 'starved a hermit-crab whom I had packed away in his shell'. Was this vivisectional nightmare a premonition of the battle he was to fight

with old Liddell, or was the dream a sign that Dodgson was not alone in being titillated by little Alice and that Ruskin was having to 'pack away' his feelings for her? Freudians could interpret it as a masterpiece of symbolic repression: 'The metaphysics of this', Ruskin notes, ' − which came to looking at the starved creature and wondering if I could revive it − are highly curious.'

41 French, *Antivivisection*, pp. 184−9.

42 Ibid., pp. 204−14.

43 Quoted by Turner, *In Pity and in Anger*, p. 176.

44 It was, however, not until murderous millinery and dove slaughter had passed out of fashion in the twentieth century that either would be entirely prohibited by law; the latter by an Act piloted through Parliament in 1921 by Lord Lambourne and Sir Burton Chadwick, the former by Lord Buckmaster and Lord Tweedsmuir's Act of 1933. Under the influence of the Swede, Axel Munthe, even Mussolini would become involved in bird protection, in 1933 declaring the island of Capri a bird sanctuary, thereby earning a congratulatory telegram from the League Against Cruel Sports and no less than the Queen Victoria Silver Medal from the RSPCA − the society's highest award.

45 Richard Thomas, *The Politics of Hunting* (Gower, 1983), p. 182.

46 Reprinted as *The Morality of Field Sports* by the Animals' Friend Society, (London, *c.* 1910, undated).

47 James Walvin, *Leisure and Society* (Longman, 1978), p. 26.

CHAPTER 8   EDWARDIAN VIGOUR AND POST-WAR
APATHY, 1900−1960

1 Henry Salt, *Animal's Rights Considered in Relation to Social Progress, with a Bibliographical Appendix* (Macmillan, 1894).

2 Stephen Winsten, *Salt and His Circle* (Hutchinson, 1951), Preface.

3 Ibid., p. 122.

4 Salt's other animal rights works include *The Humanities of Diet: Some Reasonings and Rhymings* (Vegetarian Society, 1914); *The Story of My Cousins: Brief Animal Biographies* (Watts, 1923); *The Creed of Kinship* (Constable, 1935).

5 Ernest Seton-Thompson, *Wild Animals I Have Known* (Charles Scribner's Sons, New York, 1900), pp. 12−13.

6 D. H. Lawrence, *Snake*, quoted by Jon Wynne-Tyson, 'The Extended Circle: A Dictionary of Humane Thought' (Centaur, 1985), p. 167; Albert Schweitzer, *The Philosophy of Civilization* (1923); George Orwell, quoted by Richard D. Ryder, 'Victims of Science' (Centaur, 1983), p. 143.

7 Coleridge was described by William Watson as 'The Swordsman of Mercy' − an epithet equally appropriate for many other animal rights activists.

8   The *Animal World* of July 1911 contains some lengthy correspondence between Stephen Coleridge and the RSPCA's secretary, Edward Fairholme. The former had chided the RSPCA in the pages of the *Zoophilist* for being lukewarm in the battle against vivisection and for allowing on to its council a veterinary surgeon who was also a vivisector, a Mr Stockman; a familiar tale.

9   Arthur W. Moss, *Valiant Crusade* (Cassell, 1961), p. 50.

10   Henry Salt (ed.), *Killing for Sport: Essays by Various Writers* (George Bell, 1917).

11   R. Gordon Cummings, *Five Years of a Hunter's Life in the Far Interior of South Africa* (London, 1850).

12   Maureen Duffy, *Men and Beasts* (Paladin, 1984), p. 103.

13   Henry Seton-Karr, *My Sporting Holidays* (London, 1904).

14   William Shakespeare, *Much Ado About Nothing*, III.i.

15   A. E. Freeman, 'The Morality of Field Sports', in *Fortnightly Review*, 1869–70, reprinted by the Animals' Friend Society, London, *c.* 1910.

16   Edward G. Fairholme and Wellesley Pain, *A Century of Work for Animals: The History of the RSPCA 1824–1924* (John Murray, 1924), p. 100.

17   Patrick Moore (ed.), *Against Hunting: A Symposium* (Gollancz, 1965).

18   Moss, *Valiant Crusade*, p. 174.

19   The story is given in the *Report of the Animal Defence and Anti-Vivisection Society* (1911).

20   Ibid., pp. 11, 12.

21   *Report of the Animal Defence and Anti-Vivisection Society* (1923), p. 5.

22   Richard D. French, *Antivivisection and Medical Science in Victorian Society* (Princeton University Press, Princeton, NJ, 1975), p. 260.

23   Wilfred Risdon, *Lawson Tait* (National Anti-Vivisection Society, 1967).

24   Lawson Tait, paper presented to the Birmingham Philosophical Society, 20 April 1882.

25   Bernard Shaw, 'Looking Backward', in G. H. Bowker (ed.), *Shaw on Vivisection* (Allen and Unwin, 1949), pp. 63–4.

26   Dr A. de Watteville, letter to the *Standard*, 24 November 1882.

27   Edward Carpenter, 'Vivisection and the Labour Movement', *Humanity* (November 1895), p. 68.

28   C. W. Hume, *Man and Beast* (UFAW, 1962), p. 202.

CHAPTER 9   WHY BRITAIN? PAIN, EVOLUTION AND
SECURITY

1   James Turner, *Reckoning with the Beast* (Johns Hopkins University Press, 1980), p. 27.

2   *Commons Journals*, 23 and 28 April, 1802.
3   Turner, *Reckoning with the Beast*, p. 27.
4   Nicolaas A. Rupke (ed.), *Vivisection in Historical Perspective* (Croom Helm, 1987), p. 11.
5   Keith Thomas, *Man and the Natural World: Changing Attitudes in England 1500–1800* (Allen Lane, 1983), p. 150.
6   John Pollack, *Wilberforce* (Constable, 1977), p. 80.
7   Georgina Battiscombe, *Shaftesbury* (Constable, 1975), p. 332.
8   Lord Coleridge, *The Nineteenth Century Defenders of Vivisection* (leaflet, Animals' Friend Society, London, 1882).
9   Miriam Rothschild, *Animals and Man* (Clarendon Press, 1986), p. 50.
10   Spinoza, *Ethics* (1675), part iv, prop. 37, n. 1.
11   *British Medical Journal*, no. 2, 28 May 1904.
12   Francis Darwin, 'Charles Darwin', *Dictionary of National Biography*. See also John Chancellor, *Charles Darwin* (Weidenfeld and Nicolson, 1973), pp 55–6.
13   Charles Darwin, *The Descent of Man* (1871), i, pp. 35, 48–9, 78.
14   *Report of the Royal Commission on the Practice of Subjecting Live Animals to Experiments for Scientific Purposes* (HMSO, London, 1876), C-1397, pp. 233–4, Q. 4662–6 and Q. 4672.
15   John R. Durrant, 'Darwin Unbuttoned', *New York Review of Books*, 28 April 1988.
16   M. R. L. Freshel (ed.), *Selections from Three Essays By Richard Wagner* (Millenium Guild, New York, 1933).
17   T. H. Huxley, *Evidence as to Man's Place in Nature* (1863; Macmillan edition of 1901), pp. 151–2.
18   Lauder Lindsay, *Mind in the Lower Animals* (Kegan Paul, 1879). vol. 1, pp. 118–25.
19   Charles Darwin, *The Descent of Man* (1871).
20   A. Armitt, *Man and His Relatives: A Question of Morality* (London, 1885), pp. 6–7. See also Richard D. French, *Antivivisection and Medical Science in Victorian Society* (Princeton University Press, Princeton, NJ, 1975), p. 384.
21   John Lubbock, *The Beauties of Nature* (Macmillan, London, 1892), p. 41.
22   Wilhelm Wundt, *Lectures on Human and Animal Psychology* (1892; trans. J. E. Creighton and E. B. Titchener, Swan Sonnenschein, New York, 1894), pp. 358–66.
23   C. Lloyd Morgan, *An Introduction to Comparative Psychology*, (Edward Arnold, 1894), p. 51.
24   Ivan Pavlov, *Conditioned Reflexes* (1927).
25   C. Lloyd Morgan, *Animal Sketches* (Edward Arnold, 1891). p. 5.

CHAPTER 10   THE INTERNATIONAL MOVEMENT,
1700–1960

1 Victor Hugo, *Zoophilist*, December 1884.
2 Quoted by John Vyvyan, *In Pity and in Anger* (Michael Joseph, 1969), p. 125.
3 Richard Wagner, 'Against Vivisection', reprinted in M. R. L. Freschel (ed.), *Selections from Three Essays by Richard Wagner* (Millenium Guild, Rochester, New Hampshire, 1933), p. 9.
4 Ulrich Tröhler and Andreas-Holger Maehle, 'Anti-Vivisection in Nineteenth Century Germany and Switzerland: Motives and Methods', in Nicolaas A. Rupke (ed.), *Vivisection in Historial Perspective* (Croom Helm, 1987), p. 162.
5 I am indebted to Birgitta Carlsson of the Nordiska Samfundet Mot Plågsamma Djurförsök for allowing me to examine the society's archives.
6 Quoted by Albert Leffingwell, *An Ethical Problem* (G. Bell, New York, 1916), p. 117.
7 Quoted in M. R. L. Freshel (ed.), *Selections from Three Essays by Richard Wagner*, p. 85.
8 *New York Evening Post*, 22 May 1909.
9 I am indebted to Dr John Kullberg, President of the ASPCA, for much information about this society.
10 For many years Simon and Peggy Templar, for example, have striven to protect animals in Spain, especially the chimpanzees used and abused by seaside photographers, and in India, Crystal Rogers has rescued stray dogs, bravely risking rabies.
11 J. N. P. Watson, 'Giving Tongue Abroad', *Country Life*, 8 September 1988.

CHAPTER 11   THE REVIVAL OF THE MOVEMENT AFTER
1960

1 Personal communication, April 1973.
2 The three principal histories, as previously mentioned, of the RSPCA are: Edward G. Fairholme and Wellesley Pain, *A Century of Work for Animals: The History of the RSPCA 1824–1924* (John Murray, 1924); Arthur W. Moss, *Valiant Crusade: The History of the RSPCA* (Cassell, 1961); Antony Brown, *Who Cares for Animals?* (Heinemann, 1974).
3 Brigid Brophy, 'The Rights of Animals', *Sunday Times*, 10 October 1965.
4 Personal communication, 1985.
5 Monica Hutchings and Mavis Caver, *Man's Dominion* (Hart-Davis, 1970).
6 It was after the failure of one such Bill introduced by Seymour Cocks MP in 1949 that the matter was referred to a special committee

chaired by Scott Henderson KC. Its report condemned the gin (leghold) trap and the snaring of deer, but condoned bloodsports.

7 Richard H. Thomas, *The Politics of Hunting* (Gower, 1983), p. 228.

8 The influence of the British Field Sports Society within the Conservative party still remains considerable, as was clearly demonstrated in April 1983 when the Conservative prospective parliamentary candidate for South-West Cambridge was forced to withdraw his candidacy after it was revealed that his wife had once supported the League Against Cruel Sports.

9 Thomas, *The Politics of Hunting*, p. 159.

10 Hunt Saboteurs Association Constitution, as agreed at its AGMs in 1977 and 1984.

11 Personal communication, August 1988.

12 Otters became protected in Scotland in 1981.

13 Lord Houghton of Sowerby, letter to the *Halifax Evening Courier*, 16 March 1978.

14 *Sunday Times*, 21 August 1977.

15 *Howl*, the magazine of the Hunt Saboteurs Association, Autumn 1981, Obituary, p. 6.

16 *Western Morning News*, 24 December 1986.

17 Robert Churchward, *A Master of Hounds Speaks* (National Society for the Abolition of Cruel Sports, 1960), p. 38. Churchward's real name was Paul Rycaut de Shordiche-Churchward. An explorer, soldier and big-game hunter, he denounced his 'sporting' past and became vice-president of the National Society for the Abolition of Cruel Sports in 1959 and a life patron of the League Against Cruel Sports. He contributed a chapter on fox-hunting to Patrick Moore's *Against Hunting* in 1965.

18 Vera Sheppard, *My Head Against the Wall: A Decade in the Fight Against Bloodsports* (Moonraker Press, 1979).

19 For example, Lord Halifax, then chairman of the Masters of Foxhounds' Association had written to *Horse and Hound* on 2 July 1960 stating that it was: 'absolutely essential that we should try to get foxhunting people to join the RSPCA so that they are in a position to vote'. Sheppard also referred to a letter in the *West Sussex Gazette* of 26 January 1961 from Sir Ralph Clarke, which stated that 'It was the desire of the Masters of Foxhounds' Association and the British Field Sports Society to increase the RSPCA membership in this way with the object of capturing control of the policy of the RSPCA. We are anxious to get as many members as possible.' She went on to quote more recent letters in *Horse and Hound* from John Hobhouse, the new RSPCA chairman (27 November 1970 and 1 January 1971) to the effect that he hoped that readers would join the RSPCA. (A council member defended this by asserting that by joining the society bloodsports people would in time become educated against bloodsports.) A rather similar case arose in 1988 when it was reported that members of the BFSS were urged to

join the National Trust to prevent a ban on hunting on Trust land (see *Independent*, 5 September 1988). So much for 'entryism'.

20 The Reform Group, however, went from strength to strength under its indefatigable leaders. Under John Bryant's name the group issued the following statement in 1971: 'We of the RSPCA Reform Group, representing more than one hundred RSPCA officials and other members are very concerned for the future wellbeing of the society. We believe the facts given below show that people with a vested interest in a particular form of cruelty have infiltrated the RSPCA in an effort to subdue the society's criticism of their activities. That the subject is bloodsports is not important – it could have been infiltration by the factory farming community or any large body of people who gain pleasure or profit from cruelty to animals.'

21 The group of younger and more radical members of the RSPCA council remained in a minority except from June 1979 to June 1980. The passage of their reforms throughout the period 1972–9 depended, therefore, upon the support of moderates such as Michael Kay, Lady Dunn, Marjorie Sutcliffe and Roy Crisp. The radicals included, besides those already mentioned, Jan Rennison and Robin Howard.

22 Celia Hammond, one of Britain's top models in the 'swinging sixties' and a pioneer campaigner in the modern anti-fur campaign, went on to rescue hundreds of cats in and around London, forming her own charity CHAT (the Celia Hammond Animal Trust) in 1986. Her fund-raising events were supported by many well-known people such as Joanna Lumley, Marie Helvin, Jonathan Ross, Uri Geller, Linda McCartney and Dudley Moore.

23 JACOPIS was largely the idea of Peter Mann, president of the British Small Animals Veterinary Association and, later, the Chief Veterinary Surgeon of the People's Dispensary for Sick Animals.

24 For a description of the formation of FAWCE and CRAE see Clive Hollands, *Compassion is the Bugler: The Struggle for Animal Rights* (Macdonald, 1980), pp. 73–7.

25 Speakers at the conference included Brigid Brophy, John Bryant, Stephen Clark, Maureen Duffy, Lord Houghton, Clive Hollands, the Revd Andrew Linzey, David Paterson, Tom Regan, Timothy Sprigge, John Aspinall, Michael Fox, Ruth Harrison, Peter Roberts, Jon Wynne-Tyson, Bill Jordan, David Macdonald, John Harris and myself.

26 Signatories included all the speakers and, among others, Richard Adams, Peter Singer, John Alexander-Sinclair, Raymond Frey, Ruth Plant, Angela Walder, David Wetton, Clare Druce, Violet Spalding, Ronnie Lee, Cliff Goodman, Ian Macphail, Jan Rennison and Robin Howard.

27 See, for example, *Observer*, 26 June 1977.

28 Charles Bellairs, 'Animal Welfare', *Politics Today*, no. 13, 17 September 1979.

29   One of the most effective supporters of GECCAP was Richard Course, director of the League Against Cruel Sports, which gave £20,000 to the campaign. Course's tough approach and his flair for publicity often achieved results, but sometimes controversially. Some societies, worried about GECCAP's direct lobbying of the parties at their annual conferences, objected, and the Universities Federation for Animal Welfare withdrew its support from GECCAP.

30   The parties' election promises were as follows:

Liberal party: 'Support the demand of the General Election Co-Ordinating Committee for Animal Protection for a Royal Commission on Animal Welfare. Ban the importation and manufacture of any product derived from any species whose survival is threatened, and work for a total ban on commercial whaling. We also need a co-ordinated approach to the needs of food production and conservation of natural wildlife which recognises their interdependence. Increase the number of abattoirs to EEC standard to discourage the export of live animals.'

Conservative party: 'The welfare of animals is an issue that concerns us all. There are problems in certain areas and we will act immediately where it is necessary. More specifically, we still give full support to the EEC proposals on the transportation of animals. We shall update the Brambell Report, the codes of welfare for farm animals, and the legislation on experiments on live animals. We shall also re-examine the rules and enforcement applying to the export of live animals and shall halt the export of cows and ewes recently calved and lambed.'

Labour party: 'Under Labour's new Council for Animal Welfare we will have stronger control on the export of live animals for export, on conditions of factory farms and on experiments on living animals. Legislation to end cruelty to animals will include the banning of hare-coursing and stag and deer hunting. Angling and shooting will in no way be affected by our proposals.'

31   Richard Sayer, *RSPCA Parliamentary Report* (October 1985).

32   Katya Lester and Richard D. Ryder, *Animal Protection Commission* (Liberal/SDP Alliance, August 1986).

33   Editorial, *British Farmer and Stockbreeder*, 18 August 1979.

34   Richard D. Ryder, letter to the *Daily Telegraph*, 17 December 1979.

35   The defence case rested largely on my shoulders. During the debate I was physically attacked by Frederick Burden MP. A few months later he was knighted. (See photo and report in the *Guardian*, 25 February 1980.)

36   A. L. Smith-Maxwell, letter in *Horse and Hound*, 15 February 1980.

37   'Militants Pull RSPCA Off Welfare Council', *Poultry World*, 15 November 1979.

38   For example, Mike Nelson, 'What is the RSPCA Council Really

Up To?' *Veterinary Practice*, 4 February 1980.

39   In 1979 RSPCA membership had increased to more than 65,000. By 1988 it was less than 20,000. See, for example, Richard D. Ryder, 'Animal Revolution', *Outrage*, November/December 1981.

40   'Politics and the RSPCA', *Daily Telegraph*, 1 March 1980. See also Brian Seager and Vera Sheppard's letters in reply, *Daily Telegraph*, 5 March 1980.

41   *Daily Telegraph*, 22 March 1980.

42   Personal communication, 17 March 1980.

43   BBC *Panorama*, 6 December 1982.

44   See Sir David Napley's letter, *Sunday Telegraph*, 11 November 1980, and Janet Fookes's view of the situation on 26 October. See also *Daily Telegraph*, 12 April 1980. The unsuccessful attempt to expel me from the society was on 26 November 1980. Miss Fookes's views are also reported in the *Evening Standard* of 12 December 1980. Those of the president of the society, Richard Adams, and the vice-presidents, Lord Houghton, Lady Dowding and Clive Hollands, who all supported my calls for an investigation of the society's finances, are reported in the *Daily Mail* of 12 January and 13 January 1981. See also further relevant reports in the *Daily Mail*, 1 October 1981 and 2 October 1981.

45   *Guardian*, 30 September 1982.

46   The reaction to the disputes and obvious mismanagement of the period 1980–3 was reflected in a temporary dip in legacy income in 1984; but soon legacies resumed their steady climb and by 1986 they were at a record £12 million.

47   For example, Stefan Ormrod at Wildlife, Cindy Milburn and John Callaghan, Mike Smithson, Caroline Vodden, and Gavin Grant.

48   'Blood-letting at the RSPCA', *Daily Telegraph*, 29 November 1988; BBC Radio 4 News, 30 November 1988; George Hill, 'Should You Kill a Healthy Cat?', *The Times*, 3 January 1989, p. 7.

49   Personnal communication, March 1979.

50   Personnal communication, October 1980.

51   Royal College of Veterinary Surgeons, *Guide to Professional Conduct* (1978), p. 4.

52   *Veterinary Record*, 8 April 1972, pp. 416–18.

53   *Sunday Mirror*, 26 June 1988.

54   Clive Hollands, 'What the Animal Welfare Movement Expects of the Veterinarian', Biological Council Lecture, British Veterinary Association Congress, 10 September 1987.

55   *Mail on Sunday*, 12 December 1982.

56   For example, Professor N. Anderson's comment that 'Animal welfare issues generate a puzzling lack of interest among the academic members of the veterinary profession' (*Veterinary Record*, 4 July 1987).

57   John Webster, *Veterinary Record*, 4 October 1986. Most encouraging of all was P. G. Dunn's letter to the *Veterinary Record* of 9 February

1980: 'Animal Welfare is a subject to which too little attention is paid; many have grown immune to the insidious development of unsatisfactory husbandry conditions for our farm animals. By tolerating such practices we support a system of animal agriculture which is immoral. How many veterinarians feel totally unconcerned at the sight of dry sows in confinement stalls on a cold winter's day? How many of us have a completely clear conscience when we see four layers in a small battery cage?'

58 *Sunday Times*, 12 June 1988.

59 Angela Walder at the Annual General Meeting of the RSPCA, 25 June 1988.

60 Jolyon Jenkins, *New Statesman*, 21 February 1986.

61 From the world of entertainment Doris Day, Brigitte Bardot, Joanna Lumley, Julie Christie, Judi Dench, Geraldine James, Julia McKenzie, Hayley Mills, Linda McCartney, Carol Royle, Spike Milligan, Johnny Morris, Sir John Gielgud, Dudley Moore, James Mason, Uri Geller, Virginia McKenna and Bill Travers are examples, and the writers Iris Murdoch, Fay Weldon, Jan Morris, Brigid Brophy, Gordon Newman, Rebecca Hall, Maureen Duffy, Richard Adams and Desmond Morris also stand out. Clare Francis, novelist and round-the-world yachtswoman, motivated to 'try to make the world a tiny bit better', became a leading anti-fur campaigner in the 1980s. Amongst royalty, Princess Diana has made it clear that she does not wear fur and Princess Anne and Prince Charles have made sympathetic public statements about farm animals (e.g. *Daily Telegraph*, 13 September 1986, RSPCA Statement of 24 January 1986 and *The Observer*, 8 January 1989, p. 3); and the latter has lamented that 'we see ourselves as somehow separate from and superior to nature' (*Daily Telegraph*, 23 March 1988). Prince Sadruddin Aga Khan has attacked animal experimentation (e.g. Prince Sadruddin Aga Khan, 'Penalising Animals for our Indulgence', *Observer*, 16 August 1981).

62 Hugh Hudson added to the fiction of *Greystoke* – Edgar Rice Burrough's story of the human baby Tarzan nurtured into adulthood by apes – a final chapter in which Tarzan, by this time the Earl of Greystoke, discovers his own ape foster-father in a laboratory cage in London; he at once liberates him and together they flee across Hyde Park. Hudson was here questioning human dominion and was conscious of the parallel with the Nazi ideal of the super-race (personal communication, December 1986). Spielberg, too, inserts an animal liberation theme in *E.T.*, and the late James Mason's final film performance in *The Shooting Party* subtly expresses the actor's own profound interest in animal rights.

Tarzan is one of the century's most popular fantasies and has a relevance to our story. For decades Hollywood depicted most of the nonhumans in Tarzan movies as the 'good guys' who assisted Tarzan in his battles against the (usually human) villains; in the Tarzan epic human dominion has become a friendly partnership. Also for decades Walt Disney, reportedly concerned about the mistreatment of nonhuman animals, portrayed nonhumans as the allies of humans in, for example, his *Snow White and the Seven Dwarfs* of 1938. According to Marc Davis, a Disney animator, Disney sought to combine life-like animal movement with anthropomorphic character (*The Art of Walt Disney*, ITV South Bank Show, 25 September 1988).

63   Anna Sewell's *Black Beauty*, published in 1877, had had a similar effect. Not too strenuously preaching humanity, this very popular 'auto-biography of a horse' had reminded thousands that animals can suffer, and persuaded many to change their ways accordingly. In recent times, Richard Adams's novels *Watership Down* and *The Plague Dogs* (1977), both turned into films, have had similar impacts, affecting the outlook of millions. Indeed, the twentieth century has seen a growing number of novels touching the cause of animal protection. Examples are *Crowleigh Hall* by Emily Robinson (1906); *The Difficulties of Dr. Deguerre* by Walter Hadwen (1926); *Morwyn or the Vengeance of God* by John Cowper Powys (1937); Roald Dahl's *The Magic Finger* (1966); *Doctor Rat* by William Kotzwinkle (1976); *Hackenfeller's Ape* by Brigid Brophy and *I Want to Go to Moscow* by Maureen Duffy (1973); Innis Hamilton's *The Beagle Brigade* (1980), and *Bobbie* (1986); and *Set a Thief* by G. F. Newman (1986).

64   First was Richard French's meticulous *Antivivisection and Medical Science in Victorian Society* (Princeton University Press, Princeton, NJ, 1975), which coincided with the new wave of philosophical books on animal liberation. Inspired by Bill Jordan and the new radicals within the RSPCA, there followed *Animal Marking*, edited by Bernard Stonehouse (Macmillan, 1978); *Animals in Research*, edited by David Sperlinger (John Wiley, 1981); and *The RSPCA Book of British Mammals*, edited by C. L. Boyle (Collins, 1981). Later came Mary Midgeley's *Animals and Why They Matter* (Penguin, 1983); James Serpell's stimu-lating *In the Company of Animals* (Blackwell, 1986), and the excellent *Vivisection in Historical Perspective*, edited by Nicolaas A. Rupke (Croom Helm, 1987).

65   *The Beast* in 1979 and *Black Beast* in 1985 (renamed *Turning Point* in 1986). *The Beast*, subtitled *The Magazine that Bites Back*, was pub-lished by Clanose Publishers Ltd in London between June 1979 and June 1981. Its founding editor was John May.

66   For example: BBC Radio 4's *Animals for Man*, 27 May 1975, *Woman's Hour*, 6 September 1976, *A Word in Edgeways*, 16 January 1983; LWT *Credo*, 26 February 1980; BBC 2 *Rabbits Can't Cry*, 20 October 1982; LWT *Credo*, 21 October 1982; Channel Four *The Animals Film*, 4 November 1982, and *Heart of the Matter*, 4 October 1984.

67   The 1970s had been another golden era for the animal welfare

movement in Britain and, by the end of the decade, its influence could be seen in revived movements throughout Europe and the English-speaking world. Many outstanding campaigners had emerged in Britain, among them Richard Adams, John Alexander-Sinclair, Mary-Rose Barrington, Eileen Bezet, May Bocking, Joanne Bower, John Bryant, Nick Carter, Vivien Clifford, Richard Course, Muriel Lady Dowding, Clare Druce, Lady Dunn, Roy Forster, Fay Funnell, Penny Goater, Basil Goldstone, Brian Gunn, Rebecca Hall, Celia Hammond, Dr Harold Hewitt, Cathy Hodgson, Clive Hollands, Lord Houghton, Margery Jones, Bill Jordan, Bruce Kent, Joan Latto, Dr Alan Long, Ruth Murray, Melanie Oxley, Jean Pink, Ruth Plant, Peter Roberts, Eileen Ryan, Violet Spalding, Kim Stallwood, Marjorie Sutcliffe, Betty Svendsen, Allan Thornton, Angela Walder, David Wetton, Jon Wynne-Tyson and Vera Yorke. In America there were Dr Michael Fox, Murdaugh Madden, Dr Charles Magel, Dr Dallas Pratt, Dr Tom Regan, Dr Andrew Rowan, Dr Ken Shapiro and Henry Spira. In Australia, Elizabeth Ahlston, Rosemary Bor, 'Mick' Fearnside, Richard Jones, Patty Mark, Graeme McEwan, Glenys Oogjes, Peter Singer, and Christine Townend. External constraints do not allow me the space to describe in detail all the superb work of these and other leaders of the contemporary movement.

68   A few probably already disturbed and sensitive individuals have taken their protests tragically too far. In March 1986, for example, Robert Blackman poured petrol over himself from a lemonade bottle and burned himself to death in Colchester: 'He gave his life', said his mother, 'because he thought the cruelty would never stop' (*Today*, 31 March 1986).

69   The Thatcher governments, despite constant lobbying, failed to implement the far-reaching reforms to protect farm animals recommended by their official Farm Animal Welfare Council, failed to introduce warning labels on furs that came from trapped species, failed to help charities to get to grips with the chronic problems of stray dogs and cats, and introduced new legislation affecting laboratory animals which was highly controversial. On the positive side, however, they rather reluctantly supported the European import ban on baby seal products, and supported amendments in 1988 to the Protection of Animals Act 1911 (steered through the House of Lords by the nonagenarian Lord Houghton) which made it illegal to tether equines so as to cause unnecessary suffering or to advertise or attend dog-fights, and gave powers to the courts to disqualify from ownership in first cases of cruelty to any species.

70   Speech at the Royal Society, 27 September 1988.

71   See, for example, *Daily Telegraph*, 20 October 1988; *Sunday Times*, 30 October 1988, p. A13.

CHAPTER 12   THE PROTECTION OF WILDLIFE

1   Quoted by Simon Lyster, *International Wildlife Law* (Grotius, 1985), p. 21.
2   John Bulwer, *Anthropometamorphesis* (1653).
3   Keith Thomas, *Man and the Natural World: Changing Attitudes in England 1500—1800*, p. 285.
4   Lewis Regenstein, 'Animal Rights, Endangered Species and Human Survival', in Peter Singer (ed.), *In Defence of Animals* (Basil Blackwell, 1985), pp. 118—32. In the UK alone the elk, bear, beaver, boar and wolf have become extinct over the last two thousand years, although humans have introduced new species such as rabbits, housemice and pheasants.
5   Regenstein, 'Animal Rights', p. 121.
6   Under the Nature Conservancy Act of 1973 the Nature Conservancy became the Nature Conservancy Council. Campaigns to protect landscape in Britain had been a feature of the 1870s and 1880s and, in 1894, the National Trust was founded by Octavia Hill, Robert Hunter and Hardwick Raunsley.
7   See C. W. Hume, *Man and Beast* (Universities Federation for Animal Welfare, 1962).
8   Fairfield Osborn, for example, was influential in America. In 1949 in his *Our Plundered Planet* (Boston) he challenged the old anthropocentric ethic which asserted that all wildlife was for the use of Homo Sapiens and warned that the continued extinction of wildlife species threatened the survival of the human race.
9   Following Carson's were other books in the 1960s which heralded the legislative progress of the next decade. In 1966 there were Kenneth Boulding's *The Economics of the Coming Spaceship Earth* and Barry Commoner's *Science and Survival* (New York, 1966), followed by Paul Ehrlich's *The Population Bomb* (San Francisco, 1968.)
10   George B. Schaller, *The Mountain Gorilla* (Chicago, 1963); Jane van Lawick-Goodall, *My Friends the Wild Chimpanzees* (Washington, 1967), and *In the Shadow of Man* (Collins, 1971).
11   BBC Radio 4, *Today*, 11 September 1986.
12   *Independent*, 13 August 1988. RSPB membership rose dramatically from 8,000 in 1950 to 65,000 in 1970 and 500,000 in 1988.
13   Tessa Robertson, *Natural World*, Autumn 1987.
14   Lord Medway, *Report of the Panel of Enquiry into Shooting and Angling* (RSPCA, 1979).
15   Bernard Stonehouse (ed.), *Animal Marking* (Macmillan, 1978).
16   *RSPCA Policies* (RSPCA, 1979).
17   *Country Landowner*, March 1988, p. 21.
18   *Reforming the Animal Welfare Laws* (leaflet, RSPCA, 1987).
19   *Daily Telegraph*, 15 July 1985.
20   *Daily Telegraph*, 15 July 1985.

21 *Wildlife Guardian*, no. 1, Spring 1986.

22 Bill Jordan and Stefan Ormrod, *The Last Great Wild Beast Show* (Constable, 1978).

23 Rebecca Hall, *Voiceless Victims* (Wildwood House, 1984), Foreword.

24 *Sunday Times*, 19 April 1987.

25 ITN News, 21 October 1987.

26 *East Anglian Daily Times*, 30 January 1986.

27 Joseph Collinson, *The Fate of the Fur Seal* (Humanitarian League, 1902).

28 Personal communication, 1985.

29 Robert Hunter, *The Greenpeace Chronicle* (Picador, 1980), pp. 10–15.

30 *Guardian*, 30 September 1987.

31 Personal communication, December 1986.

32 Hunter, *The Greenpeace Chronicle*, p. 136.

33 Personal communications from Dr Sidney Holt and Bill Jordan, 1986.

34 *Globe and Mail*, 30 July 1986.

35 *Daily Telegraph*, 10 November 1986.

36 *Guardian*, 1 August 1986; *Country Life*, 13 November 1986.

37 *Cape Cod Times*, 9 August 1985.

38 *Observer*, 27 December 1987, p. 11; *Washington Post*, 7 April 1988, p. A32.

39 Kieran Mulraney, *Country Life*, 24 September 1987; *Greenpeace News*, September 1987.

40 Heathcote Williams, *Whale Nation* (Jonathan Cape, 1988).

41 *Cape Times*, 14 August 1986.

42 *Lynx*, March 1986.

43 RSPCA Press Release, 24 January 1986.

44 BFSS *Annual Report* 1963.

45 Richard Thomas, *The Politics of Hunting* (Gower, 1983), p. 159.

CHAPTER 13   IN THE LABORATORY

1 Marquis de Sade, *Justine* (1787); translated by Alan Hull Watson (Corgi, 1965).

2 Richard D. Ryder, *Victims of Science* (Davis-Poynter, 1975), p. 223.

3 Peter Singer, *Animal Liberation* (Paladin, 1977), p. 86.

4 Ibid., p. 87.

5 *Sunday Times*, 31 July 1988, p. 1.

6 *Statistics of Experiments on Living Animals, Great Britain 1987* (HMSO, 1989), Cmnd 515.

7 Parliamentary Questions, Hansard, 10 May 1988.

8 Frederick King *et al.*, 'Primates', *Science*, no. 240, 10 June 1988.

9   William Russell and Rex Burch, *The Principles of Humane Experimental Techniques* (Methuen, 1959).

10   Ryder, *Victims of Science*, pp. 226–7.

11   Personal communication, 1986.

12   *FRAME News*, No. 17 (1988), p. 2.

13   Richard D. Ryder, 'Experiments on Animals', and Terence Hegarty, 'Alternatives', both in S. and R. Godlovitch and John Harris (eds), *Animals, Men and Morals: An Enquiry into the Maltreatment of Non-humans* (Gollancz, 1971).

14   Richard D. Ryder, letters to the *Daily Telegraph*, 7 April and 20 May 1969.

15   *Sunday People*, 26 January 1975 and several subsequent editions.

16   *Daily Telegraph*, 4 February 1975.

17   Brigid Brophy, 'The Silent Victims', *New Statesman*, 28 February 1975; H. E. Carter, 'A Nettle to be Grasped', *Veterinary Record*, 15 March 1975; Ronnie Lee, 'How Long Shall These Things Be?', *Peace News*, 4 April 1975; Ian Ross, 'Animal Welfare', *Scotsman*, 8 March 1975; Graham Lord, 'The Torture We Allow in the Name of Science', *Sunday Express*, 23 February 1975; 'A Disquieting Centenary', *British Journal of Hospital Medicine*, July 1975, Editorial, and Richard D. Ryder's letter in reply: September 1975; Maureen Duffy, 'Go, Poor Fly', *New Society*, 27 February 1975; P. J. Kavanagh, 'Animal Harm', *Guardian*, 26 February 1975; Donald Gould, 'The Smoking Beagles', *New Statesman*, 14 March 1975; Bernard Dixon, 'In the Name of Humanity', *New Scientist*, 20 February 1975; Rosalind Morris, 'How Live Animals Suffer Pain for Trivial Research', *Observer*, 2 March 1975; Douglas Houghton, 'Without Pity', *Spectator*, 1 March 1975; Louis Goldman, *Doctor*, 6 March 1975; Richard Body, 'An Unpleasant Necessity', *Friend*, 2 May 1975.

There were numerous published repercussions to the publication of *Victims of Science* and to its reviews, including: Professor D. H. Smyth, '*Alternatives to Animal Experiments*' (Scolar, 1978), esp. pp. 184–6; J. D. Keehn, 'In Defence of Experiments With Animals', *Bulletin of British Psychological Society*, 30 (1977), pp. 404–5, and my reply of March 1978; Richard D. Ryder, 'Vivisection: Ryder Replies', *World Medicine*, 25 January 1978 (see also Editorial, 2 November 1977); Richard D. Ryder, 'Professor Shuster – A Reply', *New Scientist*, 12 January 1976; id., 'Animal Experiments', *New Scientist*, 3 April 1975; id., 'Helpful', *Doctor*, 27 March 1975; id., letter to the *Daily Telegraph*, 30 April 1975; id., 'The Silent Scream', *Vegetarian*, April 1975; id., 'Animal Experiments', *Observer*, 6 April 1975; id., 'Experiments on Animals', *The Times*, 21 May 1975; id., 'Animal Experiments', *Lancet*, 10 December 1977 (see Editorial, 29 October 1977); id., 'Experiments: Time for Revision', *Doctor*, 5 June 1975; id., 'The Animal Laboratory', *New Statesman*, 28 March 1975; Sam Shuster, 'The Anti-Vivisectionists –

A Critique', *New Scientist*, 12 January 1978.

In particular, an interesting correspondence occurred on the letters page of the *Times Literary Supplement* following Dr Alan Cowey's review of *Victims of Science* on 18 April 1975. Cowey, an Oxford animal experimenter, had not been too kind to the book. Dr Stephen Clark replied on 2 May, Ryder on 16 May, Cowey on 6 June, Clark on 4 July, Ryder on 11 July and Cowey on 18 July.

Reviews of the revised edition of *Victims of Science* (Centaur, 1983) included: Marian Stamp Dawkins, 'How Should Humans Treat Non-Humans?', *New Scientist* 25 August 1983; Eric Ashby, 'Cause for Concern', *Nature*, 8 September 1983; Peter Singer, 'Ten Years of Animal Liberation', *New York Review of Books*, 17 January 1985.

18 For example, Richard D. Ryder, 'Animal Experimentation', *The Times*, 14 August 1975.

19 Judith Hampson, 'Animal Welfare: A Century of Conflict', *New Scientist*, 25 October 1979.

20 *The Times*, 25 June 1975.

21 Ryder, *Victims of Science*, p. 32.

22 Richard D. Ryder, letter in the *Lancet*, 10 December 1977.

23 I had first met Peter Singer four years earlier in Oxford and was happy to supply him with some material for his book, although declining his generous and flattering offer of co-authorship of *Animal Liberation* because I wanted to fight the political campaign which was, by the early 1970s, taking up so much of my time.

24 For more detail, see my *Victims of Science*, revised edition, Centaur Press and National Anti-Vivisection Society, 1983, pp. 147–63.

25 *Scientific Procedures on Living Animals* (HMSO, May 1983), Cmnd 8883, section 24, p. 9.

26 *Liberator*, magazine of the British Union for the Abolition of Vivisection, April 1986.

27 *Bitter Pills* (National Anti-Vivisection Society, 1988).

28 For example, *NAVS Annual Report* (1986); *Liberator*, July 1987.

29 For example, *Turning Point*, no. 7, 1987, and *The Campaigner*, magazine of the National Anti-Vivisection Society, March 1987.

30 Robert Sharpe, *The Cruel Deception: The Use of Animals in Medical Research* (Thorsons, 1988), p. 40.

31 Thomas McKeown, *The Role of Medicine* (Blackwell, 1979), p. 562. See also Denis Noble's hostile review in the *Observer* of 22 May 1988 and Dr Sharpe's letter in reply, and Dr Eddie Moore's review in the *Liberator* of June 1988. Sharpe's general thesis received support from Professor J. Webster in his 'Animal Welfare and Genetic Engineering', in the proceedings of the conference held by the Athene Trust, London, 7 October 1988, entitled *The Bio-Revolution: Cornucopia or Pandora's Box?*

32 Jane Goodall, *New York Times Magazine*, 24 May 1987.

33   Gill Langley, 'Establishment Reactions to Alternatives'; her contribution to the Status of Animals Conference, held by FRAME in Nottingham, September 1988.
34   Hansard, 17 February 1986, no. 59.
35   For example: *Tablet*, 1 March 1986; *Catholic Herald*, 28 February 1986; *Universe*, 7 and 21 March 1986.
36   Personal communication, 3 September 1987.
37   Quoted in the *Annual Pictorial Review* of the Scottish Society for the Prevention of Vivisection (1988), p. 46.
38   Quoted by Henry Spira in *Chemical Times and Trends*, July 1987.
39   See for example Alan Dowd, 'A Decade of Debate on Animal Research in Psychology: Room for Consensus?', contribution to the Canadian Psychological Association Convention, 1987.
40   *Sunday Times*, 18 October 1987.
41   *Observer*, 15 May 1988.

CHAPTER 14   ON THE FACTORY-FARM

1   Marian Stamp Dawkins, *Animal Suffering: The Science of Animal Welfare* (Chapman and Hall, 1980), p. 129.
2   Peter Roberts, personal communication, August 1987.
3   Ibid.
4   US Department of Agriculture figures, 1987.
5   *Farmers Weekly*, 23 February 1962.
6   Peter Roberts, personal communication, August 1987.
7   Ruth Harrison, *Animal Machines* (Vincent Stuart, 1964).
8   Jim Mason and Peter Singer, *Animal Factories* (Crown, 1980).
9   *Report of the Technical Committee to Enquire into the Welfare of Animals kept under Intensive Livestock Husbandry Systems*, chairman Professor F. W. Rogers Brambell (HMSO, 1965), Cmnd. 2836.
10   The Farm Animal Welfare Council was set up in July 1979 by the British Government after a decade of lobbying by animal welfarists and to meet, in part, the promptings of the General Election Co-ordinating Committee for Animal Protection for a permanent commission to monitor animal welfare and advise government. FAWC has performed well, but its reports have not, at the time of writing, resulted in much action from government.
11   Dawkins, *Animal Suffering*, p. 91.
12   Richard Body, *Agriculture: The Triumph and the Shame* (Temple Smith, 1982).
13   *Ag Scene* (the magazine of Compassion in World Farming), no. 77, February 1985.
14   Farm Animal Welfare Council, *Report on the Welfare of Livestock (Red Meat Animals) at the Time of Slaughter* (HMSO, 1984).
15   John Douglass, personal communication, 1986.
16   Dudley Giehl, *Vegetarianism: A Way of Life* (Harper and Row,

1979); Philip Kapleau, *To Cherish All Life* (Zen Centre, New York, 1981); Keith Akers, *A Vegetarian Source Book* (Putnam, 1983); Rynn Berry, *Famous Vegetarians and their Favourite Recipes* (Panjandrum, Los Angeles, 1988).

17 *Outrage*, February 1988.

18 See the reports of the Farm Animal Welfare Council on the *Welfare of Poultry* (January 1982), the *Welfare of Livestock (Red Meat Animals) at the Time of Slaughter* (1984), the *Welfare of Farm Deer* (1985) and the *Welfare of Livestock at Markets* (1986), all HMSO.

19 Andrew Tyler, 'Animals' Rights and Wrongs', *Independent Magazine*, 6 January 1989, p. 24.

20 *Daily Telegraph*, 11 November 1986.

21 Jim Mason, *New Scientist*, 28 March 1985.

22 For example, the Athene Trust held a conference on genetic engineering in London on 7 October 1988, entitled *The Bio-Revolution: Cornucopia or Pandora's Box?*

23 Brambell Report, p. 13, para 37.

CHAPTER 15   VIOLENCE AND THE ANIMAL LIBERATION
FRONT

1 *Sun*, 25 and 29 March 1975.

2 Ronnie Lee, 'How Long Shall These Things Be?' *Peace News*, 4 April 1975.

3 Ibid.

4 Ibid.

5 For example, Eileen Macdonald's hysterical 'Gospel of Terror', *Daily Express*, 6 May 1986.

6 Cal McCrystal, *Sunday Times Colour Supplement*, 12 October 1986.

7 *Black Beast*, no. 2, Autumn 1985. (This magazine was later renamed *Turning Point* and published by Arc Print, London.)

8 *Liberator*, August 1986.

9 *Daily Telegraph*, 6 February 1987.

10 *Outrage* (February 1988), p. 7.

11 *Daily Telegraph*, 7 February 1987.

12 *Independent*, 13 July 1987; *Daily Telegraph*, 14 June 1988.

13 *The Times*, 21 December 1988; *Daily Telegraph*, 21 December 1988.

14 Ronnie Lee, 'Personal Opinion', *Liberator*, November/December 1988.

15 *Western Morning News*, 17 November 1986; national press 23 February 1989.

16 Peter Janke, 'Europe', in Richard Clutterbuck (ed.), *The Future of Political Violence* (Royal United Services Institute, 1986), pp. 100–1.

17 For example, see 'The Nigel Hampster Diary' in *FRAME News* no. 17 (1988).

18   Jolyon Jenkins, *New Statesman*, 21 February 1986.
19   Yvonne Roberts, *The Times*, 21 May 1986.
20   'Animal Welfare', BBC *Brass Tacks*, 20 June 1986.
21   Nicholas Roe, 'Crusaders Against Cruelty', *Independent*, 12 December 1988.
22   Andrew Tyler, 'Animal Rights and Wrongs', *Independent Magazine*, 7 January 1989, pp. 20–4.
23   Ronnie Lee, 'How Long Shall These Things Be?', *Peace News*, 4 April 1975.
24   McCrystal, *Sunday Times Colour Supplement*, 12 October 1986.
25   *Today* newspaper, 18 June 1986.
26   *Howl*, no. 13 (1986).
27   *Daily Telegraph*, 17 November 1986.
28   *Western Morning News*, 20 February 1987.
29   *The Times*, 22 January 1988.
30   *Liberator*, April 1983, p. 4.
31   *Turning Point*, June 1988, p. 4.
32   Brian Davies, personal communication, April 1984 and *Red Ice* (Methuen, 1989), pp. 84–100.
33   International Primate Protection League, personal communication, May 1988.
34   Andrew Tyler, 'City Hunters', *Independent* 'Weekend', 10 September 1988.
35   Bob Harrowe, *Fur Age Weekly*, 19 August 1985.
36   Peter Singer, *Liberator*, April/May 1986.
37   Earlier unfortunate publicity for the militants had occurred in 1977 when attempts were made to disinter the bodies of two famous huntsmen, John Peel and the Duke of Beaufort, but these episodes had been reported quite neutrally by most media.
38   *Turning Point*, no. 5 (Autumn 1986), pp. 16–18.
39   International Association Against Painful Experiments on Animals leaflet, 1986.
40   *Turning Point*, no. 4 (Spring 1986).
41   *Outrage*, no. 38 (May 1985).
42   Rebecca Hall, *Voiceless Victims* (Wildwood House, 1984), p. 282.

CHAPTER 16   INTERNATIONAL PROGRESS

1   The member organizations were: from Belgium the Association Nationale de Sociétés de Protection Animale, from Denmark the Foreningen til Dyrenes Beskyttelse, from France the Conseil National de la Protection Animale (CNPA), from Italy the Ente Nazionale Protezione Animali (ENPA), from Luxembourg the Ligue Nationale pour la Protection des Animaux, from the Netherlands the Nederlandse Vereniging Tot Bescherming Van Dieren, from the Republic of West

Germany the Deutscher Tierschutzbund e.V., from the Republic of Ireland the Irish Society for the Prevention of Cruelty to Animals (ISPCA), and from the United Kingdom the RSPCA.

2   Consultative Assembly: Printed Document AS/Agr. (2)22.

3   Hans-Jurgen Weichert, in *Animal Regulation Studies*, 1 (Elsevier, Amsterdam, 1978), pp. 273–6.

4   *The Times*, 24 July 1986.

5   West Germany's revised Animal Protection Law of 1 January 1987 banned the testing on animals of weapons, cosmetics and tobacco. It restricted the infliction of pain and obliged experimenters to use alternative techniques wherever possible.

6   Caroline Vodden, personal communication, 8 June 1988.

7   The Swedish Animal Protection Act of 1988 also requires that pigs and cows should have straw and space, and that calves should remain with their mothers for at least their first two months. It prohibits the docking of dogs' tails and the administration of drugs and hormones to animals except for the treatment of disease. One of the key campaigners responsible for this major advance was the author of childrens' books, Astrid Lindgren. (John Witherow, 'Swedish Law lets Pigs Rule the Roost', *Sunday Times*, 30 October 1988.)

8   One of the principal Finnish organizations has been that concerned with the treatment of laboratory animals, Koe Elainten Suojelu, headed by campaigners such as Hannele Luukainen, Päivi Viinikainen and Raili Vesanen.

9   Christine Townend, personal communication, 1986.

10   *Daily Telegraph*, 17 November 1986.

11   *Hindustan Times*, 16 June 1985.

12   *Times of India*, 27 June 1986.

13   Ann Cottrell Free, 'Remembering Rachel Carson: A Friend of Animals', *Animal Welfare Institute Quarterly*, vol. 36, no. 2, p. 9.

14   *National Anti-Vivisection Society Bulletin*, no. 3 (1987).

15   Gill Langley, *Outrage*, no. 37 (March 1985).

16   Gavan Daws, 'Animal Liberation as Crime: The Hawaii Dolphin Case', in Harlan B. Miller and William H. Williams (eds), *Ethics and Animals* (Humana Press, 1983).

17   Culture and Animals Foundation leaflet, 22 July 1986.

18   These bodies were the American Anti-Vivisection Society, American Humane Association, American Society for the Prevention of Cruelty to Animals, Animal Protection Institute, Fund for Animals, Humane Society of the United States, International Society for Animal Rights, Massachusetts Society for the Prevention of Cruelty to Animals, Michigan Humane Society, National Anti-Vivisection Society and New England Anti-Vivisection Society.

19   *Animals' Agenda*, September 1985.

20   Joyce Tischler, personal communication, 19 March 1986.

21   *Bulletin of the British Psychological Society*, 38 (1985), pp. 289–91.
22   Society for Animal Protective Legislation information leaflet, 1987.
23   Harold Takooshian, *PsyETA Bulletin*, Spring 1988.

CHAPTER 17   SPECIESISM

1   Keith Thomas, *Man and the Natural World: Changing Attitudes in England 1500–1800* (Allen Lane, 1983), pp. 38–9.
2   Ibid., p. 38.
3   Ibid.
4   Mary Wollstonecraft, *Vindication of the Rights of Women* (1792).
5   Miriam Rothschild, *Animals and Man* (Clarendon, 1986), pp. 51–2.
6   Women have participated more during the period of their gradual social emancipation, and the unconscious emulation of the masculine role may have played a part in this; but in modern Britain, horse-riding as a leisure pursuit has become chiefly a feminine occupation, and fox-hunting happens to be one of the equestrian situations in which British women mix with male company. In primitive cultures it is usually the male who does the hunting, and it is often said that it is the males who are in at the kill in modern Western society, while the women hang back like a distant audience of camp followers.
7   Randall Lockwood, 'Pathways to Compassion', *PsyETA Bulletin*, Spring 1986, pp. 6–9.
8   Harold Takooshian, *PsyETA Bulletin*, Spring 1988, pp. 8–9.
9   Thomas, *Man and the Natural World*, p. 117.
10   *Daily Telegraph*, 18 April 1987.
11   French writers, as well as British, have extolled feline charm, among them Chateaubriand, Victor Hugo, Baudelaire and Alexandre Dumas; later still, Colette and Cocteau (Fernand Mery, *The Life, History and Magic of the Cat* (Hamlyn, 1967), pp. 223–5). In England, there have been Dickens, H. G. Wells and Hardy, and in America Mark Twain and Edgar Allan Poe; actresses, too, just as often as writers, have been outstanding cat-lovers, from Ellen Terry and Sarah Bernhardt to Sophia Loren.
12   John Chancellor, *Charles Darwin* (Weidenfeld and Nicolson, 1973) p. 76.
13   Professor Bernard Knight, BBC World Service, 25 August 1988.
14   This paper was read to the AGM of the British Psychological Society, Exeter, 1977. The sample of students was small – only 31.
15   Leo Tolstoy, 'Introduction', *The Ethics of Diet* (Russian translation). Quoted by Jon Wynne-Tyson, *Food for a Future* (Thorsons, 1988), pp. 165–6.
16   Harry Hieover, *Bipeds and Quadrupeds* (T. C. Newby, 1853), p. xi.
17   Roberta Kalechovfsky, 'Metaphors of Nature', *Behavioural and Political Animal Studies*, 1 (1) (1988).

18   James Walvin, *Leisure and Society 1830–1950* (Longman, 1978), pp. 84–5.
19   Anthony Montague Browne, letter in the *Financial Times*, 8 August 1987.
20   Geoffrey Gorer, *The Life and Ideas of the Marquis de Sade* (Peter Owen, 1934).
21   Carol McKenna, *Ag Scene*, September 1987, p. 5.
22   *RSPCA Conviction Returns*, September 1987.
23   Andrew Tyler, 'City Hunters', *Independent* 'Weekend', 10 September 1988.
24   See for example Matthew 7:12; Galatians 5:14; Leviticus 19:17–18.
25   The electro-encephalograph (EEG) record will show (a) blocking of alpha rhythm, (b) enhancement of N100 event-related potential, (c) 'Readiness Potential' and (d) P300 event-related potential. All these electrophysiological signs, which have been associated with human consciousness, have been found in nonhuman primates (Richard Latto, 'Making Decisions about the Conscious Experiences of Animals', *Behavioural and Political Animal Studies*, 1 (1) (1988), pp. 7–16).
26   Lord Medway, *RSPCA Panel Report* (1980), pp. 8–11.
27   Peter Singer, 'Ten Years of Animal Liberation', *New York Review of Books*, 17 January 1985, p. 6.
28   See Marian Stamp Dawkins, *Animal Suffering* (Chapman and Hall, 1980).
29   Peter Singer, *The Animal Liberation Movement* (Old Hammond Press, 1987), p. 8.
30   Ibid., p. 10.
31   For example, see the emphasis on 'duty' in William Smith, *Uses and Abuses of Domestic Animals* (Jarrold, 1884).
32   I coined the word speciesism in 1970. It entered the *Oxford English Dictionary* in 1986.
33   Rebecca Hall, *Voiceless Victims* (Wildwood House, 1984), p. xii.
34   Steven Walker, *Animal Thought* (Routledge and Kegan Paul, 1983).
35   Roger Fouts, *The Natural History Programme*, BBC Radio 4, 10 August 1988.
36   Richard Dawkins, *The Selfish Gene* (Oxford University Press, 1976), p. 11.
37   Richard Dawkins, *The Blind Watchmaker* (Longman 1986), p. 263.
38   Richard Leakey, 'Science Now', BBC Radio 4, 23 November 1985.
39   Karl Marx, *Early Writings*, trans. Rodney Livingstone and Gregor Benton (Penguin, 1975), p. 239. Marx was certainly a speciesist.
40   Marly Cornell, 'The Philosopher Who Came in from the Cold', *Animals Alert*, Summer 1988 (Magazine of the Australian and New Zealand Federation of Animal Societies, Collingwood, Victoria, Australia).

Index